Corners in the City of God

Corners in the City of God

Theology, Philosophy, and *The Wire*

Edited by
JONATHAN TRAN
and MYLES WERNTZ

CASCADE *Books* • Eugene, Oregon

CORNERS IN THE CITY OF GOD
Theology, Philosophy, and *The Wire*

Copyright © 2013 Wipf and Stock Publishers. All rights reserved. Except for brief quotations in critical publications or reviews, no part of this book may be reproduced in any manner without prior written permission from the publisher. Write: Permissions. Wipf and Stock Publishers, 199 W. 8th Ave., Suite 3, Eugene, OR 97401.

Cascade Books
An Imprint of Wipf and Stock Publishers
199 W. 8th Ave., Suite 3
Eugene, OR 97401

www.wipfandstock.com

ISBN 13: 978-1-60899-851-7

Cataloguing-in-Publication Data

Corners in the city of God : theology, philosophy, and The Wire / edited by Jonathan Tran and Myles Werntz.

xii + 316 p. ; 23 cm. Includes bibliographical references and index(es).

ISBN 13: 978-1-60899-851-7

1. Wire (Television program). 2. Wire (Television program)—History and criticism. 3. Television broadcasting—Religious aspects—Christianity. I. Tran, Jonathan. II. Werntz, Myles. III. Title.

PN1992.77.W53 C60 2013

Manufactured in the U.S.A.

Contents

Acknowledgments vii
Introduction ix

Part I: **Prologue**

1. The Church in *The Wire*: Prophetic Witness as a Prop in Urban America 3
   —JAMES H. COSTON

2. Living on Set: A Year Spent Living and Working in Baltimore City 17
   —WHITNEY JOHNSON

3. "Way Down in the Hole": Systemic Urban Inequality and *The Wire* 31
   —ANMOL CHADDHA and WILLIAM JULIUS WILSON

Part II: **Encountering *The Wire***

4. Marlo's City of Words: Tempting a Natural Theology of Language 59
   —JONATHAN TRAN

5. Sexual Communication and Institutional Dysfunction in *The Wire* 76
   —DAVID MATZKO MCCARTHY

6. Realism and Utopia in *The Wire* 95
   —FREDRIC JAMESON

7 "This Is Me": Ronald Pryzbylewski, Mis-Performance, and Transformation in *The Wire*   109
   —BRIAN BANTUM

8 Down in the Hole: Melancholy, Vulnerability, and the Puncturing of Black Masculinity   128
   —JOSEPH WINTERS

Part III: Engaging *The Wire*

9 The Ethics of Counter-Insurgency in *The Wire*   147
   —JACOB L. GOODSON

10 Keeping the Devil Down: The Church on *The Wire*   174
    —NEKEISHA ALEXIS-BAKER

11 Depravity and Hope in the City: Karl Barth in Conversation with *The Wire*   191
    —KEITH L. JOHNSON

12 On Naming the Work of God: Ecclesiological Witness and Theological Transformation in *The Wire*   210
    —MYLES WERNTZ

13 "It don't matter that some fool say he different...": The Pretense of Frank Sobotka's Self-Sacrifice   230
    —JOSEPH WIEBE

14 Earthly Peace in the Halls of City Schools   249
    —PETER BOUMGARDEN and KRISTEN DEEDE JOHNSON

Part IV: Life after *The Wire*

15 The Communication of the Nameless   269
    —DANIEL COLUCCIELLO BARBER

16 *The Wire*, Or, What to Do in Non-Evental Times   285
    —SLAVOJ ŽIŽEK

List of Contributors   305
Index   307

Acknowledgments

THE EDITORS OF THIS volume wish to thank Baylor University's Department of Religion and George W. Truett Theological Seminary for their support of this project. Additionally, they thank Baylor's University Research Committee for monetary support enabling the inclusion of a full range of voices in this collection. Thanks also to The University of Chicago's *Critical Inquiry*, Wayne State University's *Criticism*, and Verso Press for granting reprinting rights for previously published essays by Anmol Chadhha and William Julius Wilson, Fredric Jameson, and Slavoj Žižek, respectively. We also owe a tremendous debt to Charlie Collier, who encouraged us to pursue this project in the first place. Additionally, this project could not have been completed without the hard work of Daniel Marrs, KC Flynn, Jaqua Williams, and Jill Riley. And the editors owe much to Waco's Calvary Baptist Church, where love of neighbor, so desperately needed according to *The Wire*, remains on display going on eighty-five years now. Finally, we thank our families for more than can be said here.

Introduction

BETWEEN 2002 AND 2008 the HBO series *The Wire* offered television audiences a dystopic vision of modern-day Baltimore, a city caught between promise and peril, replete with complex characters remanded to the forgotten corners of America's beleaguered experiment with democracy. The series was named "the best show on television" (*Philadelphia Daily News, Salon, London Guardian, Time*), winning Peabody, Broadcast, and Cable Critics awards, and was nominated for Emmys as well as NAACP Image and Edgar awards. Deemed "too Black for America," the show's sustained critique of late capitalism meant that its popularity never quite matched its critical acclaim.[1] Over five seasons, the series explored the crowded intersections of poverty, drugs, sexuality, urban crime, law enforcement, race, local government, business, public education, and the media. Subtly adding nuances every episode and each season, creator David Simon and the writers of *The Wire* eventually produced one of the most ambitious projects entertainment media has ever witnessed: "We were always planning on moving further and further out, to build a whole city."[2] The breadth of the show's relational and institutional matrix borders on the brilliant and gives its viewers a glimpse inside the complexities of contemporary urban life.

Augustine of Hippo, nearly two millennia ago, similarly offered an account of cities—the earthly city of man and the heavenly city of God. Augustine narrated the political realities of his day by mapping Roman culture onto the eschatological kingdom of God that he believed the church proleptically, though imperfectly, embodied. While his political masterpiece *De Civitate Dei*'s extolment of the heavenly city came with invectives against the practices and presumptions of the earthly city, Augustine understood his task as articulating the possibilities for sanctified desire in the pilgrim

---

1. On this criticism, see Danielsen, "*The Wire*: Too Black, Too Strong?"
2. Quoted in Talbot, "Stealing Life."

cities of the temporal kingdom. Augustine thought he was calling Rome to its better self.

The Wire beautifully dramatizes the earthly city's pilgrimage in time. With its disordered loves and powerful impulses toward good, the Baltimore of *The Wire* displays desire as an urban landscape where hope dies and is born again on every corner. The death and rebirth of hope finds expression in chalked bodies and the dogged presence of children in a world where kids die too often. Not surprisingly, homicide detectives are given as the city's caretakers, as if meaning might be found in the austere narrative of the police procedural. Yet, when murder cases lead only to more murder cases, meaning gives way to larger questions and to the dawning sense that something is deeply wrong, not simply with Baltimore or inner-city America but with America as such, the inner city an unfortunate miner's canary of the American dream and maybe even the ritual sacrifice that makes for its possibility.

This volume tries to give voice to this sense of something being wrong, terribly so, but also to capacities for wonder even amidst terribly wrong conditions. It does so by reflecting (theologically, philosophically, and with whatever resources still salvageable) on *The Wire* and on the questions the show provokes, though with only the space and energy to answer a meager handful; it is the nature of the show's genius to raise more questions than can be addressed, which is both the show's virtue and its burden.

The structure of this volume consists of four parts. The first part offers three autobiographical perspectives that orient as well as disorient the reader as the authors seek to dislodge certain assumptions while calling forth attention to the city in new ways. The second part lays out thematic concerns permeating the show. Using the resources of theology and philosophy to diagnose and describe themes of structural inequity, power, and identity, the authors of these essays examine the show using specific conceptual lenses. The third part moves beyond diagnosis to engagement, once again using theological and philosophical tools to explore particular issues raised by *The Wire*. The final part, rather than offering a conclusion that neatly "solves" *The Wire*, sends the reader back out again with greater appreciation for the complexities of the world in which we find ourselves, challenged by its peril and emboldened by its promise.

The first part (Prologue) offers three autobiographical selections that reflect on the disorienting experience of living in places like Baltimore. Reverend James H. Coston's essay relates the story of someone who spent a decade in Trenton, New Jersey, as both a pastor and city council member. His essay, which describes the institutional dysfunction of a city unable to come to terms with its problems, examines *The Wire*'s depiction of the church and offers the perspective of one whose voice is largely silent in *The Wire*: the pastor. Whitney Johnson's essay tells the story of a woman who lived in Baltimore for a year as an Americorps volunteer and still struggles to name the ways that living in Baltimore's East Side still lives with her. Rounding out this opening section of the volume, a previously published essay by Drs. Anmol Chadhha and William Julius Wilson offers a descriptive account of the systemic inequalities that contribute to the difficulty of altering deep-seated social inequalities portrayed in *The Wire*.

The second group of essays (Encountering *The Wire*) moves beyond observing the events of the show's Baltimore and directly engages thematic issues that permeate the show. In Jonathan Tran's essay, the show's violence is framed as tempting a certain view of the incarnation that Tran resists by appealing to Wittgenstein's account of language as ordinary and therefore available to God's presence. David Matzko McCarthy's essay argues that *The Wire*'s highly sexualized language expresses certain power dynamics, and that coming to terms with the language means coming to terms with these power dynamics. McCarthy insists that power is communicated by language, specifically naming, which creates pathways for relational corruption. Frederic Jameson's republished essay casts *The Wire* as struggling for place along the spectrum of realism and utopianism. In Brian Bantum's essay, the figure of Roland "Prez" Pryzbylewski is seen as embodying the show's possibilities for moral transformation; as Prez transitions from cop to teacher, Bantum asks the question of what it means for transformation to occur and what, theologically speaking, transformation leaves undone. By looking at the ways in which racial and gender identity are formed and deformed in the lives of the Barksdale criminal organization, Joseph Winter's essay examines how *The Wire* scripts personhood.

From the second to the third part (Engaging *The Wire*), we turn from description to prescription regarding particular questions the show raises. Jacob L. Goodson starts things off by questioning whether locutions like "the war on drugs" condition conversations about America's drug problems in discursively disastrous ways. Joseph Wiebe's essay explores the role of sacrifice in social change, as seen in the problematic and tragic figure of Frank Sobotka, a sorry character who exemplifies the effort to remain human amidst Baltimore's equally sorry institutions. In his essay, Keith L. Johnson offers an account of human corruption, encountered so forcefully in *The Wire*, using Reformed theologian Karl Barth's construal of sin and the powers. Nekeisha Alexis-Baker's essay challenges the impotence of *The Wire*'s church with her own description of on-the-ground initiatives taken by actual Baltimore churches, offering a more hopeful picture of the church's faithfulness. Myles Werntz's essay seeks to account for *The Wire*'s dismissive view of the church by offering an alternative vision for Christian ethical engagement. In an essay by Kristen Johnson and Peter Boumgarden, the decaying educational system is subjected to an Augustinian analysis, exploring the ways in which justice is sought for the students of Baltimore and the reasons justice seems permanently out of reach. For Johnson and Boumgarden, ordering a society rightly requires not only rightly aligning educational access, but ordering the soul as well.

The final part (Life after *The Wire*) backs out of *The Wire* mindful of how *The Wire* has changed our theological and philosophical presumptions. Daniel C. Barber's essay explores what "religion" means after *The Wire*. For Barber, the show's relative absence of religion may indicate that we have misunderstood what it means for religion to be present. And in a previously published essay, Slavoj Žižek uses a materialist understanding of religion to consider how *The Wire* helps viewers deal with life in what he calls "non-evental" times.

Throughout these essays, the reader will find themselves challenged by both the ways theology offers new lenses for seeing the world of *The Wire* and the ways *The Wire* reveals that theology's gaze is in need of correction. The issues explored in this volume, though provoked by a television series, are issues of flesh and bone and of soul and spirit. Every city, whether it be Baltimore or Waco, Texas, remains *in via* and so suffers the practices and presumptions of the earthly city, as Augustine put it two millennia ago. On corners all along the way, pilgrims claiming citizenship elsewhere set up shop in hopes of bearing witness to another city.

A brief word about the format for the references to episodes of *The Wire* that appear throughout the essays in this volume: the season number is listed first, indicated by the letter *S*, followed by the episode number indicated by the letter *E*. Authors have included episode names either in the essay text or in the footnote at their discretion.

BIBLIOGRAPHY

Danielsen, Shane. "*The Wire*: Too Black, Too Strong?" *The Guardian*, July 21, 2008. Online: http://www.guardian.co.uk/culture/tvandradioblog/2008/jul/21/thewire tooblacktoostrong.

Talbot, Margaret. "Stealing Life: The Crusader behind *The Wire*." *The New Yorker*, October 22, 2007. Online: http://www.newyorker.com/reporting/2007/10/22 /071022fa_fact_talbot.

PART I
Prologue

1

The Church in *The Wire*
Prophetic Witness as a Prop in Urban America

JAMES H. COSTON

IN THE INTEREST OF full disclosure, I did not anxiously await each new Sunday night episode of *The Wire* when it originally aired from 2002 through 2008. I did not have HBO—I had television, the basic cable version, and so I came late as a convert to the show. David Simon's examination of Baltimore, and by extension urban America, soon made its way into public consciousness, and in the midst of *The Wire*'s run several friends recommended that I rent the DVDs and watch the show. Eventually I did and in short order caught up to the live broadcasts. Simon brought the dynamics of my adopted home city, Trenton, New Jersey, to a larger audience on a grand stage. Within the Baltimore towers, I saw the life of Trenton's own Miller Homes low-income housing project. The boys the show called Michael and Dukie I knew as Quon and Darrell. Officers Freamon and Greggs in Baltimore were Detectives Clayton and Reyes in Trenton. Mostly, only the names were changed.

David Simon has admitted that *The Wire* wanted to "pick a fight" regarding "the America left behind."[1] Simon does this well, offering critiques of power in all its civic forms: economic, political, educational, and social. As his critiques grew more comprehensive with each season, however, I

---

1. Simon, "Introduction," 4, 8.

noticed a frightening omission. Where was the Church within the world of *The Wire*?[2] Clergy and church buildings make several appearances in the show; however, their appearances serve only as props within the larger narrative. Simon places ministers and ministries within the world of the *The Wire* only to serve the advancement of stories, never to participate in the story itself as prime actors or agents. It is as though the Church in urban America didn't merit the airtime, or is so irrelevant that it did not warrant a critique from "the angriest man in television."[3] Why?

David Simon's service as a reporter for *The Baltimore Sun* (1982–1995) coupled with his realistic portrayal of urban grit suggests no reticence to call it as he sees it. One may then conclude that the Church as an agent of redemption and change within Baltimore—and dare I add urban America—does not effectively exist. This chapter will detail the portrayal of the Christian lay leaders, clergy, and congregations within *The Wire*. Utilizing my experience as both a local pastor and politician in Trenton, New Jersey, I will then offer explanations for this depiction. Finally, I will propose remedies for an anemic Church in urban America.

I believe that one of the strengths of *The Wire* is the quilted nature of its many characters, relationships, and narratives. These patches provide stories within the larger tale. Each has elements of independence while also serving as a piece of the completed work. The Church does not merit a square, but it does provide threads here and there for the completed piece. These threads serve the narrative arc of the series and reveal an underlying assumption about the Church: that the Church in Baltimore can serve politics but cannot transform the city.

One of these story threads centers upon the character of the Deacon.[4] In the episode "Moral Midgetry," the Deacon interacts with Dennis "Cutty" Wise[5] as Cutty begins to build his boxing gym.[6] The Deacon and Cutty talk about submission with the question centering upon surrendering to what or to whom. The camera follows Cutty's line of sight to a cross around the

---

2. I will use the term Church to signify the Church universal as manifest in congregations, formal faith associations, and houses of worship. I also will use the terms Church and Christianity interchangeably, for the purposes of this piece alone.

3. Bowden, "Angriest Man in Television," para.1.

4. The Deacon appeared in eleven episodes. Ironically, this most overtly and consistently Christian character was played by Melvin D. "Little Melvin" Williams, a convicted Baltimore drug dealer whom David Simon, as a *Baltimore Sun* reporter, and Ed Burns, as a Baltimore police detective, helped put in prison.

5. The character of Cutty appeared in twenty-six episodes and was played by Chad Coleman.

6. S3/E8.

Deacon's neck. Before the Deacon can verbalize and make explicit what is implied by this shot, namely submission to Jesus Christ, Cutty tells him to stow it "here and now." The Deacon has notable influences within the show, some of which are detailed below. However, this is, in my opinion, the closest that the series comes to a blatant and unconcealed Christian pronouncement. And yet, just as the Word was about to come forth, the episode moved on. Simon dipped his toes in the baptismal waters, then stepped back from full immersion.

Earlier in "Moral Midgetry," Lt. "Bunny" Colvin[7] gives the Deacon a tour of Hamsterdam. While the invocation of a deity as expressed by the Deacon may be dismissed as invective, the Deacon does express the societal and human cost to Colvin's open air drug market. Where the West Commander sees safer streets surrounding Hamsterdam, the Deacon sees a circle akin to Dante's *Inferno*, a place disregarding basic human needs and promoting suffering through a lack of precautions appropriate to drug use. While Colvin's end may be noble, the Deacon echoes the Apostle Paul in arguing that the end does not justify the means.[8] In this way, the Deacon serves as the moral conscience and a counterweight to Colvin. But the Deacon's presence is made to speak nothing of redemption, forgiveness, or salvation. Certainly, the Deacon wants improvement and voices that. However, he does not utter words of proclamation or grace. Here, the Deacon appears more as a moralist than "one crying out in the wilderness to prepare the way of the Lord."[9]

Simon himself has argued that in a world in which capitalism reigns people are worth less.[10] As in a Greek tragedy, the gods of *The Wire* watch human suffering not from Mount Olympus but from contemporary postmodern institutions. These institutions focus on numbers, transactions, and concrete outcomes. Society's empirical bent toward the measurable and material leaves little room for something as vague sounding as the good news of Jesus Christ. Hence, *The Wire* adds the Church to the scrapheap of the "America that got left behind."[11]

In *The Wire*, the Church exists as a political animal, ruthless like all the others. This is manifested at multiple points in the series. For example, "Margin of Error" portrays the Sunday prior to the Mayoral Primary election with the three candidates, Councilman Tommy Carcetti, Councilman

---

7. Played by Robert Wisdom in twenty-seven episodes.
8. Rom 3:8.
9. Isa 40:3.
10. Simon, "Behind the Wire," para. 5.
11. Simon, "Interview with Bill Moyers," 4:00.

Tony Gray, and Mayor Clarence Royce, attending separate worship services.[12] The local press attends as well, catching each candidate sitting with masses of congregants. Carcetti, with the Deacon and State Delegate Odell Watkins sitting nearby, has difficulty keeping the beat in an African-American church, but he listens intently as the minister, preaching from Exodus 18, speaks of Moses delivering the Israelites to the Promised Land. Upon exiting, Carcetti fails to secure more than a promise of open-mindedness from the clergyman. Simon provides watchers with a tangible instance of the political utility of the Church. The Church serves only as a prop for an urban political narrative. With what I take to be intended irony, each candidate passes corner boys while on his way to church. While the powerful prostrate themselves before power-broking pastors, parishioners-as-voters, and the press, the world outside proceeds oblivious to the songs, sermons and scripture within the respective houses of worship. The chasm between the liturgies (liturgy being "work of the people") within and the circumstances outside seems to be the point. *The Wire* depicts the two realms as utterly disconnected and foreign to one another. While they inhabit adjacent spaces, the sacred and the profane occupy different dimensions making an intersection untenable.

In the episode "Slapstick,"[13] Cutty, the Deacon, and Reverend Frank Reid[14] discuss how to secure appropriate permits for Cutty's boxing gym for youth. The chain of power proceeds to State Delegate Watkins,[15] whose influence enables Cutty to receive the needed permits. Watkins readily admits that he will help Cutty mainly because the voters like Reverend Reid. In this instance, the Deacon provides a link between Cutty's boots-on-the-ground approach to societal betterment and the powers-that-be in government. The show figures the links between the pulpit and the public square as one of political calculation and expedience. This positive outcome underscores the kind of relevance *The Wire* envisages the Church having.

Season 2 opens with a Polish Catholic parish serving as the setting for a personal dispute between Stevedore Union Head Frank Sobotka and Baltimore Police Major Stan Valcheck.[16] Sobotka has bought and placed within the church nave a stained glass piece commemorating the work of dock workers. This purchase serves posterity *and* Sobotka's political ambitions, in

---

12. S4/E6.
13. S3/E9.
14. Played by Felix Stevenson in two episodes.
15. Played by Frederick Strother in sixteen episodes.
16. "Ebb Tide," S2/E1. Played by Chris Bauer (twelve episodes) and Al Brown (nineteen episodes) respectively.

this case gaining the ear of Maryland's United States Senator, who just happens to be a member of the church, in order to secure earmarked benefits for the harbor and its workers. As Sobotka leaves, the Priest offers to hear his confession, to which Sobotka responds by chuckling to himself as he walks away. Later, Valchek arrives at the church with his own commissioned stained glass piece honoring Polish police and fire officers, only to find that the stevedores already occupy the nave window. The Priest, after expressing the appropriate decorum, wryly notes that he hasn't seen Valchek at Mass in recent memory.

This portrayal makes a case for the impotence of Christianity. The Church within *The Wire* at best fosters political connections. Valchek and Sobotka parallel one another in that they willingly purchase windows, but neither participates in the life of the church or goes to church seeking anything like God or God's gathered community. I would argue that both characters dismiss any notion that the Church has practical utility beyond fostering access to civic power. While the show makes few explicit statements about the Church, its direct participation in all manner of political graft serves as a subtext to the series, suggesting that the Church not only enables but encourages such behavior.

Season 3 has an episode ironically titled "Reformation." Cutty asks the Deacon to encourage at-risk kids into his gym in order to learn self-discipline through boxing training. The Deacon matter-of-factly admits that "no one has any idea how to go at the hoppers." The Church among other institutions lacks the knowledge and ability to impact life on the street. In "Middle Ground," Cutty approaches Avon Barksdale[17] for a donation to buy new equipment for his gym. Avon's generosity exceeds Cutty's expectations as he leaves with $15,000. This quick action is juxtaposed with a West Side meeting. Here, the police meet with the community within a church, where the community complaints are met with stock replies: inadequate manpower and a malfunctioning legal system. The disparity speaks to the larger narrative about power and its application. The fact that Avon acts while the police and community talk buttresses the portrayal of the Church as passé or ineffective. After his short meeting with the drug kingpin, Cutty leaves more than satisfied. After a longer meeting at the church with the police, the residents leave frustrated.

Consider also a scene in the fourth season where mayoral candidate Councilman Tommy Carcetti addresses the Interdenominational Ministerial Alliance. He notes that he is the third candidate they have heard and he fairly assesses the limitations of his prospects for an endorsement. Simon

---

17. Played by Wood Harris in thirty-eight episodes.

offers a vivid contrast between this receptacle of power and the reality of the corners in Baltimore. This African-American clergy association receives Carcetti in a plush, adorned conference room. With glass display cases surrounding the room, it is as though the reverends have taken every good thing from the city itself and placed them behind glass for viewing. Such is the visual contrast between the reception room and the streets. While the Barksdale crew meets above a funeral parlor and the narcotics co-op meets in a drab hotel meeting room, the Alliance space projects power and influence.

In reality, outside the façade, the reverse seems true. The drug crews own the streets. The ministers may have an impact on the occupant of the mayor's office in City Hall; but their sway over the projects, towers, and neighborhoods of Baltimore appears non-existent. In an amusing and telling irony, even those whom the church endorses politically don't always win. Even within the narrow political sphere of influence granted to the Church in *The Wire*, it is portrayed as largely impotent.

The fourth season continues to reinforce this point about the symbiosis between churches and civic power. Here, Bubbles, a hustler and drug addict, seeks retribution against police detective Thomas "Herc" Hauk[18] for events from a previous episode. Under the auspices of a police informant, Bubbles incorrectly informs Herc that a certain car contains narcotics owned by the Stanfield crew. In truth, the car, replete with "PR8ZGOD" plates, belongs to a minister who carries his Bible in an attaché case. Herc responds just as Bubbles knows he will—with unbridled enthusiasm, profanely berating and roughing up the minister. As the Bible falls out of the "drug" bag, Herc realizes his error. Later, Herc's actions become fodder for civilian complaints about police abuses. The news reaches Mayor Carcetti and Police Commissioner Ervin Burrell,[19] seriously effecting Herc's career. The point of this illustration for our present discussion centers upon Bubbles' knowledge that police harassment of a minister will have quick and specific consequences. He does not pick an average civilian at random but rather a citizen with some political and religious clout. With precision and obvious intent, Bubbles sets up Herc and it goes just as planned. Just after Bubbles calls Herc with the false information, he asks several women from a local church for food. They decline and Bubbles seems unfazed. This moment expresses *The Wire*'s view of the practical mission of the Church. Harassment of Church members is wrong; that is not in dispute and the Church confronts it, taking care of its

---

18. Played by Domenick Lombardozzi in sixty episodes.
19. Played by Frankie Faison in forty-seven episodes.

own. Yet, the Chuch lacks that same vigor in addressing needs beyond itself, typified here by its neglect of Bubbles.

These narratives provide insight into Simon's assessment of the Church in urban America. It is an institution hitched to political power but lacking the ability in either proclamation or praxis to positively and practically impact the lives of urban residents who suffer from economic, social, and political marginalization. The Church, the body of Christ-followers, exhibits as her primary objective connecting with the politically-connected, rather than building relationships of what I will describe as a vertical and horizontal nature with those all too often disconnected from the benefits of political power.

The Wire also provides commentary on the unique and not altogether holy uses of churches and clergy. In the fifth season, Prop Joe Stewart instructs the new kingpin Marlo Stanfield[20] on how to launder drug money. Prop Joe introduces Marlo to one of three ministers that the East Side dealer himself uses. The money goes through a church as a donation to build schools, hospitals, and housing in the Caribbean but nothing actually gets built. Instead, the money comes back clean to the donor, with a cut to the minister. The minister instructs Marlo on the arrangement: pay ten on the dollar; anything beyond that depends on the generosity of the donor to "save those who want to be saved." The Church here not only fails to quell urban violence but actually contributes to it by providing a front for narcotics cash.[21]

Perhaps the most blatant intersection of the Church and street life in Baltimore occurs in the third season's "Slapstick." The rogue stick-up artist Omar Little[22] takes his grandmother to church once a month. The Barksdale crew has orders from Stringer Bell[23] to assassinate Omar for his past thefts. Two Barksdale henchmen see Omar with his grandmother; however, it is a Sunday and drug battles take the Sabbath off, viewers learn. The henchmen follow protocol and ask what they should do from higher-ups: let Omar go or break the truce and take their shot at him? The question gets to Bell, oddly enough, during a meeting of all drug co-op principals. Concerned to

---

20. Played by Robert F. Chew and Jamie Hector in twenty-four and thirty-two episodes, respectively.

21. One might argue that this scene speaks allegorically to a larger narrative on the profitability of poverty. Do the church and social service agencies actually promote the sustainability of indigence and destitution through their relief work? For more on this argument, see Lupton, *Toxic Charity* or Corbett and Fikkert, *When Helping Hurts*.

22. Played by Michael Kenneth Williams in fifty-one episodes.

23. Played by Idris Elba in thirty-seven episodes.

kill Omar, Bell approves the Sunday truce-busting hit. With church buildings all around, the gangsters unload their clips but fail to hit their target.

Consequences abound for the failed Sunday targeting. Slim Charles[24] upbraids the young soldiers, berating them for wounding the "Church crown of a colored lady" on a Sunday. Avon Barksdale and Stringer Bell have a heated exchange, with Avon noting that the Sunday truce has stood since illegal narcotic sales began. Whether a primary narrative point, which I do not think is likely, or just fodder to move the story along, this scene reinforces the notion that the Church has no connection to life on the street and instead serves only as a sentimental ornament of days gone by. Omar has no use for church; his allegiance is to his beloved grandmother. This ritual could just as easily amount to a monthly meal at the local delicatessen. The observance of a Sunday truce, and its ubiquitous acknowledgment among all levels of gang hierarchy, seems pointed more toward tradition and a gang code than to any acknowledgement of God. On Sundays grandmothers go to church while drug dealers scheme. The Church may meet the needs of seniors, but for hoppers, corner boys, and the like, the idea that the Church could offer them something lies outside the show's paradigm.

The Church's impact on urban society within this world has at best political effects. Clergy and churches lack relevance, either through civic impotence or empty conviction, on the corners. This is not to say that Simon fails to implant occasions of redemption. He certainly does, particularly in the evolution of the relationship between Bubbles and the Narcotics Anonymous sponsor Walon.[25] But this thread serves only to contrast the relative impotency of the Church to offer change, be it to an individual, institutions, or a community.

In "Final Grades," viewers find Bubbles in a hospital mental health ward.[26] Bubbles sits here, distraught, having accidentally killed his friend Sherrod with a loaded drug. With no dialogue, we witness Walon entering the room and embracing Bubbles. In the midst of Bubbles' great personal suffering and guilt, Walon offers grace, understanding, and companionship through his actions. This juxtaposition is continued in "Unconfirmed Reports," in which Walon and Bubbles attend a Narcotics Anonymous meeting in a church basement.[27] A cross over a partially stained glass window frames the camera shot as Walon invites Bubbles to offer a testimony to the group. Although Bubbles cannot finish telling his story, we do learn that he

---

24. Played by Anwan Glover in twenty-six episodes.
25. Played by Steve Earle in eight episodes.
26. S4/E13.
27. S5/E2.

has fifteen months of sobriety and clean living. This is illustrated through his improved physical appearance. Bubbles is on the path to changing his life, repentance from drug enslavement, and hustling. Finally, in "Late Editions,"[28] Walon, Bubbles, and the *Sun* reporter Mike Fletcher[29] attend another NA meeting. On this occasion the cross is perfectly centered in the background as Bubbles celebrates a sobriety anniversary and shares his personal testimony to other recovering addicts. His physical transformation has progressed so that he is almost unrecognizable from the street dweller at the early stages of the show. As viewers, we are made to feel that Bubbles is on his way to being redeemed.

Redemption, both symbolically through the image of the cross and in the personal journey of Bubbles, is present in *The Wire*. In the midst of profound and seemingly comprehensive tragedy, we have an instance of comedy (Bubbles serves as the show's comic character). However, the conveyance and proclamation of this salvation does not come via the Church but through a Narcotics Anonymous sponsor. The intersection of Christianity and corners appears limited to twelve-step programs in church meeting halls. As the pastor of a church that hosts, funds, and directs a recovery ministry, I know that recovery programs provide a substantial link between churches and communities. I do not intend in any way to minimize the Narcotics Anonymous program or the work of the character Walon. I know my own Bubbles and Walons. I have seen firsthand the redemptive power of recovery communities. In many ways, recovery ministries function as parachurch organizations. These are entities with Christian values and missions yet not directly affiliated with the Church. Simon allows a place for these organizations, and in contrast to his portrayal of the Church, very directly illustrates their effectiveness.

But why is this the locus of redemption within the show? As portrayed, grace and salvation do not come from City Hall.[30] Transformation does not come from the streets.[31] And, redemption does not come from the prophetic witness of the Church. The singular instance of the transcendent power of love within *The Wire* is the relationship between Walon and Bubbles. This reality further substantiates the disconnect between the Church and urban dwellers.

28. S5/E9.

29. Played by Brandon Young in nine episodes.

30. Illustrated by Mayor Carcetti turning down state money for Baltimore schools in order to further his future political opportunities in "Final Grades," S4/E13.

31. We find Malik "Poot" Carr (played by Tray Chaney in twenty-five episodes) in "Clarifications," S5/E8, working at a Foot Locker after having left the grind of the corners.

What is the meaning of this disconnection? During *The Wire*'s airing, I served as the pastor of a small Baptist congregation in the South Ward of Trenton, New Jersey. Later I was elected Councilman for that ward. My wife and I moved to Trenton in the summer of 1998, having both graduated from Princeton Theological Seminary just weeks before. We purchased a three-bedroom semi-detached home within walking distance of our new roles at First Baptist Church of the City of Trenton. We served there until 2009.

For those eleven years, we worked and lived in a place different from Simon's "Body-more, Murdaland" in size, but not in scope. We witnessed open air drug sales in front of our church and home, knowing that the Trenton Police Department fought a courageous yet losing battle against the adaptive, organized, and seemingly ubiquitous corner boys and girls. We drove by living monuments to the death of work: old Roebling Steel factories long since idle and in decay, rows of century-old homes that once housed American Bridge factory workers now vacant, the old Trenton bridge alight with red neon providing a eulogy for a city that is no more—Trenton Makes, the World Takes—now unable, whether willing or not, to change the political dynamic of a state consumed with suburban concerns. We became friends with teachers and principals, students and parents, and learned that those who could send their children to other schools did, while those who could not sent them to Trenton public schools. And we witnessed the two regional papers of record, *The Times of Trenton* and *The Trentonian*, sensationalize symptomatic details of urban life, yet fail to initiate any discussion of the root causes of the capital city's afflictions. The themes of the show are not things we simply watch on television or write about in books but live.

I would like nothing more than to offer a robust rebuttal to Simon's portrayal of the Church in urban America. However, when it comes to political power, dissonance from street life and those doing good works in the name of Jesus Christ, the Church seems little more than a tertiary agent, a prop on the stage of urban life. At least this appeared the case in Trenton.[32]

---

32. I offer several anecdotal examples. Within Trenton, thirty or so African-American churches combined efforts to form a ministerial association that functioned primarily as an economic development organization, the Concerned Pastors of Trenton and Vicinity. In 2004, this entity partnered with a New Jersey affordable housing developer and pushed a proposal to "develop" six square blocks of housing within a low-income, heavily rental, primarily Latino section of Trenton. This development would have utilized eminent domain as its primary vehicle to move out five hundred families residing within this section. Since the project would have consisted of 80 percent affordable housing, federal and state tax credits would have provided most of the capital. Stringer Bell could only have hoped for such a deal and economic return. Trenton's City Council, with the implicit approval of the Mayoral Administration, granted exclusive development rights to this development partnership for the period of a year. Ultimately, the indigenous community of this neighborhood organized and defeated this project.

As a person of faith, I believe in redemption. I believe that the Church is an agent of Jesus Christ with a mission in the world. How then can congregations do better than urban irrelevance? First, urban Christians must expound a theology of the city. For too long, American Christianity has looked to suburban churches to define and model church, dictating faithfulness in terms of those churches that have chosen urban flight over the urban plight. Willow Creek, Saddleback, and other sprawl churches have become the predominant model of Christianity in this country. In this theology of

---

(They did this through picketing, letters to the editor, and constant attendance at City Council meetings. Currently, small developers are building on vacant lots and rehabilitating empty properties within this section, adding economic diversity to transform this neighborhood into a mixed income melting pot community. Information on the flagship property within this section may be found here: http://www.trentonlofts.com/default.php?building=26.) But, were it not for the political connections of The Concerned Pastors of Trenton and Vicinity this project would not have left the drawing board. Churches can bring votes and those votes can yield political connections.

Those connections have a price—political interests can leverage church proclamation. In the 2004–2005 school year, students at a Trenton Public Schools alternative high school on Sherman Avenue in Trenton received false grades. These grades allowed students to matriculate from ninth grade to tenth grade. This travesty came to light only after a former State History Teacher of the Year took evidence to this effect to New Jersey's Department of Education. Shortly thereafter, the Trenton Public Schools Superintendent resigned. Three administrators faced charges and received suspensions. (For more information on this sad episode, see Bob Bowden's 2009 documentary *The Cartel*.) In response to the harming of children, did the churches of Trenton demand accountability? Did they march on the Trenton Board of Education? Did they take to the streets? The Church did nothing.

This follows a general withdrawal of the Church from education in Trenton. At one time, Trenton had as many as half a dozen Catholic schools serving hundreds of children from kindergarten through eighth grade. These schools were rigorous and prepared children to succeed. As white families in the 1960s and 1970s fled to the suburbs, and upwardly economic minority families followed suit in the 1990s and 2000s, families that could afford this private tuition diminished. By 2008, the Diocese of Trenton had shuttered each school citing inadequate funding mechanisms. Thus was lost an effective alternative to the failing public schools.

Trenton does have points of light within its boundaries. Many faith-based organizations provide for daily and systemic needs of residents. The Trenton Area Soup Kitchen supplies hot meals, support and community to those in need. Habitat for Humanity Trenton Area promotes economic improvement by fostering homeownership opportunities while supplying needed elements of renewal for neighborhoods. The Catholic Youth Organization invites young people to experience teamwork, coaching and success. These are para-church organizations, not unlike Walon's NA meetings. Bruce Main and Urban Promise in Camden, New Jersey, Jimmy Dorrell and Mission Waco in Waco, Texas, and the ministry couple Bill Stanfield and Evelyn Oliveira of Metanoia in Charleston, South Carolina are leading faith-based organizations that partner with churches. While these organizations are loving, effective, and devoted, the Church should not farm out this ministry work. Churches need to be at the forefront of this engagement.

the suburbs, engagement rarely exceeds the church edifice. One can go to church on Sunday, and play in church leagues at church gymnasiums connected to church schools funded by church cafes every other day.

Rather than expanding the Kingdom of God, this mentality seeks to build earthly empires. These empires are largely indistinguishable from our prevalent materialistic culture, denoting precisely their reasons for success. Sadly, in recent decades, more and more city churches have succumbed to this false theology, uprooting themselves and leaving craters in their former communities, all to chase after grand buildings, ornate decorations, and palaces of mammon. Urban Christians must reject this country-club Christianity and proclaim without hesitation or reservation that God loves the city. Christianity began as an urban movement.[33] Given the Baltimores and the Trentons, it must once again become an urban movement.

This proclamation will demand a radical reassessment of method and methodology. The practical tenets of this theology are simple. The Church must be present in its community, or in other words: get out of the pews and on the damn corners! When my wife and I began looking at houses in Trenton in 1998, some dear souls told us that the church did not expect us to live in Trenton, much less the neighborhood immediately surrounding the church. However, it was important to us that we live amongst the community in which we worked. By living in our faith community, we came to know those outside our church body. We lived next to them; we shopped with them at the bodegas and convenience stores; we shared common urban experiences—and not all pleasant. As we breathed the same air and walked the same sidewalks, we bonded and community formed. This allowed us to engage with all elements of the street and, more importantly, provided entrance for our congregation to become involved. The community came to view our church as safe and a resource, while the church gained an appreciation and love for the community.

Because of this, our corner in front of First Baptist ceased to be a locale for open air drug sales. I began to play basketball with local gang members at the Boys & Girls Club next door to the church. Our consistent physical presence in that community gave our mission credibility and relevance. We began to know the boys and girls on the corners, gain trust, and build relationships. Another Trenton pastor asked a high-level drug dealer how he could so easily recruit lookouts, runners, and dealers. The response spoke volumes: "You're here for a few hours a couple of times a week. I'm here all day every day. You're not around; I'm always around. Who do they see more?" In the city, the Church must be seen more.

---

33. For a detailed analysis of this, see Stark, *Rise of Christianity*.

Most Trenton pastors do not live in the same communities as their churches and this residential dissonance has profound effects. First and foremost, this tendency inhibits the building of meaningful relationships among equals. As pastors choose to live in "better" communities, an attitude of servicing the subordinate may rise accompanied by the manifestation of resentment among those serviced. Non-residency also discourages church members from engaging with neighborhoods as the church becomes the totality of experience for those parishioners. Congregants drive in to church and then drive home to live. Their tie is to the building itself, not the community in which it sits. In this way, the Church is seen as an occupier of space within the community by people who live in those neighborhoods, not a part of the indigenous community per se; in other words, it fails to be Church in these important ways. These traits make outreach and gritty ministry almost impossible.

Residency matters. But more than just living within the city, the Church must serve the city. I find comfort and encouragement in the writings of the early Church as it ministered in the cities of the Roman Empire. The Church grew because it was a presence in the cities, building relationships. We may return to the origins of the Church to learn how to engage in this ministry. Tertullian wrote in 200: "To no less a post than this has God called them, and they dare not try to evade it. We have filled up every place belonging to you—islands, castles, caves, prisons, palace, city forum. We leave you your temples only."[34] Let us fill up the corners, the vacant lots, the boarded up buildings; let us take our worship outdoors for the masses; let us reside in the community and leave only political palaces behind. We must cast aside the seductive allure of political power and instead work for Kingdom power to transcend evil and transform lives through Jesus Christ.

David Simon has provided a critique of twenty-first-century American Christianity by making the Church within the world of *The Wire* little more than a stage prop. May this raw assessment rouse God's faithful from their slumber so that those on the corners of America's forgotten neighbors may say of us: Christians know and trust God. They placate those who oppose them and make them their friends. They do good to their enemies. They love one another. They do not refuse to help the widows. They rescue the orphans from those who do him violence. They have given ungrudgingly to those who have not. If they see strangers, they take them to their dwellings and rejoice over them as real brothers and sisters, for they do not call themselves brothers and sisters after the flesh, but after the spirit, and in God. If anyone among them is poor and needy, and they do not have food to spare,

---

34 Tertullian, *Apology*, 45.

they fast for two or three days, that they may supply the necessary food. They scrupulously obey the commands of their Messiah. Every morning and every hour they thank and praise God for his loving kindness toward them. Because of them, there flows forth all the beauty that there is in the world. But the good deeds they do they do not proclaim in the ears of the multitude but they take care that no one shall perceive them. Thus they labor to become righteous. Truly this is a new people, and there is something divine in them.[35]

BIBLIOGRAPHY

Aristides. "Apology." Translated by D. M. Kay. In *Ante-Nicene Fathers*, edited by Allan Menzies, 9:257–79. Online: http://www.earlychristianwritings.com/text/aristides-kay.html.

Bowden, Mark. "The Angriest Man in Television." *The Atlantic* 301 (January/February 2008) 50–57. Online: http://www.theatlantic.com/magazine/archive/2008/01/the-angriest-man-in-television/306581/.

Corbett, Steve, and Brian Fikkert. *When Helping Hurts: Alleviating Poverty Without Hurting the Poor . . . and Yourself*. Chicago: Moody, 2009.

Lupton, Robert. *Toxic Charity: How Churches and Charities Hurt Those They Help (And How to Reverse It)*. New York: HarperCollins, 2011.

Simon, David. "Behind the Wire." Interview by Meghan O'Rourke. *Slate* (December 1, 2006). Online: http://www.slate.com/articles/news_and_politics/interrogation/2006/12/behind_the_wire.html.

———. "Interview with Bill Moyers." *Bill Moyers Journal*. April 17, 2009. Video interview. Online: http://www.pbs.org/moyers/journal/04172009/watch.html.

———. "Introduction." In *The Wire: Truth Be Told*, edited by Rafael Alvarez, 2–34. New York: Pocket, 2010.

Stark, Rodney. *The Rise of Christianity: How the Obscure, Marginal Jesus Movement Became the Dominant Force in the Western World in a Few Centuries*. Princeton: Princeton University Press, 1996.

Tertullian, "Apology." In *Ante-Nicene Fathers*, edited by Alexander Roberts, James Donaldson, and Alexander Coxe, 3:17–60. Peabody, MA: Hendrickson, 1994.

---

35. Aristides, "Apology," para. 15.

2

Living on Set
A Year Spent Living and Working in Baltimore City

WHITNEY JOHNSON

"You can't trust anyone. Anyone. Remember that, okay?"

ENDINGS

AS MY FATHER PREPARED to walk into the airport, we shared our last good-byes. He looked at his youthful (read: naïve) daughter and dealt me one of his favorite mantras: *You can't trust anyone. Anyone.* I was perched on the eve of my eleven-month AmeriCorps service commitment in Baltimore, and my father was perched on the edge of all reason. He could not for the life of him understand why I needed to move halfway across the country to work, in his opinion, as a volunteer. All I knew about my impending assignment was that I would be working somewhere in the heart of the city alongside the Baltimore City Office of Sustainability. As I entertained myself with what lay ahead, I was thrilled; my father was terrified. Having almost no idea what I was getting into, I could only try to alleviate his anxieties with assurances that I was sure I would be fine. I hoped my father's troubled soul would rest easy as he flew home that night, though I was sure it would not.

Looking back on the experience, I realize now that neither my father nor I had any idea just what I was getting into. In fact, it was a good thing my father hadn't known any more about my assignment, or he may have refused to leave me on that warm night in Maryland. Little did I know that soon my ideas about race, poverty, and power would find faces and names. Little did I know I would soon come to confront my own racial identity by living and working among the racial and ethnic *other*. Little did I know I would get hooked on the HBO series, *The Wire*, as each new episode came to capture and somehow summarize snapshots of my year—portraying both the hostile street corners and barren landscapes against which my time in Baltimore came to life.

THE LANDSCAPE

On the first day of my assignment, I awoke eagerly, as I would each day over the course of the next 11 months. It was August 2009, and a Maryland Transit Authority bus rumbled past my bedroom window. I shared a classic-looking red brick Baltimore row home with two native Marylanders, taking up residence in their converted basement. My sole window to the world sat at sidewalk-level, peering into the oft-buzzing neighborhood street. My tiny window and I were tucked away on the east side of Baltimore (of Prop Joe fame), in the recently renovated (read: gentrified) neighborhood of Canton. It was a beautiful location—the backdoor of our row home was only steps away from the idyllic waterfront. As I got dressed and ate breakfast that morning, I was filled with a mixed rush of excitement and trepidation. It was the first day of my new job. My first *real* job. My professional career had begun.

I grabbed my bag and walked across the street to the bus stop. There I waited for the #7, which would take me from just across my doorstep to the Charles L. Benton, Jr., Building, where the Baltimore City Office of Sustainability was housed. As I waited for the bus, I surveyed my new neighborhood. I scanned the block, my eyes panning over a landscape of mixed residential and commercial-use buildings. A lively late-night restaurant sat immediately across from our row home, a morgue was situated two doors down and row homes in various states of renovation lay all around.

There was hardly a grassy reprieve in sight. From my brief and inexpert inventory, I could tell that the natural environment was restricted to several distinct and clearly confined spaces. There were newly installed maple and dogwood trees planted sporadically along the sidewalk, which sought to break up the concrete and offer shade and solace amidst an otherwise unforgiving landscape. Unfortunately, a few of the young trees weren't faring so well. I hoped the sickly saplings did not foretell my own future misfortune as a transplant in such a trying environment. The #7 bus rolled up, and where my excitement ended, my anxiety quickly found me again.

Just six months prior to my first day on the job, President Obama delivered on an important campaign promise. On February 13, 2009, Congress passed the American Recovery and Investment Act, and dollars quickly began funneling into the U.S. labor market.[1] This included at least twenty-five million dollars for the AmeriCorps VISTA program.[2] My assignment in the VISTA program was to act as a Program Assistant to the Baltimore Neighborhood Energy Challenge (BNEC), a pilot program collaboration among three main entities: a local non-profit, the Baltimore Office of Sustainability, and the Baltimore Community Foundation. In the Baltimore city government's own words, BNEC was formed as a project tailored to eight Baltimore neighborhoods selected for their "diversity of geography, housing type, housing size, race, income, and level of community organization."[3] The program's aim was to work alongside community groups, neighborhood volunteers, and residents to spread knowledge, resources, and motivation to help Baltimore communities save energy and money. I would be connecting residents in two of those under-resourced neighborhoods with energy-saving resources.

The experience of entering the building diverged radically depending on the point of entry. Entering from the north side of the building affords one a beautiful view of Baltimore's City Hall, which is stationed stoically just across the street. Just in front of City Hall lies a carefully manicured, grassy mall—an open and inviting stretch of green space. Outlining the mall are several large beds of edible landscaping, designed and planted by the local Master Gardeners club, which donates the fruits of each harvest to a local food bank. In that light, the garden in front of City Hall seems to present a charming picture of civic idealism: a municipal entity wielding its power to provide nourishment to its most under-resourced citizens.

When entering the Benton Building from the south, one encounters an entirely different situation. From 10 a.m. to all hours of the night, bouncers linger outside dimly lit entryways marking each establishment amid a strip of adult businesses. Catcalls and dehumanizing stares were a normal part of the commuting experience. Needless to say, it was an uncomfortable way to begin the day. At first I avoided the area entirely, but slowly my revulsion

1. Recovery.gov, "Recovery Act," lines 1–8.
2. Goren, "Senate Passes Stimulus Bill with National Service Funding," line 1.
3. Garrison Institute, *Alice Kennedy: Baltimore Neighborhood Energy Challenge.*

waned and I began to navigate my way to the office by way of the south-side circus. In a strange way, that wanton strip sort of grew on me, developing a certain charm in all of its decadence. Yet, in spite of my best efforts, I never grew comfortable with the stark juxtaposition of civility and revelry.

On the north side of the Benton Building, the rhythms of creation present in the edible garden reminded me that life was continually evolving and unfolding, creating a sense of peace and stillness. On the south side, the cycle of insatiable desire and dissatisfaction disrupted my soul. Slowly the realization emerged that this was surely a less charming, but clearly more sober picture of civic reality. The city could present a public performance of order only to the extent that it was able to conceal the underbelly of its rooted injustices, the severe socioeconomic injustices that I found so compellingly uncovered with each episode of *The Wire*.

THE BACKGROUND

It wasn't long before I began noticing that conversations around me were sprinkled with mentions of an HBO series entitled *The Wire*. Shortly thereafter, I got my hands on the series and my boyfriend and I began to make our way through the series with religious devotion. The show became the third wheel in our relationship, frequently butting into conversation and demanding we pay it an increasing amount of attention. We could spare little time away from the stories as they unfolded, consistently drawing us in. I can still remember the opening scene of the pilot episode as it filled the screen. I found myself stunned, as the setting was nearly identical to the places where I worked on a daily basis. I was fairly certain that I could actually identify which street that first scene had been filmed on, and I was convinced that I had been there within the last few days.

Throughout *The Wire*, David Simon and Edward Burns offer a vivid and layered depiction of how urban communities have materialized in the postindustrial shadow, many scenes of which are painted against the backdrop of a bleak and barren hue of concrete. Isolated, exposed, and desolate, the urban environment of inner-city Baltimore, as illuminated throughout *The Wire*, both overshadows and undergirds the lives of its inhabitants. The show draws attention to the commercially deserted neighborhoods created by the rise and fall of early twentieth-century industrialization, revealing the remains of a postindustrial wasteland stripped of its fertility. The characters living on the west side of the city are confined to and by its environmental bankruptcy. The inner-city island of cracked sidewalks and empty lots are at their most basic level the canvas upon which the story unfolds, and perhaps at a more complex level, an invitation to question just what the miles of concrete aim to conceal.

The city hasn't always looked so desolate. Like several other Northeastern cities, Baltimore experienced an explosion in both its labor market and population during the early twentieth century. Human and resource objectification, exploitation, and massive manufacturing operations drove the American industrial economy into a new age of proliferation. By 1950, however, the manufacturing industry had run much of its course and begun its grinding descent. Over the next twenty years, Baltimore saw a 74.9 percent decline in its industrial employment. The city's urban population of nearly one million was driven into the throes of joblessness, soon followed by white flight into suburbia and rapid property degradation.[4] After four decades of failed revitalization, reorganization, and reinvestment strategies, the west side of Baltimore—in the neighborhoods where I worked—continued to struggle to regain its footing and recover from its harrowing lack of resources.[5]

I was reminded of this each time I walked its streets. Hemmed in by blocks of condemned row homes and endless rivers of concrete, the environment of West Baltimore appears deprived of its natural integrity throughout *The Wire*. Void of the fertility and possibility of natural space, this environment both creates and further perpetuates the seemingly inescapable powerlessness of those who reside therein. Arguably the city's most geographically vulnerable population, residents of the inner city find themselves egregiously disconnected from the ability to experience, care for, and receive from what most take for granted: our shared natural environment. Instead, they find themselves inhabiting spaces covered in concrete.

Such concealed spaces are perhaps best illustrated by "Hamsterdam," the enforcement-free zone introduced during the third season of *The Wire*. Hamsterdam is the brainchild of Major Howard "Bunny" Colvin, District Commander for the Western District of the Baltimore Police Department, and formed with the intent to create a space where drug use and sales are tolerated, where drug laws are not enforced, and in fact, blatantly disregarded. Major Colvin hopes that in corralling the Western District's drug activity into a few concentrated areas, the rest of the community will be free to live in peace and the department can then focus on "real" police work. Hamsterdam's physical zone is one made up of seemingly vacant row homes and abandoned lots. This particular space, much like those

---

4. Levine, "Third-World City," 125–6.
5. For a more detailed account, ibid., 138–45.

found elsewhere on the west side, has been all but forgotten, until Colvin's plan gives it a "new life."

In observing the creation of Hamsterdam, I identified the intention to disregard human and environmental dignity, to simplify what was meant to remain complex by covering over or cordoning off certain parts of the city. Even though the vacant lots within Hamsterdam were covered in concrete and remnants of dilapidated structures, they still bear witness to the life confined below, however chaotic and unruly it may be. As in my own neighborhood, plants threatened to overtake the deserted buildings—life breaking through in the most unreasonable places, even through layers of concrete, relying not on human nurturing but on the most basic elements of air, water, and sunlight. While the structures of power administered an ineffective bandage as treatment for the city's most affecting issues of poverty, addiction, and violence, the natural environment breaking in reminds us that life in its messiness cannot be that easily contained.

THE STARS

I was honored to support the work of community volunteers in both Park Heights and Reservoir Hill, two very vibrant and historically rich neighborhoods on the northwest side of Baltimore. As I spent time in each neighborhood, I became more familiar with the unique environment of each, as well as with the incredible people who called those neighborhoods home. As an outsider, I had the task of approaching each individual volunteer or group of volunteers with the offer to connect them to a clearinghouse of energy-saving resources available through the city's network of energy-efficiency programs and contractors. As an AmeriCorps VISTA member, my role was limited to offering mental and relational elbow grease, rather than any physical service. Practically, this meant that I was able to connect homeowners with such resources as free basic household weatherization, connect neighborhood organizations with on-site workshops about energy-use behavior modifications, or simply perform administrative tasks that no one else had either the time or inclination to complete. A typical day included doing a few or all of these things, in addition to fielding calls from volunteers or attending community block meetings or service events.

My role as an outsider was not unique to the history of each of these neighborhoods. They seemed somewhat used to the imposition of outsiders, with some modes of presence having fared more positively than others. Luckily, I was working for a program that employed a locally sensitive and contextualized approach. The Baltimore Neighborhood Energy Challenge

(BNEC) was an asset-based community engagement initiative that built on the existing investment and involvement of community members and institutions already established within these neighborhoods. I was not surprised to learn that there was a layered history of projects, not unlike mine in their objective to help, that had been initiated and at some point abandoned. These projects presumably had been initiated with good intentions, but as the history in these communities shows, good intentions seldom prove to be enough. I often felt that by walking into those neighborhoods as a "helper," I'd inherited the burden of all the broken promises that came before me.

Knowing the ineffective or negative outcomes of many programs in the past, I could not make sense of why I was so warmly and genuinely welcomed into each of these communities. What would make *this* program different? How would I be sensitive to this history and avoid making promises that could not be fulfilled? What would sensitive and appropriate support look like? I became resentful of the short-term tourism that had contributed to the fractured relationship between service provider and recipient in these neighborhoods, and I became acutely aware of the need for long-term commitments to the kind of work I was undertaking. On the other hand, I also grew increasingly aware of the fact that there was no guarantee the program I was working for would be funded beyond its initial phase, much less a guarantee that I would personally remain in Baltimore after the completion of my eleven-month AmeriCorps commitment.

Mindful of my own transience, I was continually surprised and inspired by the *sense of place* radiating from the visionaries I met who had been living and advocating from within their neighborhoods for years. These community members seemed to possess a still and strong sense of defiant optimism in the face of decreasing property values and increasing crime rates. These folks not only remained in the neighborhood as disheartening conditions escalated, but they continued to strengthen their ties to and within their community. Many community leaders I met with did not have the luxury of calling this function their full-time job, yet this did not diminish their level of devotion. From where I stood, there seemed to be little indication of any immediate improvement or direct return on their generous and prolonged investment. And despite the odds, these leaders devoted themselves boldly to their neighborhoods, committing their emotional energies to the endless number of tasks at hand. They scattered and watered seeds of hope that they might never see break ground.

One particular neighborhood activist remains dear to me; I'll call her Iris. I met Iris at an introductory meeting in Park Heights during the first weeks of the program. She sat at the front of the room, all eyes on her as she convened and then directed the meeting. It was obvious that she had longstanding influence and was widely admired. Her personal style seemed to tell a rich and colorful story; she wore a head wrap in a striking West African print and rings on every finger. I felt instantly intrigued by her discernment and drawn in by her presence. She quickly identified herself as a strong proponent of BNEC and volunteered to impart the information the program offered to those she knew would appreciate it. I knew that her early adoption meant I would get to spend an increasing amount of time with her, and I was delighted. As she grew from an acquaintance to a friend, I began to see Iris's presence as more fierce and more gracious than I had at the start. She exuded a tenacity that was fueled not by bitterness, but by her undying commitment to her community and her hopeful vision for its future. She had a weathered collection of life experiences and on some days, if I was lucky, she would share a few of them with me.

One of my favorite excuses I used to spend time with Iris was to volunteer at the farmer's market in Park Heights. True to her spirit, Iris was at the helm of this community asset. Park Heights was one of the few neighborhoods in West Baltimore with nearby access to fresh and local foods; thanks to the work of a community alliance, Park Heights had established its very own weekly market, operating from June through November and located within walking distance of most homes in the neighborhood.[6] Iris was first to arrive at the farmer's market each week and the last to leave, acting as the market's general manager. I joined her several times at the market, which I found to be a great place to share information about BNEC with market shoppers; but even better, it was an excuse to spend time with Iris. As we sat together atop the Pimlico Race Track parking-lot-turned-farmer's-market, we chatted about the lack of community gardens and green space in Park Heights. At the time, there were plenty of vacant lots and very few unpaved spaces in the community. The idea of community gardening was a stretch even for Iris.

Park Heights, like many other Baltimore neighborhoods, had few food source options. Particular portions of the neighborhood were even defined as verifiable *food deserts*.[7] For West Baltimoreans living in Park Heights and wishing for a chance to produce, purchase, or consume healthy fare, the

---

6. Park Heights Community Health Alliance, "Park Heights Community Farmers Market @ Pimlico," line 6.

7. The official definition of *food desert* given by the Johns Hopkins Center for a Livable Future and Baltimore City's Office of Sustainability is this: "An area where the distance to a supermarket is more than one quarter of a mile; the median household income is at or below 185 percent of the Federal Poverty Level; over 40 percent of households have no vehicle available; and the average Healthy Food Availability Index score for supermarkets, convenience and corner stores is low." See Johns Hopkins Center for a Livable Future, "New Improved 'Food Desert' Map," para. 3.

farmer's market seemed to be the best, and only, option. How could this flagrant injustice be? Where I lived, I often found myself wondering which grocery store or farmer's market to visit, based on which had the *best* produce. That year, I qualified and applied for Food Stamps through the federal Supplemental Nutrition Assistance Program (SNAP). I could use my small monthly fortune to buy whatever my taste buds desired: organic, equal exchange chocolate, salmon from the other side of the country, or coffee from the other side of the world. Knowing what I knew about the food desert where I'd spent the bulk of my day, I often felt conflicted as I handed over my SNAP card to the cashier at Whole Foods. I could purchase fresh and local produce *every* day of the week; I lived in a food oasis.

On another occasion when we were working together, Iris told me about what it was like to raise her son in a place where the distractions were endless and drug-related violence ubiquitous. She told me about her resulting resolve to be involved in as many aspects of her son's life as was necessary to keep him on track and out of trouble. She volunteered at her son's schools throughout his education and made sure he completed his homework each evening before he was allowed to spend time with friends. She told me about how her son began hanging out on street corners with his friends during his teenage years—something that, from my observations, seemed a precarious but somewhat natural neighborhood activity, especially for young men. Iris made it her business to hang out alongside her son and his friends on those corners. If he headed out to the corner, she did so as well. Of course I was curious where her son had ended up after years of such attentive parenting. She told me that he was in his thirties and working as a youth counselor in a Baltimore City school. In no way was I surprised that he too was living a life of service.

For Iris, however, simply guiding her own son through the most challenging years of adolescence was not enough. Her involvement in the guidance of young lives extended beyond her son and into the lives of the youth of the neighborhood. With very few public resources available to youth in Park Heights, Iris recognized the need for "third places" in her community, community spaces outside of society's first two places, home and work. These third places were spaces for the public to engage on neutral ground, promoting social equality, commonality, and rest. In Ray Oldenburg's seminal work on the concept, he proposes that such spaces are the epicenter of the community.[8] But in Park Heights, there are no coffee shops and very few public parks. In 1998, Iris took notice of this void in her community and subsequently transformed a vacant row home into a thriving community

---

8. See Oldenburg, *Great Good Place*.

center that has since become an open and available alternative to the lure of the street corner for youth in Park Heights.[9]

Throughout *The Wire*, the lack of third places is oppressive. Beloved Bubs, for example, suffers from having no place to go besides the street. Squatting in an abandoned row home or in his sister's basement, Bubs finds little relief from the vices of the street until he finds Narcotics Anonymous. In the sanctuary of a nearby church, he finds a third place created by the meetings, providing peace, reprieve, and support. There, members found each other in order to find themselves. I was left to wonder if he would have had any hope without the availability of such a space. With the restrictive effects of having no asylum within his own neighborhood, this third space created the opportunity for Bubs to find healing and wholeness. As the show progressed, and I saw the value of these third spaces illustrated, Iris's work became even more meaningful to me.

THE CONFLICT

Before I arrived in Baltimore, I had only the vaguest sense of who I would be working alongside. I knew little about the city and was largely unaware of the incredible racial, economic, and environmental divides that plagued the city. I had never been more than a tourist in a city as large as Baltimore, nor had I experienced such a regular sense of fear while walking in a city alone. Only days into my fieldwork, I noted that an accurate internal navigation system is necessary in Baltimore. Much like the Benton building, the stark and immediate shift in conditions from one block to the next never ceased to astound me. This lack of consistency in the inner city meant that I had to know exactly where I was headed, lest I find myself in a thoroughly unrecognizable location only a few hundred feet from my actual destination.

When I found myself working late in West Baltimore, there seemed to be a general understanding among the volunteers that I was not to walk back to my car alone. Someone would either personally accompany me or at the very least stand on their front porch until I was safely inside my running and locked car on my way home. At first I politely declined the offers of security, but never protested if they insisted. While I had no empirical reason to fear for my safety, I still walked with a sense of fear. Finding myself in a near continual state of distrust, I began to question my default posture of anxiety and fear. Why did I return to fear time and time again? How could even the smallest glances from certain demographics incite in me an overpowering sense of self-preservation? Where was this coming from?

9. Neighborhood Link, "NIA Center," lines 4–7.

Something deep inside of me feared the darkness. The darkness of the night. The darkness of all my worst racial assumptions. I began to reflect more intently on the root of my discomfort.

What my father left unsaid when we exchanged our goodbyes at the airport were all the nuanced sensibilities I had inherited as a white middle-class woman growing up in the American South that did not warrant repeating. I grew up in a racially and culturally homogenous community—white and middle-class. In many ways, it was not necessary for my father to remind me to "be careful." I understood the protocol to which he was referring. I was being instructed to stay out of any "unsafe" areas of town and to watch out for myself and myself *only*. I could confidently translate the term "unsafe" to mean any area of town without middle-class white folk bustling about.

My father unashamedly expressed his desire to protect his only child, and looking back I do not blame him for his paternal instincts. I do not blame him for his distrust of the situation. Perhaps he was not even aware of the culturally racist milieu he had inherited and had inadvertently donated to his progeny. Having grown up with Southern pride, my father's warnings were informed by communities where calling someone "Black" or "Mexican" was not a harmless description, but a way to denote a set of assumptions about them. At the same time, however, I was taught to practice "colorblindness," taught not to acknowledge the racial, ethnic, and cultural differences of others; I was instructed to act as if everyone was a part of the same club.

I began to question this set of narrow assumptions earlier in life, sensing that passing judgment on someone based on race was an unfair and impractical system and that this practice indeed harms both the judged *and* the judger. And yet, on the streets of Baltimore, I still found myself reverting to ridiculous assumptions, avoiding friendly acknowledgment, eye contact, and conversation, making sure I always had my phone and keys in my hands. Did this make me neurotic or aware? Either way, I found that I was missing out on opportunities to know and understand those inhabiting the streets around me, opportunities to acknowledge and honor the uniqueness and beauty of our differences. Perhaps what is most disturbing to me is that, while living in this state of paralysis, I was not contributing to the active undoing of racism deeply etched around me, and that in my passive racism, I was actively contributing to the problem. Interpersonal, systemic, and structural systems of racism are very much alive, and whenever I found myself moving along the streets of Baltimore, I knew I was living proof that there was still work left to be done.

Most of my time in Baltimore was extremely positive. The community volunteers I worked alongside welcomed me warmly into their homes and neighborhoods, working with me to establish trust and rapport. As my term progressed, my time spent in my assigned neighborhoods came to be marked less by fear and anxiety and more by familiarity and ease. It was not until near the end of my term that an unfortunate encounter in Park Heights brought me back to a state of paralysis. I was in Park Heights dropping off some program information to one of the community volunteers. As I headed back to the office in my car, I hit a red light and idled at an intersection for a few minutes. It was the middle of the day and there were very few cars around. Like countless other times in the neighborhood, I stuck out. As I sat in my car waiting for the light to change, I noticed a group of young men standing on the corner and within seconds they noticed me also. One of the young men took a special interest in me and began yelling from the corner, "What are you doing here?" I was at first confused. He seemed angry. Was his outburst directed at me? Had I done something to offend him? I was not sure, but I began to panic. I picked up my phone and feigned a phone call. He read right through me. "Put the phone down. You ain't on the phone," he yelled. I began to sweat. Just as the light turned from red to green and I began to drive away, I could hear him hurl his final affront. "Get out of here you stupid bitch," he screamed. I picked up my phone and legitimately called my supervisor. In that moment I was convinced that I would not see the light of another Baltimore day. Why was this happening? What had I done to incite such personal bitterness and hate between myself and these strangers? Why me?

But why *not* me? I began to think of the scenes in *The Wire* as real life, perhaps unconsciously expecting that I would one day get caught up in the turf wars between Marlo and Barksdale's men and never make it out alive. Was that what was happening at that very moment? Unlike all the hours I'd spent witnessing depictions of open hostility that often escalated into gunfire, I did not have the safety of a screen between me and the world to protect me—to keep me anonymous and unknown. I was not the viewer; I was part of the show. I had often considered the sort of ethical choice I would have to make when or if I ever found myself threatened while alone in the city. I had very romantic ideas of striking up a gentle conversation with the aggressors, perhaps even becoming friends within minutes. I would tell them about my family, beg for mercy, and turn over all my possessions. But sitting there all I could think about was how to escape.

Once I escaped the situation and had time to decompress, I found myself using the show to gain a clearer perspective on the situation. *The Wire* allowed me to survey both the large and small contexts of the complex socioeconomic situation within the city. While I may not have *felt* like the problem, as a white woman I was a representation of the historical racism and structural limitations imposed on non-dominant groups by the historically white power holders. Whether I admitted it or not, the claim held true, and as long as I was not actively a part of the solution (and in many ways, even then), I was contributing to the problem.

It is difficult to imagine that the conditions of poverty, powerlessness, and racism could produce anything less intense than the episode I'd endured. The young man on the corner had perhaps felt the pangs of prejudice for as long as he could remember. I assume that the moments he felt anything other than disenfranchisement were notable anomalies. While the dramatic stop light episode certainly troubled my soul and quickened my heart rate, I imagine that my discomforts significantly paled in comparison to the number of times that young man had felt the effects of racist attitudes and power structures that I undoubtedly benefit from. And while his sensibilities were amplified overtly in that particular moment, I would argue that my countless acts of covert racism have over time amounted to something much worse.

And so how was I to respond? I felt victimized and disrespected, misrepresented and confused; but mostly, I felt sad. It was clear that as long as there were reasons for others to hate the skin I'm in, there are reasons to keep actively unraveling the racist lies that the dominant culture's history has imparted—especially those I'd told myself. These issues are as complex as they are oversimplified and I have no intention of offering any more insight into something about which I have little grounds to do so. Beverly Daniel Tatum insists that the act of moving against engrained racism is much like walking against an airport walkway: It must be intentional and it must be upstream, against the flow of racist norms. She reminds us that no member of the dominant class is without responsibility to act, for one is actively racist, passively racist, or actively antiracist.[10] We must decide and act.

BEGINNINGS

As my term drew to a close, I found myself more of a Baltimore amateur than any kind of expert. The sad irony of my time in Baltimore is that I left more afraid of the city than I was when I had arrived. Having encountered the edges of injustice, I understood the incredible cost of involvement. But I also left with a greater respect for those who are unafraid, who actively inhabit and improve the under-resourced neighborhoods and populations

---

10. Tatum, *Black Kids Sitting Together*, 15–16.

of Baltimore. My year in Baltimore was filled with vibrant personalities for whom I have great respect, and who I was fortunate to meet. But the racial, economic, and environmental issues remain complicated and twisted.

The issues that appeared fairly black and white upon my arrival I now see through a gray lens, much like the shade of concrete threatening to suffocate the life out of Hamsterdam in *The Wire*. As I continue to excavate my own suffocated and disordered perceptions of others, I continue to find plenty of space for hope and understanding buried underneath the inherited sheets of concrete, as rogue growths of life burst through the cracks towards the sun. Maybe this is just what the cracks in life invite us to do. Perhaps, after all, we can be surprised to find common elements of the human experience nestled inside us all that—given enough time, attention, and grace—will bring forth clear and expansive shades of truth and reconciliation that cannot be contained.

BIBLIOGRAPHY

Garrison Institute. *Alice Kennedy: Baltimore Neighborhood Energy Challenge* 8. Online: http://www.garrisoninstitute.org/climate-and-behavior/46-climate-mind-and-behavior-initiative/cmb-videos/climate-cities-and-behavior-videos-2011/579-alice-kennedy.

Goren, Nicola. "Senate Passes Stimulus Bill with National Service Funding." Online: http://www.nationalservice.gov/about/newsroom/statements_detail.asp?tbl_pr_id=1234.

Johns Hopkins Center for a Livable Future. "New, Improved 'Food Desert' Map." Online: http://www.jhsph.edu/research/centers-and-institutes/johns-hopkins-center-for-a-livable-future/news_events/announcement/2012/food_desert.html.

Levine, Mark V. "A Third-World City in the First World: Social Exclusion, Race, Inequality, and Sustainable Development in Baltimore." In *The Social Sustainability of Cities: Diversity and the Management of Change*, 125–26. Toronto: Toronto University Press, 2000.

Neighborhood Link. "NIA Center." Online: http://www.neighborhoodlink.com/Baltimore_MD/pages/88052.

Oldenburg, Ray. *The Great Good Place: Cafes, Coffee Shops, Bookstores, Bars, Hair Salons, and Other Hangouts at the Heart of a Community*. New York: Marlowe, 1999.

Park Heights Community Health Alliance. "Park Heights Community Farmers Market @ Pimlico." Online: http://www.phcha.org/farmersmarket.php.

Recovery.gov. *The Recovery Act*. Online: http://www.recovery.gov/About/Pages/The_Act.aspx.

Tatum, Beverly Daniel. *Why Are All the Black Kids Sitting Together in the Cafeteria? A Psychologist Explains the Development of Racial Identity*. New York: Basic, 1997.

3

"Way Down in the Hole"
Systemic Urban Inequality and *The Wire*[1]

ANMOL CHADDHA and
WILLIAM JULIUS WILSON

THE WIRE IS SET in a modern American city shaped by economic restructuring and fundamental demographic change that led to widespread job loss and the depopulation of inner-city neighborhoods.[2] While the series can be viewed as an account of the systemic failure of political, economic, and social institutions in Baltimore in particular, the fundamental principles depicted in *The Wire* certainly parallel changing conditions in other cities, especially older industrial cities in the Northeast and Midwest. Indeed, it is for this reason that *The Wire* captures the attention of social scientists concerned with a comprehensive understanding of urban inequality, poverty, and race in American cities.

In providing a sophisticated depiction of systemic urban inequality, *The Wire* investigates how key aspects of inequality are interrelated. It offers an in-depth examination of the decline of urban labor markets, crime and

---

1. Originally appeared in *Critical Inquiry* 38 (Autumn 2011) 164–88. Reprinted with permission by the University of Chicago Press.

2. The authors greatly benefited from enlightening discussions with the students in our seminar on "Urban Inequality and *The Wire*" at Harvard University. This article particularly benefited from the valuable insights of Brandon Asberry, Tony Bator, Christen Brown, Dylan Matthews, and Zoe Weinberg.

incarceration, the failure of the education system in low-income communities, and the inability of political institutions to serve the interests of the urban poor. A central theme of *The Wire* and a fundamental principle of scholarship on urban inequality is that political, social, and economic factors reinforce each other to produce profound disadvantage for the urban poor. By highlighting these connections, *The Wire* sheds light on the persistence and durability of concentrated disadvantage, which is reproduced across generations.[3]

Through the characters of *The Wire*, viewers can clearly see that various institutions work together to limit opportunities for the urban poor and that the actions, beliefs, and attitudes of individuals are shaped by their context. While scholars of inequality often take these ideas as basic assumptions, Americans remain strongly disposed to the idea that individuals are largely responsible for their own economic situations. In a recent survey of American attitudes, "fully two-thirds of those interviewed (67 percent) say blacks in this country who can't get ahead 'are mostly responsibly for their own condition' while only 18 percent say discrimination is mainly at fault." Nearly three-quarters of U.S. whites (70 percent), a large majority of Hispanics (69 percent), and even a slight majority of blacks (52 percent) believe that "blacks who can't get ahead are mostly responsible for their own condition."[4] In the face of a dominant belief system emphasizing personal inadequacies as the cause of poverty, *The Wire* effectively undermines such views by showing how the decisions people make are profoundly influenced by their environment or social circumstances.

Unlike conventional cop or crime dramas, *The Wire* develops complex characters on each side of the law who cannot be placed in unambiguous moral categories—neither castigated for criminal pathologies and the absence of mainstream values toward work nor valorized as one-dimensional hapless victims of society's cruelty who should command endless liberal sympathy.

To be sure, *The Wire* is fictional, not a documentary, though it takes inspiration from real-life events. It draws on the experiences of its creator David Simon, a former reporter at *The Baltimore Sun*, and his cowriter, Ed Burns, a former police detective and public school teacher in Baltimore. It is part of a long line of literary works that are often able to capture the complexity of urban life in ways that have eluded many social scientists.

---

3. Sampson, "Racial Stratification," 260–80; Sharkey, "Intergenerational Transmission of Context," 931–69.

4. Pew Research Center, "Blacks Upbeat about Black Progress, Prospects."

One need only consider works by Richard Wright, Italo Calvino, Ben Okri, and Charles Dickens, among many others, as examples.[5]

As a work of fiction, *The Wire* does not replace rigorous academic scholarship on the problems of urban inequality and poverty. But, more than making these issues accessible to a broader audience, the show demonstrates the interconnectedness of systemic urban inequality in a way that can be very difficult to illustrate in academic works. Due to the structure of academic research, scholarly works tend to focus on many of these issues in relative isolation.

A number of excellent studies analyze the impacts of deindustrialization, crime and incarceration, and the education system on urban inequality. It is often implicitly understood among scholars that these are deeply intertwined, but an in-depth analysis of any one of these topics requires such focused attention that other important factors necessarily receive less discussion. With the freedom of artistic expression, *The Wire* is able deftly to weave together the range of forces that shape the circumstances of the urban poor while exposing deep inequality as a fundamental feature of broader social and economic arrangements.

The idea that cities function as systems in which residents, neighborhoods, and institutions are integrated into a broader ecological unit is central to the paradigmatic Chicago school of urban sociology, led by Robert Park and his colleagues in the 1920s. Emphasizing *The Wire*'s sociological value, Nicholas Lemann argues that it

> was about as complete a realization of Park's dream of capturing the full richness and complexity of the city as anyone has ever accomplished. One of *The Wire*'s virtues was that, without denying any of its characters an iota of humanity, it resolutely kept its attention focused on Baltimore as a total system, in which every neighborhood and every institution exist in some relation to every other and people behave according to the incentives and choices they find set before them, more than according to whether they are good guys or bad guys.[6]

CRIME AND INCARCERATION

The first season of *The Wire* follows the activities of the Barksdale drug gang and the police unit that set out to bring down the criminal organization.

---

5. See Wright, *Native Son*; Okri, *Dangerous Love*; Dickens, *Tale of Two Cities*.
6. Lemann, "Charm City, USA."

The show casts a critical eye on the war on drugs, which it convincingly depicts as an ill-conceived undertaking whose primary outcome has been the mass jailing of nonviolent offenders. Street-level police officers patrol the neighborhoods where the Barksdale gang operates, and they repeatedly arrest dealers on the corners. Wee-Bey, Cutty, and the gang leader Avon Barksdale are in and out of prison throughout the series. Despite intensive policing, arrests, and jail sentences for many of the key players, the community does not seem safer. The dealers' regular customers, like Bubbles, continue to struggle with addiction, and the drug trade has hardly been curtailed.

This localized drama takes place against the backdrop of an unprecedented scale of imprisonment in the United States, where more than 2.3 million people are incarcerated.[7] The current penal regime is marked by both its magnitude and its rapid expansion in the past decades. While the incarceration rate remained relatively stable from the 1920s to the mid-1970s, it has more than tripled since 1980.[8] The United States far outpaces other countries with advanced economies; the incarceration rate is five times higher than that of England, for example, which has the highest rate in Western Europe.[9] The United States outranks all other democracies, with an incarceration rate that significantly exceeds that of Russia and South Africa.[10]

Imprisonment, however, is not spread evenly across society; it varies tremendously by race, class, and spatial location. Just less than 1 percent of the national population is incarcerated. By comparison, one in fifteen African Americans are currently in prison or jail, with even higher rates for black men under the age of thirty-five. Considering the disproportionate severity across social groups, some scholars describe the phenomenon as "racialized mass incarceration."[11] About 10 percent of young African Americans who did not complete high school were in prison or jail in 1980; by 2008, the rate had increased to 37 percent. These men, therefore, are nearly fifty times more likely to be incarcerated than the average American. Indeed, research suggests that going to prison "has become a normal life-event for African American men who have dropped out of high school."[12] Among the cohort

---

7. See Cooper et al., "Prisoners in 2008."
8. See Western and Pettit, "Incarceration and Social Inequality," 8–19.
9. See Lacey, "American Imprisonment in Comparative Perspective," 102–14.
10. See Mauer, "Comparative International Rates of Incarceration."
11. See Bobo and Thompson, "Racialized Mass Incarceration," 322–55.
12. Western and Pettit, "Incarceration and Social Inequality," 11.

of African American men now in their early thirties, 68 percent of those who dropped out of high school have spent some time in prison.

In terms of spatial location, it should not be surprising that residents of some neighborhoods are more likely to be incarcerated than others, since crime rates also vary across neighborhoods. Robert Sampson and Charles Loeffler, however, find that even among neighborhoods with comparable levels of crime, the incarceration rate is substantially higher for residents in neighborhoods with higher levels of concentrated disadvantage.[13] Taken together, this research makes clear that the incarceration boom in recent decades has been concentrated among certain social groups.

Beyond the unprecedented magnitude of the prison population, the social implications of mass incarceration extend beyond the individuals currently behind bars. Each inmate is tied to a number of people in the general population, with relationships to spouses, children, other family members, and friends in their communities. Given the disparities in incarceration, social exposure to the phenomenon of large-scale imprisonment is also felt most sharply by some sections of society. In a survey conducted in 2001–2 cited by Lawrence Bobo and Victor Thompson, one in ten whites reported having a close friend or relative who was incarcerated.[14] By comparison, half of African Americans had a friend or relative in prison. Class is also an important factor in who goes to prison and therefore who has social exposure to incarceration. Among high school dropouts with incomes below $25,000, one in five whites and nearly three in five blacks had a close relationship with someone behind bars. At higher-class positions, among college-educated respondents making at least $60,000, less than 5 percent of whites were tied to someone in prison. Among comparable African Americans, nearly one in three had a friend or relative in prison. While the higher end of the class hierarchy has less exposure to the incarcerated population in general, "the impact of racialized mass incarceration reaches across boundaries of class in black America."[15] In fact, the highest status African Americans were substantially more likely to have a close friend or relative in prison than whites at much lower class positions.

In addition to disparities in who is incarcerated and the social exposure to friends and relatives in prison, mass incarceration also has the effect of exacerbating existing social inequality. The standard economic measures mask the devastating impact on poor black communities, in particular. Official statistics reveal that joblessness and unemployment are regularly more

13. See Sampson and Loeffler, "Punishment's Place," 20–31.
14. See Bobo and Thompson, "Racialized Mass Incarceration."
15. Ibid., 350.

than twice as high for blacks as for whites. Since inmates are excluded from employment statistics, however, these troubling figures do not even fully capture the economic conditions of black communities.[16] Spending time in prison significantly hinders the future prospects of ex-offenders, which compounds disadvantages they faced before their incarceration. Using longitudinal data to isolate the impact of serving time in prison, Bruce Western and Becky Pettit find that incarceration is associated with 40-percent lower earnings and higher unemployment, corroborating similar findings by other researchers.[17]

A fundamental feature of the era of mass imprisonment is that incarceration has effectively been decoupled from crime. The dramatic expansion in the prison population is not accompanied by a corresponding increase in crime. Western shows that the incarceration rate has grown consistently since 1970, while official measures of crime increased in the 1970s and declined in the 1990s.[18] At the level of individual offenders, one might expect a direct link between crime and punishment, so that an increase in incarceration should be the result of greater crime. At the macro level, however, political shifts since the 1960s have created the climate for a more punitive approach to crime, so much so that incarceration has increased independently of trends in actual crime. Indeed, the chances of an arrest resulting in prison time and the average time served by violent offenders have risen over time despite a decline in the level of violent crime.[19] Recent research on mass incarceration explicitly draws attention to the role of state policy in generating and exacerbating key dimensions of urban inequality. Current sociological research generally emphasizes how economic and labor market processes have combined with demographic factors to produce enduring racial inequality and poverty in American cities. Through direct state action, the boom in incarceration interacts in critical ways with deindustrialization, joblessness, and other threats to family stability and the social organization of poor inner-city neighborhoods, including the significant decline in social provision through traditional social policy.[20]

Several scenes in *The Wire* connect this macrolevel analysis of mass incarceration in academic research to key processes that produce these outcomes at the micro level. Perceptions of crime and the lack of safety have

---

16. Western, *Punishment and Inequality in America*.

17. See Western and Pettit, "Incarceration and Social Inequality," and Holzer, "Collateral Costs," 239–69.

18. See Western, *Punishment and Inequality in America*.

19. See ibid.

20. See Wacquant, *Punishing the Poor*.

been consistent challenges for political leaders throughout the era of urban decline. Elected officials place pressure on their local police departments to produce measureable results in fighting crime and typically track progress with statistics. This approach was made famous by the CompStat system of the New York Police Department and was subsequently adopted by local police around the country.

Faced with the expectation of producing numbers, police departments are encouraged to focus on poor, inner-city neighborhoods to provide a greater number of arrests, especially by targeting the open-air drug trade. Much police activity in *The Wire* is intended to "juke the stats," as the officers describe it. With media attention on crime and the pursuit of measurable results, greater public pressure makes more intense policing a political necessity. Since imprisonment directly constrains the economic opportunities of ex-offenders and has deleterious consequences for their families, the social conditions of inner-city communities deteriorate even further. In cities across the country, mass incarceration has an enduring effect on the concentration of disadvantage.

GANGS AND STREET CULTURE

In his ethnographic research on the social order of an inner-city community, Elijah Anderson argues that activity and behavior in the neighborhood are characterized by one of two codes.[21] The street code places the highest value on interpersonal respect and makes the regular use of the threat of physical violence a means of self-assertion. While outsiders commonly stereotype all inner-city residents as acting in accordance with this code, Anderson argues that many residents in fact follow the decent code, which affirms middle-class values, personal responsibility, and participation in the mainstream economy. Subsequent ethnographic research has challenged this framework as overly simplistic and inadequate in explaining how the social organization of inner-city neighborhoods corresponds to greater violence.[22]

In the first two seasons of *The Wire*, viewers see the tension between D'Angelo's active participation in the worst aspects of the drug trade and his desire to pursue a different life path. As he develops sympathy for the victims of violent conflicts, he is unable to convince the gang leaders to change their approach. D'Angelo never reconciles these inner tensions, and, as he takes the fall for the gang's activities at the same time that he charts out a decent life for himself, he cannot be placed in either moral category. Wallace, a

---

21. See Anderson, *Code of the Street*.
22. See Harding, *Living Drama*, and Venkatesh, *Off the Books*.

teenager who takes orders from D'Angelo, similarly undermines this street-decent dichotomy. While he pursues a life in the drug trade and seeks to prove his street orientation to the gang leaders, he simultaneously oversees a household of several young neighborhood children. He feeds them in the mornings, gets them ready for school, and helps with their homework. Wallace is deeply troubled by the gang's killing of a perceived adversary and doubts whether he is suited to continue in the drug trade. Unable to find an exit from that trajectory, Wallace is himself killed when the gang's leaders question his loyalty to their enterprise. The moral dichotomy is perhaps most significantly undermined by Omar, a stick-up artist who regularly robs drug dealers but follows a personal code that prevents him from harming any resident not involved with the drug trade.

D'Angelo and Wallace are not able to freely act on their personal misgivings because they are both situated within the Barksdale gang. The organization of the gang is generally in line with the "business" model of street gangs described by Sudhir Venkatesh and Steven Levitt.[23] It has a well-developed internal hierarchy with high-level executives like Avon Barksdale and Stringer Bell, managers like D'Angelo, and lower-level corner dealers like Bodie and Poot. To a significant degree, the structure of the Barksdale gang parallels that of other organizations in *The Wire*, including the police department and the dockworkers union. Internal hierarchy is central to the operations of these organizations, as reflected by the entrenched norm of following the chain of command in the police department. Each organization demands unwavering loyalty from its members, although tensions inevitably arise among those at the low end, who are expected to implement the decisions made by leaders at the top, who are removed from the day-to-day reality on the ground.

Viewing the drug gang as an organization with specific objectives—in this case, maximizing profit from the sale of drugs—helps to explain many of the actions by gang members. Some of their violent acts are rooted in the organization's objectives, such as protecting its segment of the drug market from competitors and punishing those who cooperate with police efforts to obstruct its operations in the drug trade. These motivations are distinct from psychological, emotional, or cultural sources of violence. Some of the murders carried out by the Barksdale gang are not motivated by anger or a vague personal desire for respect on the street. To the extent that an analysis fails to distinguish a gang's institutional objectives from personal and individual-level factors, explanations of social organization and inner-city violence will necessarily be incomplete.

---

23. See Venkatesh and Levitt, "Are We a Family or a Business?" 427–62.

JOBLESSNESS AND WORK

The Wire also examines the declining economic prospects of Baltimore and many of its residents. Cities like Baltimore were economically devastated by deindustrialization in the 1970s and 1980s. Manufacturing jobs had been a source of decent wages, and the strong demand for labor had attracted migration to these cities in earlier decades. However, in the last quarter of the twentieth century federal transportation and highway policies made it easier for industries to relocate to cheaper labor production areas in the suburbs. And the out-migration of industries was accompanied by the out-migration of higher income families to the suburbs, aided by mortgage interest tax exemptions and home mortgages for veterans.

Improved transportation and the suburbanization of employment accelerated the out-migration of central city manufacturing. With manufacturing jobs no longer readily available in central-city and inner-city areas, the Great Migration wave of blacks from the South to northern urban areas abruptly ended around 1970. With the cessation of migration from the South and the out-migration of higher income families, many poor, black, densely populated inner-city neighborhoods were physically transformed by depopulation, as abandoned homes and storefronts became common markers of the visual landscape. By 2000, there were 60,000 abandoned buildings in Philadelphia, 40,000 in Detroit, and 20,000 in Baltimore.[24] The depopulated inner city is the visible backdrop for much of the action in *The Wire*.

In addition, the end of the Great Migration from the South and the out-migration of higher income families resulted in inner-city ghettos with a much larger proportion of poor families and significantly higher levels of joblessness. These developments were in part due to the following: (1) the exodus of higher income families who were more likely to be employed, including black middle- and working-class families whose departure was also aided by antidiscrimination measures in housing; (2) the decline of industrial employment in the inner city; and (3) the decline of local businesses that depend on the resources of higher income groups, many of whom had departed.

In previous years—prior to the cessation of the Great Migration, massive industry relocation from central city neighborhoods, and the civil rights revolution—poor, working-class, and middle-class blacks had generally lived in the same section of the city, as reflected in the classic research on

---

24. See Fox et al., *Shared Prosperity, Stronger Regions*.

race and the city during this time.[25] This class heterogeneity in black neighborhoods was rooted in the intense residential segregation whereby even black families with greater resources were confined to black neighborhoods by direct discrimination in the real estate markets: redlining practices by banks that denied home loans to black applicants and restrictive covenants that prevented the sale of designated property to black buyers.[26] However, with the gradual exodus of higher income blacks, poor blacks were left behind in neighborhoods hardest hit by the disappearance of jobs.[27]

The unprecedented concentration of poverty produced the profound social isolation of poor blacks in the inner city.[28] They had little meaningful employment nearby, inadequate schools and training opportunities for higher-skill jobs, and spatial barriers to employers that had relocated to the suburbs. As joblessness climbed, formal organizations that had depended on the support of middle-class residents were weakened, thus undermining social organization in the inner city, including important institutions such as churches, schools, businesses, and civic clubs. As a greater percentage of the residents were jobless, they had fewer social ties to individuals employed in the formal labor market who could provide information on and access to job opportunities. With all of these developments occurring simultaneously, urban sociologists developed the concept of concentration effects to signify that the various processes associated with concentrated poverty work together to produce uniquely severe disadvantage for residents of these neighborhoods.[29]

One of the greatest strengths of *The Wire* is that it captures this analytic perspective. The Barksdale gang dominates the drug trade on Baltimore's West Side, where economic decline and the failure of political institutions have had harmful social consequences that work together to constrain the opportunities of residents. As a result of the disappearance of work, there are few economic opportunities in the mainstream economy for neighborhood residents. Many poor black residents live in public housing projects where they are generally confined to interactions with their neighbors and remain socially isolated from the rest of the city. Other than the police, there are almost never visitors from other neighborhoods.

The loss of jobs was not exclusively a problem for black workers, though. White workers were also hit by the wave of factory closings across the Northeast and Midwest during this period. Deindustrialization and the decline of

25. See Drake and Cayton, *Black Metropolis*.
26. See Massey and Denton, *American Apartheid*.
27. See Wilson, *When Work Disappears*.
28. Ibid.
29. See ibid.

manufacturing fundamentally altered the economic prospects of the white working class, especially men who had not gone to college. With labor unions in decline, workers were unable to resist the downward pressure on their wages brought about by these structural economic shifts and competition through international trade.[30] These economic factors have had important social implications for white working-class communities, as shown in ethnographic research on the impact of plant closings in white towns.[31]

The Wire examines the declining fortunes of white workers through the storyline of the dockworkers in the second season of the series. The ports had long been a source of stable jobs for the white working class, who loaded and unloaded cargo from the ships that had docked in Baltimore. With the decline in production at the steel mills, a local manifestation of the nationwide deindustrialization, activity at the ports had dropped dramatically. The stevedores depicted in *The Wire* go day to day without knowing whether they will have any work. And much of the work still remaining at the port is quickly being mechanized through technological innovation. Faced with limited economic prospects, they eventually turn to illicit activities to earn money. The union itself colludes with a smuggling ring, which delivers payments in exchange for the union's assistance in moving contraband through the port. Some individual workers also look for opportunities to make money in the local drug trade.

In many ways, the experiences of the dockworkers parallel those of the black poor depicted in *The Wire*, as both groups struggle with the disappearance of work in the formal economy. In the absence of stable employment opportunities, both the white dockworkers and black residents in the show are drawn to illicit activities to provide income. There are also clear similarities in their lack of trust in mainstream institutions and the sense that they have been abandoned in the face of economic hardship. In an economy that places a much greater premium on high levels of education and credentials than on manual skills, both the white working class and inner-city black residents sense that they have been made superfluous by deindustrialization. Bodie, a teenager who works in the drug trade, likens himself to a sacrificial pawn on a chessboard.[32] Lamenting the loss of reliable employment, the leader of the dockworkers union, Frank Sobotka, complains, "We used to make shit in this country."[33] The parallel trajectories of these two groups

30. See Freeman, "How Much Has De-Unionization Contributed to the Rise in Male Earnings Inequality?" and Harrison and Bluestone, *Great U-Turn*.
31. See Dudley, *End of the Line*.
32. "The Buys," S1/E3.
33. "Bad Dreams," S2/E11.

point to important similarities based on their class position with regard to the impact of economic restructuring.

While recognizing these similarities, we need to pay special attention to the sharp impact of rising joblessness on African American communities. Indeed black workers have borne the brunt of deindustrialization. John Bound and Harry Holzer estimate that the shift away from manufacturing accounts for nearly half of the decline in employment for less-educated young black men in the 1970s.[34] The social implications of high joblessness for many African Americans, including those formerly in manufacturing jobs, are unique because the concentration of disadvantage in black neighborhoods creates fundamentally different contexts than those in urban white neighborhoods.

In an analysis of Chicago neighborhoods, Sampson found that even the poorest white neighborhood has an income level higher than that of the median black neighborhood. This stark inequality leads him to conclude that "the bottom-line result is that residents in not one white community experience what is most typical for those residing in segregated black areas with respect to the basics of income. . . . Trying to estimate the effect of concentrated disadvantage on whites is thus tantamount to estimating a phantom reality."[35]

An analysis of Baltimore neighborhoods reveals an identical pattern. Figure 1 plots Baltimore neighborhoods by their per capita income. Among black neighborhoods (that is, those in which at least 75 percent of residents are black), the median neighborhood has a per capita income of $12,588 (in 2000). The lowest per capita income of any white neighborhood is $13,550. As in Chicago, there is not a single white neighborhood in Baltimore that faces the economic conditions that characterize the typical black neighborhood (fig. 1).

When considering the neighborhood contexts of poor families, it is clear that the black poor face even greater disadvantage than poor white families in Baltimore. Among all families below the poverty line, the average poor white family lives in a neighborhood that has a poverty rate of 22.7 percent. By comparison, the average poor black family lives in a neighborhood in which 32.5 percent of the families are below the poverty line. More than a quarter of poor black families (27.7 percent) live in neighborhoods in which more than 40 percent of the residents are living below the poverty line; 6.8 percent of poor white families live in neighborhoods with such high levels of poverty. Thus, the neighborhood context differs for even poor

---

34. Bound and Holzer, "Industrial Shifts, Skills Levels, and the Labor Market."
35. Sampson, "Racial Stratification," 265.

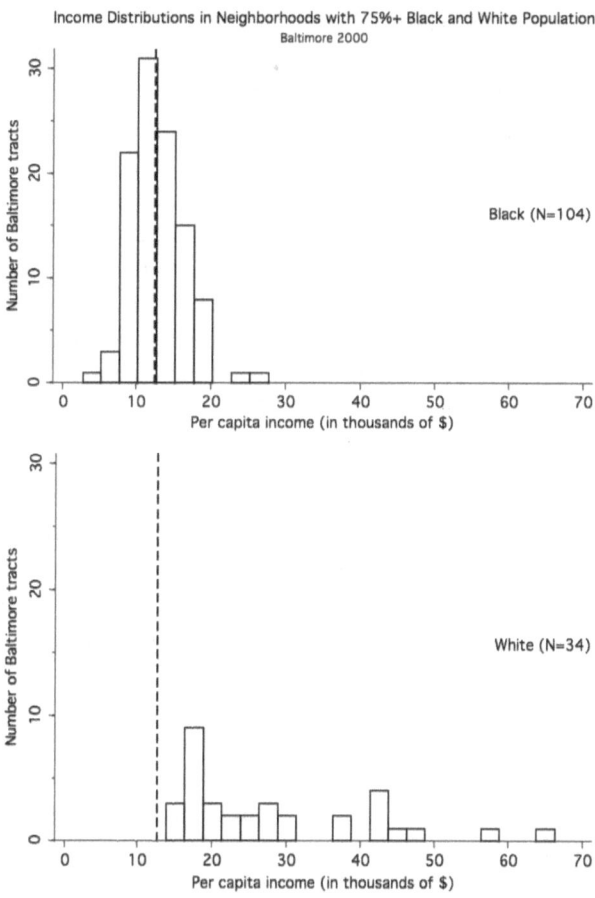

FIGURE 1: Baltimore neighborhoods by per capita income and racial composition. Note: the dashed line represents the per capita income of the median black neighborhood ($12,588).

white and poor black families. The absence of stable employment opportunities in poor black neighborhoods exacerbates this concentration of disadvantage, thereby presenting uniquely difficult challenges for its residents.

The disparate neighborhood context is not the only factor that takes us beyond the apparent similarities between the black poor and the white dockworkers in *The Wire*. The different social implications of economic hardship for the two groups are also evident. While the status of employment on the docks is certainly in decline, the stevedores maintain an attachment to jobs and are ready to report whenever work does materialize. However unpredictable their actual employment, this attachment to a job and the community of fellow union members are significant buffers against the social isolation that has accompanied economic decline in the inner city.

The union members have meaningful ties in a well-developed social network and are less isolated from mainstream institutions. The leaders of the union maintain access to political leaders in local and state government, although their political influence has diminished with their declining economic prospects. By comparison, political institutions have not been vehicles for pursuing meaningful improvements in the conditions of the black urban poor, even when black officials have been elected to office.[36] In short, whites with diminishing employment prospects still maintain fundamental advantages in social capital and access to political institutions that are not similarly available to their African American counterparts.

POLITICS AND URBAN POLICY

While economic factors are central to the urban social problems examined in *The Wire*, the political context of urban decline must also be incorporated in an analysis of systemic urban inequality. As jobs were leaving urban centers in the 1980s, the Reagan administration aggressively pursued its political project of New Federalism through which the federal government dramatically reduced fiscal support for city governments and spending on programs that mainly targeted urban residents. In 1977, federal aid accounted for 17.5 percent of local government revenues in cities; by 1990, that share had dropped to a mere 5.0 percent.[37] Without this support, cities were stripped of the capacity to deal with the serious challenges presented by the crack epidemic, public health crises, and widespread homelessness in the 1980s.[38] The economic decline that accompanied deindustrialization weakened revenues for city governments, which inevitably reduced services and programs for those in need. The drastic cuts in federal aid to cities were not restored during the Clinton administration; federal support comprised 5.4 percent of city budgets in 2000.[39]

The federal abandonment of cities at the same time that joblessness became widespread in the inner city exacerbated the problems of urban decline. This political context is essential for understanding the subsequent course of urban policy and the contemporary nature of urban inequality several decades later.

36. See Thompson, *Double Trouble*.
37. See Wallin, "Budgeting for Basics."
38. See Caraley, "Washington Abandons the Cities."
39. See Wallin, "Budgeting for Basics."

In this same period, federal urban policy underwent a fundamental shift toward an explicit emphasis on the market as the preferred source of social welfare in distressed neighborhoods. Initiated by the Carter administration in the late 1970s, the Urban Development Action Grant (UDAG) program promoted public-private coordination of local urban development and required that local authorities work with private developers in attempts to revitalize poor neighborhoods. This market-based approach was extended through the Reagan and Clinton administrations, most notably through enterprise zones that provided tax incentives to attract developers and private firms to invest in profitable opportunities in the inner city.[40]

This marked a significant break from previous federal policy. Whereas the earlier state-sponsored antipoverty programs were essentially countercyclical, the new emphasis on economic development meant that urban policy had become fundamentally procyclical. With the focus of urban policy shifting to economic development through a supply-side approach, inner-city neighborhoods would be dependent on the private sector rather than the state and therefore even more vulnerable to structural economic shifts. As this explicit turn to the private sector and a market-based approach to urban policy took place in the late 1970s, inner-city neighborhoods became particularly vulnerable to the widespread problems of joblessness, which are typically viewed as an economic process.

With the decline of their industrial sectors and federal support, cities turned to urban economic development as a source of revenues to make up for their budget deficits. These strategies increasingly emphasized commercial and housing development to generate revenues from sales and property taxes. Many cities sought to develop major projects to attract revenue from outside investors and tourists.[41] With limited capacity for redistributive policy, local governments sought to attract middle-class residents through high-end residential development that could provide increased property taxes, while giving little attention to the conditions of low-income residents.[42]

Along with the strategy to attract middle-class residents, many cities also sought to deconcentrate poverty in the 1990s—mainly through the demolition of high-rise public housing projects. In cities like Baltimore and Chicago, these buildings were home to thousands of poor residents living in highly concentrated poverty. The physical structures were often in disrepair,

---

40. See Oakley and Tsao, "New Way of Revitalizing Distressed Urban Communities?" and Porter, "Competitive Advantage of the Inner City."

41. See Hoffman et al., *Cities and Visitors*.

42. See Newman, "Newark, Decline and Avoidance, Renaissance and Desire."

and high rates of crime and violence threatened the safety of public housing residents. The demolition of public housing projects was supported by federal assistance, including the HOPE VI program that replaced the buildings with mixed-income developments. Local officials typically promoted the demolition of housing projects by highlighting the problems of concentrated poverty and the need to improve conditions for poor residents. Indeed, in the opening scene of the third season of *The Wire*, the mayor of Baltimore addresses residents and the media just before the high-rise projects are demolished. With local developers at his side, he emphasizes the detrimental social conditions of poor families as the basis for tearing down the buildings.[43]

Understood in the context of the pressures on local governments to generate sufficient revenue after the federal disinvestment from cities, the demolition of public housing projects was linked to urban economic development strategies. Many of the buildings were located near redeveloped downtown areas, which could attract middle-class residents who, unlike public housing residents, would pay property taxes on market-rate housing. In Chicago, for example, the infamous Cabrini-Green housing projects were located less than one mile from downtown; they were demolished and replaced with mixed-income housing. Considering that many former residents of public housing in cities like Baltimore, Chicago, St. Louis, and Atlanta had not been relocated to other areas several years after their public housing projects were demolished, they were apt to question whether the discourse of deconcentrating poverty had been cynically employed to promote high-end real estate development instead.[44] As the mayor in *The Wire* announces the demolition of the housing projects with great fanfare, three teenagers debate the costs and benefits of losing the towers.[45] Beyond the problems posed by the restructured labor market and broader economic forces, political institutions have also failed to improve the conditions of the urban poor.

The period of urban decline also coincided with the ascent of an urban black political elite, as black mayors were elected in many large cities for the first time. However, this apparent political empowerment has not seemed to produce meaningful improvements in the conditions of the urban black poor. In a detailed study of urban politics in postwar Atlanta, Clarence Stone describes a long-running alliance between the white business elite and black middle class that has shaped local policymaking and constrained

---

43. "Time After Time," S3/E1.
44. See Crump, "Deconcentration by Demolition," and Goetz, *Clearing the Way*.
45. "Time After Time," S3/E1.

the policy options available to elected officials.[46] This alliance has negotiated a compromise through which the white business elite benefits from pro-growth policy while the black middle class has reaped gains in minority business opportunities. Even when Maynard Jackson was elected in 1973 with the support of progressive, neighborhood-based voters, he was unable to implement redistributive policies that would have benefited poor black residents. Stone emphasizes the distinction between an electoral coalition and a governing coalition; although they may be significant in their electoral power, residents of poor, black neighborhoods cannot contribute much in governing capacity, and elected mayors are consistently dependent on the entrenched regime for governing authority.

In the fictional depiction of Baltimore politics in *The Wire*, the incumbent black mayor, Clarence Royce, makes symbolic appeals to black voters when he is threatened by an electoral challenge from a white candidate. While in office, however, Mayor Royce never prioritized policies that would benefit the black poor. The influence of governing coalitions on local policies points to the significance of political processes and shows that macroeconomic forces do not solely determine urban inequality. In analyzing the waves of black mayors in recent decades, Thompson also emphasizes the divide between the black political elite and the urban poor.[47] While the black political elite depend on low-income black voters to get elected, once in office they actually demobilize the black poor by building coalitions with business interests and the middle class; and consequently they prevent the black poor from effectively demanding policies that improve their conditions.

Even in cities with a substantial share of low-income black residents, elected officials have tended to cater to middle-class residents and business interests that can provide valuable governing capacity and economic resources that are crucial in local politics. Nonetheless, while political institutions have not effectively improved the conditions of the urban poor, the magnitude of the underlying structural problems may in fact be beyond the capacity of local government to address. Deindustrialization has devastated the economic base of many large cities, and federal disinvestment from the cities further weakened the ability of local governments to address urgent problems. The combined impact of these changes—declining economic and social institutions and the failure of political institutions—on the residents of poor inner-city neighborhoods is fully captured in *The Wire*'s portrayal of systemic urban inequality.

46. Stone, *Regime Politics*.
47. See Thompson, *Double Trouble*.

EDUCATION AND YOUTH

In his classic 1965 text on the conditions of the black poor in inner-city ghettos, Kenneth Clark devotes a chapter to "ghetto schools" and the unequal educational achievement of black and white students.[48] More than four decades later, much of his analysis applies to present-day urban schools, which are examined in the fourth season of *The Wire*. Clark points to the de facto segregation of schools as the fundamental factor at the root of educational inequality. He strongly criticizes popular arguments that emphasize cultural deprivation as the cause of lower black achievement. In his view institutional practices of schools and the structure of the education system are much more significant in explaining educational inequality than cultural explanations. As schools develop lower expectations for black students, he argues, these become self-fulfilling prophecies as black students then inevitably underachieve.

The public school depicted in *The Wire* lacks the necessary resources truly to educate students and help them develop skills that prepare them for jobs that would pay decent wages. Even before the students reach high school, their trajectories are seriously constrained by the poor quality of the elementary and middle schools and the limited economic opportunities available to them. The students themselves seem aware of their likely outcomes, and the teachers are often resigned to accept their fate. In a comment that describes the antagonistic dynamics in the school, one teacher in the show reflects, "No one wins. One side just loses more slowly."[49] The students also recognize that even if they were able to learn skills in their schools, they would be thwarted by the absence of well-paying jobs in the surrounding area.

At a systemic level, economic factors and educational institutions work together to shape this dimension of urban inequality. Although some students might overcome these obstacles and attain some upward mobility, the broad pattern of social stratification is reproduced and remains durable. The school essentially prepares the students for the social positions they occupy. For students who are already involved in the drug trade, the school is actually a site of learning the *habitus* of disobeying rules and dealing with authority.

Through an in-depth historical analysis of inner-city education, Kathryn Neckerman emphasizes that the problems of inner-city schools are fundamentally linked to policy choices made by the school system

---

48. See Clark, *Dark Ghetto*.
49. "Refugees," S4/E4.

throughout the twentieth century.[50] Using the case study of inner-city schools in Chicago, she highlights the inadequate response to de facto segregation in the school system, the implementation of vocational education that relegated black students to a lower tier of skills training, and the failure of schools to provide adequate remedial education for low-achieving students. Her analysis makes clear that the problems of inner-city schools were not necessarily and inevitably determined by the concentration of disadvantage in the surrounding communities; instead, these institutions pursued specific policies that had detrimental impacts on the achievement of black students. While urban decline was an important condition that contributed to failing schools, the practices of educational institutions resulted in even greater inequality.

This focus on institutional practices effectively challenges alternative explanations that overemphasize the role of individual actors, especially those that attribute low achievement to the behavior or attitudes of teachers, families, or students. A common view is that, in the context of racial segregation and social isolation, black students have developed an oppositional culture toward schools and teachers. According to this explanation, the cultural perspective of black students entails a devaluing of education, which is presumed to be a significant factor in their low achievement. A specific version of this explanation holds that black students stigmatize educational success as acting white; rather than accept the social penalty that supposedly comes with educational achievement, black students are hypothesized to favor social acceptance over education.[51] While there may be evidence of oppositional or antagonistic relationships between some students and the schools, these explanations do not adequately explain racial disparities in educational achievement.[52]

An overemphasis on attractive but inadequate cultural explanations mistakenly draws attention away from structural, institutional, and environmental factors that are fundamental to understanding educational inequality. Prudence Carter connects the cultural orientations of students to institutional practices of schools by demonstrating that the schools and teachers actually link cultural patterns of students to their educational outcomes. She distinguishes between "dominant" and "non-dominant" forms of cultural capital and argues that teachers mistakenly interpret the "non-dominant" cultural capital of inner-city students as evidence of lower

---

50. See Neckerman, *Schools Betrayed*.
51. See Fordham and Ogbu, "Black Students' School Success."
52. See Fryer, "Acting White."

academic ability.[53] This profoundly shapes the expectations that teachers hold, which then constrain the academic performance of poor, black students. Even if a student does value education and is committed to succeeding in an inner-city school, the structural barriers in the education system as depicted in *The Wire* present tremendous obstacles.

Outside of the schools, the neighborhood context is also an important factor in the cognitive and educational development of students. As an illustration of the impact of the neighborhood environment, researchers analyzed longitudinal data on 750 black students in Chicago and found that "residing in a severely disadvantaged neighborhood cumulatively impedes the development of academically relevant verbal ability in children."[54] An important finding in this research is that the negative effects of concentrated disadvantage on the cognitive development of the students persisted even for those who had moved out of these neighborhoods.

In addition to the economic and demographic components of neighborhood disadvantage, the high levels of violence characteristic of many poor urban neighborhoods may also adversely affect students. In a recent study, Patrick Sharkey finds that performance on cognitive assessments were significantly lower for students who lived in areas in which a homicide had occurred in the week before they were given the test.[55] This study estimates only the effect of a very recent murder near a student's home on his or her cognitive performance. The long-term effects of cumulative exposure to high levels of violence may also have significant implications for the development of children in poor urban neighborhoods.

Beyond these acute effects of violence on student achievement, the prevalence of violent conflicts has important implications for the social organization of these neighborhoods, especially for youth. Based on ethnographic research in inner-city neighborhoods, David Harding shows that the perceived threat of violence leads poor youth to seek protection by developing more neighborhood-based bonds among youth of different ages. Whereas young people in other neighborhoods tend to create relationships with peers of their same age, youth in poor neighborhoods are more likely to develop social ties with people who are a few years older. These bonds facilitate the "cross-cohort socialization" that Harding argues is an important

---

53. Carter, "'Black' Cultural Capital."

54. Sampson, Sharkey, and Raudenbush, "Durable Effects of Concentrated Disadvantage," 846.

55. See "Acute Effect of Local Homicide on Children's Cognitive Performance."

mechanism for the transmission of certain worldviews about education and the labor market.⁵⁶

In a notable scene in *The Wire*, two teenage drug dealers marvel at the ingenuity of their boneless Chicken McNuggets and imagine that they must have made their inventor extremely wealthy. An older dealer, D'Angelo, derides their naïveté. "The man who invented them things, just some sad ass down at the basement of McDonald's thinking up some shit to make money for the real players," he tells them. Disillusioned with a formal labor market comprised mainly of low-wage jobs, D'Angelo rejects it as fundamentally unfair since people are not rewarded according to their true worth. In his view, powerful institutions regularly exploit those with less power, and social inequality is the inevitable result. His understanding of how society works shapes his approach to how one should operate in such a world. When a younger dealer objects to the inadequate compensation of the McNuggets inventor, D'Angelo teaches them, "It ain't about right. It's about money." In this way, D'Angelo transmits his view of how the world works to the dealers who are several years younger.⁵⁷

Given the scale of mass imprisonment, poor urban youth are also exposed to family members and older friends who are or have been incarcerated. Christopher Wildeman estimates that 25 percent of black children born in 1990 had a parent in prison by the time they reached the age of fourteen; by comparison, approximately 4 percent of white children had a parent in prison.⁵⁸ For black children born to parents who had not completed high school, more than 50 percent had a father in prison. The risk of having a parent or family member who is incarcerated therefore is especially concentrated among low-income black youth. Having an incarcerated parent has detrimental, long-term impacts on these children, who already confront other forms of disadvantage.⁵⁹ In *The Wire*, the young character Namond is shown visiting his incarcerated father, Wee-Bey, who had been active in the drug trade. Namond is identified by the school as a particularly troubled student and soon thereafter enters the drug trade himself as a street-level dealer.⁶⁰

The low educational achievement of poor urban youth can be traced to the social dimensions of their neighborhood context, the economic factors underlying urban decline, the institutional practices of the school system,

---

56. Harding, *Living Drama*, 4.
57. "The Detail," S1/E2.
58. See Wildeman, "Parental Imprisonment."
59. See Comfort, "Punishment beyond the Legal Offender."
60. "Soft Eyes," S5/E2.

and the reliance on mass imprisonment in the criminal justice system. This set of factors undermines the "achievement ideology" that promotes a belief in the equality of opportunity and assumes that schooling itself can provide a route for upward mobility. In this framework, education is regarded as the solution to social inequality. With an understanding of how unequal education reproduces social inequality, acceptance of the "achievement ideology" is a key mechanism through which existing inequality is legitimated.[61] The entangled connections among these institutions are at the core of systemic, multigenerational urban inequality.

URBAN INEQUALITY BEYOND *THE WIRE*

By placing crime and the drug trade at the center of its depiction of urban inequality, *The Wire* runs the risk of reinforcing stereotypical depictions of the urban poor. Some writers have maintained that the show promotes biased views of poor African Americans as dependent on welfare, lazy, criminal, and immoral.[62] A degree of caution about the broader implications of how the black poor are represented is certainly well founded. These negative perceptions have dominated popular discourse on urban inequality, and they, too, often influence decisions about who is deemed worthy of assistance through social policy.[63]

A careful assessment, however, reveals that *The Wire* actually powerfully undermines these dangerous stereotypes. By examining the institutions that shape the characters, it convincingly demonstrates that the outcomes of the lives of the black poor are not the result of individual predispositions for violence, group traits, or cultural deficits. Through a scrupulous exploration of the inner workings of drug-dealing gangs, the police, politicians, unions, and public schools, *The Wire* shows that individuals' decisions and behavior are often shaped by—and indeed limited by—social, political, and economic forces beyond their control.

To be sure, *The Wire* does not provide a comprehensive portrayal of the various complex dimensions of life in the inner city. As one example, the influx of immigrants in recent decades has reshaped urban America. A thorough understanding of contemporary urban inequality needs to include an examination of how recent immigration continues to transform American cities. The racial landscape of urban inequality is far more complex than an

61. See MacLeod, *Ain't No Makin' It*.
62. See Bowden, "The Angriest Man in Television," and Reed, "Should Harvard Teach 'The Wire'?"
63. See Gilens, *Why Americans Hate Welfare*, and Katz, *The Undeserving Poor*.

exclusive focus on poor black ghettos. In its depiction of the poorest of the poor, the series does not provide an in-depth portrayal of the challenges faced by those who do hold jobs in the formal economy and who may be above the poverty line but nevertheless struggle in the context of deep urban inequality. As others have noted, many residents of these neighborhoods are actively engaged in political efforts to improve their conditions; rather than adapt to their circumstances, they work to improve the opportunities that should be available to residents.[64]

In fact, metropolitan poverty itself is no longer a fundamentally inner-city phenomenon. In recent years, the share of the nation's poor living in the suburbs has actually surpassed that of the cities. Of the 39.1 million people below the poverty line in 2008, 31.9 percent were in the suburbs, 28.0 percent lived in "primary cities," and the rest were in small metropolitan and rural areas.[65] In portraying the lives of the urban poor, *The Wire* also gives relatively little attention to families and parents, which have long been the subject of considerable research on urban poverty.

There are undoubtedly several substantive topics that are relevant to urban poverty but receive less attention in the series. That said, we must not lose sight of an important recurring theme in the series: given a limited set of available opportunities, there is often no exit from the predetermined life trajectories of residents in poor urban neighborhoods. This is vividly illustrated in the lives of D'Angelo, Wallace, and many other characters. By the end of the series, the problems remain unsolved, and the cycle repeats itself. Disadvantages become more deeply entrenched over time and across generations.

A fundamental objective of social scientists is to generate explanations of social conditions. Outside of academia, ordinary people also form explanations about their conditions and how the world works, and *The Wire* takes their explanations seriously. A key lesson from the series is that people's circumstances are shaped by the institutions that govern their lives—despite their best efforts to demonstrate individual autonomy, distinctiveness, and moral and material worth. Accordingly, the conditions of the urban poor cannot be understood as somehow existing outside the political and economic arrangements of the broader society. By depicting the interrelationship of social, political, and economic institutions that work together to constrain the lives of the urban poor, *The Wire* effectively illustrates the fundamental nature of systemic urban inequality.

---

64. See Atlas and Dreier, "Is *The Wire* Too Cynical?"
65. See Kneebone and Garr, "The Suburbanization of Poverty."

BIBLIOGRAPHY

Anderson, Elijah. *Code of the Street: Decency, Violence, and the Moral Life of the Inner City*. New York: Norton, 2000.

Atlas, John, and Peter Dreier. "Is *The Wire* Too Cynical?" *Dissent* 55 (2008) 79–82.

Bobo, Lawrence D., and Victor Thompson. "Racialized Mass Incarceration: Poverty, Prejudice, and Punishment." In *Doing Race: Twenty-One Essays for the Twenty-First Century*, edited by Hazel Rose Markus and Paula M. L. Moya, 322–55. New York: Norton, 2010.

Bound, John, and Harry J. Holzer. "Industrial Shifts, Skills Levels, and the Labor Market for White and Black Males." *The Review of Economics and Statistics* 75 (1993) 387–96.

Bowden, Mark. "The Angriest Man in Television." *The Atlantic* 301 (January/February 2008) 50–57.

Calvino, Italo. *Invisible Cities*. Translated by William Weaver. New York: Harcourt, 1974.

Caraley, Demetrios. "Washington Abandons the Cities." *Political Science Quarterly* 107 (1992) 1–30.

Carter, Prudence L. "'Black' Cultural Capital, Status Positioning, and Schooling Conflicts for Low-Income African American Youth." *Social Problems* 50 (2003) 136–55.

Clark, Kenneth B. *Dark Ghetto: Dilemmas of Social Power*. New York: Harper & Row, 1965.

Comfort, Megan. "Punishment Beyond the Legal Offender." *Annual Review of Law and Social Science* 3 (2007) 271–96.

Cooper, Matthew, et al. "Prisoners in 2008." (December 8, 2009). Online: http://bjs.ojp.usdoj.gov/content/pub/pdf/p08.pdf.

Crump, Jeff. "Deconcentration by Demolition: Public Housing, Poverty, and Urban Policy." *Environment and Planning* 20 (2002) 581–96.

Dickens, Charles. *A Tale of Two Cities*. London: Chapman & Hall, 1859.

Drake, St. Clair, and Horace R. Cayton. *Black Metropolis: A Study of Negro Life in a Northern City*. New York: Harcourt, 1945.

Dudley, Kathryn Marie. *The End of the Line: Lost Jobs, New Lives in Postindustrial America*. Chicago: University of Chicago Press, 1994.

Fordham, Signithia, and John U. Ogbu. "Black Students' School Success: Coping with the Burden of 'Acting White.'" *Urban Review* 18 (1986) 176–206.

Fox, Radhika K., et al. "Shared Prosperity, Stronger Regions: An Agenda for Rebuilding America's Older Core Cities." PolicyLink (2006). Online: http://www.policylink.org/site/apps/nlnet/content2.aspx?c=lkIXLbMNJrE&b=5136581&ct=6997657.

Freeman, Richard B. "How Much Has De-unionization Contributed to the Rise in Male Earnings Inequality?" In *Uneven Tides: Rising Inequality in America*, edited by Sheldon Danziger and Peter Gottschalk, 133–63. New York: Russell Sage, 1993.

Fryer, Roland G. "'Acting White': The Social Price Paid by the Best and Brightest Minority Students." *Education Next* 6 (2006) 53–59.

Gilens, Martin. *Why Americans Hate Welfare: Race, Media, and the Politics of Antipoverty Policy*. Chicago: University of Chicago Press, 1999.

Goetz, Edward G. *Clearing the Way: Deconcentrating the Poor in Urban America*. Washington, DC: Urban Institute Press, 2003.

Harding, David J. *The Living Drama: Community, Conflict, and Culture among Inner-City Boys*. Chicago: University of Chicago Press, 2010.

Harrison, Bennett, and Barry Bluestone. *The Great U-Turn: Corporate Restructuring and the Polarizing of America*. New York: Basic Books, 1988.

Hoffman, Lily M., et al., editors. *Cities and Visitors: Regulating People, Markets, and City Space*. Malden, MA: Blackwell, 2003.

Holzer, Harry J. "Collateral Costs: Effects of Incarceration on Employment and Earnings among Young Workers." In *Do Prisons Make Us Safer? The Benefits and Costs of the Prison Boom*, edited by Steven Raphael and Michael A. Stoll, 239–69. New York: Russell Sage, 2009.

Katz, Michael B. *The Undeserving Poor*. New York: Pantheon, 1989.

Kneebone, Elizabeth, and Emily Garr. "The Suburbanization of Poverty: Trends in Metropolitan America, 2000 to 2008." Metropolitan Opportunity Series 8. Washington, DC: Brookings Institution, 2010.

Lacey, Nicola. "American Imprisonment in Comparative Perspective." *Daedalus* 139 (2010) 102–14.

Lemann, Nicholas. "Charm City, USA." *New York Review of Books* (September 30, 2010). Online: http://www.nybooks.com/articles/archives/2010/sep/30/charm-city-usa/?pagination=false.

MacLeod, Jay. *Ain't No Makin' It: Aspirations and Attainment in a Low-Income Neighborhood*. Boulder, CO: Westview, 1987.

Massey, Douglas S., and Nancy A. Denton. *American Apartheid: Segregation and the Making of the Underclass*. Cambridge: Harvard University Press, 1993.

Mauer, Marc. "Comparative International Rates of Incarceration: An Examination of Causes and Trends" (2003). Online: http://www.sentencingproject.org/doc/publications/inc_comparative_intl.pdf.

Neckerman, Kathryn M. *Schools Betrayed: Roots of Failure in Inner-City Education*. Chicago: University of Chicago Press, 2007.

Newman, Kathe. "Newark, Decline and Avoidance, Renaissance and Desire: From Disinvestment to Reinvestment." *The Annals of the American Academy of Political and Social Science* 594 (2004) 34–48.

Oakley, Deirdre, and Hui-Shien Tsao. "A New Way of Revitalizing Distressed Urban Communities? Assessing the Impact of the Federal Empowerment Zone Program." *Journal of Urban Affairs* 28 (2006) 443–71.

Okri, Ben. *Dangerous Love*. London: Weidenfeld & Nicolson, 1996.

Pew Research Center. "Blacks Upbeat about Black Progress, Prospects." January 12, 2010. Online: http://www.pewsocialtrends.org/2010/01/12/blacks-upbeat-about-black-progress-prospects/.

Porter, Michael E. "The Competitive Advantage of the Inner City." *Harvard Business Review* 73 (1995) 55–71.

Reed, Ishmael. "Should Harvard Teach 'The Wire'? No, It Relies on Clichés about Blacks and Drugs." *Boston Globe* (September 30, 2010). Online: http://www.boston.com/bostonglobe/editorial_opinion/oped/articles/2010/09/30/no_it_relies_on_clichs_about_blacks_and_drugs/.

Sampson, Robert J. "Racial Stratification and the Durable Tangle of Neighborhood Inequality." *The Annals of the American Academy of Political and Social Science* 621 (2009) 260–80.

Sampson, Robert J., and Charles Loeffler. "Punishment's Place: The Local Concentration of Mass Incarceration." *Daedalus* 139 (2010) 20–31.

Sampson, Robert J., Patrick Sharkey, and Stephen W. Raudenbush. "Durable Effects of Concentrated Disadvantage on Verbal Ability among African-American Children." *Proceedings of the National Academy of Sciences* 105 (2008) 845–52.

Sharkey, Patrick. "The Acute Effect of Local Homicide on Children's Cognitive Performance." *Proceedings of the National Academy of Sciences* 107 (2010) 11733–38.

———. "The Intergenerational Transmission of Context." *American Journal of Sociology* 113 (2008) 931–69.

Stone, Clarence N. *Regime Politics: Governing Atlanta, 1946–1988*. Lawrence: University Press of Kansas, 1989.

Thompson, J. Phillip. *Double Trouble: Black Mayors, Black Communities, and the Call for a Deep Democracy*. New York: Oxford University Press, 2005.

Venkatesh, Sudhir Alladi. *Off the Books: The Underground Economy of the Urban Poor*. Cambridge: Harvard University Press, 2006.

Venkatesh, Sudhir Alladi, and Steven D. Levitt. "'Are We a Family or a Business?' History and Disjuncture in the Urban American Street Gang." *Theory and Society* 29 (2000) 427–62.

Wacquant, Loïc. *Punishing the Poor: The Neoliberal Government of Social Insecurity*. Durham: Duke University Press, 2009.

Wallin, Bruce A. "Budgeting for Basics: The Changing Landscape of City Finances." Discussion paper prepared for The Brookings Institution Metropolitan Policy Program. Washington, DC: Brookings Institution, 2005. Online: http://www.brookings.edu/~/media/research/files/reports/2005/8/metropolitanpolicy%20wallin/20050823_budgetingbasics.

Western, Bruce. *Punishment and Inequality in America*. New York: Russell Sage, 2006.

Western, Bruce, and Becky Pettit. "Incarceration and Social Inequality." *Daedalus* 139 (2010) 8–19.

Wildeman, Christopher. "Parental Imprisonment, the Prison Boom, and the Concentration of Childhood Disadvantage." *Demography* 46 (2008) 265–80.

Wilson, William Julius. *The Truly Disadvantaged: The Inner City, the Underclass, and Public Policy*. Chicago: University of Chicago Press, 1987.

———. *When Work Disappears: The World of the New Urban Poor*. New York: Knopf, 1996.

Wright, Richard. *Native Son*. New York: Harper, 1940.

PART II
Encountering *The Wire*

4

Marlo's City of Words
Tempting a Natural Theology of Language

JONATHAN TRAN

THE INCARNATION TEMPTS US to think we have God in a way we don't. The temptation is a uniquely metaphysical one, where God's revelation in Christ is taken as authorizing our life in words, and if not authorizing at least constraining what words might otherwise mean. God in Christ as the verbalization of the divine mind, we think, tells us what God is or is not (God, for example, does not answer to human bidding) and so Christian use of "God" cannot go anywhere (by "God" for example we don't mean someone who answers to human bidding). Then one of the tasks of theology is to discover what that verbalization, ensconced as it is in scripture, must imply metaphysically (metaphysics subsequent to scripture's grammar in the order of theological investigation). This is all straightforward enough. The pull comes when the giving of the one Word is seen as authorizing all words, as if God in Christ as revelation of the divine mind tells us something essential about cats on mats or brains in vats (if cats and brains exist anywhere, the thinking goes, they first exist in God's mind and only secondarily on mats and in vats). Here the notion is that one word serves as the key to all words. This notion is predicated on the idea that a word means just one thing (or just a few things) and that one thing is decoded by Christ. If what a cat or a brain *is* is what it is in the divine mind, then the Word gives access to the divine and by correspondence access to the essence of cats or brains. Here is a picture of language as encoded and Christ as cypher; figure out the cypher and you figure out what all other words mean, delimiting the possibilities of how one might appropriately use them.

This is important because linguistic use conditions human life. The possibilities of one's language are the possibilities of one's world. Without some constraint on what a word can mean, the tempting notion continues, we lack the capacity to delimit human speech and therefore human action (human speech and human action rendering each other intelligible). And here is where a certain fantasy of the incarnation cashes out. Insofar as Christ as cypher maps onto all words, that Word can then be used to judge what other words mean. We freely admit that without something like divine revelation language and interpretation go on and on. Since the meaning of a word is determined by use there is no telling where or how far from the familiar our language will stray, what a word might come to mean; we might be able to say what a use has derived *from* (the natural history of a word, as in "we used to mean this by this word") but not what it will derive *to*. And so it is for words, where "God" can be made to mean just about anything (well, as far as the grammar of one's scripture allows, which taking Christian scripture as an example can be quite a ways). And so too with other words—cats, brains, love, history, and so on. We find ourselves flummoxed by the range of linguistic derivation and think we have found in Christ a stopgap to derivation and so think we can use Christ to get behind words and then proclaim and then protest, "This is what 'God' means and so your use of 'God' is not authorized!" And so on with cats, brains, love, and history.

I am concerned in this essay with resisting this temptation by arguing that neither the doctrine of the incarnation works this way nor do words. I make this argument by rejecting not the notion that the Word *can* have a controlling relationship on all our words (that after all is what Christians call discipleship) but that it *necessarily* does; but first I dismantle the fantasy that the incarnation gives God into our hands, that we so possess God in Christ that we are given handles on human language. If anything, Christ is cypher not for what words mean but how words work. The working out of language is such that the Word *can* be made to rule other words, not that it has too. If, and this is critical, it was the case that human language relied on God for its authority, then the incarnation would be redundant; that it was not redundant is shown in the features of its history, the life, death, and resurrection of Christ. The tortured drama of Christ's (and Israel's) history exemplifies how language works, where words can come to mean anything and only as such does the Word become flesh and make its home among us; it then becomes (became) up to us to figure out what that word means (meant). As such is language available to us, and God. I want to say that if not for language working just this way, the Word would not be the Word for us; we certainly could not do to him what we did; he certainly would not have become for us what he has. It is only because words can be made to mean anything that the enjoining of Christian words to the Word proves so momentous (the church being the momentous if provisional occasion of the Word's reign). The wonder of the incarnation is precisely that God submits himself to the derivations of human speech, deriving what we took "God" and "human" to mean (and hence what "cat," "brain," "love" and "history" *can* come to mean). To get to this, I need first describe what the incarnation tempts, as I do below by considering how the violence confronted in *The Wire* tempts a natural theology of language. By a natural theology of language I mean the sense Rowan Williams has about how we tend to respond to the facts of language, facts I have described as derivation. The unbearable facts of language make us wish for an essence of words similar to how the slippery facts of life make natural theologians seek after the essence of things ostensibly available in nature. I turn to Williams in a bit, after first discussing *The Wire*'s violence in terms of commitments shared with ordinary language philosophy.

MARLO'S CITY OF WORDS

The Wire is a show of unspeakable violence. It is the kind of violence (picture the show's only true hero, Omar, his brains splattered on a wall, shot dead by a random twelve-year old) most people lack words for; except for empty gestures (imagine suburban pontifications on the evils of the inner city) they would not know how to speak about it. When people speak of such violence as "meaningless," what they mean is that it is hard for them to imagine the violence as part of a coherent moral universe that would render it defensible and therefore meaningful, even responsible, inspirational, and enjoyable. Again, certain thinned out descriptions of violence seek to opine in this direction but can venture only the most abstract speculations. When the reality of urban violence is confronted (*The Wire*) and the splattered aspects of violence come to the fore, pontification gives way to ascriptions of meaninglessness. And this is the way it should be; we should not be able to speak well of *The Wire*'s violence; it is a virtue of society that it does not know what to say when confronted by it. Our speechlessness in these moments tells us that our moral universe has reached its limit, telling us our moral universe remains intact. No moral universe should be able to comprehend everything.

The difficulty with a show like *The Wire* is that, apparently, some moral universes do allow such things. I said *The Wire* portrays violence *most* people lack words for. But what about those whose words prove adequate for this violence, words that sound like ours but are used so very differently, used to make acts of violence defensible and hence meaningful, even responsible, inspirational, and enjoyable? What about those whose language extends far beyond ours on the scale of allowable possibilities? What about those who call acts of egregious violence "love" or use "God" to authorize what we otherwise consider apathetic or godless? What do we do then? To what are we tempted in such moments? What do we do when faced with monsters?

Marlo Stanfield, the chief antagonist of *The Wire*'s final three seasons, is a monster, in the words of the show's writers, "terrifying in every way . . . a psychopath: devoid of the capacity for empathy, without restraint in exploitation and cruelty."[1] The creators of *The Wire* intended as much. David Simon says of Marlo, "He represented the ultimate totalitarian impulse—beyond money, beyond power or the exercise of power for its own sake, but instead that strange combination of self-love and self-loathing that rarely dares speak its name openly."[2] Part of what makes Marlo a terrifying personality in the show and a dominating figure in its fictional Baltimore is the inevitability with which he carries his power. Unlike those groping after power (from the local corner boys to the city's political players), Marlo wields power with a degree of frightful casualness that is unique among television characters in recent memory. We never see him angry or even emotionally invested; he does not need to carry weapons or raise his voice; he never utters a threat and yet comes off as the show's most threatening character. Unlike fellow criminals Avon Barksdale or Stringer Bell, the character of Marlo Stanfield elicits no sympathy; he is a sociopath who operates at a level of brazen nonchalance. Dennis Lehane, writer of the episode "Refugees," which I discuss momentarily, said of him:

> Marlo is very de-human. That's different than subhuman which suggest an evolutionary disconnect or an insult in regard to intelligence. Marlo is exceptionally intelligent and in an evolutionary sense he's Machiavelli's ideal . . . he's been dehumanized to the point where he's incapable of understanding why he should care about anyone or anything that doesn't enrich his bottom line. Where other characters on the show had a lot of flesh—I'm talking about everyone from Omar to Bunk to McNulty, even Bodie—Marlo is practically Stalinist in his lack of it. That makes

---

1. Alvarez, *The Wire: Truth Be Told*, 476.
2. Ibid., 333.

him all the more terrifying. It's hard to expect mercy from someone you can't imagine telling a joke or having a mother.[3]

Marlo, with his slight persona, preppy pastel polos, and mild voice, is the show's least imposing criminal, a jagged scar the only hint of menace.

In a scene early in the fourth season, Marlo enters a local convenience store. This one has private security. As is the case here, the people employed to provide security for these businesses are no less desperate than those who would rob them. "Rent-a-cops" play an unfortunate role in the power matrix of inner city Baltimore, despised for policing one's own people while never attaining the transcending power and respect of real police. They stand in as capitalism's laughable attempt at imposing traditional markets on the city. Marlo, the kingpin of West Baltimore, will have none of it, and while he could easily afford it, intentionally steals candy *so that* the security guard can see, in order to let the hired security guard know who's in charge, who actually runs the store and the city. As Marlo nonchalantly walks out of the store the security guard follows him.

> Security Guard: What the fuck? You think I dream of coming to work up in this shit on a Sunday morning? Tell all my friends what a good job I got? I'm working to support a family, man. [After Marlo turns away] Pretend I ain't talking to you. Pretend like I ain't even on this earth. [Marlo coolly makes eye contact after shamelessly putting the stolen candy in his mouth] I know what you are. And I ain't stepping to, but I am a man. And you just clip that shit and act like you don't even know I'm there.
>
> Marlo: I don't.
>
> Security Guard: [After moving to stand directly in front of Marlo] I'm here. [Now Marlo steps forward so that the two are only inches apart] Look, I told you I wasn't stepping to you. I ain't disrespecting you, son.
>
> Marlo: You want it to be one way.
>
> Security Guard: What?
>
> Marlo: You want it to be one way.
>
> Security Guard: Man, I don't know what you're –
>
> Marlo: You want it to be one way.

---

3. Ibid., 322–3

> Security Guard: Man, stop. [A finger pointed at Marlo] Stop saying that.
>
> Marlo: But it's the other way.

Marlo's enforcers Chris and Snoop pull up and without making eye contact, Marlo gets in and is driven away. Marlo's flippant authority is chilling; the security guard will later be killed by Chris and Snoop for "talking back." The scene is remarkably frustrating. Viewers identify with the security guard, coming face to face with our impotence, our inability do anything, faced as we are with the lame choice between turning a blind eye or getting killed for a trifle (candy).

We want it one way. We want the basic laws of human decency to apply or at least the rule of law. We want for the barest of local economies to sustain themselves, for those courageous enough to brave work for their families to get back to those families. We want the rich not to steal from the poor. We want stealing to bear the marks of purpose (to feed a family or make one rich). We want for killing to be necessary, and if necessary, coupled with some measure of regret, if only regret for the necessity of killing. We want it one way. But it's another way. In Baltimore, where corruption and political ambition serve one another, there is no one to whom we might appeal to tell us how things ought to be even if it isn't always that way. We want at least to know it should be this other way. Marlo tells us, "You want it to be one way. But it's the other way." The other way is what *The Wire* so powerfully portrays. There are of course many ways, as many ways as ways of speaking about the world, and I am interested in the way in which Marlo's ways are made familiar, how the unspeakable is made speakable, how violence becomes ordinary.

Season 4 starts with Snoop walking through Home Depot. Snoop and Chris serve as the main enforcers of the Marlo Stanfield criminal organization. In previous seasons, Marlo's gang beat out rivals primarily by a willingness to perpetrate its criminal activities at a level of audacity and violence unmatched by previous generations of drug dealers. In Chris and the androgynous Snoop, the drug trade has gone off the rails of anything approaching morality. The Stanfield gang operates at a level of extraordinary violence, making for an extraordinary moral universe. And yet we find Snoop shopping at Home Depot, the most ordinary of places. Specifically, she is considering the Dewalt cordless nail gun.

> Snoop: The trouble is you leave it in the trunk for a while and you need to step and use the bitch, the battery don't hold up, you know?

Salesman: Yeah. Cordless will do that. You might want to consider the power-actuated tool. The Hilti 460 MX or the Simpson PTP.

Taking Snoop for a local contractor rather than a murderous enforcer with "about five just last month," the salesman goes on to pitch power tools he extols as "my Cadillacs." When he begins on the Hilti's light recoil, Snoop throws him for a loop:

Snoop: Man, shit. I seen a tiny-ass .22 round-nose drop a nigga plenty of days, man. Motherfuckers get up in you like a pinball, rip your ass up. Big-joints though, big joints, man, just break up your bones, you say "Fuck it."

After paying the salesman $800 cash for the $669 Hilti, Snoop says, "You earned that buck like a motherfucker. Keep that shit." The scene is comic, a hilarious collision of Snoop's extraordinary gang world with the ordinary culture of Home Depot (or is it Home Depot that is extraordinary? which one serves as the common, the baseline?). Until we realize what the nail gun is purchased for. Talking to enforcer partner Chris, Snoop jokes about the nail gun's many features, "This here is gunpowder-activated, .27 caliber, full auto, no kickback, nail-throwing mayhem, man. Shit right here is tight. Fuck just nailing up boards. We could kill a couple motherfuckers with this right here." We discover what Snoop means by "nailing up boards" when Chris and Snoop murder people and hide their bodies in the walls of abandoned homes, using the nail gun to seal the makeshift mausoleum.

In one scene Chris and Snoop are about to murder someone. As the victim begs for his life, the two methodically cover him in plastic and quicklime, Chris calmly assures the victim, "Quick and clean, I promise." When the victim vomits from fear, Chris and Snoop look at each other exasperation, as if imminent murder should not warrant so much drama. (Right before Snoop is later executed she asks with equal detachment, "How's my hair look?") By the time the police discover the ploy, the vacant neighborhood has become a macabre cemetery, bodies literally coming out of the walls. The abandoned homes prove the perfect place to dispose of victims exactly because the buildings are visible but abandoned—"We got vacants on both sides. He'll stink is all"—a convenience made possible by neglect, serving the show's ongoing commentary about the desperately ordinary violence of American urban life.

By ordinary violence, I mean the shocking violence that occurs within ordinary everyday places where we expect the absence of violence (in neighborhoods where children play, at Home Depot, in convenience stores) but more so the philosophical sense, what some have called ordinary language philosophy following Wittgenstein's attempt to return words from their metaphysical to their everyday home. One guiding sense there is that the meaning of a word is its use, and so that the rule, or criterion, for a word's or an utterance's right use is none other than that which the users of that language establish and maintain. Claiming that words don't have meanings detachable from use might suggest a certain rulelessness to language, as if language lacked grammar. It is the opposite, that language is ruled by none other than grammar and grammar is not ruled by God (in contrast to Nietzsche's instructively askew dictum that as long as we have grammar we will have God). This is not at all to say that language cannot speak about God (obviously it does) nor that God cannot be present to human language (Jews, Christians, and Muslims think it obvious that God is), but only that humans rule language, grant it its sense, authorize its use. So if we take the basic claim that words and utterances have their meaning by way of use, that the criteria that rule a language are granted and governed by those who share the language in common, then we have come to terms with the fact that language can go as far as its use and that a word can go any way we use it. Again, this is not to say that anything is correct, for certainly a community's grammar can rule out a use (we rule in partly by ruling out); only that anything can be correct, that anything can be ruled into a grammar or out of it, that anything *can* be made to mean anything (that some things mean some things at all tells us this). To be sure we tend to use words reflective of the kinds of lives we live and the things such lives cause us to think and care about and so while use is conventional, convention is natural (to the lives we live) rather than arbitrary. Words can come to mean anything, but the process by which new uses are derived is as thick as biography. Another way to put this is to say that grammars and meanings are constitutive of the lives of those who share those languages.

There is no essential limit to one's language and therefore one's world except that which is natural for one's community to talk about and natural to the commitments certain ways of speaking commit one *to*. Taking all of this, violence can be understood as an utterance of language, a kind of speech. The implications here can be unsettling. As Sandra Laugier writes, "We have not yet understood, or we have quickly forgotten, the original point of departure for analytic philosophy, the linguistic turn, and we have not understood or have forgotten what it *means* to be interested in language."[4] To be so interested in language is to be interested in those who

---

4. Laugier, "Rethinking the Ordinary," 84. Emphasis original.

order its ways, to pursue language is to fall back on ourselves. Consider this comment from Stanley Cavell:

> We learn and teach words in certain contexts, and then we are expected and expect others, to be able to project them into further contexts. Nothing insures that this projection will take place (in particular, not the grasping of universals nor the grasping of books of rules), just as nothing insures that we will make, and understand, the same projections.... Human speech and activity, sanity and community, rest upon nothing more, but nothing less, than this. It is a vision as simple as it is difficult, and as difficult as it is (and because it is) terrifying.[5]

Again, "ordinary" indicates not so much the commonplace or common sense as much as this manner in which a word's use is determined by criteria maintained by us. And so it is we who determine (and discover) what we mean by "good" or "evil," we who set the criteria for what is to be identified as "good" or "evil." By returning words from their metaphysical to their everyday uses, Wittgenstein meant to return to us the maintenance of language, or more precisely, sought to return *us* to its maintenance, hoping we might come to terms with our language, come to terms with ourselves (our words speak us as much as we speak them—Herbert McCabe adds the important point that words grow and we grow into our words).[6] What is a nail gun for? What is the criterion by which we assess its use? Well, it is not so simple as deciphering the purpose for which it was made, for who can determine such things as intentions and how far those reasons should carry (we may want it one way; someone else, another way). A good many things come to us without purpose; there is often no point where intention comes into view; our use imbues things with purpose. As examples, though we might get away with asking, "For what use was the nail gun made?" it would not be so easy to ask, "What is the proper use of money?" and nonsensical to question, "What is the point of jealousy?" In adjudicating right use of a nail gun, we are thrown back on Chris and Snoop and their uses. Now we could disqualify Chris and Snoop from its maintenance (this has been deemed as a reason for prison) but such a move only furthers the point, that we return to us as the givers of criteria. Hence, by "ordinary" I mean the "we" of attunement in language. To underscore how far derivation can migrate, consider these reflections on the Partition of India and Pakistan and its many violences, about which the anthropologist Veena Das writes,

---

5. Cavell, *Must We Mean What We Say?*, 52.
6. McCabe, *Law, Love and Language*, 18.

> [I]t is because the range and scale of the human that is tested and defined and extended in the disputations proper to everyday life move through the unimaginable violence of the Partition into forms of life that are seen as not belonging to life proper. That is to say, these experiments with violence raise certain doubts about life itself, and not only about the *forms* it could take. Was it a man or a machine that plunged a knife into the private parts of a woman after raping her? Were those men or animals that went around killing and collecting castrated penises as signs of their prowess? These are not, however, simply places of doubt about the human—for the terror of the violation of the Partition was precisely that victims *knew* their perpetrators to be human: that is what puts life itself into question . . . The precise range and scale of the *human* form of life is not knowable in advance, any more than the precise range of the meaning of a word is knowable in advance . . . What I found compelling in my relations with Manjit [a victim of the Partition that Das comes to befriend in her research] was her recognition that her violation was of an order that the whole principle of life stood violated and that to put it back into words could not be done except with extreme hesitation.[7]

The situating of violence into normal patterns of life, its normalization, occurs through linguistic impartation; when we begin to speak thus, things have been made possible for us, and when we speak again and again about it, the abnormal has been made normal. *The Wire* portrays how violence has been instilled in the regular patterns of life by ensconcing itself in regular speech. In discussing everyday violence and death, anthropologist Nancy Scheper-Hughes speaks of trying to "uncover and call attention to forms and spaces of hitherto unrecognized, gratuitous and useless social suffering by referring to them as invisible genocides and small holocausts." Scheper-Hughes offers a depiction eerily similar to Chris and Snoop's makeshift mausoleum: "The paradox is that they are not invisible because they are secreted away and hidden from view, but quite the reverse. As Wittgenstein noted, the things that are hardest to perceive are often those which are right before our eyes and therefore simply taken for granted."[8] This paradox of visibility and invisibility gets to the heart of what Scheper-Hughes intimates by these invisible and small events that take place so near us (nothing is nearer to us than our speech, and nothing so hidden as that secreted in what

---

7. Das, *Life and Words*, 90, 92. Emphasis original.
8. Nancy Scheper-Hughes, "Small Wars and Invisible Genocides," 889. Matthew Whelan pointed me in Scheper-Hughes' direction.

we say). Chris and Snoop are exasperated by their victims' terror because for them murdering people and burying their bodies in abandoned homes occur "as if they were the most normal and expected behaviors."[9] The writers of the show tell of "how cheap life can be out there" as "people die over stupid shit." Speaking of Omar's death, Lehane says, "There's zero nobility in it. That's the street."[10]

It is helpful to examine the conditions under which linguistic—and therefore, imaginative—change occurs. On the one hand, language change occurs constantly if not noticeably. According to linguist John McWhorter, "To be a language, then, is to be a mess, and the only question is to what extent. As you might suppose, irregularity decreases to the extent that adult learners have smoothed it out over time. This means that a hideous amount of irregularity is, like an equal amount of ingrowness, the default state of language."[11] On the other hand, intense cultural circumstances put pressures on language to meet the descriptive needs of its speakers, making change more rapid and noticeable. Studying gang and drug culture in Harlem, anthropologist Phillippe Bourgois summarizes, "In the particular case of the United States, the concentration of social marginalized populations into politically and ecologically isolated inner-city enclaves has fomented an especially explosive cultural creativity that is in defiance of racism and economic marginalization."[12] Language serves everyday life, and if one's everyday involves regular violence, language will serve life by giving it place within the common parlance. Of course this has a circular effect; insofar as language is available, so then will be the practices imagined in that language. The unimaginable becomes routinized through language, which isn't to say that unimaginable violence becomes imaginable to everyone, just everyone who speaks that way. Hence, the collision of ways: "You want it to be one way. But it's the other way." The point here is not that urban America is more violent than elsewhere; whatever "violent" comes to denote (whatever the criteria for "violent") is determined locally and provisionally, making judgments like "more violent" themselves local and provisional. It is the nature of violence, insofar as "violence" is a word at all, to have a vague (to use Peter Och's semiotics) future, even if our retrospective use of the word grants the semblance of certainty.[13]

---

9. Ibid., 890.
10. Alvarez, 324.
11. McWhorter, *What Language Is*, 73. I am indebted to KC Flynn for this point.
12. Bourgois, *In Search of Respect*, 8, 9.
13. See, for example, Ochs, "Theosemiotics and Pragmatism," 59–81.

What is terrifying about Marlo Stanfield is not that his language plays fast and loose with the world, but precisely that it matches onto the world, that it bespeaks a reality of things we don't want to acknowledge (that violence and speech about violence avail one another). Marlo has worded his city (as we each word our worlds) in his image, and this city, and hence Marlo's moral universe, is not easily dismantled. As Cavell writes, "The conventions which control the application of grammatical criteria are fixed not by customs or some particular concord or agreement which might, without disrupting the texture of our lives, be changed where conveniences suggest a change."[14] Marlo Stanfield's existence would be less frightening if it *were* arbitrary. That it is not, that Marlo is natural to our world, to the human form of *life*, tells us things we don't want to know about ourselves, that the violence he ushers in is not only coherent but natural to the world in which we find ourselves. It is not that Marlo puts it in his head to speak and act in a way different than how others might wish *it* to be, nor the security guard who may, as Marlo rightly surmises, want it "the other way." What terrifies us about Marlo is that while his way is strange to us, it is continuous with a history we find ourselves part of (it is telling that the older drug lords refer to Marlo as "Youngin"). As Cavell writes, "I cannot decide what I take as a matter of course, any more than I can decide what interests me. . . . What I take as a matter of course is not itself a matter of course. It is a matter of history."[15]

TEMPTING NATURAL THEOLOGY

I have been saying that *The Wire*'s transmutation of language tempts something. I think it makes us wish language didn't work this way, that words were not as pliable to human touch as they are. I am trying to say that this temptation presses in on something about our life in words, that we are tempted out of it, out of life. It is not just the show that tempts us, but the

---

14. Cavell, *Claim of Reason*, 110.

15. Ibid., 122–23. Questions as to how accurately *The Wire* portrays "reality" often turn out to be red herrings. The show certainly has been lauded for its "realistic" depiction of urban poverty and violence and for how that depiction raises awareness of the realities of urban poverty and violence. Such appraisals harbor a latent empiricist allure. That is, we can begin to think that reality is the goal (where some people "get it" and some don't), a thought which quickly yields to the regression that something as banal as entertainment television will always miss the mark because it can never capture "what life is really like in the inner city." Hence Cavell referred to film as "a moving image of skepticism" by which he meant that such habits of thought distract from one's responsibility to one's words (meaning what one says) by raising the specter of realism/anti-realism. Cavell, *World Viewed*, 188.

show insofar as it lays bare a temptation for life as other than created, and so tempting a moral life without God.

Working through Augustine's *De Doctrina Christiana*, Rowan Williams identifies this temptation. Williams reads Augustine as figuring epistemology as an issue of desire, such that to understand language is to understand how human creatures (those creatures with language) move about the world as drawn forward by love. Only within this account of desire does it make sense to speak of words, to offer up a view of language only after first having set the context as one of love. Otherwise we might think that what is important about the world can be spoken of outside our relationship to it. According to Williams,

> Augustine assumes that "signifying" is a threefold, not a twofold, affair, involving the subject *for* whom signs signify. We cannot miss the point that discussion of signification is also discussion of those beings who are involved in meaning or "intending" or understanding. The distinction between *frui* and *uti* (I.iii) is thus superimposed on the *res-signum* distinction, and will pervade the whole of DDC; it is the means whereby Augustine links what he has to say about language with what he has to say about beings who "mean" and about the fundamentally desirous nature of those beings—a link which is undoubtedly the most original and interesting feature of the treatise.[16]

While no sign adequately signifies God as *res* and while God as *res* signifies no further *res*, God as supreme *res* provided his own sign in the divine Word. To understand Williams on this point one needs to understand inadequacy beyond its narrow Platonic scope. The emphasis here is not the basic sense that God exceeds every signification; any theology that majors on God's transcendence and hence the inadequacy of language qua language has ripped the theological notion of transcendence from its conceptual context—it has not only minimized the incarnation but forgotten it altogether. The point about the inadequacy of signs is not that "God" cannot mount up to (is not expansive enough for) all that God is. Casting the incarnation as solving the problem of language's inadequacy would have the theologically fatal effect of denigrating our life in words as if what is important about the incarnation is that it conveys information rather than expresses love. Our words are adequate to our life with God because of God's con-descending availability to them. No sign signifies God not because God is information and our language is not up the task of that

---

16. Williams, "Language, Reality and Desire," 140. Emphasis original. I am much indebted to Natalie Carnes for many helpful conversations about this essay.

information but because God is the very form of love and love is known in its actuality, the Word made flesh.[17]

This is where the superimposition of desire onto the *res-signum* scheme begins to pay off, helping us understand that things are enjoyed insofar as they enthrall us toward final enjoyment and signs signify things in terms of this enjoyment. Williams gives us nothing less than an erotic account of language whereupon words are indexed to human desire such that not only do we have the world through words but the world in terms of our desirous relationship to it. All signs—signs being relays of desire—therefore gesture to God just as all desire ends in God. The incarnation fires the sacramental imagination, rendering the world sign, as this supreme *res* is made sign. To confess the incarnation is to see the world operating in just this way, as replete in its multifarious *res* as divine script, the flesh made word.

Notice, however, that none of this is to deny that creation with full integrity and resounding intelligibility subscribes to and for itself meaning through its respective languages; doing that just is the work of any natural language, the human occupation of wording the world according to desire. It is only that in its desire meaning reaches beyond itself. This point is critical, not something that Williams takes much time to underline but which serves as the basis of his labored distinction between use and usury. It cannot be that the words we use or the concepts we employ have meaning only when they indicate God as supreme *res*; no, such words and concepts have a present unity even if not yet made subject to this final signification. If they did not, critically, they would have no use at all and would have no place in our life in words. If these concepts and words did not already work *for* us, did not already do the work of conceptualizing the world, then they could not do the further work of pointing to God. It is exactly that language works as it does (is available as it is) that it can be made to work for the purpose of revealing God. Only insofar as our words give us the world can they also give us God. It is just that no matter how much our words give us a grip on the world, their futures are through and through vague, continuously opening up to new uses and meanings, and hence continuously opening up new worlds.

There is something unsettling about this. Words that give us the world can also give us God; words that give us the world can also give us monsters. We want it one way but more often it's the other way. And so nails are used to build homes, and they are used to murder and hide bodies. When Marlo's city of words "steps to us" we are tempted by what Williams calls "a 'natural

---

17. This is not to deny knowledge in the sense of *aedequatio mentis ad rem* but only to underscore knowledge of God as relationally constituted. On this point, see Griffiths, *Intellectual Appetite*, 135.

theology' grounded in the facts of language." This temptation goes two ways, both trying to get around language. First, the thought that language's derivation reveals to us God as likewise derivative, with the added effect of rendering the incarnation redundant—i.e., we don't need the incarnation if we can read the same stuff off the surface of our life in words. Second, that despite language's derivation, it is not so hopelessly (and dangerously) open, that there is a ground to it. Both temptations relocate the theological relevance of language away from its unsettling fluidity. The first, harkening on surfaces as it does, claims that what is important about language is not what it gives us (e.g., the world, God, monsters, etc.) but its fluidity as such. The second promises us that at bottom all is solid, rendering fluidity trivial. In both instances the attempt to still the "restless fluidities in meaning" takes us out of life and forfeits the manner in which we might have the world at all, and so God.

Williams helps us understand the temptation by engaging literary theorist Geoffrey Hartman's claim, "There is no absolute knowledge but rather a textual infinite, an interminable web of texts or interpretations." Contending that "no worldly *res* is securely settled as fixed object 'meaning' itself, or tied to in a fixed designation, that no worldly state of affairs can be allowed to terminate human desire, that all that is present to us in and as language is potentially *signum* in respect of the unrepresentable God," Augustine on Williams' reading "certainly has affinities with the popular notion that everything is language."[18] But Williams departs from Hartman, and it is important to note where this departure takes place and what Williams means and doesn't mean by it. For Hartman, there is no key that proves normative for the interpretation of texts, no one text that decodes all other texts. For Williams, there is "the canonical text that witnesses to the canonical (normative) representation, Christ."[19] It is what Williams calls "the definitive sign." Let me consider two divergent ways one can read Williams on his difference with Hartman. This is a crucial point not so much in regards to Williams and Hartman (Christian orthodoxy and contemporary linguistic and literary theory) but more so for my present concern, coming to terms with wanting it one way when it is the other.

---

18. Williams, "Language, Reality and Desire," 145. Williams quotes from Hartman, *Criticism in the Wilderness*, 202. By "absolute knowledge" Hartman is referring specifically to Hegel's notion and continues, "the fact that we discern periods or sentences or genres or individual outlines or unities of various kinds is somewhat like computing time. We can insist that time has a beginning and an end; or more modestly, that Romanticism, for example, began circa 1770 and ended 1830; but this is a silly if provoking mimicry of providential or historical determinism" (ibid.).

19. Williams, "Language, Reality and Desire," 146.

Williams could be arguing that no matter the range of linguistic possibility (what I have been calling derivation) there is a base of meaning settled before use takes words afield, a center to linguistic range, and a necessary commitment of all grammar. This base, center, and commitment is none other than God and at the incarnation God gave what Williams caricatures as "a breakthrough into clear metaphysical knowledge" that rescues language from the realm of infinite derivation and interpretation from infinite regression. Because Christ anchors language as its base, center, and commitment, all language not only points to God in Christ, but God through Christ grounds all language. How this anchoring works can be worked out in any number of suggestive arrangements that we need not get into here. The important point is that whereas Hartman thinks language can go anywhere Williams, on this reading, thinks that the doctrine of the incarnation commits one to language's metaphysical delimitation. This is one way to read Williams' (Christianity's) difference with Hartman.

I take Williams conversely, as challenging the likes of Hartman but in the opposite direction, not by showing forth an anchor to language such that Hartman and Marlo Stanfield go too far, but by unleashing language from any one base, center, or commitment, such that Hartman and Marlo stop too short. This has to do with what one thinks animates language's derivation. Hartman bases the derivation of language on language qua language whereas Williams bases the derivation of language on human desire for God's infinite triune life. The problem with any account of language fixed on finite affairs (language qua language) is that it settles in finite political arrangements; it simply is not up to the task of its projected infinitude (Hartman's "textual infinity") precisely because it will repeatedly settle for finite desire (a basic Augustinian claim). Marlo wants it one way, but there are other ways. When another way "steps to" Marlo he is killed; this will happen whenever one speaks the world differently in a city of words that allows no "talking back."

Another way, one that properly respects God's infinitude, has been given. It is the life of the one who properly signified that life in his very body (a genuine textual infinite) first in his carnal fleshy body and then the body of the church that continues as sign of this supreme *res* made flesh. In being so given, the divine Word is given to human wording and hence is called variously "Emmanuel," "drunkard and glutton," "Messiah," "Beelzebul," "King of the Jews," and so on and so forth. Submitted to our wording of the world, Christ—what Williams describes as "the central displacement of fixed concepts"—is killed; this will happen whenever one speaks the world differently in a city of words that allows no "talking back." God speaks again and rewords the world in a syntax of resurrection, though some remain in their city of words, for it is the nature of words to allow every possibility.

For Christians the giving of the one supreme *res* in Christ reinterprets all language as infinite desire for Father, Son, and Holy Spirit, making that which comes through language beyond possession. Marlo is to viewers of *The Wire* as the security guard is to Marlo, something wished not there. Which is to say we sometimes wish God not there when indeed God is as close to us as our words. Christ is the sign of the supereme *res*, and so the sign of the unpossessable God (demonstrating in the form of this sign that we have been given God in Christ and yet can never possess God in Christ). Williams says it best: "Wisdom elects to be mortal; and what prevents this from being a straightforward theophany that would lead us to *identify* Wisdom with the world of mortality is that it is precisely *mortality* itself, limit, incompletion, absence, that is the speech of Wisdom with us."[20]

BIBLIOGRAPHY

Alvarez, Rafael. *The Wire: Truth Be Told*. New York: Grove, 2009.
Bourgois, Phillippe. *In Search of Respect: Selling Crack in El Barrio*. Cambridge: Cambridge University Press, 2003.
Cavell, Stanley. *The Claim of Reason*. Oxford: Oxford University Press, 1979.
———. *Must We Mean What We Say? A Book of Essays*. Cambridge: Cambridge University Press, 2002.
———. *The World Viewed: Reflections on the Ontology of Film*. Enlarged ed. Cambridge: Harvard University Press, 1979.
Das, Veena. *Life and Words: Violence and the Descent into the Ordinary*. Berkeley: University of California Press, 2007.
Griffiths, Paul. *Intellectual Appetite: A Theological Grammar*. Washington, DC: Catholic University of America Press, 2009.
Hartman, Geoffrey H. *Criticism in the Wilderness: The Study of Literature Today*. New Haven: Yale University Press, 1980.
Laugier, Sandra. "Rethinking the Ordinary: Austin *after* Cavell." In *Contending with Stanley Cavell*, edited by Russell B. Goodman, 82–99. Oxford: Oxford University Press, 2005.
McCabe, Herbert. *Law, Love and Language*. New York: Continuum, 2003.
McWhorter, John. *What Language Is (And What It Isn't and What It Could Be)*. New York: Gotham, 2011.
Ochs, Peter. "Theosemiotics and Pragmatism." *Journal of Religion* 72 (1992) 59–81.
Scheper-Hughes, Nancy. "Small Wars and Invisible Genocides." *Social Science & Medicine* 43 (1993) 339–900.
Williams, Rowan. "Language, Reality, and Desire in Augustine's De Doctrina." *Theology & Literature* 3 (1989) 138–50.

---

20. Ibid., 149.

5

Sexual Communication and Institutional Dysfunction in *The Wire*

DAVID MATZKO MCCARTHY

INTRODUCTION

IN FILM AND TELEVISION, as well as popular attitudes, sex is usually thought to be unproblematic on a social level, pursued for the sake of pleasure, self-expression, or love. Individual persons act foolishly or destructively, but sex is assumed to be under the control and management of the agent, defined by the self. In *Sex and the City,* one of the consistent themes is that each of us decides what sex will be for us, such that sexuality is the medium for self-actualization. As women struggle to define themselves in a world of men, sex is set apart from the antagonisms of class, race, and economic segregation. In *Sex and the City*, sex is an activity of the fashionable bedroom.[1] In *The Wire*, by contrast, sex is usually drunken, sloppy, and/or meaningless, highlighting how sex is not a medium for self-actualization, but for acting out (making evident) social tensions and institutional dysfunctions, as well as conflicts of economic inequality, class, and race.

---

1. Brasfield, "Sex and the City," 130–39; Cramer, "Discourses of Sexual Morality," 409–32.

In this essay, I will explore how sex—both the act itself and how it is used conversationally—illuminates the networks of association within which the characters are trapped in a variety of institutional frameworks. In the series, sex is not the only medium for social commentary, but it is an important medium; analyzing its use within the series thus reveals the complexities of social relations as well as the ambiguities and contradictions of personal roles and intentions amid institutional life. The first section of the chapter deals with sexual expressions used among men as a language of domination and authenticity, antagonism and collegiality; these ways of speaking, I argue, reinforce a person's relationship to the institution, and form how sexual relationships are conducted. From there, I will outline the way in which the characters' interpersonal bonds and sexual relationships are caught up into larger institutional networks, for better or for worse.

The underlying theological angle of the chapter is this: Within Christianity (and religions in general) sexual activity is not private but fits with the contours of common life—with communal and institutional embodiments that are accountable to God's faithfulness. As properly directed to God's faithfulness, sexual expression (like other institutional embodiments) also communicates personal and social frailty. The drama of human aspirations, desires, sin, and redemption marks our sexual relations. Sex is not private but communicates (even in our failures) moral and theological goods. To say "not private" is not to say "exhibitionist." The description "private" or "institutional" identifies purposes and ends. Sex, in the church, is framed and infused with the common end and goods of fidelity, steadfast love, and generativity. Indeed, it is the private character of contemporary sex that leads to its dominant exhibitionist and voyeuristic expressions. If sex is private, each individual determines his or her own sexual purposes and ends; then, sexual expression becomes (as in *Sex and the City*) a basic means of self-expression *over against institutions and social life*. In effect, sex becomes a form of conspicuous consumption. Because of its realism, *The Wire* avoids the naïveté of privatized sex. For this reason, theological realism about the institutional and social character of sexual activity provides a useful approach to sex in *The Wire*. The theologian is well situated to see what is going on.

THE SEXUAL AND THE SOCIAL

The sex scenes in *The Wire* are often illustrative of more complex social problems. Two examples will suffice to begin the larger exploration here. First, consider how the relationship between Nick Sobotka (a dockworker) and his girlfriend is set within a frame of social and economic displacement.[2] Nick and Aimee have an ongoing relationship and expect to be married. They are raising their child but do not have enough money to set up a home and begin a family in earnest; with little seniority at the dock amid a weak economy, Nick is given only infrequent work at the docks. Waking up together in the basement of his parents' house, Nick asks Aimee to sneak out the back door because, according to him, his parents are "decent people," as opposed to the economically disadvantaged Nick and Aimee, with their "abnormal" sexual relationship. Likewise, consider how, in West Baltimore, Cutty Wise's relationships with women undermine his credibility with the boys he is trying to get off the streets.[3] He is attractive to single mothers because he is a decent (drug- and crime-free) man of the neighborhood. But because he is intimate with their mothers, the boys do not want to get close to him. His sincerity with them only arouses suspicions about what he is really after, and frustrates his attempts to reform both himself and the neighborhood around him.

The various institutions within *The Wire* function, in part, to perpetuate certain sexual parameters, often to the detriment of those dwelling within these institutions. These networks are largely homosocial, framed in terms of how a man can sexually possess and dominate a woman, and perpetuated through a discursive medium of heterosexual mastery. A full break with the dysfunctions of homosocial institutions is possible, as I will describe in the concluding section of the chapter. But within *The Wire*, these examples are the exception to the rule; in the world of *The Wire*, institutions perpetuate themselves not only through overt displays of sexualized power, but through the invisible institutions and networks which make up Baltimore. While programs like *Sex and the City* highlight the idealism of sex as self-actualization, *The Wire* reveals the seamy and destructive side of sex amid real social and economic dysfunction.

EVERYDAY DOMINATION . . . OR AUTHENTIC BONDS?

In *The Wire*, the language of sex is used in day-to-day interactions to communicate power dynamics; phrases related to sodomy, and other sexual insinuations like "kiss my ass" are necessary to communicating the status of specific persons and the relationship of one organization to another. Throughout the series, to "fuck" another can be—among other things—equivalent to doing a good job. To "be fucked" might be to fail in one's role

---

2. "Hard Cases," S2/E4.
3. "Unto Others," S4/E7.

or to be mastered by another; to be a "bitch" is to be one who is mastered.[4] Consider, for example, the opening scene in the narcotics unit. Thomas "Herc" Hauk and Ellis Carver pal around with Kima Greggs. Herc wants Carver to do menial paperwork for him. Carver's refuses, asking, "Am I your bitch?" Greggs is frustrated with her labors at the typewriter. When she makes a mistake, she mutters, "Fuck me." With good humor, Herc and Carver brag that their real job is not in the office pushing paper, but on the streets, "Fucking the motherfuckers up."[5]

In male organizations, sexual language functions to express both aggression and social equilibrium. The language of dominance is, by necessity, impolite; it offers no dignity to the dominated, and among friends, it puts on no airs. In most male-oriented institutions, both hostility and friendship are expressed through the language of aggression, sometimes taking the place of real battle. At times, it is used to denounce, challenge, and overpower with words without other acts of revenge or control, maintaining peace by containing the violence within words, a performance of posturing and chest pounding.

The antagonism perpetrated by sexual language occurs at a variety of levels. Within the police department, this is seen in the perennial power struggles between the rank-and-file and the officers. Early in the series, Major Rawls orders Officer Santangelo in order to get him to incriminate Jimmy McNulty.[6] Santangelo says that it is not his job to "fuck another cop." Later in the episode, McNulty is talking to his partner, Bunk Moreland, about his problems with Rawls; McNulty concludes that he is going to have to "kiss Rawls' ass" for about four months. McNulty tells Bunk that he respects Bunk because, "When it came time for you to fuck me, you were very gentle." The inference is that McNulty, when newbie or virgin in homicide, had to be put in his place, with Bunk the perpetrator of pseudo-sexual violence upon McNulty. At the end of the episode, McNulty learns from Santangelo that Rawls wants his badge. In McNulty's words, "they're going to do me."

Though functioning as a conduit of dominance and submission, the language of sex also paradoxically communicates social bonds. Various partners within the series develop their own sexual banter, focusing their antagonisms toward superiors, inferiors, enemies, or their institution as a whole. Sexually charged language is also the medium of interpersonal-yet-professional relationships, as seen in the Bunk-McNulty example above. The

4. When their stash of drugs is stolen, Wee-Bey Brice says to D'Angelo Barksdale, "We look like bitches" ("Old Cases," S1/E4).
5. "The Target," S1/E1.
6. "One Arrest," S1/E7.

backdrop of this friendship and warm regard is a kind of solidarity (whether real or contrived) of mutual subjection—a union from being dominated by the same forces or institutions.

Consider also the banter which Bunk and Lester Freamon have when Freamon is leaving the homicide unit.[7] Bunk speculates that Lester wants to leave because he doesn't like "the smell of pussy" on Bunk, the implication being that Bunk is virile, while Lester finds the smell of women objectionable and, thus, is not a real man. Lester responds, "I am going to miss you too, bitch." The exchange continues with Bunk then calling Lester a pervert for wanting to listen to phone calls on the wiretap; at this point, Kima breaks in and suggests that the wiretap would do Bunk good; it would broaden his horizons. Far from being degrading, the entire exchange reveals only respect and friendship.[8]

As such, sexual language is the vocabulary of the "real" community within the cold and antagonistic institution. Institutions often "fuck" with their members, and to be part of organizations is to be "fucked" along with others. In a poignant scene at the onset of Season 5, Carver endures his first roll call as the Sergeant-In-Charge of the Western District.[9] The scene opens with his patrolmen and plainclothes officers waiting in the meeting room, with Carver called a "pretty bitch" and accused of being an institutional climber. He defuses the accusation with good humor: "If I were minding my career, would I be in the Western commanding you useless fucking humps."

In this way, Carver effectively expresses his solidarity with them; he shares their degradation; he, like them, is dominated by the hierarchy. But Carver's expression of solidarity (shared humiliation) is effective only for a moment. As the patrolmen's anger over lack of overtime mounts, Carver no longer talks like one of them. His language becomes clean and professional, bereft of swearing and full of talk about duty and a higher calling.

This example of Carver reveals another aspect of how this sexual language functions institutionally. In contrast to the solidarity created by sexual talk, official institutional language is clean, but only *artificially* so. The institutional position is constructed for the sake of politics, policy, and public consumption; in reality, however, the inner workings of institutions

---

7. "A New Day," S4/E11.

8. The language of sexual domination, even here, is volatile. The conversation ends when Carver enters the office to discuss a case with Bunk, in which they realize that Herc had failed to deliver a witness to Bunk, and the meaning of the foul language quickly turns. Words that had been used just before in play suddenly become bitter as Bunk calls Herc a "motherfucker."

9. "More with Less," S5/E1.

are full of ambiguities, mixed motives, and personal antagonisms. While presented (as with Carver) as clean, the reality of institutions is messy like sexual language—like Herc walking into Mayor Royce's office when his secretary is performing fellatio.[10] Herc, at first, thinks that his career is ruined. But when Herc acts as though nothing has happened, Royce uses his influence to have Herc promoted to sergeant. What could have been a public scandal (as sexually degrading to women) bonds Royce and Herc. Likewise, foul language of both Mayors Royce and Carcetti is reserved for their inner circles and their institutional antagonists when behind closed doors, where the language used by the institutions is indistinguishable from that of the subordinates.

This imposition of clean but artificial and inauthentic speech is not limited to the police institution, but is shown in the tensions between the city editor of *The Baltimore Sun*, Gus Haynes, and managing editor Thomas Klebanow. Haynes sustains institutional memory, defends practices of good reporting, and demands excellence of his writers. Klebanow (along with the executive editor Whiting) represents the absentee ownership and cheaper (both shallow and less expensive) forms of journalism. Where Haynes looks for truth, Klebanow lives on the surface of public opinion and cost-cutting measures and is willing to overlook shortcuts in pursuit of a Pulitzer. As such, Klebanow's concern for appearances is reflected in his clean language, and Haynes' authenticity is expressed through his foul mouth.[11]

In contrast to Haynes' language, Klebanow's concern for appearances and civility as the Pulitzer Prize candidate intrudes as hypocrisy. As the newsroom watches Mayor Carcetti announce Commissioner Burrell's retirement on TV, Haynes gives a running commentary on Baltimore politics.[12] Klebanow is impressed and asks if Haynes' analysis will make it into the morning's paper. Haynes says, "No," because of the cutbacks in staff; to do the story, the newspaper would need a veteran with connections and respect on the police force, and "fuck if we didn't buy ours out." Klebanow, defending the institutional values of the paper, dodges the substance of Haynes' statement and criticizes Haynes' language.[13] After Klebanow walks away, Haynes reacts. "Collegial. I fucking failed out of journalism school. What does collegial mean?" The official institution, represented by Klebanow, is undermining good journalism and arguing for appearances of civility.

10. "Soft Eyes," S4/E2.

11. There is a connection between swearing and perceptions of authenticity. See Rassin and Heijden, "Appearing Credible? Swearing Helps!" 177–82.

12. "Transitions," S5/E4.

13. "I understand your frustration with the cutbacks, but civility is important. I have been meaning to talk to you about your profanity. A collegial atmosphere is essential."

Klebanow will accept fabricated stories (by reporter Scott Templeton) in hope of winning a Pulitzer.[14] Once again, foul language expresses bonds of mutual subjugation to institutions, subjection to both their corruption and their possibilities for good work.

INSTITUTIONAL INFIDELITY AND SEXUAL INFIDELITY

Institutions are constituted by individuals, their mixed motives, uneven talents, and sometimes contradictory purposes and ambitions. The conflicts between institutions (e.g., law and organized crime) are settings for deeper struggles within institutions, among individuals, and within individual persons. Persons must struggle between what is required for personal advancement in the institutions and their ideals for what the institutions ought to be. To which will a person be subject? Consider Councilman Tommy Carcetti. He has high ideals about what city government can and should do, but wins the mayor's office by cold ambition and cynical political maneuvering. Similar contradictions affect the Barksdale drug organization's "CEO" and "CFO," Avon Barksdale and Stringer Bell; while loyal to each other, their struggles over what the drug organization will become leads each to betray the other. The genius of David Simon's storytelling is that these figures are shown to be as much caught by their institutions as they are shapers of it.

In the same way that sexual language tends to govern how persons interact within institutions, the infidelity of persons in institutions and the infidelity of institutions as a whole are often enacted sexually. Jimmy McNulty's status as the central figure through the five seasons of *The Wire* is perhaps best seen here, in his confusing amalgam of fidelity and infidelity, both sexually toward loved ones, and institutionally toward his partners, good police work, and the law. In McNulty, there is a crisscrossing of duty, self-centeredness, faithfulness, and betrayal, making him the paramount Augustinian anti-hero, as his contentious relationship with the politics of police life spill out into his sexual relationships. During a tryst with Rhonda Pearlman, for example, he paradoxically talks about hoping to redeem his marriage. But when his wife, Elena, refuses to get back together with him, he and Elena have passionate sex, an act which communicates not fidelity to

---

14. Both Haynes and reporter Alma Gutierrez convey their suspicions that Templeton is making up quotations and stories. In the last episode, both are demoted by Whiting and Klebanow, Haynes to the copy desk and Gutierrez to Carroll County. Templeton, who fabricates the news, stands with Whiting and Klebanow to receive the Pulitzer Prize.

each other, but rather their *lack* of fidelity to each other or marriage, in ways mirroring the infidelity expressed in the relationship between Jimmy and Rhonda.[15] And yet, surprisingly, when political consultant Terry D'Agostino expects from him only casual sex for the sake of furthering her political cause, he feels used and ends the relationship.[16]

While McNulty's personal and institutional dysfunctions which manifest themselves in sexual behavior sprawl across five seasons, a more manageable presentation of these struggles is found in D'Angelo Barksdale. He is a soldier in the Barksdale drug organization, but has acted impulsively and foolishly, shooting another dealer in front of civilians. Demoted to dealing in the low-rise projects, he takes the role as the experienced, vigilant, and wise elder to his crew as his former immaturity turns to scruples about the drug trade and its violence. Like McNulty, his desire for personal integrity forms the foundation of his unfaithfulness to the organization. When one of his crew mistreats a junkie, he argues that "the game ain't gotta be played like that, you can't tell me that this shit can't get done without people beatin' on each other, killing each other, doing each other like dogs." Such an opinion about how the drug trade could be conducted runs directly counter to the expected norm, and as such, is dismissed.

D'Angelo's emerging conscience sets him apart from his Uncle Avon and the other officers of the Barksdale organization, an instability which plays itself out against a sexual backdrop. When on his way to see his uncle at Orlando's Strip Club (the Barksdale headquarters), D'Angelo expresses awe to Orlando and envy about his easy access to the strippers. But later, he witnesses a dancer, Shardene, setting herself apart from the other girls in the club; rather than employ her as a stripper (as one would expect from the intertwining of the Barksdale headquarters with a strip club), D'Angelo asks her out on a date.[17]

In a subsequent episode, we learn what we had already suspected: that she doesn't take drugs and she isn't a prostitute; in other words, Shardene does not conform to the sexual norms of the Barksdale organization. D'Angelo already has a girlfriend, Donette, and a child that are already within the purview of the Barksdale organization, but he moves in with Shardene instead (without Donette's knowledge)—setting up, in a sense, an alternative to the strip club, Donette, and the Barksdale way of life. To take the alternative (a life of sexual fidelity outside the Barksdale organizational

---

15. "All Prologue," S2/E6.

16. These instances continue, as McNulty attempts to have a domestic relationship with Beadie Russell, only to continue to struggle with infidelity.

17. "The Pager," S1/E5.

assumption of infidelity) is to betray the Barksdale organization. At one level, D'Angelo's action is unfaithful to Donette, mother of his child, but among the Barksdales, faithfulness to women has never been expected of him, making his move to fidelity all the more traitorous. Thus, D'Angelo's sexual behavior follows his institutional infidelity.

The hope for an alternative ends when Shardene learns that a friend of hers from Orlando's has overdosed at a Barksdale party and is found naked, rolled up in a carpet, and thrown out with the trash.[18] Days before, D'Angelo and Shardene had talked about leaving the Barksdale life together; now she leaves him because he is part of the cruelty and indignity that she wants to leave behind.[19] Arrested for trafficking again, D'Angelo shows loyalty to his family (though not directly to the Barksdale organization) by accepting a longer prison sentence for not testifying against the Barksdales.

Sexual relationships, which signified D'Angelo's breaking with the Barksdale organization, likewise signify the ways in which D'Angelo is subjugated by that institution. Avon Barksdale is convicted along with D'Angelo, leaving Stringer Bell in command of the Barksdale organization. Stringer is worried about D'Angelo's commitment during his long prison sentence, and arranges to have D'Angelo murdered in prison. But first, Stringer begins a sexual relationship with Donette. While visiting Donette in her apartment in order to convince her to visit D'Angelo in prison, a sexual relationship begins.[20] Though others (Donette, D'Angelo's family) want to give D'Angelo time to work out his own commitments, Stringer poignantly is depicted contemplating murder while D'Angelo's son sits in his lap and Donette cooks dinner in the kitchen.[21] He turns D'Angelo first into a cuckold and then a murder victim, staged—with even greater indignity—as a suicide. The organization, here led by Stringer, also destroys the loyalties and bonds of home, using sexual relationships to display the power dynamics of the Barksdale organization; in the same way that D'Angelo attempted to leave the organization, displaying this through the establishment of a sexual relationship of respect and fidelity, so Stringer reasserts the Barksdale authority as he transgresses D'Angelo's family relations.

From a theological perspective, we can see the complexity of *The Wire*'s use of sexual acts and practices as social commentary. Sexual activity and self-assertion are shaped by and sometimes shape institutional practices

---

18. "Game Day," S1/E9.

19. In "Cleaning Up," S1/E12, Shardene will play a role in D'Angelo's arrest on drug distribution charges.

20. "Hot Shots," S2/E3.

21. "Undertow," S2/E5.

and ends. The sexual struggles and hopes of D'Angelo (as well as McNulty, Greggs, Pearlman, etc.) reflect social dysfunction and aspiration for institutional reform. Sex is clearly the union of bodies, and as "embodiment," it is also a union of persons, who are inescapably bound within common life. Within the church, the simple word is marriage. The struggles and hope for faithful, steadfast, and generative sexual unions is fundamental to the practices of common life. Sexuality and sexual activity have the power to build or destroy social bonds. *The Wire* gives a new perspective to consider the Apostle Paul's claim: "Because of the temptation to immortality, each man should have his own wife and each woman her own husband" (1 Cor 7:2 RSV). This claim is not a puritanical degradation of sex; it is a clear sense that sexual practices have the power to express either God's faithfulness or the fractures within human community (as exhibited in Paul's main concerns in writing to the church in Corinth).

THE INSTITUTION AS HOMOSOCIAL SYSTEM

The twin functions of sex and sexual language (communicating both authenticity and infidelity, both friendship and belligerence) might seem to be contradictory. But, in *The Wire*, the contradictions are consistent with the tensions within male homosocial networks (i.e., within social systems that are maintained exclusively as relationships between men). In other words, so long as the systems are run by heterosexual males, sex is used in powerful and controlling ways which both bind people together as it dominates their existence.

The dominant forms of homosocial institutions are heterosexual and regulated by clear strictures against homosexuality.[22] In a violent sport like football, strict rules are established to disallow intentional brutality; to hurt another person is applauded unless harm is one's primary aim, in which case players are excluded from the game. Likewise, male homosocial institutions are regulated by the overt slandering of the homosexual male, using sex as a part of the "game," with a corresponding ban on men whose acts make homosocial relations their primary aim. As the sexual language of *The Wire* indicates, the currency of exchange is what a man does to a woman, and the means of mastery is sexual penetration. Insiders must be "heterosexualized." Outsiders, thus, are often "feminized" or constructed as passively homosexual.

Women in enclosed male-homosocial networks like Snoop Pearson (the street soldier) and Kima Greggs (the detective) often have to be men

22. Sedgwick, *Between Men*; see also Sedgwick, *Epistemology of the Closet*.

for all practical purposes. Snoop looks androgynous, but her bravado and brutality match the best of Marlo Standfield's solders. Her single gesture of femininity comes when she bravely, almost indifferently, accepts her death. At the moment that she is about to be shot by Michael Lee (her apprentice), she asks, "How's my hair look, Mike?" He tells her, "You look good, girl," and he shoots her in the head.[23] She is a girl only at the moment when she is "screwed."

Kima, in contrast, exudes femininity. In the first episode, we catch Carver admiring her buttocks. When she becomes a homicide detective, she starts to wear high heels. But like her male counter-parts, she has sex with women and is not against "objectifying" women in her manner of speaking and in her gaze. McNulty remarks that he knows one other female cop that is any good, and she is also a lesbian. "It figures," he says. Early on in the series, she is in a domestic relationship that parallels Lieutenant Daniels' marriage, with scenes of the two couples at their homes set side by side. But when Kima's partner gives birth, Kima becomes aloof and unfaithful, commenting despairingly, "I am turning into McNulty."[24] Both Snoop and Kima are male character types in female skin.

Unlike the insular institutions of the drug families and the police, the courts, city hall, and the newspaper are less cordoned off. Being more porous to outside socialization, they tend to be more heterosocial, or at least less seamlessly homosocial. Women in these institutions do not have to be men, but they must know how to operate in a man's world. This overlapping identity is the situation for attorney Rhonda Pearlman and port authority officer Beadie Russell. Both begin as outsiders and both have to deal—in very different ways—with McNulty's infidelity and his struggles with domestic life; both become part of a police team in relationship to surveillance operations and their central figure, Lester Freamon.[25]

Part of the way that Pearlman and Russell are able to negotiate these institutions is by connecting the sphere of work to the sphere of home, the alternative to the male homosocial spheres—the streets, police offices, docks, and bars. Pearlman, with Lieutenant Daniels, survives the courts in part through her relationship and home life which is kept from public

---

23. "Late Editions," S5/E9.
24. "Dead Soldiers," S3/E3.
25. Lester Freamon is a mediating figure and his tinkering with doll furniture puts him in a pliable (translatable) discursive space. With him, Prez finds a place; Shardene starts a new domestic life, and Beadie and Rhonda become part of a law enforcement team. In him, McNulty has an advocate and conspirator against the system (especially in Season 5).

view.[26] Likewise for Russell, home life is the touchstone which orients her engagements as an officer, which makes her attempts to incorporate McNulty into the home all the more problematic; as McNulty struggles to leave behind the police as his primary institution of reference toward the close of the series, it is not without significant disruptions within Russell's home life.

The school and classroom likewise constitute a heterosocial sphere. Men like Prez and "Bunny" Colvin learn to cultivate their domestic abilities within the school system, which provides an opportunity to break from the dysfunctions of the male homosocial world. In contrast to McNulty, Prez is able to sustain a home. And accordingly, Prez is overwhelmed by police work, able to negotiate police work only with the protection from a domestic relation, his father-in-law Major Valchek. Unlike McNulty, Prez cannot manage the violence of the street—blinding a boy in one eye with the butt of his pistol and killing an undercover officer. Neither is he comfortable with homosocial exchange: he is embarrassed when he goes to a strip club with Kima Greggs. (Greggs, the woman cast as a man, is not embarrassed at all.) But away from the street, Prez starts to find a place, in the office monitoring the wiretap and "following the paper trail." His flourishing continues when he teaches at a middle school and takes a parental role with his students, as he arranges to feed and do laundry for virtually homeless Dukie Weems. In sum, Prez's bi-location in both home and police station is ultimately what allows him to escape to a more humanizing institution: the school.

Prez's domestication and escape from the homosocial control of the world of the police has parallels in Dukie, who is much like Prez in being unable to negotiate the masculine streets.[27] Dukie is practically homeless, living with parents who sell his clothes for drugs, and thus immersed in the streets though constantly exhibiting an inability to negotiate the streets. When Dukie's family is evicted, for example, he says, "dag," not "fuck" or even "damn,"[28] unable to communicate in the language of the

---

26. Daniels and Pearlman have, perhaps, the most functional relationship in the series. But it must be hidden because their relationship will hurt the public image of Daniels' estranged wife, Councilwoman Marla Daniels.

27. Dukie's other friends suffer the same struggles as Dukie in not being able to negotiate the streets, becoming either subsumed by the streets or escaping them. Namond Brice, for example, is continually criticized by his mother because he lacks the toughness and street smarts to be a dealer. He is not man enough; his pony tail marks him on the street. But he finds a way out as he is adopted by Bunny Colvin. Randy Wagstaff likewise wants a home, but is mistreated and lost by the system. He ends up hardened in a group home. Michael Lee, similarly, wants to maintain a family structure, but is increasingly drawn into the conflicts of the streets as he becomes a part of Marlo Stanfield's crew to provide for his family.

28. "That's Got His Own," S4/E12.

streets. His failure to be a man on the streets and to gain respect selling drugs in Michael's crew leads to his domestication, paid to be a nanny for Michael's little brother. When Michael goes into hiding, Dukie is homeless again—with the junkman, living among the discarded things of various homes and shooting heroin.

While we would like to think that one can live between these worlds, as seen in the examples of Rhonda, Beadie, and Prez, the story of Dukie shows that there is little middle ground between the heterosocial home and the agonism of the homosocial streets. For those attempting to live within the institutions, the options are most often abandoning one sphere (Prez), living fully within another (Dukie), or precariously remaining in both at the cost of keeping one allegiance invisible (Rhonda).

MAINTAINING THE HETEROSOCIAL SYSTEM: BETWEEN THE AUTOEROTIC AND COVERTLY GAY

In providing an account of how these systems function, it is important to recognize that there is within these institutions a range of sexual identity, but only a limited range of sexual identity. In this section, I will describe this range vis-à-vis the two standard bearers of sexuality: Jay Landsman and Bill Rawls. Both men live within the institution of the police and occupy its sexual behavior, albeit in different ways; ultimately, however, both men's sexual lives are reflective of the power dynamics of the institution. First, we will consider Landsman as a discursive center, and then Rawls as the outer limit of the homosocial sphere.[29]

Sergeant Jay Landsman, supervisor of the homicide unit, maintains the equilibrium of the male world. While Jimmy McNulty's sexual exploits communicate institutional infidelity, Landsman is, in a sense, the gatekeeper of the homicide unit. He is frequently eating and looking at pornographic magazines, and takes mild but sadistic pleasure in the failures of his subordinates; yet, he usually protects his subordinates from aggression (from being "fucked") by the likes of Major Rawls. Amid homosocial tensions—as officers attempt to dominate one another—he maintains the harmony of the homosocial group by the suggestion of an autoerotic orientation, displaying his allegiance to the institution through overt self-sexualization (his use of pornography).

Landsman doesn't really fuck anyone (neither literally nor figuratively). Landsman admits to McNulty that he told Rawls that the marine

---

29. HBO's online character biography for Rawls notes that he is married and has children.

unit is the last place where McNulty would want to work.[30] Rawls assigns him to the boat patrol because of his disloyalty during the Barksdale case and his refusal to respect the chain of command. Landsman concedes that he told Rawls, but he claims that he had no hostile intentions. Most others would not only admit hostility, but also be proud of it and lord it over the victim. For example, McNulty manages to prove that fourteen deaths at the docks were not accidental but homicides. When Bunk Moreland and Lester Freamon describe the degree to which he has angered and upset Rawls, McNulty responds, "Careful, you're giving me an erection."

In this and other exchanges, Landsman diffuses tensions with McNulty, and at the same time he preserves the homosocial exchange. In Season 3, for example, Landsman is clearly angry with Bunk for failing to find a police pistol (lost when a cop is victimized on the street).[31] But he again defuses his antagonism homosocially, telling Bunk, "Rawls and [Major Raymond] Foerster have crawled up my backside and they're going to stay there until you find Dozerman's gun. Now, I would like it very much if I could unclench my ample ass cheeks, if you don't mind, and rid myself of that discomfort."

In contrast to Landsman, who uses sexual language to communicate solidarity, Rawls threatens and dominates with resolute animosity. If Landsman makes sexual language self-referential, Rawls directs it fully toward his subordinates. Similarly, to his superiors, Rawls is obedient, maintaining the coherence of the institution through the chain of command. For a time in Season 4, he plots surreptitiously against Burrell, but he soon falls back in line behind him, as Rawls (unlike McNulty) is not prone to setting policy which he doesn't answer to. McNulty is the anti-institutional type, and it is no mistake that Rawls finds McNulty to be disloyal, self-centered, and cancerous.

Rawls' institutional character is complicated, however, by a quick glimpse of him at a gay bar.[32] The effect of the scene, as I see it, is not to expose him as gay. Although he may very well be gay, he is not "outed" among his associates on the police force. The point of the scene is that he sits fully at ease in a homosexual setting—or better, in a homosocial setting without pretense—in a homosocial setting without the limit of homophobia and strictures against homosexual acts. As we glimpse him in the bar, he is not interacting with anyone, but simply sitting calm and composed in an environment where men are taking active and passive sexual roles. He is fully comfortable in an institution where men are figuratively fucked (as

30. "Ebb Tide," S2/E1.
31. "Dead Soldiers," S3/E3.
32. "Reformation," S3/E10.

he threatens McNulty and several others), and he is equally comfortable in a setting where this is literally the case (the gay bar). This comfort is what makes Rawls a threat to his subordinates and an asset to his superiors. He exemplifies the institutional mode of homosocial agonism at the limits of its intensity, embodying the homosociality of the police both in his demeanor toward his subordinates and in his own sexuality.

OUTSIDE THE LINES: OPENLY GAY, HYPERSEXUAL, AND CELIBATE

If the center and reach of homosocial systems are represented by male autoeroticism and covert homosexuality, the outside of these institutions is characterized by the overtly gay, the autoerotic lampoon, and the celibate seeking wisdom. In these three types, we find possibilities for stepping outside the institutional controls of *The Wire*. As I have indicated already, any number of characters seek to use sexuality as expressions of their distaste for institutional control (e.g., McNulty, D'Angelo). But these characters, in one way or another, find ways to exist within these institutions, for better or worse. What I will describe here are the options, as presented by *The Wire*, which attempt to move beyond institutional control in their sexual communication.

Omar Little, as openly gay, has a distinct discursive function. He dominates the drug overlords. He thrives by robbing drug dealers. Taking money and drugs by force, brutally if necessary, he shows dominance over virtually everyone on the street. It is fitting that he is finally gunned down unawares by another outsider—by a young boy, who has no authority or connections with street organizations. As gay, Omar is outside their homosocial world, and as aggressive and fearless, he is above it.

As both gay and fearless, however, Omar arouses intense enmity. As outside and above the homosocial world, he is able to display fair-mindedness and good will to potential adversaries (i.e., Brother Mouzone and the police) without needing to entertain the sexual power dynamics intrinsic to it. Take, for example, Omar's dislike of swearing. When his boyfriend, Brandon, uses "fuck" in a series of phrases, Omar chastises him, saying that he does not like to hear it.[33] As seen already, the frequent use of "fuck" and other elastic profanities fosters unimaginative and derivative habits of speech typical of those within the systems; insiders on the police force and in the drug trade operate, for the most part, with a hackneyed language of "fuck" and "bitch." Omar, as an outsider, has a wider perspective and more

---

33. "The Pager," S1/E5.

articulate, sophisticated sense of how things work. Omar has a distinctive lexicon and independent understanding of what he calls "the game," its boundaries, and his own rules of engagement, and does not transgress these rules, either in his conduct according to "the game," or in the language appropriate to his position vis-à-vis "the game." Being gay in a heterosexual/homosocial world makes him nomadic, a perpetual outsider with a flexible, always changing network of relations, and a paramount threat to others in the game, both because of his violence and his refusal to conform to the homosocial norms of other powers.

By contrast, the young stevedore and pubescent prankster Ziggy Sobotka is, strictly speaking, an insider. But his sexual expression, as hypersexualized, casts him as an erratic court jester who is unable to thrive within a world governed by particular sexual expressions. He becomes an annoyance and is pushed to the outside. Ziggy, as jester, entertains by lampooning the less noble inclinations and habits of the stevedores. Part of his play is to exaggerate and satirize homosocial relations. He often makes a show of his penis, but, as a professional fool, his performances are devoid of sexual intent and overt aggression. His play, like Landsman's, is finally autoerotic, albeit harmless. To make it in the world, he tries to convert his satirical swagger into real bravado on the street. But he turns out to be too weak and vulnerable. In frustration at his powerlessness, he murders George Glekas over the price for stolen cars. Rather than accept his fate stoically like the other dockworkers, Ziggy's reaction is to weep and confess. In prison, he is visited by his father who tries to bolster him by reminding him of his status as a union man and a stevedore: "You're a Sobotka," to which Ziggy replies, "Fucked is what I am."[34]

If Omar represents the gay outsider, and Ziggy the hypersexual insider, Reginald "Bubbles" Cousins signifies the sagacious celibate. Like Omar, he charts an alternative to homosocial membership; but whereas Omar's sexuality leads him to a nomadic flux, Bubbles' celibate existence is characterized by a kind of pilgrimage toward a new alternative, characterized by sobriety and home. As McNulty asks him, "Hey, Bubbs, how is it that you have all this wisdom and your life is so fucking hard?" Bubbles answers, "I have been wondering on that myself."[35]

Like a religious celibate, his life apart from sexual relations makes him more available and porous to persons of various walks of life. He is a friend of addicts, the police, a newspaper reporter, and guests of the Catholic Worker House dining room. As a celibate, we find Bubbles responsive to

---

34. "Bad Dreams," S2/E11.
35. "The Buys," S1/E3.

suffering and open to the world. His friendship with Johnny Weeks and his parental affection for Sherrod are based on genuine care. Bubbles is one of the few characters in *The Wire* who is without pervasively selfish motives, and more significantly, is openly repentant of his past.

His sexual abstinence also fits with his journey to be free of his addiction and the ways of the street. His one act of violence goes terribly wrong: Sherrod pilfers a poisoned dose of heroin, which was intended for an addict who repeatedly robs and beats Bubbles. Sherrod's accidental death occasions a deep sense of guilt and despair. But Bubbles finds healing in various kinds of confession: to the police, through Alcoholics Anonymous, and in telling his story to *Sun* reporter Mike Fletcher. He is on a pilgrimage from addiction and life on the street to sobriety in his sister's basement to her trust at her kitchen table.[36] He makes it home.

Bubbles' story fits with a profound sense within early Christianity that life in a community of monastic celibates and life in marriage and family are a lot alike.[37] They are alike as faithful alternatives to "the city"—to corruption and vice. In both celibacy and Christian marriage, higher and greater goods set the contours of sexual practices. Both sexual activity and abstinence from sexual activity are called to serve a life of hospitality, reconciliation, and works of mercy. For example, in John Chrysostom (c. 347–407), we find that the faithfulness and hospitality of religious communities sets the goals for marriage and family life. In *The Wire*, Bubbles offers a clear expression of sin, failure, repentance and the way of reconciliation. Theologians have a great deal to learn from *The Wire* and its realism about sexual practices and common life. The series offers the artistic alternative to *Sex and the City*, casting sex in terms which theologically resist reducing sex to a private good, and offer up sex as one of the many vehicles by which persons are turned toward grace.

IN A FEW WORDS

If this chapter could be reduced to a few quotations, they might be "Drinking. Crack Smoking. Whoring myself on the streets of Baltimore,"[38] "I am turning into McNulty,"[39] and "Larry, let's go home."[40] In terms of sexual and

---

36. "–30–," S5/E10.

37. See Chrysostom, *On Marriage and Family Life*; Augustine, *Treatises on Marriage and Other Subjects*.

38. "The Target," S1/E1.

39. "Dead Soldiers," S3/E3.

40. "–30–," S5/E10.

social dysfunction, they establish the beginning, middle, and end of *The Wire*, describing the complex relationship between a person's institutional involvement and his or her corresponding sexual dysfunction.

The first line is said by McNulty when Sergeant Landsman asks him where he has been.[41] Far from "whoring," though, this statement emphasizes McNulty's integrity, good policing, and shrewd understanding of the streets, which comes with the attendant sexual behavior. As characters repeatedly point out, the better McNulty gets at police work, the worse his sexual behavior becomes, to the point that he nearly destroys his salvific relationship with Beadie Russell over his need to do "real police work," sleeping with random strangers as his involvement in the serial killer case of Season 5 escalates.

By the end of *The Wire*, McNulty has been unfaithful to just about everyone and everything, including his own commitments to good police work. He has been, now, truly whoring, by betraying his own relationships and his own institutions in an attempt to get free of the politics of police life. In this, McNulty is the Everyman, in that there is a degree to which everyone who is part of the main institutions of *The Wire* is likewise prostituted or sells out; as Kima Greggs says, she is "turning into McNulty." We must remember, however, that stepping outside the domination of the institution can be a moment of destruction or the first step toward freedom: it can be a turn toward further destructiveness (as with McNulty) or it can be the attempt to establish something new (as with D'Angelo or with Bubbles).

Finally, on the horizon, outside the mastery of dysfunctional institutions, is the image of home, whether conceived as "domesticity" (as with Prez) or simply "stability" (as with Bubbles). Tragically, some of the characters never reach home. Dukie becomes lost to the streets; Omar is gunned down in a convenience store; Kima remains estranged from her child. Amid social dysfunctions and a desire for home, sex is symptomatic of deeper problems, and is not itself the way home. If we are to clear the thickets created by misappropriated sexual existence, we must begin with substantive social reform, which addresses the structural roots which continually create and re-create new forms of sexual violence, tragedy, and isolation.

BIBLIOGRAPHY

Augustine. *Treatises on Marriage and Other Subjects*. Translated by Roy J. Deferrari. Fathers of the Church 27. New York: Fathers of the Church, 1995.

---

41. "The Target," S1/E1.

Brasfield, Rebecca. "Sex and the City: Exposing the Hegemonic Feminist Narrative." *Journal of Popular Film and Television* 34 (2006) 130–39.

Chrysostom, John. *On Marriage and Family Life*. Translated by Catharine P. Roth and David Anderson. Crestwood, NY: St. Vladimir's Seminary Press, 1997.

Cramer, Janet M. "Discourses of Sexual Morality in 'Sex and the City' and 'Queer as Folk.'" *Journal of Popular Culture* 40 (2007) 409–32.

Rassin, Eric, and Simone Van Der Heijden. "Appearing Credible? Swearing Helps!" *Psychology, Crime and Law* 11 (2005) 177–82.

Sedgwick, Eve Kosofsky. *Between Men: English Literature and Male Homosocial Desire*. New York: Columbia University Press, 1985.

———. *Epistemology of the Closet*. Berkeley: University of California Press, 1990.

6

Realism and Utopia in *The Wire*[1]

FREDRIC JAMESON

GENERIC CLASSIFICATIONS ARE INDISPENSABLE to mass or commercial culture at the same time that their practice in postmodernity grows more and more complex or hybrid. Is *The Wire* a police procedural, for example? No doubt, but it is also a version of the organized crime story. The majority of its actors and characters are black, which nonetheless does not exactly make it a black film (a film for black audiences). There is a political drama going on here, as well, but its nature as local politics reminds us that it is also very much a local series, one framed in Baltimore and very much about Baltimore (something not always to the liking of Baltimore's elites). It is, however, also the case that most detective or crime literature today (as well as its filmic offshoots or inspirations) is local and based on the consumption of a specific landscape (whether a foreign country—Swedish detective stories, Italian ones, even Chinese detective stories—or regional—Montana, Louisiana, Los Angeles, Toronto, etc.). The broadest categories would then be that of the thriller or that of the action film (although there are few chase scenes, no cliff-hangers, few-enough mass action or carnage scenes).

Each of the five years of the TV series is a unit in terms of plot and theme; and there are at least a hundred characters deployed in each season,

---

1. Reprinted from "Realism and Utopia in *The Wire*" by Frederick Jameson in *Criticism: A Quarterly for Literature and the Arts*, Vol. 52 No 3&4. Copyright © 2010 Wayne State University Press, with the permission of Wayne State University Press.

many of whom carry their own independent plotlines. It may be argued that there is a single major protagonist, the Irish American detective Jimmy McNulty (Dominic West), even though his status fluctuates over the five years of the series and is often eclipsed by other characters. This is to say that a work of this kind challenges and problematizes the distinction between protagonists and "secondary characters" (or stars and "character actors"), in ways most often described, I guess, as "epic" (*War and Peace, Gone with the Wind*)—a characterization that does not help to underscore what may be a historical development in the evolution of this kind of plot (see Alexander Woloch on secondary characters).

The episodes in each series are not separate and freestanding as they were in *Homicide* (screenwriter/producer David Simon's previous series, also set in Baltimore and using some of the same actors); so this is a series, or serial, like those by Dickens, and an inquiry into a specifically televisual aesthetic would want to interrogate the fascination with individual actor-characters (pleasures of recognition and repetition), alongside the development of a distinct plot, where frustration and the week-by-week postponement (even the sense of deliberate retardation and the impossibility of closure)—all of this put back into question by DVD rentals—work in the direction of a difference stamped with a unique temporality, whose rhythm is, however, then reorganized into a repetition. Repetition enhances the function of the television set as consolation and security: you are not alone when it is on in the house with you, and you are not lonely or isolated when your space is peopled by so many familiar faces and characters. On the other hand, since both these features can function as neurotic denial, television carries with it a permanent possibility of boredom and sterile or neurotic repetition or paralysis. The program must then have available a secondary ideological pretext, the window dressing of a "value": art or quality would be one of those, but also "entertainment" or relaxation-distraction (after a long day at work, for example)—a pseudo-concept if there ever was one. And there is also the alibi of the political or social message, and the "cultural capital" of the cable channel (HBO in this case, which of course claims to be something more than mere television). There could also be an artistic bonus, owing to the fact that each of the episodes is written and/or directed by different people, some of them distinguished visitors (George Pelecanos, Agnieszka Holland).

But initially we approach *The Wire* as a crime story; that is, a struggle between two collectivities: the police and the crime gangs (for the most part, the crime is drug trafficking). Each of these groups has its representational history: it was not terribly long ago in popular culture that the institutional police emerged from the tradition of the private detective, while organized crime gradually became an object of representation during Prohibition (its ethnic identification with the "mafia," "cosa nostra," etc., comes later). Mass-cultural representation of this kind is a kind of recognition: it confers something like an institutional status on the group or entity in question, and such groups are accorded objective social reality (and so we understand that real-life members of the so-called mafia regularly watched *The Sopranos* (1999–2007); the incidence of police watching procedurals is unrecorded). At any rate, such recognition confirms a feeling that society is static and stable; its neighborhoods have long since been mapped out, and if there are shifts or changes in this social geography, they will have been well publicized, so everyone knows that Lexington Terrace is no longer Polish but black, etc.

But mapping is not so simple: spatial it may be, but it does not inventory objects and substances but rather flows and energies. Yet the essential raw material of any social representation is bound to be that of social types, of stereotypes as well as generic types (like the "protagonist") or as psychological ones; and *The Wire* is no exception, multiplying its recognizable entities on all these levels. To what degree it is original and innovative will depend on the revisions it is able to bring to these levels and perhaps even on the new types it is able to invent. A certain modernism was able to deal with the problem of types by dissolving them into individualities and singularities, by approaching them so microscopically that their basis in the general or the universal gradually disappears; yet even this operation must take the familiar type as its starting point and is menaced by the twin dangers of the emergence of new and more subjective types, on the one hand, and of the ironic return to the external social starting point, on the other. The word "type" is of course inescapably associated with Georg Lukács's theory of realism, but I think we do his immense culture and theoretical sophistication no service by assuming that this was a conception of pre-given social or class types rather than an attention to their historical emergence.

At any rate, *The Wire* dramatically unsettles our typological expectations and habits by at once drawing us into an epistemological exploration that greatly transcends the usual whodunit formula. To be sure, the series begins with a banal murder whose principal novelty lies in the victim's race (white) and whose solution seems obviously enough related to his forthcoming testimony in another gangland murder trial. But what we are quickly made to understand is that the police themselves are almost wholly ignorant of the structure of the gangs and the very names of the people who control them, let alone the latter's faces and localities. The uniform cops simply know the neighborhoods and the corners on which the drugs are finally sold to customers by teams of juveniles, some of them too young to be prosecuted. But this is, as it were, simply the *appearance* of the reality, the empirical or sensory form it takes in daily life; it is the most superficial approach to this reality, whose ultimate structure (source, refinement, transportation, sales network, and bulk or wholesale distribution) must remain too abstract for any single observer to experience, although it may be known and studied—and also occasionally sensed in a representational way, as later on in *The Wire* in various forms and probes. But the intermediate reality—the so-called drug lords themselves, here Avon Barksdale (Wood Harris)—are certainly knowable but not yet known by the street cops, who learn his name in an early episode and finally manage to glimpse his face and person when he organizes a basketball game with a rival gang. Is this because his rise to power is so recent or simply because the police have not concentrated on this level of the organization before? Or perhaps, since the drug trade is a business, police observers have not attributed to it the forms and structure of legal businesses before and have therefore not asked the right questions. Whatever the reason, this ignorance of their own city suddenly opens up a space for realism: for seeing things, finding out things, that have not been registered before; and for investigation, for solving problems and tracking down causes as in scientific experiment or classical detective procedures. But here it is not an individual criminal responsible for an enigmatic crime, but rather a whole society that must be opened up to representation and tracked down, identified, explored, mapped like a new dimension or a foreign culture. "Barksdale" is only one component of that whole social complex, which now demands new instruments of detection and registration (just as ever-newer realisms constantly have to be invented to trace new social dynamics).

    To what degree is this sociological mystery reducible to the standard plot forms of the detective search or the solving of a puzzle? I tend to think that the deeper motivation of such forms—or, it might be better to say, our pleasure in such forms—has something to do with Freud's primal scene (which also underpinned the scientist's passion at unveiling Nature). One would want to add that the Freudian-type satisfaction is never complete: just as no desire can ever really be satisfied, so also this one leaves a sense of disappointment. "Who cares who killed Roger Ackroyd?" famously cried Edmund Wilson in denouncing the detective story as a trivial genre;[2] and it is certain that there will also be a discrepancy between the passion of the chase and the contingency and triviality of the quarry. But this very discrepancy in the content plays into the form itself—the television serial—

---

    2. The reference is to Agatha Christie's ingenious breakthrough novel *The Murder of Roger Ackroyd*.

for its ultimate satisfactions must never be complete, and we must also be motivated to come back for more in hopes of greater ones. And perhaps the appropriation of these dissatisfactions for high culture or high literature would then consist in affirming that incompleteness: we never do catch the Greek, the ending remains unknown—save that, here, that incompleteness simply means the drug trade will rebound, start all over again, continue, no matter who is finally brought to justice. But *The Wire* inscribes this fatal recurrence in social history when it shows the passionate but superficial Barksdale eventually succeeded by the ruthless and dispassionate Marlo Stanfield (who finally, albeit awkwardly, becomes a bourgeois businessman).

There is necessarily a tension here between the mystery and the agon, since we also see things through the villains' eyes and thus know some solutions the police have not yet worked out. Still, what saves the mystery format is that the discoveries are made successively like links in a chain, knots on a cord: they lead us closer and closer, and so some of the suspense is displaced from the Who to the How along with the modalities of legal proof. And here we must remark on the other specificity of *The Wire*.

Not only is the "discovery" or solution a whole milieu, the world of a whole society or subsociety cordoned off from the peace-loving bourgeois civilian public (of whatever color), but the "detective" is also a group and a conspiratorial one at that. The police as a whole is an institution and, as such, moves in the direction of a properly political plot (networks, personal relations either of services rendered or of personal animosity, taking credit, passing the buck, ducking blame, etc.), and it is a political dimension that in the last seasons and episodes will come to the surface and be transformed into an official political campaign.

But this is that institutional police that has little capability of identifying its targets since, on the one hand, it does not even know their names and, on the other, has not yet even grasped the nature of the crimes it is investigating or their interrelationship. The lonely private detective or committed police officer offers a familiar plot that goes back to romantic heroes and rebels (beginning, I suppose, with Milton's Satan). Here, in this increasingly socialized and collective historical space, it slowly becomes clear that genuine revolt and resistance must take the form of a conspiratorial group, of a true collective (Sartre would call it the fused group forming within the serial mass society). Here Jimmy's own rebelliousness (no respect for authority, alcoholism, sexual infidelities, along with his ineradicable idealism) meets an unlikely set of comrades and fellow conspirators—a lesbian police officer, a pair of smart but undependable cops, a lieutenant with a secret in his past but with the hunch that only this unlikely venture can give him advancement, a slow-witted nepotistic appointment who turns out to have a remarkable gift for numbers, various judicial assistants, and finally a quiet and unassuming fixer.

This last—the ultimate hero of *The Wire*—leads us to say something about the title, which rarely means a wire you wear on your body, but in general wiretapping as such. The older movies, seen today, make it clear how the introduction of cell phones radically transformed the constructional problems involved in plotting a mystery or adventure film, as well as in tracing calls and wiretapping as such—complexities that are here explored in detail. But it is the genius of Lester Freamon (Clarke Peters) not only to solve these problems in ingenious ways, but also to displace some of the purely mystery and detective interest onto a fascination with construction and physical or engineering problem solving—that is to say, something much closer to handicraft than to abstract deduction. In fact, when first discovered and invited to join the special investigative unit, Freamon is a virtually unemployed officer who spends his spare time making miniature copies of antique furniture (which he sells): it is a parable of the waste of human and intelligence productivity and its displacement—fortunate in this case—onto more trivial activities that nonetheless absorb his energy and creative powers more productively than crossword puzzles, say. But Lester is also the type of the archivist-scholar capable of spending long hours on minutiae and in dusty files, which ultimately cracks open financial conspiracies all over the city; and he has deep, unostentatious, yet invaluable, roots in the community, as when he first uncovers an old photo of the youthful Barksdale in an old boxing hangout not many of his fellow officers would be likely to have any knowledge of: and to many of them he is also an inestimable mentor. This is then the sense in which *The Wire* not only offers a representation of collective dynamics (on both sides) but also one of work and productivity, of praxis. In both instances, then, there is at work a virtual Utopianism, a Utopian impulse, even though that somewhat different thing, the Utopian project or program, has yet to declare itself.

But Lester's creativity may also be said to have a counterpart on the other side. We have not yet mentioned Barksdale's sidekick, Stringer Bell (Idris Elba), who is something like his executive officer or prime minister in the classic political situation: the police themselves also have a degraded version of this dual structure, where the second in command is however by no means as disinterested or as efficient as Bell. Stringer is in fact a real intellectual, and when the police (and the viewers) finally do penetrate his private apartment, they find modernist furniture and a décor of unexpectedly enlightened artistic taste. Yet, although this figure may thereby come to seem a positive one, he gives all the most lethal killing orders without a moment of remorse. Still, the interplay with Barksdale, to whom he is absolutely devoted, but who envies his intelligence and sometimes seems to resent it, is characteristic of the extraordinarily dense and minute interpersonal situations through which *The Wire* plays out its larger plot.

Obviously enough, not only do the police not initially even know who Barksdale is, they have no inkling of Stringer's existence, save in those rare moments in which he has to visit the corners and monitor the operation on the street personally. Then one day, Jimmy takes it on himself to follow this so far unidentified figure (it will later on transpire that he is administering a whole expanding real estate investment development for Barksdale, something only gradually revealed by Lester's extraordinarily creative curiosity and know-how). At any rate, the car leads Jimmy to a university and thence to a classroom, in which, through the window, he can observe the drug kingpin and gangster taking a course in the business school and obediently answering questions and doing his homework. To be sure, the comparison of the mafia with a business enterprise is hardly metaphoric or figurative, although we sometimes omit to think historically and to identify those who actually reorganized the crime gangs in this way, along the lines of profitability (Lucky Luciano, I believe, for the mafia; but see Roberto Saviano's 2007 film *Gomorrah* for a vivid contemporary example). But here, *sur le vif*, we see something of the same well-nigh aesthetic creativity: Stringer will gradually reorganize the Barksdale mob; he uses words like product, competition, investment; he brings the gangs together to eliminate the kind of internecine warfare that is always bad for business (*la douceur du commerce*: its historic taming of feudal savagery). I have deliberately used the word *creativity* several times in this context: how can this element not be seen as somehow proto-Utopian on both sides in a bureaucratic society for the most part static and content to run in the normal time-honored way, with all the old problems and malfunctions? At this early point already, *The Wire* can be observed to be ceasing to replicate a static reality or to be "realist" in the traditional mimetic and replicative sense. Here society, on microlevels of various dimensions, is finding itself subject to deliberate processes of transformation, to human projects, to the working out of Utopian intentions that are not simply the forces of gravity of habit and tradition.

But I want first to situate this discussion of Utopianism within the context of plot construction, and to show that this is not only a purely academic matter (which it also is, of course). I want to situate both these issues within the even larger context of mass culture as a whole. Plot construction is obviously a matter of practical importance in mass culture, as witness all the books and seminars on writing a script or a scenario, but it clearly has a theoretical or philosophical dimension that is not exhausted by these technical recipes and handbooks on the matter.

The philosophical meaning of plot construction has to start from what stands in the way of constructing a plot or story; and that obviously also has its historical side. The literary past—particularly the past of theatrical spectacle but also the surviving popular literature of various bygone cultures—offers abundant examples of plots that would no longer work for us today. There is, for example, the history of feelings and their expression and evolution: Adorno remarks that the teleology of modernist literature was governed by taboo, by what you could no longer use in an artwork because it had become too sentimental and too familiar, too hackneyed and stereotypical; and that teleology no doubt also holds for the history of popular or mass culture, despite the far more central role within it of the pleasures of repetition. For where the modernist novel sought to flee repetition, or at least to translate it into something more lofty and aesthetically worthy, mass culture thrives on what used to be called the *formulaic:* you want to see over and over again the same situations, the same plots, the same kinds of characters, with enough cosmetic modifications that you can reassure yourself you are no longer seeing the same thing all over again, that interesting twists and variations have freshened your interest. Yet a time comes when the paradigm succumbs under the sheer weight of the cumulative and the fatigue of the overfamiliar.

But I want to look for another kind of explanation for such formal exhaustion—and that is to be found in its raw material. If raw material can be readily adapted to older paradigms, its absence can also modify them in striking ways. We all know the variety of historical and social situations that have provided raw material in the past: country versus city, for one thing, and the growth of the new city as a consequence; industrialism, foreign travel and immigration, imperialism, new kinds of wars, colonization, the country house and the urban slum of the "lower depths," a "picturesque peasantry" as Henry James called it. (Indeed, his little book *Hawthorne* is a founding document on what the unavailability of certain kinds of raw material does to literary and formal possibility—he is thinking of the advantages of Europe over America.)[3]

But let's turn to a less literary and more conventional mass-cultural genre or subgenre: the detective story. The absence of sleepy English towns and villages, of cloistered settings and vicarages, has obviously made the (older) practice of the English-type detective story difficult in the United States. But we must also enumerate the shrinkage of motives for that indispensable ingredient: the murder. Not only did there used to exist an interesting variety of motives, they could be investigated by an interesting variety

---

3. James, *Hawthorne*.

of private detectives, a species that seems to have become extinct. Social respectability—that is, the possibility of scandal and its damages; family structure and dynastic or clan systems; passions and obsessions of all kinds, from hatred and revenge to other complex psychic mechanisms—these are only some of the interesting sources for motivation that have become increasingly irrelevant in the permissiveness of contemporary society, its rootless and restless movement and post-regionalism, its loss of individualism and of bizarre eccentrics and obsessives—in short, its increasing one-dimensionality. Thus today, paradoxically, the multiplication of consumer niches and the differentiation of "lifestyles" go hand in hand with the reduction of everything to the price tag and the flattening out of motivations to the sheerly financial: money, which used to be interesting in the variety of its pursuits, now becoming supremely boring as the universal source of action. The omnipresence of the word *greed* in all national political vocabularies recently disguises the flatness of this motivation, which has none of the passionate or obsessive quality of older social drives and the older literature that drew on them as its source. Meanwhile, the psychic realm has also been drastically reduced, perhaps in part as a result of the omnipresence of money as an all-purpose motivation, perhaps also as a result of the familiarities of universal information and communication and the flattening of the individualisms. I have observed elsewhere that that universal communicational equality that Jürgen Habermas associates with the spread of a new kind of reason also makes for a widening of the acts we can now understand;[4] what used to be thought of as pathology, as rarer mental states and acts beyond the pale—all these are now human, all too human, in such a way that the very category of evil or absolute otherness has drastically been reduced, as well. That the organizers of the Holocaust were mere bureaucrats certainly diminishes their chances of representing absolute evil; that most pathologies are pathetic and provincial rather than frightening is a triumph of reason and liberal tolerance but also a loss for those still clinging to some outmoded ethical binary of good and evil. I have elsewhere argued against this binary system: Nietzsche was perhaps only the most dramatic prophet to have demonstrated that it is little more than an afterimage of that otherness it also seeks to produce—the good is ourselves and the people like us, the evil is other people in their radical difference from us (of whatever type). But society today is one from which, for all kinds of reasons (and probably good ones), difference is vanishing and, along with it, evil itself.

This means that the melodramatic plot, the staple of mass culture (along with romance), becomes increasingly unsustainable. If there is no

---

4. Habermas, *Theory of Communicative Action*.

evil any longer, then villains become impossible too; and for money to be interesting, it has to happen on some immense scale of robber barons or oligarchs, for whom, to be sure, there are fewer and fewer dramatic possibilities today, and whose presence in any case recasts traditional plots in political terms, where they are less suitable for a mass culture that seeks to ignore politics. (Or when it turns to politics, then we may begin to wonder whether something has not also happened to politics itself: the reign of Cynical Reason is also the omnipresence of the disabused conviction about the corruption of the political generally, and its complicity with the financial system and its corruptions—so virtually by definition this universal cynical knowledge does not seem to project any political consequences any longer.)

We therefore have here two converging problems: on the one hand, the repetition of the older melodramatic plot form becomes more and more tiresome, and more difficult to sustain. On the other, the raw material or content for such a practice of form is becoming uni-dimensionalized: evil is vanishing socially, villains are few and far between, everybody is alike. The Utopian writers already had a problem with the possibility of literature in their perfect world; now we have a problem with it in our imperfect one.

This explains why villainy in mass culture has been reduced to two lone survivors of the category of evil: these two representations of the truly antisocial are, on the one hand, serial killers and, on the other, terrorists (mostly of the religious persuasion, as ethnicity has become identified with religion, and secular political protagonists like the communists and the anarchists no longer seem to be available). Everything else in sexuality or so-called passional motivation has long since been domesticated: we understand it all, from sadomasochists to homosexuals—pedophilia being a minor exception here, to be classed as a kind of subgroup or sub-possibility within the larger category of serial killers (who are generally, but not always, understood as sexually motivated). It is true that with mass murderers of the Columbine type we begin to shade over towards the political and here terrorism reappears, but the latter organized in terms of the radical otherness of belief and religious fanaticism, since little else remains. If we really grasped terrorism as a purely political strategy, then somehow its frisson also evaporates, and we can consign it to debates on Machiavelli, on political strategy and tactics, or on history.

I need not add that these two staples—terrorists and serial killers—have become as boring as the villains driven by "greed." Alas, as with the disappearance of the spy novel after the end of the Cold War, that boredom would seem to betoken an end of melodrama, which threatens to become the end of mass culture itself.

It is in the context of these dilemmas of plot construction that we now turn to Season 2 and the first non-virtual appearance of a certain Utopianism in *The Wire*. This season deals with the port of Baltimore, with labor unions and corruption, and with a whole outside network of drug suppliers (the Greek!). The magnificent landscape of the increasingly obsolescent port and its container technology perhaps requires a detour through the whole question of place and scene (in Kenneth Burke's sense) in *The Wire*. The place is, to be sure, Baltimore; and anyone's first and quite understandable impulse would be to classify this series as part of the "postmodern" return to regionalism, and not only in "high literature" (Raymond Carver, etc.). I've already mentioned the now constitutive relationship of detective stories and procedurals all over the world to local or regional commitments; meanwhile, "world cinema" makes those commitments virtually by definition, however its works might strike local audiences, since globalized film festival culture is organized by national production.

But, in *The Wire*, there are some interesting distinctions to be made. For one thing, the regional is always implicitly comparative: not the corrupt old eastern big cities, but Montana or the South, where we live differently, and so forth, with an emphasis on the small town, or the desert landscape, or even the suburb. Here in *The Wire* nobody knows that other landscapes, other cities, exist: Baltimore is a complete world in itself; it is not a closed world but merely conveys the conviction that nothing exists outside it. (It is not provincial, no one feels isolated or far from this or that center where things are supposed to be really happening.) To be sure, Annapolis (the state capital) is a reference, since it is where budgetary decisions are made (especially for the police force); Philadelphia is a distant reference, since occasionally gang members have to make a drop-off there; New York City is the place you have to hire killers from, in very special instances where you need someone unfamiliar from the outside. Where the Greek gets his drugs is absolutely not a matter of conjecture (or of subjective mapping). Even nature (and the shoreline) does not exist, as witness the bewilderment of the one unhappy youngster (Wallace, played by Michael B. Jordan) shipped off to hide out with his grandmother for a while before going back to Baltimore to be killed. Baltimore is the corners—it is the police headquarters, occasionally the courts and city hall— and this is why the very name of Baltimore is irrelevant (except for local patriotism and the TV viewers) and also why the docks and the port come as a real spatial opening, even though they are fully integrated into the web of interest and corruption as anything else, and even though the distant ports of call or whatever vessels still put in here are also absolutely unrecorded, unimagined, and so irrelevant as to be virtually nonexistent.

The labor leader is a Pole, and this is then also the moment to evoke the ethnic in *The Wire*. "Baltimore" is a nonexistent concept, but the ethnic still very much exists here, particularly if you include the police as an ethnic category, both in some figurative or moral sense, and also on account of the Irish tradition still very much in evidence among them. But are black people "ethnic" in any of these senses? We have already seen that the drug scene, run by Barksdale, is not only black, but exists like a foreign city within the official one: it is a whole other world, into which you do not go unless you have business there ("you" here standing for the officially dominant white culture). So here, in absolute geographical propinquity, two whole cultures exist without contact and without interaction, even without any knowledge of each other: like Harlem and the rest of Manhattan, like the West Bank and the Israeli cities that, once part of it, are now still a few miles away; even like East and West Berlin today, where older East Berliners are still reluctant to travel to the former West, with its opulent shops they have no tradition of, and with a whole capitalist culture alien to them for most of their lives.

Still, this might be considered essentially a black series—the bulk of its cast is black, drawing on scores not only of underemployed black actors but also local nonprofessionals—just as Baltimore itself is a predominantly black city. But as has been observed of its predecessor series, *Homicide: Life on the Street* (1993–99), this very preponderance means that you see so many different types of black people (social, professional, even physical) as to utterly dissolve the category. Here there is no longer any such thing as "black" people, and by the same token no such thing as black political or social solidarity. These former "black people" are now in the police; they can be criminals or prison inmates, educators, mayors, and politicians; *The Wire* is in that sense what is now called *postracial* (something that might be sure to have its political effect on the U.S. viewing public at large, just as the presence of TV or so many black entertainment celebrities has had its own impact on racial stereotypes and on the unfamiliarity essential to racisms).

But the Poles are still an ethnic group, as witness the ferocious vendetta waged against the labor leader Frank Sobotka by a Polish police major, which is one of the causes of Frank's eventual downfall. His ethnicity is at some distance, however slight, from his role as labor leader; and it is around this last that a certain Utopianism begins to gather. For the demise of the port of Baltimore has to do with the postmodern technology of containerization[5] and its impact on the labor movement (many fewer workers needed, leading to the fall of once immensely powerful unions like the longshoremen's), as well as on cities (the post-container development of the port

---

5. See Levinson, *Box*.

of Newark, New Jersey, having suddenly rendered a host of other competing East Coast ports obsolete, very much including Baltimore), the old port now seemingly reserved for police boats, such as the one to which Jimmy has been demoted. This is then an interesting case where the destructive force of globalization has been, as it were, interiorized along with a more general deindustrialization: it is not only the movement of work to other, cheaper countries that has ruined Baltimore, but rather our own technology (which of course amplifies the impact of globalization generally, as containerization develops foreign ports and modifies industrial production and what can be shipped, as well). But this historical story is part of the background of *The Wire*, and not its primary lesson or message.

The message is in part elsewhere, and it lies in the recontextualization of Frank Sobotka's alleged corruption (stereotypically associated with labor unions today, at least since Jimmy Hoffa); and it is certain that Frank is deeply implicated in the drug trade and lets the Greek use his container traffic. But Frank is not interested in money (and I suppose you could argue that Stringer Bell is not interested in money either and, maybe beyond that, that the excitement of finance capital itself is not really about money, in its older sense of riches and wealth). Frank uses the money to build up his own contacts, in view of a supreme project, which is the rebuilding and revitalization of the port of Baltimore. He understands history and knows that the labor movement and the whole society organized around it cannot continue to exist unless the port comes back. This is then his Utopian project, Utopian even in the stereotypical sense in which it is impractical and improbable—history never moving backwards in this way—and in fact an idle dream that will eventually destroy him and his family.

But I mean something more than that, and this enlarged conception of Utopianism has to do with plot construction. Realism was always somehow a matter of necessity: why it had to happen like that and why reality itself is both the irresistible force and the unmovable obstacle. To include Frank's pipe dream in a purely realistic work, we would have to see it (as Balzac so often did) as a mania, a psychological obsession, a purely subjective drive and character peculiarity. But this dream is not like that; it is not only objective; it draws all of objectivity within itself such that, if the plot of *The Wire* were to show its success, the representation would imply the Utopian (or revolutionary) transformation and reconstruction of all of society itself. Nor is it political pleading, a political program cooked up by *The Wire*'s writers and producers and endorsed by the public as a desirable political and social improvement. It cannot be all that—no viewer will understand this episode in that practical light, because it involves not an individual reform but rather a collective and historical reversal—but it introduces a slight crack or rift into the seamless necessity of *The Wire* and its realism or reality. This episode then adds something to *The Wire* that cannot be found in most other mass-cultural narratives: a plot in which Utopian elements are introduced, without fantasy or wish fulfillment, into the construction of the fictive, yet utterly realistic, events.

Yet Sobotka's Utopianism would remain a mere fluke or idiosyncrasy if it did not have its equivalents in later seasons of *The Wire*. (We could write it off, for example, by observing that the creators of the show, in their local patriotism, had taken this occasion to add in some more purely local statement.) But in fact it does, and at this point I can only enumerate the later incidence of a Utopian dimension in succeeding seasons. In Season 3, Utopianism is certainly present in Major Colvin's "legalization" of drugs; that is, his creation of an enclave of drug use closed to police intervention. In Season 4, on education, it is to be found in Pryzbylewski's classroom experiments with computers and his repudiation of the exam evaluation system imposed by state and federal political entities. Finally, in Season 5, the most problematical, it is to be located in Jimmy's invention of a secret source for funding real and serious police operations outside the bureaucracy and its budget—and this, despite the artificial crime panic he deliberately fosters, and also somewhat on the margins of what was to have been a series dominated by the newspaper and the media (for each season of *The Wire*, like Zola's great series, or like Sara Paretsky's Chicago crime novels, is also organized around a specific industry).

The future and future history have broken open both high- and mass-cultural narratives in the form of dystopian science fiction and future catastrophe narratives. But in *The Wire*, exceptionally, it is the Utopian future that here and there breaks through, before reality and the present again close it down.

BIBLIOGRAPHY

Christie, Agatha. *The Murder of Roger Ackroyd*. London: William Collins, 1926.
Habermas, Jürgen. *The Theory of Communicative Action*. 2 vols. Translated by Thomas McCarthy. Boston: Beacon, 1984.
James, Henry. *Hawthorne*. London: Macmillan, 1879.
Levinson, Marc. *The Box: How the Shipping Container Made the World Smaller and the World Economy Bigger*. Princeton: Princeton University Press, 2006.

7

"This Is Me"
Roland Pryzbylewski, Mis-Performance, and Transformation in *The Wire*

BRIAN BANTUM

INTRODUCTION

CREATOR AND PRODUCER DAVID Simon's groundbreaking series, *The Wire*, draws the viewer into the difficult and daunting realities of the modern American city. Through multiple and interconnecting urban narratives police, street life, political institutions, public schools, and journalism, producer David Simon asks us, "What does it mean to live together?" Even more, Simon asks this question in the dimming light of hope and possibility that marks so many postindustrial cities. Simon's brilliant exploration of this question highlights how particularities of race, ethnicity, class, and gender do not singularly mark any character or person in the city. These particularities constitute a complex constellation of commitments that are navigated each day in response to a rapidly changing city and the enduring challenges that press themselves upon the citizens of Baltimore.

The Wire adeptly displays the challenges facing the city through the concentric themes of belonging and power. Throughout the course of the series, *The Wire*'s characters navigate this world with cunning or skill, often with glaring miscues, but nonetheless speaking the "language" of the city. In doing so, notions of power and belonging are never static realities. Instead, the inhabitants of this city are on a journey; they move, adapt, and grow through the course of the series. But where are they going? While *The Wire* highlights the indelible power and presence of institutions within the city, it also displays how citizens negotiate these realities, oftentimes succumbing to a tragic nihilism or driven by what political theorist Frederic Jameson has called a "Utopianism," an ideal which animates a character's actions and realities. Through questions of belonging and power *The Wire* does more than examine the city. *The Wire* draws the viewer into the wake of our modern world.[1]

The citizens who negotiate the city's reality highlight a need to "speak the language of the city." Whether displaying tragic nihilism or a distorted Utopianism,[2] most characters understand how to play "the game," using various physical, linguistic, or intellectual tools to work their way towards particular goals or resist being used by others. In the midst of the myriad performances the figure of Roland Pryzbylewski or "Prez" is distinguished by a lack of belonging, a strangeness to the culture of power and self-protection that pervades the city. Prez's discomfited presence both highlights his own inarticulateness with the language *and* lays bare the folly of power and belonging exercised within the city. To make sense of these conflicting notions of the city that *The Wire* displays we must read these portrayals of power not only through the lenses of social science and cultural theory, but theologically in order to discern how belonging and power are articulated in an urban space that is represented as seemingly without God.

Theologically speaking, to associate the city of *The Wire* with the fall or the earthly city as Augustine describes in the *City of God* is by no means a stretch. The city of *The Wire* is a city where desire, power, and domination materialize in promotions (vocational signs of power) and corners (geographical signals of power.) Augustine, describing the folly of Rome, suggests that the Romans depend upon gods ill prepared to protect them; promotions, corners, offices, no matter appearances, do not protect, but only

---

1. While *The Wire* focuses upon the postindustrial city, Simon's question about life together is fundamentally a question for all contemporary society. For this reason I will begin to use language of the city to refer to an urban social space, as well as in a theological sense to refer to humanity's attempts to create lives and meaning in light of God's work and reality.

2. For a now classic account of nihilism in the city see West, *Race Matters*, 19–20. Political theorist Frederic Jameson points to the show's underlying utopianism in Jameson, "Realism and Utopia," 359–72. Jameson's essay is reprinted in this volume, 95–108.

raise greater peril. The city of *The Wire* is undoubtedly a fractured, fallen city tied to a fallen fractured world. Within this fallen space Roland "Prez" Pryzbylewski is an incongruous and therefore revelatory figure, unveiling the shape and practices of citizenship implicit to life in the modern city.

This chapter explores the question of living within the fracture through the lens of Prez as one who highlights the absurdity of power in the city (surviving through force and/or manipulation) with tools he does not much understand much less possess and whose displacement allows him, and the viewer through him, to imagine a different enactment of power within the same city. After briefly examining the city Prez journeys within, this chapter examines Prez's development of belonging as police in the first three seasons of *The Wire* and his transformation into a teacher in the fourth season.

THE WIRE, THE CITY, AND THEOLOGY

Prez's life in the police force displays an utter mis-performance of what it means to be a citizen of the city, inept with the languages of power that circulate throughout the city's many institutions. But what is this city? One of the show's regular characters refers to Baltimore as "this dark corner of the American experiment,"[3] a notion that exemplifies Cornel West's account of nihilism as "a profound sense of psychological depression, personal worthlessness, and social despair."[4] What makes *The Wire*'s strain of depression and despair remarkable is its ability to energize a city where power and a new kind of certainty thrive. New and novel identities (Omar, McNulty, Bubbles, Marlo Stanfield, Landsman, Michael, and so on and so forth) prove irrepressible, generating and regenerating constantly and rapidly, albeit tragically. The city exists, much like the Barksdale criminal organization itself, fluctuating between the loci of the strip club and the morgue, between consumption and death where men (and I do mean men) count money behind walls and plan for a new day. In this "city of man" the attempts to secure one's life and possibilities are drawn into a perpetual contestation over and against others—recall what Augustine called the "*libido dominandi*"—outside and within its institutions. In *The Wire*, the city exists as dark shadow bound by the occasional reference to "the county," a distant land where peace resides as boredom. And yet the nihilism of the city is not

---

3. This was Landsman's description of Baltimore in his eulogy of a fellow detective in "Dead Soldiers," S3/E3.

4. West, *Race Matters*, 13.

without gestures of hope as it grasps toward an undefined "Utopianism,"[5] albeit one remaining in a tragic key.

The city is a decaying and developing dream tied to the local, the suburban, the national, and the global. The city in this way is an icon of the modern predicament where "progress" has its priests and its sacrifices. The local attempts to navigate these varying realities while the global arrives in "packages" and containers whose contents (everything from illegal narcotics to digital cameras) become the currency of power and possibility of institutions and individuals alike. The containers represent a differing vision of the world and the forces that press themselves into people's lives. The narratives that are so often given regarding the modern predicament move between abstracted notions such as "modernity," where certain forces or ideas (truth, God, citizenship) are overbearing certainties, or "postmodernity," where notions of truth, God, or nation can no longer organize the world. Instead the world is seen as a radical multiplicity. But these abstract ideas of certainty or multiplicity are distilled and reconfigured with one another in the city of *The Wire* as its citizens struggle to discern and resist powers that seem to pervade everything.[6] The realities of the modern and the postmodern are material realities that organize urban space even as these realities seem to evade coherent meaning for the city's inhabitants.

In these ways David Simon's realism (or cynicism) is instructive. The city is not a place of progress, but a "dark corner of the American experiment" where what did not succeed is left to fend for itself. Baltimore lies in the wake, the refuse of progress and globalization. *The Wire* presses a complicated question: "How does one live in this wake?" or "How are realities of abstracted institutional power negotiated?" The city of *The Wire* displays practices of power that animate institutions, drawing its adherents into logics and practices of domination, and yet these practices are rarely seen as power, but as simply "rules of the game." Simon dramatizes Michel Foucault's crucial observation regarding institutions, societies, and power:

---

5. See Jameson, "Realism and Utopia," 364.

6. *The Wire* provides insightful observations reflecting urban sociological analysis and political theory. But at the same time, some have suggested that the city observed in *The Wire* has been stripped of black spirituality and effectively marginalized the Black Church (and all religion) as little more than a political constituency to be appeased while the Polish Catholic Church is the toy fought over between Valchek and Sobotka. While black spirituality is notably absent, Simon's representation of the church could be interpreted not as the marginalization of spirituality but its relocation to the institutions of the city. While some may attend church or other religious ceremony, most of *The Wire*'s characters bend themselves into the expectations, rigors, and practices of their various institutions hoping, settling for a certainty only those institutions can offer, but also being exposed to a grim truth—these institutions are false gods.

> Rules are empty in themselves, violent and unfinalized; they are impersonal and can be bent to any purpose. The successes of history belong to those who are capable of seizing these rules, to replace those who had used them, to disguise themselves so as to pervert them, invert their meaning, and redirect them against those who had initially imposed them; controlling this complex mechanism, they make it function so as to overcome the rulers through their own rules.[7]

Simon adroitly displays how police, drug dealers, and politicians perpetually seek to bend spoken and unspoken rules to their favor, establishing and maintaining themselves within these Foucauldian semblances of power. As if following Foucault, Simon casts his vision of the city so that it is not reduced to an abstract power or institution. The reality of these powers and rules (and the fractures they create) reside concretely in the lives of its citizens and inhabitants.

The characters of *The Wire* indicate various but interconnected answers to the question of living in the reality of the city. Through the arc of its five seasons each character wrestles with the realities of a fractured city. The city and its characters change and adapt while remaining tragically mired in the same problems of violence and control.

The Wire's depiction of the city does not leave us far from theological interpretations of the city that often associated the city with Cain, as a place of self-preservation, self-establishment, and pride. Through the lives of Deputy Commissioner William Rawls, Colonel Cedric Daniels, Avon Barksdale, Stringer Bell, and Omar Little, we see a city replete with figures conversant in languages of power. In *The Wire* the grammar of power can be seen articulated in several ways: a power of force, of information, and of bodies. Powers of force might include the use of physical violence to intimidate or coerce towards particular ends. Powers of information include the capacity to use information to manipulate others (and thus institutions) in order to avoid negative consequences or achieve positions or benefits. Powers of bodies entail the capacity to utilize and manipulate human needs (for drugs or sex specifically) by utilizing power of physical force or information to manipulate bodies to consume or be consumed.[8]

Each of these powers contains within it practices (and with these practices an implicit grammar of power) that are mastered to varying degrees by the characters of *The Wire*. The characters of *The Wire* aim to ascend within

---

7. Foucault, "Nietzsche, Genealogy, History," 141.

8 These categories are not intended to be seen as a strict classification, *per se*, but simply illustrate the various ways power is inflected and enacted within the city of *The Wire*.

the various institutions of the city, to attain a level of peace (which often means self-determination) that only these institutions can seemingly provide: rank, pension, a corner, a name. *The Wire* depicts a city where people work not only to preserve themselves but also thrive within the city. But in the confines of this urban space, thriving necessitates a certain control over another to draw the city, money, the towers into submission. Thriving is a self-preservation that feeds upon others. To return to Foucault's description of power and rules, these practices of power have been incorporated into a widely shared grammar of living with one another in the city.

But in the midst of these overt exercises of power we also see people seeking to protect themselves, to gather some semblance of meaning and hope in a world marked by perpetual violence and uncertainty. They do not seek to dominate, they simply do not want to die. In these cases *The Wire* offers glimpses of people who are merely trying to negotiate the realities of power they find around them and grasp at any tools available to preserve their lives.

The Wire slowly uncovers how the various institutions of the city press in on its citizens while failing to provide the basic protections and certainties they are meant to offer. This disclosure of the city's institutions and its citizens can be understood as the drama's center as each season is punctuated by progressions of unknowing to knowing, the discovery of facts, the garnering of skill to translate these "truths" into commodities to sell, convict, or parlay into promotions, elections, or corners.

This depiction characterizes a persistent theological theme regarding cities in particular and life apart from God generally. The association of cities with humanity's fallenness has been a dominant theme of theological reflection. Such a view is summarized well by French theologian Jacques Ellul, who points to the folly of the first city, Enoch, founded by Cain: "The city for Cain is first of all the place where he can be himself—his homeland, the one settled spot in his wandering. Secondly, it is a material sign of his security. He is responsible for himself and for his life. He is far from the Lord's face, and so he will shift for himself. Cain sought security not so much from God, whom he was trying to escape, as from the world, hostile since Abel's murder."[9] Ellul points to the allure of the city as a space of belonging, where one no longer has to wander and be uncertain of what one's day-to-day existence will be. But this desire for belonging also necessitates self-protection, maintaining belonging over against those who would seemingly deprive one of certainty within these spaces of belonging.

---

9. Ellul, *Meaning of the City*, 5.

Augustine's *City of God* widens this indictment not only to the urban, but also to human society itself, which globalization now projects widely as we see Augustine's critique materializing in the "urbanization" of the world. That is, as the world becomes more connected, its various spaces become, for good and ill, bound to one another, much like the various institutions of Baltimore. In this way, *The Wire* is a microcosm of a globalized urban.[10] For Augustine the problem is not so much the city of urbanization, but a humanity who "love[s] this present life, while they ought to hold it cheap."[11]

The Wire offers a depiction not only of the postindustrial city, but also, more profoundly, of what life in the world, the reality of power, so often requires of us as we journey through its streets and how the costs of certainty in some spaces create corners of nihilism and perpetual estrangement in others. While *The Wire* offers a realistic depiction of the city's institutions, it also highlights the paradox of life in the city and so much of the modern world. The more power one accumulates and the more adept at negotiating (or manipulating) people one becomes, the more vulnerable one becomes. In this way, *The Wire* demonstrates the reality of city life and the difficulty its citizens have in perceiving the city and its institutions for what they are, failing to truly see one another.

This paradox of belonging and perception is displayed in *The Wire* not through expertise, but through incompetence and here we return to the main topic of this inquiry. In the narrative arc of Roland "Prez" Pryzbylewski, *The Wire* displays the grammar of power and belonging that animates the city by imaging the exercise of power *ad absurdum* in Prez. The show highlights the fundamental limits and distortions of human life that have become engrained in life together in the urban world. In Prez, Simon displays how the nihilism depicted in *The Wire* extends beyond a loss of hope among black Americans toward a more complicated question about what happens when hope as something beyond oneself (in a nation, an industry, in one another) is seemingly lost in vast swaths of citizens, and the inflection of power becomes oriented toward what is left as an atomized and self-generated hope in one's own possibilities.

---

10. Of course it should be noted here that to understand the city as a fundamental mark of the fall would be shortsighted. For instance, James Donald describes the city as a place of imaginative possibility where "the city becomes the symbolic space in which we act out our more or less imaginative answers to the question which defines our *ethos*: 'how to be "at home" in a world where our identity is not given, our being together in question, our destiny contingent or uncertain: the world of violence of our own self-constitution.'" Donald, *Imagining the Modern City*, 145. Donald here quotes John Rajchman; see Rajchman, *Truth and Eros*, 144.

11. Augustine, *City of God*, 14.

THE REVELATORY STRANGER: PREZ AS POLICE

The nihilism that pervades the city of *The Wire*, for Simon, is a mark of a tragic reciprocity that runs between individuals and the institutions governing them. In the city violence is not merely the act of a gun, but practices of intimidation that are systematized as rules, as part of the given order. Foucault describes this relationship between violence and rules in this way: "Humanity does not gradually progress from combat to combat until it arrives at universal reciprocity, where the rule of law finally replaces warfare; humanity installs each of its violences in a system of rules and thus proceeds from domination to domination."[12] It is in the midst of this dynamic of power and belonging in the city that Prez's presence as well as his various enactments of power for the sake of belonging leave one bewildered and confused. Does this man even belong here?

The character of Prez enters the show in Season 1 as an unwanted presence. Introduced by words *about* him, Prez is a chip bartered between two veteran colonels. By what others say about him, we find out that Prez is in the Baltimore City Police Department only because of the nepotism of his father-in-law, Deputy Commissioner Stanislaus Valchek. From the outset, Prez's presentation to the viewer, his place within the department, is under question. When Prez shows up in Daniel's special detail his presence is equally ill-fitted. Prez's clothes are too neat (no one else in the Baltimore PD presses his pants), his eyes too nervous and language too clean. These fine though noticeable gaps in Prez's presence contrasts with the standard operating procedure of life in the police department and the realities of urban life in general. As Prez ventures out with his new partners he immerses himself into the city's circuits of power.

Prez's ineptitude at playing "police" occurs in concert with Sergeant Ellis Carver and Officer Thomas "Herc" Hauk, real police characteristically dissatisfied with their assignments, viewing their work as petty and insignificant. Allegedly looking for evidence that can break a case, Carver and Herc take Prez on an ill-advised late-night raid of the towers. In actuality, they venture to the towers to raise their profile within the detail. But in the midst of this "routine" exercise of police force, Prez hits a teenager with the butt of his gun, blinding him in one eye and sparking a minor riot in the plaza of the towers. Prez's career as street police ends as absurdly as it begins.

Herc and Carver's charge into the towers displays important elements of the police force's grammar of power. The authority of the badge derives from the power the police have to arrest or forcefully harass seemingly

---

12. Foucault, "Nietzsche, Genealogy, History," 151.

without probable cause and with impunity. Their power extends through a continual threat of greater police presence and surveillance, with further arrests and more violence. While Herc and Carver's calculating attempts end in laughable and deplorable police behavior, Prez proves unable to achieve even that.

Prez's sad attempt at being police is instructive in two ways. Prez's actions highlight his lack of understanding regarding the exercise of force and the delicate balance required to maintain control. A similar balance is mirrored within the drug organizations where enough force must be exerted in order to maintain territory, but without "bodies" and the police attention such force inevitably draws. Prez does not understand how to exercise the power he possesses as a member of the police department and so estranges himself from all sides of the police/criminal social order.

While Daniels censures Herc and Carver for their clumsy "police work," Prez's actions are highlighted as particularly egregious and disciplined immediately. Only because Daniels instructs him on the language necessary to avoid punishment for his excessive use of force is Prez allowed to remain on the force, albeit as a desk cop stripped of his gun, no longer real police, making official what was already the case. Power comes by adhering to the rules respective of each position. Prez's failure in the tower courtyard was a failure to manage properly the power (its uses and limits) available to him by virtue of his position. This incapacity leads to a double delimitation, being confined to the office and stripped of his weapon.

The arc of Season 1 articulates in various ways this grammar of belonging and power for both the police department and drug organization. In so doing, *The Wire* demonstrates how the grammars of power remain universal within the city. Both the police and the drug organization exert control over or manipulate others in attempts to maintain or establish standing. For example, while police establish themselves by harassing the people of the towers, the drug dealers establish their own brand of power by exploiting drug addicts, "fiends" too ignorant and weak to master the rules of the game.

D'Angelo Barksdale's Season 1 explanation of chess is instructive in describing the rules in the city.[13] Persons are like chess pieces, respectively inhabiting various positions with their proper powers and possibilities. Both Wallace and Preston "Bodie" Broadhus understand the danger of being pawns, those whose available moves are limited, those perpetually subject to the power of the other pieces on the board. Properly disposed police officers and drug dealers come to understand the game; others resist

---

13. See Anderson, "The Game Is the Game."

inculcation and pay the consequences (e.g., drug underling Wallace's reaction to Brandon's death mirrors Prez's misuse of power; both are exiled, Wallace to the "country" and Prez to the office).

Desire drives the various exercises of power—consumption, control, manipulation, and so on. Fiends do not recognize how their broken desires empower others; police and drug dealers deride addicts because they fail to recognize this, even as their own power profits off these failures. Desire sits at the heart of every enactment of power: the fiend's need for a fix, police harassment of innocent citizens, warring over corners. Theologian Graham Ward describes this dynamic in terms of late capitalism: "Desire in a postmodern culture can never come to an end or the market would cease. Desire here operates because we always sense, or are made to sense privation, and we always are attempting to fill that lack or find compensations for unfulfillment."[14]

The context of a postindustrial urban landscape pushes Ward's observation regarding the consumptive nature of the earthly city, broadly speaking, further still. *The Wire* highlights how institutional realities create and sustain its citizens, shaping them into pawns for the game. Put differently, *The Wire* asks, "Who isn't a fiend?" The people of the towers inhabit an ambivalent personhood in the eyes of the police and the Barksdale organization. In institutions of "law" and "crime," the desire that drives practices of control or certainty—resisting vulnerability—mimic one another as hope, now confused and obfuscated, surrenders to immediate material realities.

For the Barksdales, the inhabitants of the towers are cheap labor, or "fiends." For the police, they are bodies that exist to be thrown around to buttress an image of being "in control." The inhabitants, charged with ordering the desires of the city and fulfilling its interests, shuttle between these competing claims. Belonging within these spaces requires fealty to "the game," which entails using weaker pieces and dodging more powerful ones. At Orlando's Strip Club, the headquarters of the Barksdale organization, Avon and Stringer count money, respond to threats, and plan their organization's expansion behind sealed doors, while women's bodies are paraded and consumed. This depersonalizing of women's bodies mirrors the police department's, which is evident in Landsman's constant and casual pornographic magazines and in the ubiquitous sexual banter between officers. Within the city, power embodies the desire which circumscribes individuals within promises of fulfillment. Prez's strangeness is again demonstrated when he ventures into Orlando's with Kima Greggs. His discomfort, an inability to look at the strippers, is physically tangible.

---

14. Ward, *Cities of God*, 76.

None of this is to suggest that belonging goes without conflict. When their authority is challenged, the Barksdale organization utters, "Do they know what I'm about?" and when an officer is shot, the police commissioner declares, "We will show them what we are about." Belonging means ensconcing oneself amidst practices that pronounce one's bare allegiance in a totalizing system of real consequence. By failing to gawk at a stripper or balance intimidation and restraint, Prez transgresses the allowances of belonging and what it means to be a citizen of the city.

D'Angelo proves his belonging when he refuses to testify against the organization even when faced with a long prison sentence. This leads to his final break with the organization and he is left to languish unprotected (eventually murdered) in prison. Prez, on the other hand, discovers a new mode (beyond intimidation and restraint) of being police. When Daniels' detail turns to electronic surveillance work (one of the reasons for the show's title), Prez finds he is quite expert in deciphering, translating, and discovering patterns. He likes to "figure shit out." Even though he never learns to deploy these skills for political advancement in "the game," Prez comes to be a crucial part of Daniels' detail, his analysis contributing to the defeat of the Barksdale organization.

While Prez demonstrates the capacity to contribute and belong, Season 2 displays the limited nature of his understanding; after manipulating his connections to do "real police work," he ultimately punches his father-in-law and is once again stripped of his gun and exiled to an office. Prez's absurd use of force again displays a profound misconception of the tools necessary to thrive and belong as police. However, Prez's use of force cannot be understood as an anomaly but as a magnification of the grammars of power he sees exercised around him each day. As a tragic/comical mis-performance of power, Prez's punch is a prefiguration of the various exaggerations such power must become (such as Stringer Bell's various attempts to manipulate Avon and reform his organization into a corporate-style entity, or Freamon's and McNulty's scheme to "create" a serial killer).

The folly of violence and power enacted throughout the series highlights how, within both the nihilistic and utopian poles, sight becomes distorted to a degree that its citizens fall into tragic attempts to gain meaning or place within their institutions and their city. The characters misperceive, are unable to disentangle the availability of power and coercion from the grammars and rhythms of the game, which seemingly always has a bigger, more powerful player behind a guarded door. Prez's presence and enactment of policing in the city highlights the grammar of power that accompanies the implicit and explicit declarations of "what we're about."

The misrepresentation finally materializes for Prez in Season 3 as Prez's police life takes a sudden turn. Prez has demonstrated excellent analytical skills and alongside Freamon seems even to flourish in his place within the detail (and thus the police force implicitly.) But in the midst of this apparent belonging, the gap between Prez and his identity as police once again collapses without warning. Prez's enactments of power magnify these practices of announcement and demonstrate how such grammars work against attaining certainty. Prez could never truly recognize a police officer.

In the episode "Slapstick,"[15] the everyday is drawn into the absurd. Prez and McNulty, while out on a seemingly benign trip for dinner, hear a call for assistance nearby. In responding to the call, Prez shoots an armed man, believing him to be a drug dealer; he is actually a black undercover police officer. While the gap between Prez and police had been relatively obscured throughout the season, the gap is gestured towards again immediately prior to the shooting. Prez, eating a fortune cookie, reads his fortune: "You will have company tonight." McNulty alludes to the possibility of a sexual rendezvous with a woman, and Prez responds, "I'm married with lawn furniture."[16] Even in innocent banter Prez reveals his strangeness; working in a city with no grass and no lawns, he comes from a place where lawn furniture makes sense. Prez's eschewing the sexual innuendo that punctuates virtually all of the conversations among police highlights his misperception and disconnection even while he attempts to serve his colleagues and find a place among them. This strangeness will explode to the surface in the aftermath of the shooting, revealing Prez's doubts about his identity as a police officer and reiterating his fellow police officer's doubts about him.

The gap between intent and enactment, how life in the city confuses and obscures these with only death, becomes clear in Season 3, and the shooting of the cop makes apparent the gap that Prez always understood was present between him and his vocation as a police officer. While Prez can analyze, he cannot distill power from this analysis when policing on the streets.

But this disequilibrium is wound throughout the city's inner workings and its citizens and the city's place within the nation. In the same episode that explores the aftermath of Prez's shooting we also see the gap between Dennis "Cutty" Wise's desire to start a gym and the reality of a bureaucracy that actually operates with phone calls and favors. Cutty's desire was simply not enough. Similarly, McNulty's attempt to seek after a relationship with Theresa D'Agostino rather than a midnight rendezvous (this is itself

15. "Slapstick," S3/E9.
16. "Slapstick," S3/E9.

a transformation worth exploring) reveals a profound difference between Baltimore and Washington, the local and the national. Reeling a bit from the awkward conversation of politics with D'Agostino at dinner, McNulty tries to enter into her world, turning on a political talk show when he returns to his apartment. But it is a world he cannot enter. Instead he settles for a documentary on World War II, about the trenches where people fought and died. *The Wire* can be seen as an attempt to narrate the varying ways these gaps are seen and negotiated, but often not resisted. Ultimately, Prez will come to confess a fundamental gap between his vernacular and the language of police work in the city. Prez is "married with lawn furniture."

Following the shooting, Prez's misplacement is clear to himself and he no longer seeks to find a place within the police, but resists its inflections of power (he does not want to be represented by the F.O.P., and doesn't enlist his father-in-law Valchek to help him). Prez is again introduced to the viewer through the words of fellow cops in contrast to the "real'" cop who was killed. Prez is little more than a "clusterfuck," an amalgamation of many ill-fitting pieces making him seemingly unuseful in a multitude of ways. Prez recognizes the end of his attempt to live into police work: "I'm done," he says simply.[17] Reflecting on his life as a cop, Prez acknowledges the gaps, begins to see the sensibilities required to do police work in a particular world, in the world of Augustine's earthly city, a city where control, power, and self-assertion are the primary tools of belonging and establishing one's credentials as well as one's future.

In actuality, Prez's work was central to the very successes that brought Daniels, McNulty, and Freamon back from the dead. But this kind of work, oriented toward uncovering truth, is not what police work of the city is actually about. Vocation in the city is about mastery of facts, of the rules that govern the institution and the bodies that inhabit it. It was these implicit and explicit rules of mastery over others that Prez could not master, or seemingly never recognized.

Prez's shooting represents the height of his inability to perform the grammar of power. Prez could not see properly in this city; on that dark night he could not identify whom he supposedly belonged to. But Prez's misperceptions are emblematic of an urban space that perpetually wounds itself, destroying both those whom it serves and its own purposes. The city does not recognize its own and kills that which it cannot discern as friend or foe. The culture of power and self-protection always works against itself as it must work to establish its power over-against. As it does so, it deepens the injuries to the world and to itself. This becomes an image of the city of

---

17. "Slapstick," S3/E9.

man, but also of Baltimore in the context of a United States that attempts to retain power by killing "terrorists" (those who are not recognized as citizens), that alleviates debt by requiring more of the poor, and that demands human rights while imprisoning perceived threats to national security. We do not properly apprehend one another or ourselves.

In reflecting upon what happened, Prez confesses to Freamon, "Guilty of failing to identify yourself as a police officer. Sounds like what I've been guilty of my whole career.... I'm not sure I was supposed to be police, not really."[18] Prez's recognition of his own strangeness or mis-placedness marks an important transformation. This transformation is not a transformation of character (as we see in McNulty, perhaps) or vocation (as in Colvin or Cutty), but in sight (self-perception and recognition of the world). Prez recognizes his own blindness in the alley, but also a profound incapacity to truly see as a police officer sees, to inhabit the various subtle practices through which he would declare himself a police officer (to those in the department and in the city.)

The irony of this statement comes from the fact that Prez did excellent police work within a certain context, certain boundaries. Analyzing patterns, organizing information, reading people through their monetary and linguistic nuances. Along with Freamon, Prez's contribution was critical. But the city obfuscates Prez's self-perception. The power of the city draws its inhabitants into *its* logic of survival, twisting power into weakness and weakness into power. The world of *The Wire,* in this way, displays the profound difficulty of discerning belonging in our modern world. How do we begin to "see" truthfully without death?

MIDDLE SCHOOL TEACHER—PRIEST OF THE IN-BETWEEN?

Season 4 finds Prez post-confession, seeking a new vocation, a new sense of place as a teacher in a middle school. The vice principal takes him to his dilapidated classroom, saying, "This is you." Prez replies, "This is me."[19] Prez's response here is emptied of the heroic teacher complex of *Stand and Deliver* or *Freedom Writers*. In fact, Prez's response is a statement of neither certainty or nor fear. "This is me" is a statement of belonging that is not achieved, but into which he is invited and must discover.

Prez's sense of place does not translate into an ease of work. In fact, Prez is confronted with patterns of behavior and networks of power that

---

18. "Mission Accomplished," S3/E12.
19. "The Boys of Summer," S4/E1.

continue to echo the life of the city into the classroom. And yet within this space Prez exercises a restraint that allows him to be present to his students. Within the school Prez comes to understand power as subjection, interconnection, care, being-for in such a way that allows his penchant for "figuring shit out" to uncover patterns of possibility in his students, whether it is Duquan "Dukie" Weems' mind for computers or the use of street games to teach probability.

Prez's tasks are no longer monitoring daily conversations or evaluating financial transactions that can ultimately "break the case." Instead, Prez becomes enveloped in a new mundane: how to get Dukie food and clean clothes without his mother selling them, and how to cultivate Randy's entrepreneurship and loyalty. Within the space of the middle school, Prez exercises power no longer to determine and control in service to his professional thriving or survival. Prez attempts to create a space within his classroom that can allow students to imagine different possibilities for themselves. In this middle space, Prez is confronted by the realities of the city in a new key, the families struggling to maintain normalcy despite the various instantiations of power represented in the police, City Hall, or the Barksdales and the Marlo Stanfields.

As a "priest of the in-between," Prez cannot determine or create, he can only shepherd. But for most of Prez's students the realities of the city cannot be overcome solely by Prez's attentiveness or a few dollars for food. Dukie, at the end of the series, is shooting heroin, Randy is the victim of a violent retaliation from a rival drug organization whom he testified against, and Michael reemerges at the end of a series as a stick-up man.

Prez's statement of belonging ("This is me") that begins his vocation as a teacher is not an identity of power or certainty; rather he is identifying with the subjection his students constantly endure. But ultimately, his statement of identity is also a confession of his own limitations and belonging. His classroom will become a perpetual middle space with new students again and again navigating the same challenges and temptations. Some students may find new opportunities or new possibilities, but others will find themselves inescapably subject to the city's logics of power.

In this middle space no amount of manipulation, no amount of cunning can create certainty because the ends do not reside in the accumulation of respect, money, blocks, or promotions. Rather the middle space is one that is radically bound to the personhood of the inhabitants. The vocation of the teacher is bound to the belonging of the students within that particular classroom. But because the students arrive in the classroom carrying with them the realities of the city, the teacher is also bound to the city, to its realities and its powers. As such, the middle school is space antithetical to the city itself in that its safety is predicated not on the perfection of power, but the persistence of presence. Prez's vocation is not to save but to be present, to see, to attend where he can—never knowing what the end will be.

Prez's reorientation of skills used as a police officer is also mirrored in Lt. Colvin's transition into the same middle school. Colvin, having lost hope in the "rip and runs" that were the defining characteristic of his district for so long, begins to draw upon the experiment of "Hamsterdam" and the discovery of police work that relies upon relationships and restraint. Operating within this new space, Colvin begins to read, hear his students. Through these interconnections, Prez does not see the students as ends for his own advancement but as people to be cared for, to be poured into, heard and seen.[20]

Prez's and Colvin's transitions into middle school disclose the ubiquity of institutional power in all aspects of citizens' lives, but also how this peculiar institution, the middle school, harbors the powers of the "earthly city" and requires an alternative enactment of power by those in authority. Interestingly, the school is an institution run by women, whether the vice principal's constant presence or Ms. Sampson's unquestioned authority among students. The school represents a space in the city where possibility and hope still linger, but as a current beneath a surface dominated by competing institutions with means and powers whose sole aim is self-preservation under the guise of service. The inevitable failure of institutions to see these students is highlighted by Prez and Colvin's desire to *see* students (this could also be said of Carver as he progresses through Seasons 4 and 5) even in the midst of the educational systems systemic need to "socially promote." But *The Wire* is quite clear that one's capacity to see is different than salvation.

The school exists as a mediating space (a middle place) where children are themselves navigating the transition from childhood and possibility to seeing the reality of their lives and the lives of those around them truthfully, in all of its tragedy. As a middle space the school attempts to ward off the realities of the city. With its locked doors the school draws in the youth—the newly entered, those who are deciding so much—but the school cannot lock out the realities of the city that abide in the lives of the students.

In this regard Prez's and Colvin's transformations exemplify a modest crack of hope and perhaps *even* religious commentary on what Christians might call a "conversion," as the former citizens of the world enter into a

---

20. This is not to say Prez is a hero or a savior. Dukie, a student into whom Prez pours a great deal, eventually chooses the street rather than school when no longer under the care of Prez. Prez reads this, not ignorant of the choices Dukie makes, but also not unwilling to be duped in the hope that something good might come from one good turn.

new world and must now navigate this *middle* space. "What they are about" can no longer be determined and defined through their own power. Prez's and Colvin's positions as teachers and mentors give them a bit of authority, but it is always an authority that is subject, working through relationships where power is never clearly in their possession and thus their vocation is predicated on seeing in a new way. They must see *who* they are even while constantly being reminded of their own limitations in the face of a violent and dark world.

CONCLUSION

Within the institutions of the city, the question of belonging is constantly highlighted in the estrangements that arise with Prez's attempts to articulate himself within the city. But in this process, Prez comes to recognize his ill-fittedness, the absurdity of the power he wields so awkwardly, which results in his own exile or the death of innocents. He understands a distinction between the power he believed he had and the power he actually has.

Within the walls of the school, another city within a city, Prez cannot intimidate through violence or force, he can only call students into a possibility through a perpetual presence and invitation. He must "see" the students and the complicated reality they bring with them into the school, that the two cities are bound together and he is bound to them. The middle school is a space where the city of God and city of man coalesce and contest in the lives of these dual citizens. Baltimore grinds even on these little ones, obscuring sight into nihilism or a too-distant utopia that allows for tragic and terrible choices for the sake of the "good" (Michael's promise and tragic choices figure prominently here).

The city is an extension of what we try to establish for ourselves—but it is also an inevitable fact of our lives. Prez does not leave for "the county." Like Colvin, Prez must reimagine his power and presence within the city. This reality is not a certain path or precise calculation of actions and reactions in a game, it is the garnering of our peculiar powers and laying them down as an invitation.

Augustine observes that the folly of those who lived in the city of man was their understanding of the world: "They love this present life, when they ought to hold it cheap."[21] But perhaps the sojourn through this place is not so quick, and the distinction between this world and another world is too clean. If we must travel lightly, perhaps the journey also requires us to pick up travelers along the way, to make camp in strange places, and

---

21. Augustine, *City of God*, 13.

among strange people to discover new uses for tools and words we thought we understood so well.

David Simon's Baltimore at once demonstrates the seemingly enduring power of institutions to preserve themselves and bend its inhabitants into a mode of belonging that both upholds the institutions while destroying its people. And yet, within Simon's city there also emerge small cracks of resistance, attempts to carve out or even undo these machinations. While it is unclear whether the institutions themselves will be reformed, the beginnings of transformation in Prez, Colvin, McNulty, and others suggest that the power of these institutions is not complete and irrevocable.

The middle school is hardly a salvific space and Prez and Colvin are hardly messianic figures. But in this space they find what they are about. The middle school is a space of shepherds where there is no neat distinction between street and government, crime and law enforcement. In the middle school they are all painfully present within one locked building trying desperately to figure it out.

The Wire indicates the difficulty the earthly city confronts us with—that we so often fail to see the seduction of the power, violence, and control that seem necessary to live and thrive in this world. Prez's mis-performance of belonging in the city, his transformation into un-knowing, is not a place of promise in the earthly city but a space of perpetual vulnerability. His is not the heroic reversal of the earthly city's perpetual demise. Rather, Prez becomes present to the death the city produces; he participates in the institutions, but in ways that disrupt its logic, finding partnerships with others who see both possibility and their limitations within the locked but tragically permeable doors of the middle school.

BIBLIOGRAPHY

Anderson, Paul Allen. "'The Game Is the Game': Tautology and Allegory in *The Wire*." *Criticism* 52 (2010) 373–98.
Appiah, Kwame Anthony. *Cosmopolitanism: Ethics in a World of Strangers*. New York: Norton, 2006.
Augustine. *City of God*. New York: Modern Library, 1950.
Donald, James. *Imagining the Modern City*. Minneapolis: University of Minnesota Press, 1999.
Ellul, Jacques. *The Meaning of the City*. Translated by Dennis Pardee. Grand Rapids: Eerdmans, 1970.
Foucault, Michel. "Nietzsche, Genealogy, History." In *Language, Counter-Memory, Practice: Selected Essays and Interviews*, edited by Donald F. Bouchard, 139–64. Ithaca: Cornell University Press, 1977.
Jameson, Fredric. "Realism and Utopia in *The Wire*." *Criticism* 52 (2010) 359–72.

Rajchman, John. *Truth and Eros: Foucault, Lacan, and the Question of Ethics.* New York: Routledge, 1991.
Ward, Graham. *Cities of God.* New York: Routledge, 2000.
West, Cornel. *Race Matters.* New York: Vintage, 1994.

8

Down in the Hole
Melancholy, Vulnerability, and the Puncturing of Black Masculinity

JOSEPH WINTERS

IN RECENT YEARS, THERE has been a heightened interest in the categories of mourning and melancholy. Authors from a variety of disciplines and fields (theology, literary theory, psychology) have drawn from Freud's well-known "Mourning and Melancholia" essay to address historical forms of loss, suffering, and trauma.[1] Judith Butler, for instance, appropriates the category of mourning in order to unveil the hierarchies of grief produced within everyday discourses about war and terror. According to Butler, the refusal by Americans to acknowledge and lament the loss of non-American Muslim lives is connected to the pervasive denial of our shared vulnerability to injury, suffering, and death. Anne Cheng similarly uses Freud's notion of melancholy to reframe discussions about racial injustice. By foregrounding the grief involved in being both assimilated into *and* excluded from the racial imaginary, Cheng is able to keep track of the psychological wounds that remain after "successful" attempts to redress race-inflected grievances. What is significant about this recent investment in the theorization of loss

---

1. See, for instance, Butler, *Precarious Life*; Cheng, *The Melancholy of Race*; Eng and Kazanjian, *Loss*; Kim, *Melancholic Freedom*.

and vulnerability is its incompatibility with triumphant cultural narratives and practices that both deny and reproduce death.[2]

There is an indirect relationship between this heightened interest in the ethical/political implications of mourning and discourses concerned with the performance of black masculinity. Authors such as bell hooks have demonstrated how contemporary black male culture is defined by an ethos of cool, an ethos that valorizes being in control, exhibiting power over others (especially women), and concealing weakness.[3] Although she refuses to place all of the blame on hip hop culture, hooks chastises young black males for their desire to hear and digest "rap music with its aggressive presentation of invulnerability."[4] This "presentation of invulnerability" is presumably designed to protect black males from being perceived as weak and can therefore be interpreted as a survival tactic. In what follows, I attempt to show how the HBO series, *The Wire*, unwittingly connects these two discursive strands—the one dealing with the ethical dimensions of mourning/melancholy and the other addressing the so-called crisis of black masculinity. As the series delves into the ambiguities and contradictions of the drug trade, law enforcement, and the postindustrial urban environment, *The Wire* reframes and alters the way we see, imagine, and hear black males dwelling in the proverbial concrete jungle. Most significantly, the series exhibits how the aforementioned performance of invulnerability founders, how the posture of invincibility and hardness within black male culture both conceals and reveals a recognition of weakness and exposure to forces that are beyond our control. In accomplishing this, *The Wire* also unsettles the viewer, compelling the spectator to be more attentive to the wounds and fissures that mark our social worlds.

This chapter consists of three sections. In the first section, I provide a brief historical and theoretical context for my foray into the complexities of black masculinity. In the second section, I analyze the characters of D'Angelo and Wallace, two members of the Barksdale drug organization whose salient sensitivity to the suffering of others threatens the stability of the organization. By situating these characters against the backdrop of broader discussions about black masculinity, I show how *The Wire* complicates contemporary assumptions about young black men. In the third section of the chapter, I examine the series as an aesthetic object, paying attention to the ways in which the show attempts to figuratively wound the

---

2. This is an idea that that is articulated powerfully in Hauerwas and Coles, *Christianity, Democracy, and the Radical Ordinary*.

3. See especially hooks, *We Real Cool*.

4. hooks, *We Real Cool*, 99.

viewer, opening us up to the suffering of those who reside on the corners and edges of our lifeworlds. Drawing from Theodor Adorno's aesthetic theory, I suggest that *The Wire* embodies a mode of melancholic hope—the flickering possibility of a better, less violent world that is tethered to the memory of suffering (and not to the optimistic vision of a society that will eventually resolve its social conflicts).

CONTEXTUALIZING THE BLACK MALE SUBJECT

bell hooks' concerns about contemporary black male culture can be read as an extension of Michelle Wallace's analysis of "Black Macho," an attitude/mode of being that takes on a heightened valence during the black freedom struggles in the late 60s.[5] According to Wallace, the Black Power movement was largely motivated by the desire to display and project a particular conception of black manhood. Well-known activists such as Huey Newton and Eldridge Cleaver associated power with assertiveness, control, and sexual virility. A liberated black male, according to the logic of Black Power, is one who no longer grovels at the feet of white people, who no longer turns the other cheek when attacked or harassed, and who no longer depends on the institutions, values, and ideals of the dominant culture. Similarly, this liberated black man is also one who is willing to defend and protect his community against external and internal threats. Racial authenticity is therefore tethered to a rigid vision of manhood, a narrow understanding of being a strong, self-possessed man.[6] Insofar as this version of manhood is consolidated by the possession and deployment of the phallus/master signifier, sexual penetration (and in some cases, rape) becomes a significant vehicle of liberation for some proponents of Black Power.[7] To some extent, the valorization of black male virility within this movement can be interpreted as a compensatory response to a history of being the object of systemic violence, a history of being wounded, humiliated, lynched, and so forth. Yet the triumphant notion of masculinity put forth by Black Power proponents can also be read as a denial of this history and an attempt to relocate the qualities of weakness and vulnerability to other groups (white men, women, homosexuals). Although Wallace sees the hypermasculine performance and rhetoric of Black Power activists as a necessary moment within the black freedom struggle, she claims that ultimately the Black Macho ethos

5. See Wallace, *Black Macho and the Myth of the Superwoman*, 3–85.

6. For a brilliant analysis of how notions of racial authenticity have traditionally been intertwined with rigid notions of manhood, see Harper, *Are We Not Men?*

7. See for instance Cleaver, *Soul on Ice*.

produced men who were "frequently cruel, narcissistic, and shortsighted."[8] I am particularly interested in the accusation of cruelty insofar as it denotes a disregard for the pain and suffering of others.

As William Van Deburg has pointed out, although the tactics and political aims of the Black Power movement were fleeting, this movement has had a major influence on everyday black cultural practices —language, slang, styles, attitudes, aesthetic sensibilities, music, films, and so forth.[9] For instance, the interplay between race, gender, and power that Wallace examines is evident in the Blaxploitation films of the early 1970s, films that often depicted the black male protagonist as violent, indomitable, hypersexual, and in control (an attribute that always extended to women as objects of possession).[10] In Gordon Parks' 1971 classic, *Shaft*, the audience is introduced to a heroic black detective whose assertive, cool attitude clashes with the more submissive quality of earlier black male characters and personas within the film industry.[11] Shaft's heroism is not only secured by his willingness to violently defy and undermine white authority (he eventually saves a black mobster's daughter from white mobsters by overcoming the white adversaries). His power is also reinforced by the way he treats, manipulates, and uses women in the film. The audience is supposed to identity with the protagonist's ability to saunter through various situations and contexts, a mode of freedom that involves fleeting interactions with black and white women when they are sexually useful. Finally, Shaft's heroic quality seems to rely on his tendency to survive violent altercations relatively unscathed. Even when he is shot during the initial battle with the white mobsters, he recovers quickly and immediately proceeds to rescue the female victim. Compare Shaft's "imperviousness" with the torment and pain that the female protagonist endures in *Foxy Brown*, another significant film within the Blaxploitation genre. Before Foxy Brown defeats the crime organization that is responsible for the murder of her brother and boyfriend, she is tortured, raped, and drugged by her adversaries. Whereas the black female body becomes the object/occasion for the depiction of torture, Shaft's heroism is predicated on his relative invulnerability to pain and suffering.

8. Wallace, *Black Macho and the Myth of the Superwoman*, 73.

9. See Van DeBurg, *New Day in Babylon*.

10. For a clear analysis of the Blaxploitation genre, see Guerrero, *Framing Blackness*, 69–111.

11. Think, for instance, of Steppin Fetchit or Bill Bojangles Robinson, actors who were consigned to the role of the submissive jester, coon, and so forth. For an analysis of the various personas that blacks have been consigned to in the film industry, see Bogle, *Toms, Coons, Mulattoes, Mammies, and Bucks*.

This connection between masculinity, power, and the semblance of invulnerability is evident within contemporary black male cultures, especially those influenced by hip hop. Here we might think initially about the abundance of songs and videos performed by black males that glorify violence, that use female bodies as visible signs of male power and wealth, and that equate authentic masculinity with being "hard," invincible, and so forth. According to Imani Perry, "masculinity in hip hop reflects the desire to assert black male subjectivity, and it sometimes does so at the expense of black female subjectivity, while at other times it simply reveals the complexity of black male identity."[12] Part of this complexity involves the fact that the lurid display of wealth and power within hip hop culture is often a response to what Perry calls "racialized economic powerlessness."[13] More generally, the self-aggrandizing dimensions of hip hop (where possessions, including women, become indicative of a certain kind of power and control) tend to compensate for and dissimulate past and present experiences of deprivation and loss.

Black males who participate in hip hop culture often assume rigid masculine roles in order to avoid appearing weak and vulnerable. What is interesting is that some male artists occasionally voice this complexity. Think for instance of Jay-Z's "Song Cry," a track in which the rapper mournfully recounts the way he mistreated a past girlfriend, a love interest who returns the favor by secretly finding herself a "special friend." The song's hook is telling: "I can't see 'em coming down my eyes, so I gotta make the song cry."[14] Here the song as a whole becomes the substitution for Jay-Z's tears. The song enables him to express feelings of remorse, guilt, and sorrow while also concealing the physical marks of these emotions (the tears). Jay-Z is implicitly aware that existing codes of masculinity constrain and enable his capacity to mourn. He writes: "Though I can't let you know it, pride won't let me show it, pretend to be heroic, that's just one to grow with, but deep inside a nigga's so sick."[15] Here Jay-Z suggests that "appearing heroic" entails the public denial of those aspects of our lives, relationships, and experiences that disrupt, undo, and even "sicken" us.

---

12. Perry, *Prophets of the Hood*, 118.
13. Ibid., 127.
14. Jay-Z, "Song Cry."
15. Ibid.

D'ANGELO, WALLACE, AND THE THREAT OF VULNERABILITY

Similar to Imani Perry's aforementioned reading of hip hop culture, I argue that *The Wire* expresses the "complexity of black male identity." Throughout the series, we are introduced to black male characters that both reinforce and undermine standard codes of manhood. While Omar Little might exemplify this ambiguity most provocatively (he robs and murders other participants in the drug game while defying the heteronormative expectations that are typically associated with the assertive black male), I am interested in drawing attention to D'Angelo Barksdale's character. I also examine Wallace's horrified response to the corpse of Omar's boyfriend, Brandon. In examining these characters, I am particularly interested in the interplay between acting tough, detached, and hard and moments that betray vulnerability and weakness. I suggest that the rejection and stigmatization of the latter moments is essential to the stability of "the game" and the overall order of things.[16]

We are introduced to D'Angelo in the first episode of the series as he is acquitted of murder only after members of the Barksdale organization violently tamper with key witnesses. When Avon, D'Angelo's uncle and the head of the drug organization, chastises his nephew for killing Pooh Blanchard in front of security cameras, it becomes clear that D'Angelo killed his adversary in a moment of panic and fear. In fact, Avon suggests that his nephew was afraid of "taking a beating."[17] It is as if violence in this case is a way to compensate for vulnerability and preempt injury. Yet when one of his subordinates asks him why he has been demoted from being a drug lieutenant in the Towers to being in charge of the Pit, he responds in a cold, phlegmatic manner: "I killed a nigga."[18] Here D'Angelo begins to secure his authority over his subordinates (Bodie, Poot, and Wallace) by alluding to the murder in a particular way, as if the act came naturally to him, as if he can own the deed with no qualms. This speech act enables him to appear as if he is in control of things even though his uncle berated him earlier for being over-emotional and out of control.

To consolidate his authority, D'Angelo tells a story to his subordinates about the murder of Deirdre Kresson, one of Avon's girlfriends. Although

---

16. My analysis dovetails with the arguments expressed in Peterson, "Corner-Boy Masculinity." In this essay, Peterson creatively uses the idea of the "corner" to signify the intersection of different identities, characteristics, attitudes, and dispositions, an intersection that the male characters in *The Wire* inhabit and embody.

17. "The Target," S1/E1.

18. "The Target," S1/E1.

we eventually find out that Wee-Bey Brice murdered Deirdre because she threatened to expose the Barksdale organization, D'Angelo claims her body. What is significant is that he claims her body/corpse after Bodie challenges his authority and trivializes the aforementioned murder of Pooh. Bodie, boasting about his escape from a juvenile prison, says to D'Angelo, "If you was me, you would still be down there."[19] D'Angelo responds: "Have you ever seen a city jail? You ever caught a body?"[20] An unimpressed Bodie replies: "Yeah, you got the one."[21] D'Angelo then asserts: "Yeah the one you know about, man you all need to ask around."[22] As he draws Bodie, Poot, and Wallace into his story (a story that falsely portrays D'Angelo carrying and using a "big gun" to murder Deirdre Kresson), it becomes clear that D'Angelo's triumph over Bodie's skepticism is facilitated by the characters' cold indifference to the death of Deirdre Kresson. Telling stories about "catching bodies," about taking another's life, becomes a form of self-aggrandizement, a way for D'Angelo to re-assert and reinforce his manhood. This scene also constitutes a kind of bonding moment between these young males, a moment that solidifies D'Angelo's position within the Pit hierarchy. This bonding moment entails a refusal by all of the participants in the scene to be affected or moved by the suffering/cry of the female victim of violence within D'Angelo's narrative. This is why Poot can ask D'Angelo in a flippant manner, "If she [Deirdre] was all that, why didn't you fuck her first?"[23] Poot's question suggests an analogy between "fucking her" and "killing her" insofar as both acts involve treating the female body as prey, as a disposable object of male dominance. This theme of female disposability reaches an apex later on in Season 1 when Wee-Bey discards/dumps the body of Keisha, an exotic dancer who dies of an overdose at a house party.

Throughout Season 1, we see another side to D'Angelo, a more vulnerable side that threatens to undermine the stability of the Barksdale organization. For instance, after his crew severely injures Johnny Weeks, Bubbles' friend, for trying to buy drugs with counterfeit money, D'Angelo complains to Stringer that the punishment far exceeded the infraction. He laments, "It was only a couple of dollars . . . they fucked him up so bad."[24] Stringer, Avon's right hand and the organization's second in command, reminds D'Angelo that "its all in the game. It ain't the money, it's the message,

19. "Old Cases," S1/E4.
20. "Old Cases," S1/E4.
21. "Old Cases," S1/E4.
22. "Old Cases," S1/E4.
23. "Old Cases," S1/E4.
24. "The Target," S1/E1.

D. You can't show no weakness."²⁵ Notice how Stringer attempts to mitigate D'Angelo's concern by alluding to the rules of "the game," a trope that reverberates throughout the series. Violent reprisal or sending a message to those who violate the rules is often necessary to reestablish the order of things. To maintain the order and success of the drug organization, weakness cannot be "shown," vulnerability cannot be exposed to others. Survival in the drug trade and in the streets apparently relies on the semblance of invincibility.

After this dialogue between D'Angelo and Stringer, a conversation that takes place in Orlando's Strip Club, the camera briefly turns to the television and we see a news headline, "America at War." The brief allusion to the invasion of Afghanistan suggests that the use of excessive violence to conceal or compensate for signs of weakness applies to American foreign policy, the political realm, and the "game outside of the game." As Judith Butler points out, in reference to America's response to the 9/11 attacks, collective experiences of loss and vulnerability typically lead to immediate military retribution, a tendency that betrays a nation's anxiety over being exposed to injury, invasion, and death.²⁶ By juxtaposing the drug game with the image of war, *The Wire* suggests that violent masculine codes and norms are entrenched in the broader practices and activities of the nation-state.

In addition to the brutal beating of Johnny Weeks, D'Angelo is visibly shaken by the murder of William Gant, a state's witness who previously testified against D'Angelo. In the final scene of episode one, we see D'Angelo in a crowd of onlookers as police officers reveal the face and bullet-punctured head of Gant. A flashback to the moment in the trial when Gant identifies D'Angelo as the assailant of Pooh Blanchard indicates that the murder of Gant is retaliation by the Barksdale organization. After witnessing the dead body, D'Angelo stumbles backward, bumping into another onlooker. He is visibly stunned and unsettled; he knows that he is implicated in the witness's murder. When McNulty and Bunk, the homicide detectives investigating the murder, coerce D'Angelo into the interrogation room, they exploit his "weakness." The detectives fabricate a story about Gant leaving behind orphaned children. To make the story more credible, Bunk uses a photograph of his own children. Deceived into thinking that the images represent Gant's fatherless children, D'Angelo cries out "Lord Jesus."²⁷ Throughout the scene, we see D'Angelo break down and cry as the detectives probe into the violence that marks the drug game.

25. "The Target," S1/E1.
26. See the author's preface in Butler, *Precarious Life*.
27. "The Detail," S1/E2.

Borrowing from Freud's definition of melancholy, we might say that D'Angelo begins to internalize the loss of William Gant.[28] This melancholic internalization is mediated by D'Angelo's compassion toward those presumably impacted the most by Gant's death. Whereas the aforementioned notion of catching a body connotes a possessive, triumphant attitude toward one's victim, melancholy signifies a more receptive stance regarding the victims of violence. In fact, it suggests that the lost object might haunt and possess the living, especially those immediately responsible for the loss. The detectives ultimately convince D'Angelo to write an apology to Gant's family but his written confession is interrupted by Maurice Levy, the lawyer for the Barksdale organization. As Levy leads D'Angelo out of the interrogation room, he slaps D'Angelo over the head with the letter, chastising him as if D'Angelo was a child. Levy's paternal act suggests that D'Angelo stepped out of line and violated the rules when he decided to express remorse through the letter. Being affected by the suffering of others threatens to destabilize the order of things.

D'Angelo's response to the Gant murder anticipates Wallace's response to the tortured corpse of Brandon. In retaliation to the robbery executed by Omar's stick up crew (which included Brandon and Bailey), members of the Barksdale organization capture Brandon, torture him, mutilate his body, and then leave the corpse in an alley beside Wallace and Poot's house. As Poot confirms that the corpse is "Omar's boy," the camera draws our attention to Wallace's facial expression, a countenance marked by disgust, shock, and lament. The camera quickly shifts to Brandon's body and we see that one of his eyes has been gouged out, while the other seems to be staring at Wallace, figuratively piercing and indicting him. As Wallace walks away, he flails his arm against a branch. His visible anger indicates that he acknowledges his complicity in Brandon's death (Wallace and Poot identified Brandon at a diner and contacted other members of the Barksdale organization to carry out the retaliation).

In a later scene, Wallace reveals his disgust to D'Angelo, saying, "He was all cut up; his insides were hanging out."[29] Both ironic and telling, D'Angelo justifies the brutal act using the same logic that Stringer deployed earlier—"Sometimes you got to send a message yo . . . all that shit is in the game."[30] Although D'Angelo urges Wallace to forget about Brandon's mutilated body, the latter persists, "His eye was blown out, and the other one was open . . . and yo D it fucks me up. Its like he's looking out, like he

28. See Freud, "Mourning and Melancholia."
29. "The Wire," S1/E6.
30. "The Wire," S1/E6.

sees everything."³¹ Here Wallace suggests that what is so unsettling about Brandon's corpse is that it appears to inhabit a liminal position between life and death. Resembling Freud's notion of the uncanny, Brandon's inanimate body haunts Wallace, gazes at him, and therefore takes on a quasi-animate quality. Because one eye is open and the other mutilated, the body becomes a vivid reminder to Wallace of the life that preceded the murder, a life that has been lost, a life that partially remains through its haunting effect.

Brandon's pierced body disorients Wallace. After his conversation with D'Angelo, he alienates himself from the members of the Pit and begins to consume drugs to cope with his pain. Because Wallace temporarily leaves the game, Stringer doubts that he can be trusted when he decides to return. Stringer therefore orders Bodie and Poot to get rid of Wallace. While trying to convince Poot that Stringer's order is justified, Bodie says, "If he using, you know he ain't reliable. Look, the man gave the word. We either step up or step off. It's the game."³² Here he makes an implicit connection between using drugs, weakness, and instability. Wallace is considered to be weak and a potential threat to the organization not primarily because of his drug use but because of his sensitivity to the pain and suffering of others, a character trait/flaw expressed and indicated by his drug use. The game, as Bodie reminds Poot, compels its participants to step up, to be assertive and to accept the course of things, even if this course involves taking the life of a friend. Yet this acceptance of the game and the overall course of things can be interpreted as an indication of the players' lack of control and a recognition that each participant in the game is subject to intractable forces, rules, constraints, and arrangements.

What I am arguing is that the rules of the drug game require its male participants to deny their vulnerability or stigmatize the vulnerability of others when this quality threatens to undermine the game and its order. In Wallace's penultimate scene, for instance, Bodie derisively calls Wallace a child and refers to him as soft after he makes a wistful allusion to his mother. When he asks Wallace, "So what are you, a boy or a man?," Bodie suggests that weakness/softness is not an attribute of proper manhood. Wallace's weakness has something to do with him not performing masculinity properly. And he must be eliminated because as Bodie says, "A soft link breaks the chain."³³ More significantly, getting rid of the weak link means removing that part of the chain that reminds us of our own exposure to injury, suffering, and pain, a condition that is interminable and that defines

31. "The Wire," S1/E6.
32. "Cleaning Up," S1/E12.
33. "Cleaning Up," S1/E12.

us as contingent beings in the world. Ironically, Bodie's death in Season 4 is a result of his fragility, a result of his dismay and sadness over seeing the draped corpse of his friend, Little Kevin.[34]

In Wallace's final scene, Bodie and Poot follow him upstairs as Wallace searches for the children that reside with him. Throughout the first season we see Wallace as the caretaker for several children who have been abandoned; he prepares the children's lunches, provides them dinner, and reluctantly helps them complete their homework. Wallace adopts a quasi-maternal role with respect to the younger children, which potentially reinforces the perception that he lacks "proper" male qualities and therefore constitutes a weak link in the Barksdale organization. When the three reach the top of the stairs, Bodie pulls out a gun while Poot watches Wallace with tear in his eyes. Bodie says to Wallace, "You's a weak ass nigga man . . . wetting your pants like a little boy, be a man. Stand up like a fuckin man, stand up straight."[35] What is important here is that Wallace's fragility is again attributed to his deficient manhood. At the same time, Poot is in tears and Bodie's hand is shaking as he wields the gun. If Wallace cannot stand up straight/erect and take his death like a proper man, Bodie cannot commit the murderous act without quivering, without showing signs of uncertainty and fear. Wallace pleads, "Ya'll my niggas yo," indicating that even as Bodie and Poot are about to betray him, he affirms his intimate connection with his childhood friends. As Bodie pulls the trigger, we see him jump back, startled, his body recoiling with the gun. Poot then takes the gun from Bodie and reluctantly finishes the deed; as he does this, we see the traces of tears in his eyes. What the scene visualizes is an example of assertiveness that undermines itself, a violent act that is inflected with the anticipation of loss, remorse, and guilt. Bodie and Poot exhibit the same qualities—ambivalence, fear, and vulnerability—that render Wallace a threat to the Barksdale organization.

Black men residing in urban areas are often depicted as violent, cold, aggressive, and so forth. As literary critic Maurice Wallace argues, the representation of black males is marked by a dialectic between hypervisibility and invisibility.[36] Wallace urges us to be attentive to the ways in which black male bodies are imagined within everyday culture insofar as dominant discourses typically saturate these bodies with meaning (the black male represents all the fears and anxieties of the broader culture) while preventing us from seeing the complexities and nuances of black male subjectivity.

---

34. For a very insightful essay on Bodie's character that deals with the themes of memory and vulnerability, see Bonjean, "After the Towers Fell."

35. "Cleaning Up," S1/E12.

36. See Wallace, *Constructing the Black Masculine*, 19–50.

My analysis in this section has endeavored to show how *The Wire* presents us with complex characters that both embody and defy standard codes of black masculinity. Even though the drug dealers in the Pit enact a macho, cool attitude, an attitude that tends to conceal vulnerability to pain and to the suffering of others, this mode of being often undermines itself. Season 1 of *The Wire* visualizes this tension; it depicts black males being affected and torn by the suffering of others, particularly suffering that their actions contributed to bringing about.

At the same time, we come to realize that "the game," a term that refers to the drug trade as well as the broader social processes and arrangements that traverse and inform the drug game, imposes serious constraints on participants' capacity to display weakness and vulnerability. As Bodie points out, "The game is rigged."[37] D'Angelo and Wallace are unreliable soldiers (a quality that leads to their demise) within the Barksdale camp because they are visibly affected and undone by the violence that maintains the order of things within the drug game. But is this relationship between order, reliability, and affectivity unique to the drug dealers in *The Wire* and to black male cultures in general? Isn't the broader game and order dependent on producing reliable subjects who don't break the rules? Isn't McNulty, for instance, accused of "giving a fuck when he's not supposed to" after he attempts to find a home/proper burial for the murdered victim of the sex slave trade? Doesn't the smooth flow of things rely on our insensitivity to the dissonant qualities of our lifeworlds that this smooth flow tends to conceal? Doesn't the production of social life depend on a pervasive denial of various forms of death and loss? In the next section, I show how the series as a whole addresses these broader questions and issues.

ART, MELANCHOLY, AND HOPE: THE WIRE AS AN AESTHETIC OBJECT

During interviews, writer David Simon repeatedly claims that one of the aims of *The Wire* is to draw attention to the neglected problems, disparities, and conflicts that beset America's inner cities. Simon suggests that our lack of attention and responsiveness to the violence that marks postindustrial urban America contributes to the reproduction of the state of things. If Simon is right, then indifference to the suffering of others is not unique to urban black male cultures; coldness is not a quality that the audience can exclusively attribute to characters like Wee-Bey and Marlo (we are all involved). In response to an American culture that is motivated by triumphant

---

37. "Final Grades," S4/E13.

narratives of progress and achievement, that claims to be in a post-racial state, that avoids the use of terms like "class" and "economic inequality," and that generally tends to forget elements of the recent past and present that are painful and dissonant, *The Wire* offers us a form of melancholic hope. Melancholic hope, I suggest, entails a vision of a better world that is motivated by our openness to the suffering of others, particularly those residing on the corners and edges of our urban landscapes. This concept provides an alternative to unduly optimistic attitudes and dispositions that rely on the denial of loss, violence, and painful memories. This concept becomes more apparent as we examine the artistic dimensions of the show.

Theodor Adorno's reflections on modern life and his understanding of art provide a helpful way to frame our discussion of *The Wire's* aesthetic dimensions and its embodiment of a different kind of hope. Although Adorno is typically known for his pessimistic view of the world and his dismissal of popular culture, my use of Adorno offers a more productive reading of his concerns and insights.[38] In *Dialectic of Enlightenment*, Adorno puts forth a provocative, if not persuasive, account of the underside of modernity's progressive path toward freedom.[39] According to the critical theorist, modern notions of freedom are predicated on the repression of nature and those bodies associated with nature, such as women and non-European others. Similar to Marx, Adorno contends that for some modern subjects to flourish and prosper, others must be exploited, manipulated, and subjugated. While freedom and suffering form a negative dialectic, our arrangements and practices render us less receptive and attuned to the violence that these arrangements rely on. As Adorno points out, "It is part of the mechanism of domination to forbid recognition of the suffering it produces."[40] Insofar as we are shaped to desire consistency and clarity, to develop a harmonious relationship with our environments, and to be happy subjects, we typically avoid dimensions, aspects, and subjects of our lifeworlds that appear opaque, dissonant, or out of place. Individuals understandably strive to find a stable abode in the world while the suffering of others threatens to undermine our sense of home, to take us outside of ourselves and into uncomfortable terrains. Similarly, because we are trained to keep moving forward, to celebrate

---

38. My analysis is indebted to other authors who have opened up space to read Adorno against the grain. For a reading of Adorno that emphasizes the resources he offers for ethics and politics, see Coles, *Rethinking Generosity*, 75–137. For an insightful essay that underscores the nuances of Adorno's critique of popular culture, see Levin, "For the Record."

39. This provocative text is coauthored by Adorno and Horkheimer but for the sake of convenience, I privilege Adorno's contributions.

40. Adorno, *Minima Moralia*, 63.

futurity and novelty, people tend to deny painful elements of the past, elements that haunt and linger in the present. A major part of this shaping of reliable subjects occurs through the culture industry (film, radio, television, advertisements, magazines), a mechanism that thrives by producing material that is easy to "consume."

Certain kinds of art, according to Adorno, promise and gesture toward a different predicament. According to Adorno scholar Lambert Zuidervaart, art for Adorno "creates a space where societal wounds can be exposed and alternative arrangements imagined."[41] Art is able to accomplish this because it "assimilates itself to the non-identical."[42] One way in which art embodies the non-identical is by reconfiguring the elements and relationships of everyday life. In other words, the artwork is able to express something new and different because it incorporates familiar images, objects, sounds, and ideas while placing these elements in unfamiliar relationships. "The nonexisting in artworks is a constellation of the existing."[43] Even though many praise *The Wire* for its realism, what is fascinating about the show is its ability to juxtapose stories, events, and relationships in novel ways, compelling the viewer to relate to the everyday world differently.

Think, for instance, of Season 1's tendency to relate the hierarchy within the police department with that of the Barksdale organization. By showing that participants on both sides of the law are similarly constrained by rules, codes, and expectations, *The Wire* refuses to cast the drug war as a Manichean struggle between the good cops and the evil drug dealers. Think also of the previously mentioned scene in which a televisual image of America's war against terror emerges after Stringer admonishes D'Angelo about showing weakness. This juxtaposition enables the viewer to see that the rules governing the drug game are not unlike those that regulate decisions and actions in the political realm. In the same way that the Barksdale organization cannot show weakness, the nation-state must compensate any display of weakness with excessive violence and retribution. As Zenobia, one of the students and corner kids in Season 4, astutely points out, "We got our thing, but its just part of the big thing."[44] *The Wire* might incorporate elements from the everyday world, but what makes the show "more than the everyday world" is its capacity to place these elements in new relationships and configurations (enabling the viewer to experience and relate to her world in unprecedented ways).

41. Zuidervaart, "Introduction," 4.
42. Adorno, *Aesthetic Theory*, 134.
43. Ibid., 135.
44. "Corner Boys," S4/E8.

Yet the non-identical has another sense for Adorno. Because art incorporates the tensions and antagonisms of the empirical world, the form or structure of the artwork reflects the world's broken quality. According to Adorno, "The unresolved antagonisms of reality return to artworks as problems of form."[45] In opposition to the tendency to deny or cover over the dissonant features of our lifeworlds, art embodies this dissonance in its form and content. Art therefore endeavors to express the suffering that would otherwise remain unarticulated. As Adorno puts it, "The socially critical zones of artworks are those where it hurts."[46] While watching *The Wire*, the viewer is not only affected by the death of characters that she might identify with (Wallace, D'Angelo, Omar), the viewer is also unsettled by the show's tendency to defy our desire for narrative harmony and closure. According to Amanda Klein, *The Wire* draws from the genre of melodrama, with its characteristics of individual heroism, catharsis, and narrative closure, while also departing from this familiar genre. She writes, "Because the series constantly challenges its own affect, the audience is left feeling dissatisfied and agitated; anger, sadness, and outrage are not purged in a moment of intense emotional release. This uneasy viewing position is a central part of the specific audience engagement that is created by the series."[47] This uneasiness is not only an effect of the show's depiction of uncomfortable dimensions of our social worlds. It is also a result of the show's narrative structure, a structure that reflects the broken quality of these worlds. Each episode consists of a constellation of relatively brief scenes that don't always seem to connect or cohere. The viewer is compelled to connect the fragments, to be an active participant in the gathering of different stories and subplots. There are moments in the series when a subplot gets unexpectedly interrupted—like when Omar is murdered by Kenard, defying our wish to see a showdown between Omar and Marlo. These breaks of linear narrative don't allow for the kinds of pleasures and satisfactions that accompany predictable, teleologically driven storylines. The show's form, I am suggesting, refracts the broken world that is being represented.

Think for instance of the montage that concludes the series. In one shot, we see the character Bubbles finally being permitted to leave his sister's basement and join his family for dinner. He has successfully overcome his drug addiction and his ascension up the basement stairs signifies this triumph. Those of us who have uneasily identified with Bubbles' perpetual struggle with his addiction, his grief over accidentally killing Sherrod, and

---

45. Adorno, *Aesthetic Theory*, 6.
46. Ibid., 237.
47. Klein, "Dickensian Aspect," 179–80.

his ability to survive the streets of Baltimore with compassion and generosity certainly feel a moment of pleasure, satisfaction, and even closure. It is a promising moment no doubt. Yet prior to this segment of the montage, we briefly see an image of Duquan injecting heroin into his veins, as if to indicate an ongoing cycle or repetition. What kind of note then does the show end on? I suggest that if there is hope in this concluding montage, it lies not merely in Bubbles reuniting with his family but at the discordant edge of this segment and the fragment showing Duquan repeating Bubbles' recent past. In other words, hope lies not only in the vision of drug addicts receiving the care and support that they need for transformation but also in the viewers' capacity to remember the ongoing conditions that produce alienation, desperation, and addiction. This is what Adorno might call a "hope draped in black,"[48] a hope that is motivated by and tethered to the memory of loss and suffering.

In this chapter, I attempted to show how *The Wire* prompts us to examine the intersection between discussions about black masculinity and broader discussions about the ethical implications of melancholy. I argued that the show not only exhibits the ways in which black male identity is often marked by anxieties over showing weakness and vulnerability but that the series also implicates the viewer in the charge of being impervious to the violence that punctuates our social worlds. I ultimately contend that the show's hope relies on the viewer's capacity to be affected and figuratively wounded by the dissonant qualities of our lifeworlds, qualities that *The Wire* beautifully and tragically depicts.

BIBLIOGRAPHY

Adorno, Theodor. *Aesthetic Theory*. Translated by Robert Hullot-Kentor. Minneapolis: University of Minnesota Press, 1997.
———. *Dialectic of Enlightenment*. Translated by Edmund Jephcott. Stanford: Stanford University Press, 2002.
———. *Minima Moralia*. Translated by Edmund Jephcott. New York: Verso, 1978.
Bogle, Donald. *Toms, Coons, Mulattoes, Mammies, and Bucks: An Interpretive History of Blacks in American Films*. New York: Bantam, 1973.
Bonjean, Elizabeth. "After the Towers Fell: Bodie Broadus and the Space of Memory." In *The Wire: Urban Decay and American Television*, edited by Tiffany Potter and C. W. Marshall, 162–74. New York: Continuum, 2009.
Butler, Judith. *Precarious Life: The Powers of Mourning and Violence*. New York: Verso, 2004.
Cheng, Anne. *The Melancholy of Race: Psychoanalysis, Assimilation, and Hidden Grief*. New York: Oxford University Press, 2001.

---

48. Adorno, *Aesthetic Theory*, 135.

Cleaver, Eldridge. *Soul on Ice*. New York: Ramparts, 1968.
Coles, Romand. *Rethinking Generosity: Critical Theory and the Politics of Caritas*. Ithaca: Cornell University Press, 1997.
Eng, David, and David Kazanjian, editors. *Loss: The Politics of Mourning*. Berkeley: University of California Press, 2003.
Freud, Sigmund. "Mourning and Melancholia." In *The Freud Reader*, edited by Peter Gay, 584–89. New York: Norton, 1989.
Guerrero, Ed. *Framing Blackness: The African American Image in Film*. Philadelphia: Temple University Press, 1993.
Harper, Phillip Brian. *Are We Not Men? Masculine Anxiety and the Problem of African-American Identity*. New York: Oxford University Press, 1996.
Hauerwas, Stanley, and Romand Coles. *Christianity, Democracy, and the Radical Ordinary*. Eugene, OR: Cascade, 2008.
hooks, bell. *We Real Cool: Black Men and Masculinity*. New York: Routledge, 2004.
Jay-Z. "Song Cry." *Blueprint*. Def Jam, 2001. Compact disc.
Kim, David. *Melancholic Freedom: Agency and the Spirit of Politics*. Oxford: Oxford University Press, 2007.
Klein, Amanda. "'The Dickensian Aspect': Melodrama, Viewer Engagement, and the Socially Conscious Text." In *The Wire: Urban Decay and American Television*, edited by Tiffany Potter and C. W. Marshall, 177–89. New York: Continuum, 2009.
Levin, Tom. "For the Record: Adorno on Music in the Age of Its Technological Reproducibility." *October* 55 (1990) 23–47.
Perry, Imani. *Prophets of the Hood: Politics and Poetics in Hip Hop*. Durham: Duke University Press, 2004.
Peterson, James. "Corner-Boy Masculinity: Intersections of Inner-City Manhood." In *The Wire: Urban Decay and American Television*, edited by Tiffany Potter and C. W. Marshall, 107–21. New York: Continuum, 2009.
Van DeBurg, William L. *New Day in Babylon: The Black Power Movement and American Culture, 1965–1975*. Chicago: University of Chicago Press, 1992.
Wallace, Maurice O. *Constructing the Black Masculine: Identity and Ideality in African-American Men's Literature and Culture, 1775–1995*. Durham: Duke University Press, 2002.
Wallace, Michelle. *Black Macho and the Myth of the Superwoman*. New York: Verso, 1999.
Zuidervaart, Lambert. "Introduction." In *The Semblance of Subjectivity: Essays in Adorno's Aesthetic Theory*, edited by Tom Huhn and Lambert Zuidervaart, 1–28. Cambridge: MIT Press, 1997.

PART III
Engaging *The Wire*

9

The Ethics of Counter-Insurgency in *The Wire*

JACOB L. GOODSON

INTRODUCTION

The HBO television drama *The Wire* narrates the difficulties of reality on the streets, as well as in the political offices and on the police force, of Baltimore. I use this phrase, "the difficulties of reality,"[1] in order to stress how *The Wire* refuses to represent drug trafficking in any idealized or over-simplistic way: *The Wire* provides a realistic portrayal of the drug industry within Baltimore and emphasizes the actual on-the-ground difficulties of being caught up in neighborhoods where drugs are dealt and used. In regards to *The Wire*, the phrase "the difficulties of reality" names how our perceptions concerning this representation of reality—the housing projects and streets of Baltimore—actively and strongly resist our own conceptions of and desires

---

1. I borrow this phrase from Diamond, "The Difficulty of Reality and the Difficulty of Philosophy."

for how explainable and simple we want life to be.[2] Life is neither easy nor orderly within *The Wire*; it is difficult and unbearable.[3]

What should the conflicts between the Baltimore Police Department and drug dealers look like within their city? Oftentimes, the character dispositions or virtues that we think are necessary within times of conflict are courage and justice: courage helps us know *when* to face a criminal, and justice teaches us *how* to handle a criminal. However, according to the Christian Bishop and theologian St. Augustine of Hippo (354–430 CE), the virtue of charity works as the primary virtue within times of conflict.[4] This Augustinian emphasis on the virtue of charity clarifies a Christian understanding of how to engage in conflicts;[5] it thus provides us with a way to approach the question of how the Baltimore Police Department might handle and negotiate with the criminal drug traffickers within Baltimore who cause injury and injustice on the city's streets.[6]

Additionally, the Augustinian account of charity offers us a reason for why the Baltimore Police Department—and other concerned citizens of Baltimore—ought to care and deliberate about the problem of drug trafficking: not out of the kind of self-interest that seeks power within Baltimore's economic and political elite but out of charity for those trapped within and victimized by the horrors and tragedies of the drug industry. Charity should function as the primary motivation for going after drug dealers, and charity should be the character disposition maintained within the strategies

---

2. Cf. Tran, *Foucault and Theology*, 126: "By this difficulty, Diamond means the inexorable nature of bodied existence that resists analysis yet remains critical parts of who we are as persons."

3. For significant reflections on how the discipline of ethics ought to concern learning to "bear reality," see Hauerwas, *Approaching the End*, 154–73.

4. For St. Augustine, this means that a just war is best described in terms of exercising and promoting charity between neighbors and enemies. For instance, Country A fights Country B out of charity toward those injured or oppressed by Country B—which makes the war one of necessity and not one fought in terms of national interests or self-defense. See the selections from Augustine's writings in Holmes, *War and Christian Ethics*, 61–83.

5. Ethicist G. Scott Davis explains what the virtue of charity adds to the virtues of faith and hope within the Christian tradition: "Hope without faith is unreasonable; hope and faith without charity can become demonic" (Davis, *Warcraft and the Fragility of Virtue*, 77). Davis' explanation provides us with a reason for why the Augustinian tradition of just war reasoning emphasizes the virtue of charity within times of conflict: conflict tempts us to become "demonic" and perhaps to fall back, viciously, only on our faith and hope. In the name of faith or hope alone, Christians are tempted to give up on helping those oppressed or victimized.

6. I recognize the ambiguity of the claim that drug traffickers cause injury and injustice, and I hope to clarify how this is the case within my analysis of the individual characters.

employed by the Baltimore Police Department in relation to the players in the game of drug trafficking.[7]

For the purpose of making proper and prudential judgments on the characters and plots depicted within *The Wire*, we need a contemporary moral framework that builds from this Augustinian emphasis on charity in times of conflict. The twentieth-century Christian ethicists Paul Ramsey and Oliver O'Donovan address questions within the ethics of counter-insurgency in ways that draw upon an Augustinian account of charity.[8] Because their arguments are shaped by the Augustinian understanding of charity, I argue that O'Donovan's and Ramsey's reflections on the role of charity in the ethics of counter-insurgency provide us with the best arguments possible for understanding the justice and legitimacy of the war on drugs within the city of Baltimore—as this "war" is represented by *The Wire*.

In order to defend this argument, I address the following questions. First, is it morally proper to employ the language of "war" for thinking about the relationship between police departments and drug traffickers; how does *The Wire* provide clarity for this question? Second, are drug dealers best described as insurgents? If so, then what kind of insurgents do we find within *The Wire*? Third, how does the debate between O'Donovan and Ramsey on the ethics of counter-insurgency provide us with the best arguments possible for understanding the justice and legitimacy of the war on drugs within *The Wire*?

THE WAR ON DRUGS?

In the eleventh episode of the first season, Police Commissioner Ervin Burrell and his deputy Bill Rawls respond to the shooting of Detective Kima Greggs by ordering raids all across the city of Baltimore. The purpose of these raids does not include investigating Officer Greggs' shooter but to seize as much of the drug product as possible. Also, hurting and injuring citizens and drug dealers does not matter for Burrell and Rawls. Limitations

---

7. According to Augustine, both courage and justice can be defined in terms of the virtue of charity; see Augustine, "Catholic Way of Life and the Manichean Way of Life," 43.

8. Paul Ramsey is an American Christian ethicist who spent most of his teaching career at Princeton University; for Ramsey's explicitly Augustinian account of war, see Ramsey, *War and the Christian Conscience*. Oliver O'Donovan is a British Christian ethicist who currently teaches at the University of Edinburgh; for O'Donovan's reflections on the Augustinian understanding of charity, see O'Donovan, *Problem of Self-Love in St. Augustine*.

and rules no longer apply. Burrell's explanation is that the police must let the city know they are taking action in response to the shooting of a detective.

Working under Burrell and Rawls, Lieutenant Cedric Daniels questions the message that this strategy sends. Daniels runs a team of investigative police who are using wiretaps to follow the drug dealers. He meets with his team and tells them, against Burrell's and Rawls' order, the precise locations that they should raid. Daniels' own strategy is that the Baltimore Police Department should not march into any and every area of drug trafficking within Baltimore. Rather, they should invade only those places where there is no existing or functioning wiretap. Daniels' rationale is that raiding the places with the wiretap will hurt their long-term strategy concerning the information gained from the wiretap. Commissioner Burrell responds to Daniels' explanation of his own strategy by saying, "Cedric, we want to see dope on the table." The implication is that the wiretap is not the proper strategy because it is too demanding, ineffective, and slow; it lacks immediate results.

While Daniels is not necessarily against the notion of a "war on drugs," he consistently questions the expectations and methods of the authorities—within the Baltimore Police Department—for how this "war" is being executed. Cedric Daniels remains skeptical about Police Commissioner Burrell's order for "dope on the table" because he thinks that it displays impatience and imprudence within waging their "war" on drugs within Baltimore.

Moral reflections on the characters and the plot of *The Wire* demonstrate the need for a midway point between extremes when approaching the war on drugs within the city of Baltimore. When policy-makers and political scientists reflect on the war on drugs, we find that their claims tend to be excessive in one direction or another. What are the two extremes? At one extreme is William Bennett's defense of an "anything goes" war against drug trafficking.[9] Political theorist William Connolly names the problem with Bennett's approach to the war on drugs when he observes: "Bennett's command of the drug war resembles the relation of a blockbuster filmmaker to the film audience more than that of a policy-maker to a [concrete and]

---

9. William Bennett, the Director of National Drug Control Policy during President George H. W. Bush's term in office, strongly and unapologetically defends the language of the "war on drugs" (see Bennett et al., *Body Count*). Bennett advocates how the problem of drugs in the United States is a battle, and the battle centers on how to keep drugs away from children. According to Bennett, both the federal government and local police departments need to approach drug trafficking in terms of a war in which there are no limits and no rules, because drug dealers must be defeated and executed.

discrete problem."[10] At the other extreme are the conclusions of the political scientists Andrew Whitford and Jeff Yates. They conclude that the police and political leaders use the language of "the war on drugs for political gain."[11] While a commendable and impressive study, Whitford and Yates' book leaves us in a state of despair and hopelessness concerning the potential for a moral approach to the war on drugs.[12] The police officers on Daniels' detail, especially Jimmy McNulty and Lester Freamon, remain hopeful about engaging in the war on drugs in terms that are not completely hellish and impossible. *The Wire* illustrates that, while it has significant problems, the language and logic of the war on drugs is not necessarily a hopeless and vicious endeavor. We should neither give up on this domestic war nor increase malicious strategies and the use of violent tactics within the war on drugs. Rather, what we need is a moral approach to the war on drugs that serves as a realistic and virtuous framework for the Baltimore Police Department to respond to the drug dealers within their city.

I argue that, as a domestic war, the war on drugs is best understood in terms of a counter-insurgency effort.[13] The debate concerning how counter-insurgency ought to be achieved offers the framework required for thinking morally and realistically about the war on drugs in Baltimore. Reflecting on the war on drugs in terms of Christian approaches to counter-insurgency, where charity serves as the motivation and sustaining reason for curtailing and engaging drug traffickers, provides important corrections to the two extreme sides on the war on drugs.

ARE DRUG DEALERS INSURGENTS?

Within *The Wire*, the drug lords Avon Barksdale and Marlo Stanfield resemble traditional understandings of insurgents. Avon Barksdale thinks of himself as a soldier who maintains the rules and traditions of the game,

10. Connolly, "Drugs, the Nation, and Freelancing," 182–3.
11. Whitford and Yates, *Presidential Rhetoric and the Public Agenda*, 34.
12. According to Whitford and Yates, the war on drugs remains a social construct that has no meaning and no reality outside of the political manipulation of power. While Whitford and Yates maintain that the goal of their study is to "focus on how the president . . . move[s] the political agenda and change[s] the implementation of policy" (Whitfield and Yates, *Presidential Rhetoric and the Public Agenda*, 74), and to reserve moral and political judgment on these presidential abuses of power, they begin with the assumption and end with the conclusion that the "war on drugs" ought to be understood exclusively as a "rhetorical" tool to gain and maintain power.
13. For an insightful study on how the war on drugs is an effort of counter-insurgency, both domestically and abroad, see Felbab-Brown, *Shooting Up*.

and the game serves as shorthand for the nature and purpose of drug trafficking. For Avon, drug trafficking works as a rule-governed activity where the players in the game either excel or fail. Marlo Stanfield approaches the game in war-like terms, but he does not think that the rules and traditions of the game apply to him. Marlo is best described as a "terrorist." Stringer Bell, another drug lord on *The Wire*, complicates the typical depictions of an insurgent by making his job more like a CEO of a company than a "soldier" or a "terrorist." In this section, I attend to the habits and practices of these three characters in order to display how *The Wire* reveals that while the category of "insurgent" accurately describes drug dealers and drug lords, it cannot and does not apply univocally to them.

Avon Barksdale as Soldier

Avon Barksdale is an insurgent who understands that he is part of a violent network; however, the violence does not make the game of drug trafficking an "anything goes" activity. How does Avon understand himself as an insurgent? Political philosopher Jason Read observes that, from the very beginning of *The Wire*, "Avon is presented as a 'soldier,' as someone whose control of the drug trade is less about turning a profit than it is about controlling territory and [demanding] respect."[14] Avon understands himself as an insurgent whose primary purpose is not economic but, instead, to maintain the nature and purpose of the game. Emphasizing this point, Read remarks that for Avon, "conflict and violence are not subject to calculations that measure cost against benefits, but to a tradition that establishes the rules and conditions of respect. Conflict takes place within particular rules and traditions."[15] But how can drug deals be dictated by rules? Read answers this question clearly: "These rules provide no instrumental purpose; they do not serve the ends of profit or even dominance. The rules reveal that violence is not just a strategy, but it is constitutive of reputation, inseparable from the ends it serves."[16]

Avon Barksdale approaches the game deontologically, in the sense that the game works only because the players follow particular rules and patterns of behavior. For Avon, loyalty and respect become the highest goods. According to Read,

---

14. Read, "Stringer Bell's Lament," 128.
15. Ibid.
16. Ibid.

> Being a soldier, or a gangster, is not just about using violence to solve problems: it requires restricting that violence with specific rules in order to gain respect. [For example,] Avon is enraged when Stringer orders a hit on Omar on Sunday: "Sunday truce been there as long as the game itself" (S3/E9). In order to gain respect, to earn a name, it is necessary to maintain territory within certain respected traditions and rules. . . . For Avon the rules of the game are the very conditions for recognition, for the constitution of a reputation. . . . The conflict between Avon and Stringer is not just between different means, violence or negotiations, but between the ends those means serve, reputation [vs.] accumulation.[17]

Avon's insurgency is not based upon an ends-justify-the-means mentality. Rather, Avon recognizes that the world of drugs has its own normative logic. He wants to maintain the patterns and rationale of the game *for the sake of the game.*

Violence is a necessary part of the game, but it is neither a meaningless activity nor an empty sign. Read claims that, for Avon, "all violence is caught up in the drama of recognition; it is visible and overt, functioning as a sign as much as the simple elimination of an adversary."[18] Read contrasts Avon from Stringer on how they differ in their approaches to the use of violence: "Stringer utilizes a different mode of violence . . . [where it] is transformed from an activity to what is at once a strategy and a symbol, to a way of dealing with the risks of doing business."[19] While violence does eliminate the adversary, for Avon, it also remains significant as a necessary feature of the game. Killing others should never cease as a practice within the game because that would change the nature and purpose of drug trafficking. The world of drugs is a type of insurgency where both drug dealers, who stray from the rules of the game, and police officers, who challenge the normal functions of the game, must be eliminated. Neither of these groups should be killed arbitrarily but with purpose and reason, as well as within a set of rules—as in refraining from killing on Sundays. As a soldier, Avon demands loyalty from other players in the game; he demands respect from the Baltimore Police Department. He must be dealt with as a soldier, not as a terrorist. Avon reciprocates this respectfulness, which is why he does not resist arrest when "he's got." However, he does not "cooperate" with the police through giving them information. This is part of Avon's self-understanding

17. Ibid., 129–30.
18. Ibid., 131.
19. Ibid.

as a soldier: like a POW in war does not give information to the enemy, Avon refuses to answer the questions asked of him by Officers Bunk and McNulty. Avon consistently and deliberately remains a soldier and a warrior within *The Wire*.

Stringer Bell's Moral Intentions

In "The Detail,"[20] Officer McNulty makes the observation: "Everything else in this country gets sold without people shooting each other behind it."[21] Stringer Bell's life becomes an attempt to practice this observation. In this sense, Stringer's intentions for the game can be described as "moral." *The Wire* portrays Stringer as the character who hopes to legitimize the world of drugs by turning it into a "world of legal business."[22] While "Stringer's story reveals . . . the unstable nature of the border that separates the drug trade from the world of legitimate business," according to Read, it ultimately displays "the way in which the relationship between the two [the drug trade and the world of legitimate business] is sustained as much by narratives and fictions as by their actual material relations."[23] Stringer finds himself caught up within the hierarchies of the game, and he attempts to make Baltimore drug transactions less of a concern for the Baltimore Police Department.

In order to accomplish this task, Stringer employs three strategies. First, Stringer works on the "inside" of the drug industry. He hopes to correct the practices of drug dealers from his inside position. Stringer recognizes the bad habits and unnecessary practices of violence that are part of Baltimore drug dealing. He wants to correct both the bad habits and the unnecessary practices of violence, and he tries to make his case from inside the logic and rationale of the game itself. In relation to Avon Barksdale, Stringer does not think that violence is a necessary part of the game; the game can be the game without the killing.[24] Stringer thinks that once the killing ceases, then the game will become a legitimate business.

The second strategy that Stringer employs is to seek sources and resources outside of the drug industry to repair the unnecessary vices and

---

20. S1/E2.

21. See Read, "Stringer Bell's Lament," 125.

22. Ibid., 122. Read observes that *The Wire* presents Stringer "as the character most enamored of the legitimate world of business, taking economics classes at community college and applying the lessons to the world of the drug trade."

23. Ibid., 123.

24. Stringer does not want all killing to cease, but he does want to limit the killing to those who represent a clear and present danger to drug transactions. For instance, Stringer thinks that killing Omar Little is justified.

practices of violence within the drug trade.²⁵ In particular, he draws from the principles of free market economics.²⁶ Stringer prioritizes economic gain over the virtue of loyalty. The classical statement on the virtue of loyalty comes from the American philosopher Josiah Royce's *The Philosophy of Loyalty*, where he defines loyalty as a virtue that displays a "willing and practical and thoroughgoing devotion of a person to a cause."²⁷ Royce emphasizes that the object of loyalty must be an objective cause, which he contrasts from the subjectivity of the self. However, the causes that call for absolute loyalty must be good and avoid evil or else they no longer require our loyalty. How does this apply to *The Wire*? Avon Barksdale expects Stringer Bell's loyalty, for the sake of loyalty and for the sake of the game, but Stringer thinks that Avon's commitment to violence is irrational and unnecessary. In Royce's terms, Stringer makes the moral judgment that Avon's "cause" involves evil; therefore, it no longer requires his loyalty. Stringer thinks it makes more business sense to partner with a rival, Proposition Joe, for the sake of financial success. Continuing gang rivalries risks profit. Rather than rely on internal practices and tactics of drug trafficking, he pulls from outside economic models in order to increase profit and decrease violence. All of this comes at the expense of loyalty, both to Avon and to the rules of the game, because he has deemed that loyalty predatory or vicious.

While Stringer does not give up on the virtues altogether, he exercises a different set of virtues than Avon expects him to have. Stringer cultivates and displays the virtues of pride and self-preservation.²⁸ There are two instances within *The Wire* where we see Stringer embodying the virtues of pride and self-preservation. Stringer justifies his "anything goes" mentality in terms of self-preservation. He attempts to set Brother Mouzone and Omar Little against each other by telling Omar Little that Brother Mouzone is responsible for his (Omar's) boyfriend's death. For Stringer, this is not a "lie" but only an act of self-preservation against Avon Barksdale and Brother Mouzone. Avon hired Brother Mouzone to take out Stringer, and Stringer acts for the purpose of self-preservation. Stringer believes that self-preservation also helps the larger game, because he brings legitimacy to the game whereas Avon remains too "gangster."

---

25. For instance, *The Wire* depicts Stringer reading and studying Adam Smith's *The Wealth of Nations*.

26. See Read, "Stringer Bell's Lament," 129.

27. Royce, *Philosophy of Loyalty*, 117–8.

28. For the classical statement on how the virtues of pride and self-preservation function as cardinal virtues, see Spinoza, *Ethics*, part IV.

Significantly, Stringer's death—which ironically comes at the hands of Omar Little and Brother Mouzone—displays Stringer's appropriate or moderate levels of pride.[29] Stringer's final conversation goes like this:

> Stringer Bell: I ain't strapped. [Long pause.] Look man, I ain't involved. I ain't involved in that gangster bullshit no more. [Long pause.] What do ya'll niggas want, man. Money? Is that it?!? [Long pause, with heavy breathing.] 'Cause if it is, man, I could be a better friend to y'all alive.
>
> Omar Little: You still don't get it, do you? This ain't about your money, bro. Your boy gave you up. That's right. And we didn't have to torch his ass neither.
>
> [Very long pause.]
>
> Stringer Bell: Well, it seems like I can't say nothin' to change y'all minds. Well, get on with it motherfu . . .[30]

Stringer displays pride in overcoming "that gangster bullshit." This is a real accomplishment in his mind, and he thinks it provides a legitimate reason for them to refrain from killing him. He also displays pride in his wealth, to the point of offering it as a peace settlement. After hearing from Omar that Avon ordered the hit, Stringer admits his limitations. This is not quite humility, but it shows that Stringer recognizes his place within the game. Earlier in *The Wire*, Stringer displayed excessive pride by thinking that he stands above the rules by ordering a hit on Omar on a Sunday. Now, he understands that he is part of the game and hence determined by the rules of the game.

Third, Stringer thinks that his deliberate attempts at reforming the Baltimore drug scene should make him—and eventually the entire drug organization—exempt from police hostility and investigation. *Stringer represents either a "virtuous" insurgent or a drug trafficker who is not an actual insurgent.* If the latter, which seems to reflect Stringer's deepest intentions, then Stringer's character seeks to become part of the wealthy elite of Baltimore. He desires no resemblance of a gangster, an insurgent, but only to be a 'normal' and regular businessman. He wants to be known by making his money, not from selling drugs, but from profitable investments that he makes with the money he earned from drug trafficking. In Stringer's mind, this requires a different response to him, as well as an alternative strategy,

---

29. When Spinoza defends pride as virtue, his discussion on pride resembles Aristotle's reflections upon the virtue of temperance: the virtue of pride ought to find the mean between the vice of humility and having an unreasonable amount of pride.

30. "Middle Ground," S3/E11.

from the Baltimore Police Department in their role as counter-insurgents. We see this when McNulty comes into Stringer's copy shop. Stringer expects McNulty to perceive him as a legitimate business owner, and McNulty displays obvious confusion within this situation. Stringer's body language and his presence relay to McNulty: "I am not a gangster. I own a copy shop. How can I help you as my customer? You should not think that you are a police officer investigating me. You are a consumer in my store, and you are not a counter-insurgent participating in a war on drugs against *me*." Stringer seeks to overcome his insurgent status and be perceived as a CEO running multiple corporations, some legal and some illegal.

Marlo Stanfield as Terrorist

Marlo Stanfield is a terrorist. He does not discriminate in whom he kills, and he does not exercise proportionality in how people are killed. Stringer Bell failed to display proportionality in killing Omar Little's boyfriend, Brandon, but Stringer does not habituate violating proportionality in how he kills others. Marlo makes this violation the norm, and he has hired hands do the vicious work.

His primary hired hands are named Chris and Snoop, and they kill anyone on Marlo's command. Chris and Snoop excel at killing. However, like Thomas Aquinas' claims that a thief's actions might resemble courage but actually lack courage because his actions lack charity toward the farmer that the thief steals from, Chris' and Snoop's skills for killing should not be described as excellent. Chris and Snoop are morally reprehensible characters who are best understood more as beast-like than as human. But they are not exclusively responsible for the blood that they accumulate on their hands. Marlo is equally responsible, and his actions and dispositions are abhorrent and troubling. Whether or not Marlo is a product of an overzealous war on drugs in America does not make Marlo any less blameworthy and culpable.

One storyline, in particular, illustrates this depiction of Marlo. Bodie Broadus was one of the more complex and interesting drug trafficking characters. Unquestionably loyal to Avon Barksdale, Bodie found himself at odds with Marlo and his people. However, Bodie stayed strong and manned his corner effectively and without trouble. In Season 4, Bodie was spotted by one of Marlo's men, Monk, getting into Detective McNulty's vehicle. McNulty wanted Bodie to serve as an informant for the Baltimore Police Department's developing case against Marlo, but Bodie refused. Without knowing the conversation between Bodie and McNulty, Monk informed Marlo and

Chris (Marlo's primary hitman) that Bodie was interacting with McNulty. Upon hearing from Monk, Chris reminds Marlo, "We ain't sure it's that," referencing the fact of their uncertainty in regards to what Bodie said—or did not say—to Detective McNulty. Marlo responds to Chris, "What, you want to let him go? Risk it? Nah, send him a message." By "send him a message," Marlo means kill him. Thus Marlo orders Bodie's death, regardless of what Bodie actually did. While Bodie is manning his corner and complaining about the lack of customers, Chris and Snoop strategically approach him in the dark. Two other drug dealers, Poot and Spider, are with Bodie. After seeing Chris and Snoop in the shadows, Poot begs Bodie to find cover. Bodie refuses Poot's advice, retrieves a gun from under a car on his corner, and begins to fire in Chris' and Snoop's direction. While Bodie unloads his bullets into the night air, another one of Marlo's men called O'Dog comes from behind and shoots Bodie point-blank in the back of head. Although Bodie is already dead and lying in his own blood on the sidewalk, O'Dog shoots him once again in the head. O'Dog's decision to shoot Bodie postmortem reflects the vicious habits started and sustained by Marlo.

Later on, McNulty pulls up to Poot's corner in his squad car and pretends to put Poot under arrest. McNulty, however, only wants information about Bodie's death.

> McNulty: Sorry about, Bodie. I ain't jacking you up, I'm trying to do right for your boy. Who dropped him?
>
> Poot: Y'all did. They took him out because he was talkin' to y'all. Word is they seen him down at police with central booking. So cuff me, or take my ass off this corner before you do me the same.[31]

Poot does not tell McNulty that O'Dog killed Bodie; instead, Poot blames McNulty for Bodie's death. Poot does not take this opportunity to "do right" for his friend, Bodie, by putting blame on Marlo and his people. Rather, Poot places all of the responsibility on McNulty for talking with Bodie. No matter what McNulty and Bodie talked about, McNulty put Bodie in harm's way simply based on appearances. Now, McNulty is doing the same to Poot. Poot recognizes Marlo's capabilities and tendencies, and Marlo's terrorism makes Poot distrust the police even more than usual.

By calling Marlo a terrorist, therefore, I mean that he perpetuates fear by killing "symbolic victims" for instrumental purposes. Alex P. Schmid and A. J. Jongman define terrorism in these terms:

---

31. "Final Grades," S4/E13.

> Terrorism is a method of combat in which random or symbolic victims serve as an instrumental *target of violence*. These instrumental victims share group or class characteristics which form the basis for their selection for victimization. Through previous use of violence or the credible threat of violence other members of that group or class are put in a *state of chronic fear (terror)*. This group, or class, whose members' sense of security is purposefully undermined, is the *target of terror*. The victimization of the target of violence is considered extranormal by most observers from the witnessing audience on the basis of its . . . disregard for rules of combat accepted in conventional warfare. The norm violation creates an attentive audience beyond the target of terror; sectors of this audience might in turn form the main object of manipulation. The purpose of this indirect method of combat is . . . to immobilize the target of terror in order to produce disorientation and/or compliance.[32]

Marlo's character fits this definition of a terrorist. Recognizing this aspect of Marlo's role within *The Wire* raises questions concerning how drug traffickers might represent different versions of insurgency. While not all drug dealers are terrorists, what kind of response is required to those who terrorize their own people as well as others?

COUNTER-INSURGENCY AND THE WAR ON DRUGS

Avon Barksdale is a self-described "soldier" and "warrior." These terms represent the traditional understanding of an insurgent. Stringer Bell is an insurgent who makes it look like he is not an insurgent. Marlo Stanfield is an insurgent who is a terrorist. If the police are counter-insurgents, then how should they respond to these three different kinds of insurgents? Do all three require the same counter-insurgency effort and response, or do their differences in habit and pattern necessitate making careful moral distinctions? What would such distinctions look like?

Within the discipline of Christian ethics, the debate on counter-insurgency focuses on the just war principles of discrimination and proportionality. For Oliver O'Donovan and Paul Ramsey, these principles result from the role of charity within the ethics of warfare. Ramsey emphasizes how counter-insurgency needs to maintain the principle of proportionality; O'Donovan argues for the principle of discrimination within efforts of counter-insurgency. Neither O'Donovan nor Ramsey supports an "all-out"

32. Schmid and Jongman, *Political Terrorism*, 1–2.

war against insurgency; counter-insurgency remains a rule-governed activity. However, a significant difference between their approaches concerns the question of where blame lies for the brutalities and tragedies that occur within insurgency/counter-insurgency conflicts. In Augustinian terms, *Ramsey finds that following the principle of proportionality helps us direct the virtue of charity toward the insurgents; non-combatants deserve charity, too, but this is found mostly in defeating the insurgents. For O'Donovan, the principle of discrimination displays charity toward the citizens who are victims of the violence of the insurgency; the principle of proportionality exhibits charity toward the insurgents.*

Because of its emphasis on the virtue of charity, as well as the principles that follow,[33] the debate on counter-insurgency provides a significant correction (*a*) to those who defend the language of the war of drugs and (*b*) to those who think that the language and logic of the war of drugs is merely a social construct based on manipulation and a political abuse of power. My claim is that the debate on counter-insurgency clarifies our language concerning the war on drugs, specifically what type of "war" is depicted within Baltimore. In this final section, I present and examine Ramsey's and O'Donovan's arguments concerning counter-insurgency and suggest ways in which their reflections apply to characters and storylines within *The Wire*. In particular: I demonstrate how Ramsey's approach to the ethics of counter-insurgency makes Stringer Bell's character the most immoral and problematic insurgent within Baltimore's war on drugs, and I illustrate how O'Donovan's moral reasoning concerning counter-insurgency renders Marlo Stanfield's character the most dangerous and immoral insurgent within Baltimore's war on drugs.

Paul Ramsey and the Ethics of Counter-Insurgency

In his reflections on the ethics of counter-insurgency, Paul Ramsey forwards three arguments: first, he emphasizes the principle of proportionality within counter-insurgency efforts; second, he downplays the principle of discrimination within counter-insurgency efforts; and third, he places blame for

---

33. I concur with Hilary Putnam's argument that principles and virtues do not necessarily conflict within moral reasoning; see Putnam, "Taking Rules Seriously," 193–200. On how Putnam's argument relates to methodological questions within Christian ethics, see Porter, *Moral Action and Christian Ethics*, 41–83. I understand Paul Ramsey's work as exemplary, within the discipline of Christian ethics, because he properly negotiates deontological and virtue-centered reasoning; currently, I am spelling this out in an essay tentatively entitled, "Idealism, Indeterminacy, and Virtue in Paul Ramsey's Moral Reasoning."

injustice and vice on the insurgents themselves, and not on the counter-insurgents (if they follow the principle of proportionality). I stay close to Ramsey's arguments in his essay "How Shall Counter-Insurgency War Be Conducted Justly?" and use them to suggest ways in which they can be applied to the characters and plot of *The Wire*—especially Stringer Bell's story.

Paul Ramsey begins his reflections on counter-insurgency by asking, "How is it possible . . . to mount an *effective* counter-insurgency war, and to deliver such retribution upon it that future insurgency will be deterred, and thus the precarious, politically-embodied justice in the world be given some protection?"[34] He then argues that this is, in fact, the wrong question to ask. But what is the right question to ask concerning the ethics of counter-insurgency? Ramsey claims that the correct question is, "How is it possible, if indeed it is possible, to mount a *morally acceptable* counter-insurgency operation?"[35] The difference between these questions marks the significant shift from thinking that counter-insurgency ought to be "effective" in relation to insurgency to thinking of counter-insurgency in terms of what is "morally acceptable." For Ramsey, being "effective" is not the proper goal for counter-insurgent forces; rather, maintaining moral acceptability ought to be the goal for counter-insurgent forces. How should this be achieved?

Ramsey recognizes "two ingredients in the moral economy governing the use of force: discrimination and proportion." Discrimination concerns non-combatant immunity: "Non-combatant immunity assesses the action itself with no prudential reference yet to the totality of the consequences." Proportionality governs how we control damage done within acts of conflict and war: "the principle of proportion takes all the effects for the first time into account." According to Ramsey, since actions within war have "multiple consequences, some of which are evil," then *morally acceptable* actions "must pass both tests before it should ever be actually done. Since prudence is a virtue, to do deliberately an imprudent or disproportionate evil is vicious."[36] Traditionally, therefore, both principles of discrimination and proportion serve as the checks against attacks on and within civilian populations. However, Ramsey claims that when considering responses to insurgency, the military "deliberately strikes the civil population." Such a strike is not necessarily vicious. The burden, within Ramsey's essay becomes, *how can deliberate strikes against civilian populations be considered morally acceptable acts within counter-insurgency?*

---

34. Ramsey, "How Shall Counter-Insurgency War Be Conducted Justly?" 428.
35. Ibid.
36. Ibid., 431.

In order to address this question, Ramsey encourages us to "focus attention upon what happens when insurgency resorts to arms." What happens when insurgency opts for violence? Ramsey observes:

> The fact that insurgency wins by many other appeals; and resorts to terror, when it does, only in the form of *selective* terror, may be sufficient to qualify it under the requirement that cost-effects be wisely proportioned to what are believed to be good-effects. But consequences are not the only test. There is also the principle of discrimination, and this cannot justify selecting only a comparatively few among the non-combatant population to be made the direct object of attack.[37]

This is Ramsey's description of insurgency resorting to violence. At this point in his essay, Ramsey seemingly promotes the principle of discrimination. To follow this principle means that we lose the ability of directly attacking any non-combatants.

While this point deserves our attention, according to Ramsey, it is not the chief question concerning the ethics of counter-insurgency. Rather,

> The chief question . . . concerning any *counter*-insurgency operation is whether it can be effective without adopting a military strategy that is, like that of insurgency, morally intolerable. Can insurgency be countered only by strikes deliberately directed upon the civil population, or select portions of it, as a means of getting at the insurgency forces? Is it possible successfully to oppose these revolutionary wars without joining them in direct attacks upon the very people we are undertaking to protect? Are insurgency and counter-insurgency *both* bound to be warfare over people as a means of getting at the other forces?[38]

This passage from Ramsey's essay is quite telling about Ramsey's own assumptions and tendencies within this debate. There are three features worthy of consideration. First, insurgency is always "morally intolerable." Second, the primary task of counter-insurgency is not to become "morally intolerable" like the insurgency. The third feature names a specific implication that Ramsey draws from the first two: insurgency is bound to use people as means; *can counter-insurgency also use people as means for the purpose of protecting those who are being used as means by the insurgency?*[39] Perhaps

37. Ibid., 432.
38. Ibid., 433.
39. Ramsey asks this question thus: "Can counter-insurgency abide by the distinction between legitimate and illegitimate military objectives while insurgency deliberately does not?" (ibid.).

surprisingly, Ramsey answers these questions by claiming that counter-insurgency may use citizens victimized by insurgency, non-combatants, as a means in order to secure their own protection. Why is this morally acceptable?

It is not morally acceptable based upon an "anything goes" moral reasoning within counter-insurgency. Concerning counter-insurgency, Ramsey remarks that if "an act of war is *malum in se* [evil in itself], if selective terror is intrinsically wrong conduct, then the doing of such an evil by one side can never justify the doing of the same evil by the other side in return."[40] Returning evil for evil is never morally acceptable, for Ramsey.[41] Ramsey's argument for why counter-insurgents may use non-combatants as a means must be understood in relation to his conviction that we should never return evil for evil.

Why is it morally acceptable to use non-combatants as a means when fighting insurgents? Our answer to this question depends upon where we place the italics within the phrase "counter-insurgency." Ramsey writes,

> I believe that there can be and should be a counter-*insurgency* that meets the tests of just conduct in war, while insurgency does not . . . The meaning of a morally acceptable "counter-*insurgency*" operation is suggested by where [we] place the italics . . . This entails, of course, that counter-insurgency should primarily be directed to defeating insurgency by political and economic means, since that is the challenge thrown down by insurgency and the only way finally to come to grips with it. But we are prescinding from that in order to concentrate attention on the use of armed force that is needed in extension and in defense of even the best political purposes. Counter-insurgency as a military operation can and should make the insurgent forces the primary object of attack. That it *should* do so is clear . . . That it *can* do so becomes clear if only we have in mind a correct understanding of the meaning of the principle of discrimination as we to seek to apply it to the admittedly difficult situation and turmoil . . . created by insurgency.[42]

If we emphasize *counter*-insurgency, then we will tend to view the goal of counter-insurgency in terms not of defeat but appeasement and reaction. If we think of counter-insurgency simply as *countering* the insurgency, based

---

40. Ibid., 434.
41. See Ramsey, "Incommensurability and Indeterminacy," 69–144.
42. Ramsey, "How Shall Counter-Insurgency War Be Conducted Justly?" 434.

on their actions and deliberations, then we will only achieve countering them but never defeating them.

The goal within counter-insurgency ought to be defeating the insurgency, for the sake of protecting the non-combatants whose lives the insurgents put at risk. For the sake of remembering the task of counter-insurgency, we ought to emphasize counter-*insurgency* where the insurgency remains "the primary object of attack." What is the task of counter-insurgency? *The task of counter-insurgency concerns defeating, not merely countering, insurgency.* Insurgency challenges the military, and this challenge ought to be defeated "by political and economic means."

Within the previous passage, Ramsey mentions that "a correct understanding of the meaning of the principle of discrimination" serves to clarify how counter-insurgency *can* "make the insurgent forces the primary object of attack." The principle of discrimination limits what counter-insurgency can do, but what do these limitations actually involve? According to Ramsey,

> the decision of the insurgents to conduct war by selective terror results in a situation in which a whole area is inhabited mainly by "combatants" in the ethically and politically relevant sense that a great number of the people *are* from consent of from constraint the bearers of the force to be repressed ... The *insurgents themselves* have enlarged the target it is legitimate for counter-insurgents to attack, so far as the principle of discrimination is concerned; and it is therefore mainly the principle of proportion that limits what should be done to oppose them. Since in the nature of insurgency the line between combatant and non-combatant runs right through a great number of the able-bodied people in a given area ... above, say, ten years of age, and since anyone may cross over this line in either direction by the hour, it is not the business of any moralist to tell the soldiers and military commanders who are attempting to mount an effective counter-insurgency operation that this cannot be done in a morally acceptable way because under these circumstances they have no legitimate military target. In devising a military riposte, it will not be those who are directing the counter-insurgency who illicitly enlarged the target and chose to fight the war indiscriminately. Instead the tragedy is that they *have* an enlarged legitimate target because of the decision of the insurgency to fight the war by means of peasants.[43]

How does counter-insurgency defeat insurgency justly, in a morally acceptable way? According to Ramsey, they follow the principle of

---

43. Ibid., 435.

proportionality but not necessarily the principle of discrimination. How does this approach maintain the strict demands for morality within warfare, which remains a mark of Ramsey's reflections on the ethics of warfare? Because the insurgents are the ones who make discrimination difficult, if not impossible, by committing acts of "selective terror" in public areas. They enlarge the military targets. Insurgency makes non-combatants potential combatants, which means that discriminating between combatants and non-combatants becomes too demanding to accomplish. If the goal of counter-insurgency is to defeat insurgency and not simply to "counter" it, then discrimination unrealistically and unreasonably limits efforts of counter-*insurgency*.

However, Ramsey does not completely dismiss the principle of discrimination. While "the line between combatant and non-combatant runs right through a great number of the able-bodied people in a given area,"[44] anyone under the age of 10 years old (or around there) maintains their non-combatant status. Counter-insurgency must discriminate in terms of age, according to Ramsey. This means that, within *The Wire*, Marlo's youngest hired hand Michael makes the right decision as an insurgent when he moves his little brother, Bug, out of the housing projects and into his Aunt's house in the suburbs. Michael may have done this too late, in fact, because he waits until after Snoop's death to take Bug away from the housing projects. Ultimately, insurgency broadens the military target; with this enlarged target, discrimination loses its primacy and significance concerning the moral acceptability for counter-insurgency.

For our purposes, Ramsey's final point is that responsibility for injustice and viciousness is primarily on the efforts of insurgency. *Counter-insurgency becomes morally responsible if and only if the counter-insurgents violate the principle of proportionality.* For Ramsey, insurgency is morally blameworthy for the deaths of non-combatants.

> Also it is the insurgency and not the counter-insurgency that has enlarged the area of civilian death and damage that is legitimately collateral . . . In other words, again it is proportion and not discrimination which counter-insurgency is in peril of violating. . . . It is therefore the shape of insurgency warfare that defines the contours of the legitimate combatant destruction with its associated civil damage that it may be just to exact in order to oppose it, subject to the limits of proportionately lesser evil. . . . [T]he just-war theory establishes the limits and tests that should surround justified resorts to arms in a world where

44. Ibid.

there is yet no peace and many new wars, in order to insure that the precarious justice politically embodied in this world can be preserved and not left defenseless in the face of selective or non-selective terror.[45]

The function of counter-insurgency involves countering the insurgency as well as defeating insurgency. Counter-insurgency ensures "that the precarious justice politically embodied in this world can be preserved and not left defenseless in the face of selective or non-selective terror."[46] There are limits that counter-insurgency must maintain, in order to sustain moral acceptability and refrain from the immoral agents that insurgency necessarily fosters, and these limits are provided through the principle of proportionality.

In relation to the characters and plot of *The Wire*, the implication of Ramsey's position is that Avon Barksdale, Stringer Bell, and Marlo Stanfield all should be held primarily responsible for the injustices that occur within the "game" of drugs. I take this implication to be uncontroversial. The more controversial element, resulting from the application of Ramsey's moral reasoning to *The Wire*, is found in the implication concerning Stringer Bell's character: the *more* that Stringer's character becomes integrated into "normal life" within Baltimore the *less* the police are bound to the principle of discrimination. Why? Because Stringer's attempt to change drug trafficking into a capitalistic business venture, that follows the rules of corporations and not the rules of the street, makes it harder to distinguish between combatants and non-combatants. Stringer's actions and motivations enlarge the target. Take, for instance, the employee in Stringer's copy shop. When Detective McNulty goes into the copy shop, and Stringer's employee greets him, should McNulty see that employee as a clerk in a retail store who honestly wants to serve McNulty as a consumer? Or should McNulty see Stringer's employee as a criminal insurgent who might be a potential threat to McNulty? The more difficult that it becomes to distinguish between combatant and non-combatant, the more killing and violence might occur. This killing and violence does not violate the grounds of moral acceptability. If it does violate the standards of moral acceptability, then that responsibility rests on the viciousness of Stringer Bell and his cohorts.[47] Not following the

---

45. Ibid., 436.

46. Ibid.

47. Through personal correspondence, Andrea Gregory writes: "Seems ironic: Stringer's the one trying to make things a safer place in the world of drug dealing, but in fact he is responsible for enlarging the field and putting the most people into harm's way" (personal correspondence with the author on June 5, 2012).

principle of proportionality is all that infringes upon the moral acceptability of counter-insurgency.

The Baltimore Police Department ought to follow the principle of proportionality by not over-stepping the bounds of *what* they use as tactics—not *who* they use within their strategies. From a Ramseyan perspective, it is immoral to blow up all of the housing projects within Baltimore in order to "send a message" to the insurgent criminals. However, if there are known insurgent criminals within one housing project who actively disrupt order within Baltimore and consistently cause injustice as a result of their drug trafficking, then it is morally acceptable to bomb or destroy that particular housing project. That housing project becomes a military target, on Ramseyan terms. If non-combatants die, then the insurgent criminals are responsible for their deaths—not the Baltimore Police Department.

Oliver O'Donovan and the Ethics of Counter-Insurgency

In response to Paul Ramsey, Oliver O'Donovan addresses the questions of *if*, and *how*, the principle of discrimination might be maintained within counter-insurgency warfare. He claims that the "first moral question that arises from this practice is how counter-insurgency force can operate effectively while maintaining a respect for discrimination which insurgency does not share."[48] In question form, "can the conduct of counter-insurgency be conducted in such a way as to persuade insurgents to abide by the principle of discrimination?"[49] Within his chapter on counter-insurgency, O'Donovan (1) emphasizes the principle of discrimination, (2) distinguishes between "a gang of criminals," "an insurgent army," and "terrorists," and (3) requires counter-insurgents to maintain responsibility and virtue in relation to criminal and military insurgency efforts.

Concerning the principle of discrimination, O'Donovan reasons that the difference between insurgency and counter-insurgency is the following: insurgency may or may not discriminate between combatants and non-combatants; counter-insurgency *must* discriminate between combatants and non-combatants. If counter-insurgency fails in this requirement, then it becomes impossible to distinguish morally between insurgency and counter-insurgency. In other words, O'Donovan seeks to define the differences between insurgency and counter-insurgency in terms of *who maintains the principle of discrimination*. A police or military force who counters insurgency becomes another form of insurgency, or an illegitimate/immoral

48. O'Donovan, *Just War Revisited*, 64.
49. Ibid.

counter-insurgency, if they fail to discriminate between combatants and non-combatants. The principle of discrimination provides the grounds for demarcating between insurgency attacks and counter-insurgency efforts.

O'Donovan also distinguishes between types of insurgency: criminals, insurgent militias, and terrorists. Counter-insurgency must account for the differences between these types of insurgency, or we risk reducing the purpose of counter-insurgency to one end (like mere defeat). O'Donovan describes the different types in these terms:

> The essential difference between a gang of criminals and an insurgent army is simply that the latter can act upon a wider supportive community, in relation to which it occupies something of a representative role. Where such a community exists, and the inter-communal enmity is woven into the fabric of society, it does no good at all to ignore the fact, and to pretend that it is not civil strife but merely criminality that has to be overcome.[50]

According to O'Donovan, countering "civil strife" requires different skills and strategies than countering "criminality." Counter-insurgency efforts need to distinguish between these two in their engagements with insurgency. For instance,

> In insurgency and counter-insurgency war . . . the powers of death and the power of restraint are separated. The insurgent militia, if it employs guerilla tactics, has a virtual monopoly of the power to kill, for it is not often that an active unit will get squarely within its opponents' sights; while counter-insurgency, in countries where the criminal law has renounced the death penalty for murder, is largely dependent upon arrest and imprisonment.[51]

Countering insurgent militias is a more difficult task because they work with no limits in terms of killing and the threat to kill. Maintaining discrimination in regards to non-combatants, counter-insurgency efforts might involve killing combatants participating in an insurgent militia. O'Donovan rightly observes that the failure to distinguish between these two becomes "one of the unsatisfactory features of counter-revolutionary strategies in liberal societies. *The very disequilibrium may tempt security forces to resort to murder rather than entrust their adversaries to the over-tender care of the criminal justice system.*"[52]

50. Ibid., 73.
51. Ibid.
52. Ibid., 74.

Insurgency involving criminality does not require killing those who participate within the "gang of criminals" but arresting, imprisoning, and trying them. In this sense, O'Donovan provides a helpful moral framework for thinking about what kind of counter-insurgency efforts ought to be cultivated and maintained within the Baltimore Police Department. When Avon Barksdale and Stringer Bell are in charge of the drug world within Baltimore they ought to be treated as a "gang of criminals" who need to be arrested and imprisoned. The tactics used to arrest them should follow the principles of discrimination and proportionality. However, Marlo Stanfield's character presents a different case:

> The strategy of penetrating the civil population is already different from 'terrorism.' *The terrorist makes his point by slaughtering the innocent intentionally; the insurgent makes his by forcing his opponent to slaughter the innocent unintentionally.* Insurgents may also be terrorists in fact; in the public mind . . . they are so almost by definition. Yet the difference is not to be dismissed lightly; every step towards restraint gains some ground for the civilising of armed conflict. To the extent that insurgents desist from immediate acts of terror, they display a higher level of respect for the demands of justice, even if their exploitation of the civil population as hostages fails to display respect at a very high level.[53]

Arresting Marlo Stanfield might not be sufficient, on O'Donovan's terms. Within *The Wire*, Marlo is arrested yet released because of a lack of evidence against him. His extended gun hand, Chris, takes the fall and serves the prison sentence for Marlo. After Marlo is released, he attempts to find his way within the wealthiest members of society in Baltimore. Stringer Bell wanted this crowd to be his circle of friends, but Marlo has a different reaction. Marlo is not a businessman; he is a gangster. But Marlo is not the kind of gangster that Avon Barksdale is; Marlo does not follow the rules of the game. Marlo is a terrorist who knows no limits when it comes to "slaughtering the innocent," both inside and outside the world of drugs.

To handle Marlo as a terrorist requires the principles of discrimination and proportionality. On O'Donovan's terms, the Baltimore Police Department is justified in killing Marlo, but only with proper proportionality: Marlo's body should be neither annihilated through excessive use of explosives nor viciously mutilated. His death should be clean, deliberate, and quick—perhaps the result of a sniper's bullet. Additionally, non-combatants should be neither injured nor killed in relation to Marlo's death. Within

---

53. Ibid., 64–65; emphasis added.

O'Donovan's moral framework concerning counter-insurgency, if the principle of discrimination is violated by the counter-insurgency then it is the counter-insurgents themselves who are morally responsible for the deaths of the non-combatants—not the group of insurgents, not the individual terrorist.

Within O'Donovan's moral reasoning, counter-insurgency must maintain responsibility and virtue within their efforts toward limiting and defeating insurgency. The sole purpose of counter-insurgency, according to Ramsey, involves defeating the insurgency. For O'Donovan, however, counter-insurgency remains morally distinguishable from insurgency only when it exercises and sustains the principles of discrimination and proportionality within the insurgent conflict. *Both the insurgency and the citizens, who are victims of the insurgency, are the objects of charity.* Ramsey also thinks that counter-insurgents ought to maintain responsibility and virtue, but only in terms of proportionality, not discrimination.

If we adopt O'Donovan's approach to counter-insurgency, then we should recognize that the Baltimore Police Department does not display a moral counter-insurgency effort in relation to the insurgent criminals within Baltimore's drug world. However, if we employ Ramsey's reflections on counter-insurgency, then we can make the judgment that at times the Baltimore Police Department displays a moral counter-insurgency effort in relation to the insurgent criminals within Baltimore.[54]

CONCLUSION

This debate concerning the ethics of counter-insurgency provides the most helpful framework for making sense of the language and logic concerning "the war on drugs," because it helps us answer the following questions: What kind of war is it? It is a war between a criminal insurgency and a counter-insurgency comprised mostly of police officers. If it is a war, then how can the war be fought justly? According to Ramsey, counter-insurgency war is fought justly when the principle of proportionality is maintained. For O'Donovan, counter-insurgency war is executed justly when both principles of discrimination and proportionality are displayed and sustained throughout the conflict. What is the purpose of the war on drugs, as a war of counter-insurgency? Building from Ramsey's moral reasoning, the purpose of the war on drugs is to defeat the drug traffickers who bring

---

54. In terms of character analysis and moral judgment: on Ramsey's logic, Stringer Bell is the most problematic character; on O'Donovan's logic, Marlo Stanfield is the most problematic character.

about disorder within their city and cause injustices for those living in the neighborhoods where drug trafficking occurs. The logic of O'Donovan's approach to counter-insurgency, however, helps us see that the purpose of the war of drugs ought to entail police departments acting virtuously and taking responsibility in relation to the irresponsibility and viciousness of the drug traffickers. O'Donovan makes the further claim that counter-insurgency must model the virtues with the *hope* that the insurgency also will exercise the principles of discrimination and proportionality. Resulting from O'Donovan's approach, the question becomes, what kind of insurgents are the drug traffickers? Knowing precisely what to do, within the war on drugs, depends on the kind of insurgents the drug traffickers are: criminals, militants, or terrorists? Stringer Bell is best described as a criminal; Avon Barksdale as a militant; and Marlo as a terrorist. If they are criminals and/or militia (like Avon and Stringer), then the police ought to arrest, imprison, and try them fairly and justly—which entails not tampering with the evidence or the witnesses, as well as protecting the witnesses to the best of their ability. If they are terrorists (like Marlo), within O'Donovan's moral reasoning, the police are justified in killing them (or him) as long as they display and maintain discrimination and proportionality. Neither O'Donovan's nor Ramsey's moral reasoning allows for the beheading of drug lords or drug traffickers. To behead them violates proportionality, which is problematic because it does not display charity towards drug dealers as insurgents.

Marlo's release back into society, whether he finds himself on the streets or with wealthy real estate businesspeople, becomes equally problematic—on O'Donovan's terms—because it does not exercise charity toward the citizens. When we apply O'Donovan's moral reasoning to *The Wire*, Marlo's release turns out to be the primary injustice within the fifth season of *The Wire*.[55] This is the primary injustice because it does not display an Augustinian understanding of charity as a form of "kind harshness." If properly executed, Marlo's death would be considered an act of kind harshness.[56] The

---

55. My claim is not that this is the primary injustice in general, only that it is the primary injustice when understood in relation to the ethics of counter-insurgency.

56. This claim does not provide justification for police officers to execute whomever they choose. Rather, from an Augustinian perspective, Marlo's death is a form of charity toward Marlo because it is "for the sake of the enemy's repentance and reformation" (Bell, *Just War as Christian Discipleship*, 31). This Augustinian reasoning requires thinking in terms of how the human virtues enable divine judgment: God will deal with Marlo on God's terms. Furthermore, from an Augustinian perspective, Marlo's death is an act of charity toward the citizens who live "in a *state of chronic fear*" (Schmid and Jongman, *Political Terrorism*, 1) because of Marlo's vicious actions. In short: if done properly, Marlo's execution would be considered an act of kind harshness because it restores the peace that Marlo has unjustly distorted.

Christian ethicist Daniel Bell's description of how Augustine reasons concerning charity serves as an apt conclusion for my reflections on *The Wire*:

> In Augustine's view, just war is a form of [charity] insofar as it is a sort of "kind harshness." It is a kind harshness in the sense that the intent in waging a just war is . . . love of enemy for the sake of the enemy's repentance and reformation. It is harsh because it is an effort to help one's enemies against their will by punishment. But it is nevertheless a kindness because this punishment is a service to the defeated in the form of restoring justice and peace and depriving persons of the license to act wickedly.[57]

Within *The Wire*, the war on drugs can be a moral and virtuous counter-insurgency effort if Cedric Daniels, Lester Freamon, Jimmy McNulty, and other Baltimore police officers act with kind harshness toward Avon Barksdale, Stringer Bell, and Marlo Stanfield. I believe this is as far as Christian just war thinking gets us in terms of addressing the characters and plot of *The Wire*.[58]

BIBLIOGRAPHY

Augustine. "The Catholic Way of Life and the Manichean Way of Life." In *The Manichean Debate*, edited by Boniface Ramsey, 17–103. Hyde Park, NY: New City, 2006.

Bell, Daniel. *Just War as Christian Discipleship: Recentering the Tradition in the Church Rather Than the State*. Grand Rapids: Brazos, 2009.

Bennett, William J., with John J. Dilulio Jr. and John P. Walters. *Body Count: Moral Poverty . . . and How to Win America's War Against Crime and Drugs*. New York: Simon & Schuster, 1996.

Connolly, William E. "Drugs, the Nation, and Freelancing: Decoding the Moral Universe of William Bennett." In *Drugs and the Limits of Liberalism: Moral and Legal Issues*, edited by Pablo de Greiff, 173–90. Ithaca: Cornell University Press, 1999.

Davis, G. Scott. *Warcraft and the Fragility of Virtue: An Essay in Aristotelian Ethics*. Foreword by Jacob L. Goodson. Eugene, OR: Wipf & Stock, 2010.

Diamond, Cora. "The Difficulty of Reality and the Difficulty of Philosophy." In *Philosophy and Animal Life*, by Stanley Cavell et al., 43–90. New York: Columbia University Press, 2008.

Felbab-Brown, Vanda. *Shooting Up: Counterinsurgency and the War on Drugs*. Washington, DC: Brookings Institution, 2010.

Hauerwas, Stanley. "Bearing Reality." In *Approaching the End: Eschatological Reflections on Church, Politics, and Life*, 154–73. Grand Rapids: Eerdmans, 2013.

57. Bell, *Just War as Christian Discipleship*, 31.

58. Andrea Gregory, Sean Sweeney, and Seth Vannatta paid close attention to the details of this essay and offered comments and suggestions that vastly improved the analysis and the prose. I take responsibility for the remaining mistakes.

Holmes, Arthur, editor. *War and Christian Ethics: Classic and Contemporary Readings on the Morality of War*. 2nd ed. Grand Rapids: Baker Academic, 2006.
O'Donovan, Oliver. *The Just War Revisited*. New York: Cambridge University Press, 2003.
———. *The Problem of Self-Love in St. Augustine*. 1980. Reprint, Eugene, OR: Wipf & Stock, 2006.
Porter, Jean. *Moral Action and Christian Ethics*. New York: Cambridge University Press, 1995.
Putnam, Hilary. "Taking Rules Seriously." In *Realism with a Human Face*, edited by James Conant, 193–200. Cambridge: Harvard University Press, 1990.
Ramsey, Paul. "Incommensurability and Indeterminacy in Moral Choice." In *Doing Good to Achieve Evil: Moral Choice in Conflict Situations*, edited by Richard McCormick and Paul Ramsey, 69–144. Chicago: Loyola University Press, 1978.
———. *The Just War: Force and Political Responsibility*. Foreword by Stanley M. Hauerwas. Lanham, MD: Rowman & Littlefield, 2002.
———. *War and the Christian Conscience: How Can Modern War Be Conducted Justly?* Durham: Duke University Press, 1967.
Read, Jason. "Stringer Bell's Lament: Violence and Legitimacy in Contemporary Capitalism." In *The Wire: Urban Decay and American Television*, edited by Tiffany Potter and C. W. Marshall, 122–34. New York: Continuum, 2009.
Royce, Josiah. *The Philosophy of Loyalty*. Nashville: Vanderbilt University Press, 1995.
Schmid, Alex P., and Albert J. Jongman. *Political Terrorism: A New Guide to Actors, Authors, Concepts, Data Bases, Theories, and Literature*. Rev. ed. Amsterdam: Transaction, 1988.
Spinoza, Baruch. *Ethics*. Translated by Stuart Hampshire. New York: Penguin, 1996.
Tran, Jonathan. *Foucault and Theology*. New York: T. & T. Clark, 2011.
Whitford, Andrew B., and Jeff Yates. *Presidential Rhetoric and the Public Agenda: Constructing the War on Drugs*. Baltimore: Johns Hopkins University Press, 2009.

10

Keeping the Devil Down
The Church on *The Wire*

NEKEISHA ALEXIS-BAKER

FOR FIVE SEASONS, THE *Wire* revealed to audiences a truth that this nation's underclass already knows—namely, that America's major institutions are dysfunctional machines that disadvantage the vulnerable. The police, the illegal drug trade, the government, the educational system, and the news industry are different players in the same game in which the illusion of progress is the goal. In contrast to this devastating indictment of the systems that claim to protect and serve, the series maintains a relatively hopeful outlook through the enjoyable and complicated characters that rebel against institutional rules and seek to make a difference in spite of them. In a world where everyone and everything to which one is loyal "will somehow find a way to fuck you,"[1] *The Wire* highlights those people who refuse to play along with society's lie that life is better than we know it to be.

Although intricate storytelling and well-rounded characters make *The Wire* a critically acclaimed show, the series still presents viewers with a clear, binary choice. On one hand, there are institutions whose policies and practices swallow up the individuals who serve them, and the power-holders and power-seekers who are beholden to them. On the other hand, there are individuals within and outside of the system that question, critique

1. Simon, *Tapping the Wire*, 18:02.

and challenge the institutions's norms. Those who attempt to straddle the middle are quickly absorbed into the institution or, in the case of corner boy Michael, become outcasts. One can either surrender to the institution or remain an individual. There are few, if any, options in between.

Reflecting on the individual-versus-institution theme of *The Wire*, co-creator David Simon stated, "I am very cynical about institutions and their willingness to address themselves to reform. For their willingness to do what they're supposed to do in American life. I am not cynical when it comes to individuals and people. And I think the reason *The Wire* is watchable, even tolerable, to viewers is that it has great affection for individuals."[2] However, this institution-versus-individual motif that saturates *The Wire* overlooks the community as another possibility for resisting the current shape of urban life.

Communities transgress the dichotomy of *The Wire* because they are bigger than an individual but often more flexible, more diversified, and less bureaucratic than institutions. They are comprised of people whose commitment to one another shapes how they live out a common vision in a common place. Unlike institutions, which are rigid and demand conformity, communities are most successful when the people that shape them value one another for their distinctive contributions and are open to change as individual gifts and ideas, and the group's experiences shift over time. Family networks, grassroots organizations, fraternal organizations, and other voluntary associations are examples of communities that exist in various forms within urban spaces. One such communal body that is essential to the inner-city American landscape, especially within predominantly black areas, is the church. In spite of the challenges they face, "black churches are still the central institutions in their communities."[3]

Unfortunately, *The Wire* reduces Baltimore's vibrant church communities to ministerial bureaucrats, painting an incomplete picture of what the body of Christ can do in places where life is hardest. Consequently, the show lacks the stories of lay church folks and congregational networks coming together to transform their neglected but not lost neighborhoods. This gap is noticeable because the series strives to give an authentic if not factual look at life in Baltimore and because of all the real-life stories of vibrant, transforming church communities in that city from which to choose. Therefore, I will examine how *The Wire* represents the church and its effectiveness as

---

2. Simon, "Interview with Bill Moyers," 40:51.

3. Lincoln and Mamiya, *Black Church*, 160. Reliable research has consistently shown "that black churches were one of the few stable and coherent institutions to emerge from slavery" (7). Lincoln and Mamiya also suggest that "the Black Church has no challenger as the cultural womb of the black community" (8).

THE CHURCH ON *THE WIRE*

From the third season on, the most prominent representation of the church on *The Wire* is the Deacon, played by ex-drug lord Melvin Williams. The Deacon is the kind of man who is "always up in everybody's shit"[4] and for that reason often knows who people need to see, what people need to do, and where they need to go before those people know it for themselves. Throughout the series, the Deacon assumes various roles to help people reorient their lives and accomplish their goals. He is a connector, putting former street soldier Dennis "Cutty" Wise in touch with the political movers that can back his boxing gym. He is an interpreter, translating heady academic social work speech into a language that Bunny Colvin understands. He is a teacher, schooling a young man at the pool table. He is a voice of reason, calling on Colvin to stand by his drug legalization experiment until it is inevitably exposed. As an elder in the urban black vernacular community, the Deacon uses "styles of speech, techniques for building relationships, and modes of organization and networking" native to the culture of which he is a part.[5] As a leader in the black church tradition, he also carries out priestly and prophetic functions, maintains a this-worldly focus driven by otherworldly concerns, and has a communal orientation.[6]

While the Deacon assumes a priestly role when ministering to Dennis, his prophetic, this-worldly, and communal dimensions are most apparent in his response to Hamsterdam. After touring the abandoned areas turned open drug markets, the Deacon confronts Colvin for rounding up the addicts and dealers without attending to their needs. In the Deacon's eyes,

---

4. "Refugees," S4/E4.

5. McDougall. *Black Baltimore*, 2. Following Ivan Illich, McDougall describes vernacular "as an entire culture, 'home-made, homespun, home-grown,' developing gender roles, home life, and gossip as well as community institutions such as churches and civic associations" (2).

6. Lincoln and Mamiya, *Black Church*, 12–13. In their extensive study of historically black churches, Lincoln and Mamiya categorize the black church as an institution that negotiates between at least six different spectrums, including priestly and prophetic, otherworldly and this-worldly, universalism and particularism, communal and privatistic, and charismatic and bureaucratic. The Deacon is shown most clearly adopting some of these roles within his person.

Colvin is mayor of a village of pain called hell.[7] When Colvin attempts to sidestep his moral responsibility for Hamsterdam's heinous conditions by hiding behind his badge, the Deacon persists and brings in reinforcements. Within days, the Deacon enlists a friend to teach the now unemployed hoppers basketball and asks a contact from the school of public health to provide needle exchanges, condom distribution, disease treatment, and health education. In these scenes, *The Wire* dares viewers to see hell as a place where basic needs such as sanitation and water access go unmet, preventable diseases go untreated, human beings are discarded, and death lurks near every vacant building. Hell is a place where people are stuck in vicious cycles like caged hamsters on a treadmill, even when solutions to their problems are readily available.

Because *The Wire*'s critique of America's drug war extends beyond Baltimore to include inner cities across the nation, the Deacon's critique of Hamsterdam also condemns all the economically and social-service deprived neighborhoods created by systemic and systematic oppression. Through the Deacon, *The Wire* declares the condition of all Hamsterdam-like places to be immoral and unethical. By using the Deacon to bring a measure of dignity back into Hamsterdam, *The Wire* also sends the message that society's response to the drug epidemic should be rehabilitation, education, and harm reduction—not criminalization. We should treat those who participate in the drug trade's "inverted form of capitalism"[8] as human beings and citizens, and assume shared responsibility for their well-being.[9]

Although the Deacon helps Dennis and Colvin get fresh starts, and helps Colvin improve Hamsterdam and Edward Tighlman Middle School, he is inexplicably absent when Dennis needs financial support for his new gym. When Dennis needs to purchase new equipment at a cost of $10,000, his first and only stop is former employer and drug kingpin Avon Barksdale, who gives him $15,000. The show offers no clear explanation for why Dennis asks Avon rather than the Deacon, who has been steadfastly supportive, especially when the boxing program targets the corner kids Avon and other dealers use for their businesses. It is also unclear why the same

---

7. "Moral Midgetry," S3/E8.

8. Simon, "Interview with Bill Moyers," 6:31.

9. This message is the same as executive producer David Simon's personal position. In a 2009 interview, Simon avidly argues for decriminalizing drugs saying, "I would decriminalize drugs in a heartbeat. I would put all the interdiction money, all the incarceration money, all the enforcement money, all of the pretrial, all the prep, all of that cash, I would hurl it, as fast as I could, into drug treatment and job training and jobs programs . . . it would be doing less damage than creating a war syndrome, where we're basically treating our underclass." Simon, "Interview with Bill Moyers," 21:41.

Deacon who asked whether Dennis was paying the gym renovators with his own money would not also ask where Dennis got the funds to buy new gear. One way to understand Dennis's reluctance to "go around and collect a dollar here and a dollar there" is that the church cannot compete financially with the drug trade when it comes to delivering fast money.[10] Another possible interpretation may be that the church would not provide money to an unsaved non-member like Dennis, even if it could. In either case, by contrasting the well-meaning but financially limited Deacon (an individual) with a wealthy illegal drug organization (an institution), while ignoring the local congregation (the community), *The Wire* misses the opportunity to showcase the economic resourcefulness that exists in many inner-city Baltimore congregations.

Despite the writers' decision to leave the Deacon and his church community out of Dennis's fundraising efforts, the character is still the most influential church-going *man* of the series. Women clergy and laity are noticeably absent from any prominent roles, which is perplexing given women's numerical and organizational power in black church life. Furthermore, "the major programs of the Black Church in politics, economics, or music depend heavily upon women for their promotion and success."[11] The presence of women has been so strong within black churches that on a survey conducted by Project Joseph, an organization aimed at understanding the rise of Islam within black communities, black men who had become Muslim blamed the church for being "too female" as one of the reasons they left Christianity.[12] Attracting more men was also a priority at Bethel African Methodist Episcopal Church, where Reverend Reid "mobilized and encouraged the men in the congregation to develop lay organizations for men."[13] By focusing primarily on official church leaders and overlooking church communities as a whole, *The Wire* ends up disregarding women who have also been instrumental in church-related efforts to renew their city.

Among the male leaders on *The Wire*, the Deacon is more connected to the everyday realities of the Western District than the leaders who form the Interdenominational Ministerial Alliance (IMA). From the IMA's initial appearance onward, the series suggests that the group's strength is not their impact on the lives of struggling Baltimoreans, but in their electoral power. Like other candidates and mayors before him, Tommy Carcetti tries to appease and appeal to the ministers because of their authority in the black

---

10. "Middle Ground," S3/E11.
11. Lincoln and Mamiya, *Black Church*, 275.
12. Tapia, "Churches Wary of Inner-City Islamic Inroads," 37.
13. Mamiya, "Social History of Bethel African Methodist Episcopal," 280.

voting community. However, he and his handlers also attempt to outmaneuver the ministers and shape their perception to his advantage. That the IMA is not taken seriously beyond their electoral capital is manifest in the way white characters on the campaign trail and black power brokers like Commissioner Burrell, Senator Davis, and adviser Norman Wilson often speak strategically *about* the ministers, instead of strategizing *with* them as partners. Although the ministers can call in favors based on their ability to determine which officials will have their chance to fail at government-based reform, they are not portrayed as useful for anything else.

The first appearance by an IMA representative takes place in Season 3 when Reverend Reid, pastor of the Deacon's church and presumably the head of the alliance, calls Odell Watkins to vouch for Dennis's gym. When Dennis asks Watkins why he fast-tracked the permit process, Watkins' response is that the voters in his district know Reverend Reid.[14] The electoral power of the ministers is also confirmed when campaign manager Theresa D'Agostino explains her strategy for getting a white man elected in Baltimore: "We gotta start thinking about endorsements by black leaders. Ministers, community people, elected officials. But here comes the hard part. Splitting the black vote is the only way to make the math work."[15] The IMA inevitably becomes part of that strategy after Carcetti admits that he needs to meet with them, albeit toward the end of his campaign. During his visit, Carcetti recites a monologue that concludes with the promise that his door will always be open, with or without their endorsement. The ministers sit and listen silently.

Perhaps the episode that most effectively communicates the ministers' absorption into the political machine and their detachment from the people's needs takes place in Season 4. After a minister and three churchgoing women refuse to give Bubbles, a heroin addict, food or to acknowledge his presence, he calls Sergeant Hauk with a false tip implicating the minister in drug trafficking. In the wake of Hauk's rough treatment of the minister, Reid and the minister receive a private hearing with Mayor Carcetti. Against the backdrop of Bubbles' suffering at the hands of an addict that beats him daily and the show's repeated depiction of cops roughing up corner boys, the minister's charge of police brutality and outrage at Hauk's "affront to the cloth"[16] sounds selfish and absurd. Where are the ministers when Bubbles needs protection from real brutality? Where are they when officers patrol their streets using the violence of "the Western District way"? Why is it that

---

14. "Slapstick," S3/E9.
15. "Reformation," S3/E10.
16. "Middle Ground," S3/11.

PART III: Engaging *The Wire*

the only time we see them at City Hall, their top priorities are an accidental traffic stop and Burrell's employment? How is it that a church leader who is so concerned with his religious status refuses to show mercy to a hungry, hurting man right before his eyes? On *The Wire*, the ministers are more interested in defending the honor of one of their members than defending those who suffer from racial and economic oppression. Ironically, they are ineffective on both fronts. Following their visit, Norman takes steps to make the ministers think that Carcetti takes their concerns seriously without giving them what they have asked. The system ignores the IMA as surely as the minister ignored Bubbles.

While there is truth to *The Wire*'s depiction of the ministers, it seems to lack the same texture the series gives to other areas. Although their power has been absorbed by government institutions in many ways, the Alliance has also participated in initiatives that address the needs of Baltimore's most vulnerable. For example, when real-life former mayor Kurt Schmoke decided to tackle the spread of AIDS among drug users during his tenure, he went to pastors in the city seeking support for a syringe exchange program. As Schmoke describes it, a few of the pastors "wanted me *under* the church."[17] However, after additional conversations about the effect of AIDS in their congregations and communities, church leaders backed the program. When it was time to take his proposal to the legislature, Schmoke recounts,

> the clergy became the primary advocates for the needle exchange program. They went down to the legislature and became a simply irresistible force. I had lobbied the legislature myself for three years with no results. What turned the tide was an enormous outpouring from the Interdenominational Ministerial Alliance. Leaders of more than 150 churches, synagogues, and mosques asked the legislature for a chance to try our idea.[18]

They succeeded in getting legislation passed and three years later a study showed a significant decrease in the spread of HIV in Baltimore. When fictional Mayor Royce tries to recast Hamsterdam as something other than drug legalization, *The Wire* instead paints the IMA in an antagonistic light. Delegate Watkins cautions Royce, saying, "When the story breaks, the ministers will surely be against you."[19] Ironically, Schmoke plays an extra during these City Hall scenes.

In addition to their work on the needle exchange, the real-life IMA was also instrumental in creating Baltimoreans United in Leadership

17. Schmoke, "Learning from Nehemiah," 70.
18. Ibid.
19. "Middle Ground," S3/11.

Development (BUILD), an ecumenical, multiracial organization that began in the early 1980s as a way to empower poor, working- and middle-class residents and change the institutions that shape their lives. Within a decade, BUILD had become "the mainstream voice of thousands of previously voiceless Baltimoreans,"[20] positively affecting housing, industry, jobs, and programming for youth.[21] In spite of these accomplishments, however, the IMA has become less effective over time. Its membership has dwindled from 250 members in its heyday to approximately ten to fifteen active members currently, many of them retired. A more recent sign of weakness came when its tradition of endorsing electoral candidates came under fire. At issue was the group's decision to back 2011 mayoral candidate Stephanie Rawlings-Blake, without waiting for other candidates to announce their bid or meeting the other candidates after they had entered the race. Former IMA vice president and "clergy-activist" Heber Brown III responded to the action, saying, "For *at least* the past 4 years, the Alliance has been faltering. Its leadership process is questionable and its public action is largely symbolic and absent of substance or follow up. It has no agenda to hold anyone accountable."[22] Brown also called the IMA to take a number of steps, including a moratorium on endorsing candidates, launching a campaign to actively recruit younger church leaders, and going on a listening tour to reconnect with the wider community. At least in these ways, *The Wire*'s portrayal of the IMA is not far from reality.

With the exception of the Deacon, most depictions of the church are unflattering. For example, Season 2 opens with a brewing war between dockworker Frank Sobotka and Major Valcheck over whose stained glass window should have the most coveted place in the sanctuary of a local parish. Frank sees the expensive window primarily as a means of getting "facetime"[23] with a senator who is also a member. Meanwhile, Valchek, who is only moderately involved in church life, sees having prime window space as a sign of Polish police pride. Father Lewandowsky, who appears early in the conflict, does not press Frank on how he has funded his window or advise absentee parishioner Valchek to accept the "less honorable" position. Then, as the contest becomes more hostile, "Father Lew" is nowhere to be found. *The Wire*'s perspective on the church is also noticeable in its use of church settings. The only times people fill the pews are during pre-election worship

---

20. McDougall, *Black Baltimore*, 130.

21. Ibid., 132. For a historical overview of BUILD's work, see also McDougall, *Black Baltimore*, 126–35, and Schmoke, "Learning from Nehemiah," 68–71.

22. Brown, "IMA Endorsement Should Be Thrown Out," para. 5.

23. "Ebb Tide," S2/E1.

and community meetings on the state of the Western District. In the first case, the church functions as a stage for false hope in government officials and promises of reform. In the latter case, the church becomes a platform for talking heads to deliver false promises and juked stats. Otherwise, sanctuaries, when they appear at all, are basically empty.

By the end of the series, the church moves from being largely unmindful of the drug war to being an active part of the problem. Early in Season 5, drug supplier Proposition Joe takes ruthless upstart Marlo Stanfield to one of the three pastors he uses for money laundering services. The dialogue is rich with cynicism as Joe explains that the pastor is "down with all kinds of missionary work going on down in the islands: building a church for some folk; a school house for some other folks; all kinda good shit like that."[24] There is a hospital in the works too, "'Cept they been building that mess for about ten years now and nothing ever actually get finished."[25] The pastor closes the scene by outlining his fees: "You can pay ten on the dollar. Anything beyond that depends on your generosity. To save those who wanna be saved."[26] In *The Wire*, salvation is as spiritually bankrupt as it is financially lucrative and "good news" is in short supply.

THE CHURCH ON THE HIGH WIRE

After five seasons of beloved characters falling victim to murder, well-meaning people failing at other people's expense, institutions resisting reform, and church leaders bringing little positive change, it would be easy to conclude that the devil goes unchallenged in America's inner cities. Yet, many urban churches in areas of concentrated poverty across the nation practice sacrificial care for and dedication to their neighborhoods. Three of these Baltimore congregations include Bethel African Methodist Episcopal Church, New Song Community Church, and Garden of Prayer Baptist Church. By highlighting these churches, I do not intend to suggest that they are the only or the best congregations trying to heal Baltimore neighborhoods. Instead, I have chosen these congregations because of the frequency with which they appear in literature about Baltimore, and the similarities in their ministries despite denominational differences. Many of these ministries were alive or were being conceived during Simon's tenure with *The Baltimore Sun*, during Burns's twenty-year career on the Baltimore police force, and during the filming of all five seasons of the series. Like any human

24. "Unconfirmed Reports," S5/E2.
25. "Unconfirmed Reports," S5/E2.
26. "Unconfirmed Reports," S5/E2.

endeavor, these churches are undoubtedly flawed. However, my aim is not to judge the effectiveness of their ministries or to evaluate them in light of my own theological and political views. My primary goal is to notice these "paragovernmental"[27] church communities in a way *The Wire* does not.

Bethel A. M. E. Church

Since its inception, Bethel has been "a central holistic institution in the black community, constantly involving itself in political, economic, and social issues as well as in the tasks of spiritual nurture."[28] This mission goes back to the church's founding in 1815 as a response to racism by their white Methodist counterparts. Early in its history, Bethel provided the underclass of its day with a place that respected their humanity and recognized their gifts.[29] The congregation met individual and communal needs as "spiritual nurturer, comforter in times of sorrow and death, house of mercy for the suffering, provider of role models for young people and counselor for the distraught. . . . It was the place where God's spirit could renew the souls of black folk in worship to face another day."[30] Bethel was also the site for social agitation against racism, segregation, and economic inequality. It started the tradition of indignation services, which encouraged black folks to speak out against the abuses they suffered at the hands of white society, and birthed the first black-owned shipyard to be "managed and operated by lay people from one church."[31] For well over a century, Bethel was a hub for fraternal orders, mutual aid societies, programs for the poor, and other initiatives.

During his visit to Bethel in early 1990, researcher Lawrence Mamiya discovered approximately fifty internal and external ministries. These programs and services focused on "the needs of women, pregnant teenagers, drug addicts, the homeless and the hungry, former convicts, prisoners, students, senior citizens and the deaf."[32] The congregation had a credit union, an economic development committee, scholarship funding for college-

27. McDougall, *Black Baltimore*, 11. McDougall describes paragovernmental organizations as voluntary associations that try to change the way government functions through interventionist politics like protest and advocacy, and that work parallel to the government by providing basic services for the people when government refuses to address their needs.
28. Mamiya, "Social History of the Bethel African Methodist Episcopal Church," 222.
29. Ibid., 228.
30. Ibid., 245.
31. Ibid., 241.
32. Ibid., 276.

bound youth, a Black Men's Chorus, a Manhood Rites of Initiation group, and the Food Co-op (which briefly appeared on Season 3 of *The Wire*). Bethel's Freedom Now substance abuse ministry, run at the time by two female lay leaders, modified the Alcoholics Anonymous program to include Bible study, prayer, song, and testimony. Bethel's impact on the surrounding community was so significant that *The Chronicle of Philanthropy* recognized it as "a *dominant influence* in the neighborhood" that "touches people of every age and class."[33] Despite the male-dominated hierarchy of the A.M.E. denomination, male and female clergy and laity were all instrumental for developing and maintaining Bethel's work in West Baltimore. It is disappointing that these insights into Bethel's life are largely absent from *The Wire*, especially since the producers filmed in the sanctuary, used a Bethel member to play the Deacon,[34] and featured a character based on its pastor.

New Song Community Church

Like Bethel, the more recently established New Song Community Church had a commitment to justice and holistic mission from the beginning. Founded in 1986 by two white couples from the Baltimore suburbs, New Song formed using principles from the Christian Community Development Association and the base community models of Central America. With a focus on relocating to the area they wished to serve; redistributing economic, political, and social resources; and racial reconciliation, Allan and Susan Tibbels and Mark Gornik and his spouse rooted themselves in one of the city's poorest neighborhoods. Faced with their neighbors' skepticism, Allan Tibbels, who was paralyzed and used a wheelchair, began by reaching out to Sandtown youth. By 1992, the church had gained enough trust to establish a headquarters for their New Song Urban Ministries organization in a previously abandoned two-hundred-year-old convent in the neighborhood. The project brought together the pastor, church members, and neighbors for thousands of volunteer hours. The effort impressed and inspired the community "with the changes that can be made in the physical—and spiritual tenor—of the neighborhood if people get inspired and work together."[35]

Since their early days, New Song Community Church's urban ministry arm has joined community residents in developing much-needed services. The Eden Job Center trains people and places them in jobs that suit their skills while the New Song Family Health Center offers health care using

33. Stehle, "Church in Depressed Baltimore Neighborhood," 9. Emphasis mine.
34. Blount, "Respect," para. 2,
35. McDougall, *Black Baltimore*, 176. See also Silver, "Allan Tibbels," pars. 6–8.

paid and volunteer pediatricians, nurses, internists, and other physicians. In 1989, New Song also established the Sandtown Habitat for Humanity, which created 160 homes in the neighborhood over twelve years. In addition to providing suitable housing for people with low incomes—the first house went to a working mother with four children who had an annual salary of $8,000[36]—sixty of the organization's eighty employees are lifelong Sandtown residents. More recently, the church community supports Martha's Place, a recovery program started in 2000 for women overcoming addiction that includes six months of transitional living and a second long-term phase of independent housing. The project has involved renovating buildings for homes and converting vacant lots into a meditative garden and green space.

Garden of Prayer Baptist Church

A third church community that is resisting systemic evil in Baltimore is Garden of Prayer Baptist Church. Located in a neighborhood that suffered economically after the Colts and Orioles professional sports teams relocated to new stadiums, the church and their neighbors contended with increases in drugs, gangs, violence, rising student dropout rates, and early pregnancy among youth. To address these issues, Garden of Prayer began to "experiment with their own holistic remedies,"[37] instead of waiting for city government to do its part. When Reverend Melvin B. Tuggle II and his spouse, Brenda, came to the church, it consisted of six adults and six children worshipping in a garage. Within a decade, the group restored a narrow lot filled with old cars located in the midst of crack houses and established a new church community that serves its multiracial neighbors.

Garden of Prayer has fostered community through an annual summer camp for kids, a boys and girls club, a drama club, a mentoring program for mothers and daughters, an annual fishing trip for youth, and a choir that provides mentoring opportunities. Its social service ministries also include a food pantry, clothing distribution in the winter, health awareness activities, and a college scholarship program. All of the congregation-sponsored programs are free and available to members and nonmembers alike. Garden of Prayer prefers to pour all its resources into its ministries, counting on God to help them meet the needs. As Tuggle said in a 1996 interview, "I have a problem with churches that have money in the bank. We're broke every Monday after we pay the bills, and that's the way I like it."[38]

36. McDougall, *Black Baltimore*, 175.
37. Drennan, "Spiritual Healing," para. 7.
38. Ibid., para. 75.

With the exception of brief scenes like those at Bethel's Food Co-op and an unidentified soup kitchen line, these diverse ministries are largely invisible in *The Wire*'s rendition of Baltimore, raising the question of just how "realistic" the show is. These ministries do not touch the lives of the characters, either in passing or in more noticeable ways; they are not a part of the dialogue or the scenery. Even the Deacon's interactions with these church community efforts are limited as he interacts primarily with people outside his congregation and with secular institutions. Omitting these examples of resistance, small as they may be, heightens the tragedy within the series. Yet, at the same time, the omission denies the bits of hope that real Baltimoreans have managed to cultivate, and makes both individuals and communities seem more helpless than they really are.

Case Study: Filling the Gaps in Baltimore's Schools

As *The Wire* revealed in its fourth season, the school system shares the same institutional plagues as the police, drug organizations, city government, and corporate-driven journalism. When disgraced police officer Roland Pryzbylewski becomes a teacher at Edward Tilghman Middle School, he quickly discovers that the same game of "juking the stats" that destroyed "real police work" also undermines quality teaching. During his tenure, he learns to teach to the test to promote the idea that students are learning, teachers are performing well, and education as a whole is a success. Concern for how things look rather than how things really are causes one of Prez's most promising students to be socially promoted before he is ready, while the fear of tracking ends a program that reaches corner kids. Meanwhile, custodial staff round up missing children to check into class long enough for the school to receive funding. Although administrators and teachers try to do their best, they and the students know everyone is being played.[39]

In the face of an abysmal public school system, *The Wire* offers little in the way of alternatives. Although Naymond makes the exodus into middle class life thanks to Colvin's belief in his potential, he is the only one of his friends—and likely the only one in his school—to escape the corner. But here is another area in the series' individual-versus-institution narrative that fails to examine the grassroots, community-based initiatives serving the children that the system leaves behind. In addition to all their other

---

39. "Refugees," S4/E4. Colvin explains the situation best: "Their brothers and sisters, shit, their parents, they came through these same classrooms didn't they? We pretended to teach them, they pretended to learn, where'd they end up? Same damn corners. They're not fools, these kids . . . I mean, Jesus, they see right through us."

social ministries, Bethel A.M.E. Church, New Song Community Church, and Garden of Prayer Baptist Church each have programs that work to close the educational gap. What distinguishes them from the middle school on *The Wire* is student-centered learning strategies, small sizes that facilitate that goal, and a community that wants to see their youth reach their fullest potential—not just pass standardized exams and boost statistics.

In 1983, Bethel started a private elementary school "out of a concern about the decline in quality of Baltimore's public schools."[40] By 1994, the academy had grown from eighteen students to 130, with a waiting list of 100 children. Like the Freedom Now ministry, two women spearheaded the school, including Peggy Wall-Neal, who resigned from a well-paid job at Maryland State Department of Education to become principal, and Beatrice Avery, a retiree from the Baltimore City Board of Education.[41] A few years before opening the school, Bethel also ran a tutoring program in math and reading that included personal attention from a reading specialist. Also available were a dance and drama group and professional counseling.[42]

Similarly, in 1991 New Song started a preschool and after-school program that developed into New Song Academy, an independently operated K through 8 public school. In 2001, the school and its 110 students moved into the New Song Center, a $5.4 million, three-story community and learning center that the urban ministry organization built on a formerly vacant lot. The school serves only Sandtown children in spacious classrooms that are limited to fifteen students. The approach to teaching and learning is the Workshop Model, which involves a combination of teaching state curricula with individually paced work, student constructed meaning, self-assessment, and individualized learning and evaluation. Among its accomplishments, New Song Academy counts high attendance and graduation rates, and creating an environment where school police are unnecessary despite the high level of violence in the surrounding community.[43]

Finally, Garden of Prayer also renovated several former crack houses to create the Calvin W. Williams Reading Center. The center, which focused on literacy skills, homework assistance, and other educational support, featured class sizes of two to eight students with several volunteer instructors per group. Children also spent time with volunteers outside of the classroom, helping the youth foster intergenerational relationships. Program

---

40. Mamiya, "Social History of Bethel African Methodist Episcopal Church," 279.
41. Stehle, "Church in Depressed Baltimore Neighborhood," 9.
42. Bryant, "Black Church in Baltimore," 44.
43. For details on New Song Academy, see http://www.newsonglc.org/academy.htm.

coordinator Brenda Tuggle consulted teachers to determine the children's strengths and need-areas, and developed a training program for volunteers. This model not only provided supplemental help to students and teachers; it also empowered people in the neighborhood to help educate their youth.[44]

Congregations in other inner cities have also created educational alternatives to schools that underserve their youth. In 1992, a group of Cincinnati Baptist pastors became frustrated with the rates at which schools were suspending and expelling black males. They opened their churches to create learning centers where members tutored the youth and instructed them in conflict resolution skills. The success of the venture inspired conference ministers to develop plans for Project Succeed Academy, a school to meet the needs of youth who have been ostracized by public schools. Meanwhile, the One Church/One School Program in Gary, Indiana created citywide church-school partnerships. The initiative, which spread to Dallas, Chicago, and Cleveland after debuting in 1992, brought together pastors and principals to determine how church members could provide schools with additional resources. The first year, the program focused on the theme "Stop the Violence," which helped one of the participating schools develop a student-run disciplinary committee. Focusing on more than exams and test scores has brought less statistically measurable results and significant changes in the youth's lives. As then Superintendent James Hawkins noted, "If one were to ask can you tangibly measure the academic gains the kids make, no one could answer that. But in terms of changes in attitude, behaviors, and relationships, it has made a huge difference."[45]

In spite of all these attempts to create community-based alternatives to a failing educational institution, none of these projects are featured or alluded to on *The Wire*'s fourth season. There is no after-school program helping Michael's little brother with math. No church ladies trying to breathe new life in Tilghman Middle. No place outside of the classroom for Duquan to develop his computer skills. No church organizations renovating vacant lots for a learning center or church programs opening their doors to corner kids like Naymond. The efforts of these congregations to help their children learn and develop, like their other ministries, are missing from the series' landscape. And *The Wire*, gripping as it may be, loses some of its authenticity as a result.

---

44. Drennan, "Spiritual Healing," para. 12–21.

45. Superintendent Hawkins' comments can be accessed from a sidebar link in Drennan, "Spiritual Healing."

CONCLUSION

When *The Wire* began filming its first season at the housing projects near Pennsylvania and Druid Hill Avenues, reporter Ericka Blount Danois spoke to resident Sharron Dawkins about her feelings on the show. Dawkins said, "Overall I'm upset because it will show this area as nothing but drugs and violence, and there's more to it than that."[46] Although the series is not that limited in scope and it does get much of its subject matter right, its "focus on the individuals within the institutions and what institutions do to individuals"[47] does exclude vital aspects of community life that paint a less grim picture than what we see on screen. Although people in economically deprived Baltimore and other places like it are struggling under the weight of a bankrupt drug war, related violence, and other social ills, church communities are fostering hope and keeping the devil at bay. These spiritual havens serve as connectors, mediators, translators, priests, and prophets as they nurture grassroots action against the powers that negatively affect people's lives. Their impact may be modest compared to what comprehensive drug law reform, economic redistribution, and an end to systemic racism can accomplish. Yet, their work is still greater than what an individual can achieve by taking on these massive problems alone. That so little of these inspiring stories make it on screen is one of *The Wire*'s few weaknesses.

BIBLIOGRAPHY

Blount, Ericka. "Respect." *Baltimore Magazine* (September 2004). Online: http://www.erickablount.com/melvin.htm.

Blount Danois, Ericka. "Gray Areas: HBO Returns to Baltimore's Corners with *The Wire*." *Baltimore City Paper* (May 29, 2002). Online: http://www2.citypaper.com/news/story.asp?id=4515.

Brown, Heber. "IMA Endorsement Should Be Thrown Out: Alliance Has Lost Its Way." *Faith in Action* (July 12, 2011). Online: http://faithinactiononline.com/2011/07/ima-endorsement-should-be-thrown-out-alliance-has-lost-its-way.

Bryant, John. "A Black Church in Baltimore." In *See How They Grow*, edited by Anthony Walker, 39–46. Glasgow: Fount, 1979.

Drennan, Megan. "Spiritual Healing." *Education Week* (June 5, 1996) 35–39. Online: http://search.ebscohost.com/login.aspx?direct=true&db=aph&AN=9606156623&site=ehost-live.

Jaudon, Stacey. "New Song Community Church: Baltimore, Maryland." *Family Ministry* 1 (1999) 69–70.

Lincoln, C. Eric, and Lawrence H. Mamiya. *The Black Church in the African American Experience*. Durham: Duke University Press, 1990.

46. Blount Danois, "Gray Areas," para. 25.
47. Ibid., para. 6.

Mamiya, Lawrence H. "A Social History of the Bethel African Methodist Episcopal Church in Baltimore: The House of God and the Struggle for Freedom." In *American Congregations: Portraits of Twelve Religious Communities*, edited by James P. Wind and James W. Lewis, 1:221–92. Chicago: University of Chicago Press, 1994.

McDougall, Harold. *Black Baltimore: A New Theory of Community*. Philadelphia: Temple University Press, 1993.

Schmoke, Kurt L. "Learning from Nehemiah." In *What's God Got to Do with The American Experiment?*, edited by E. J. Dionne Jr. and John J. Dilulio Jr., 67–71. Washington: Brookings Institution, 2000.

Silver, Marc. "Heroes: Crusaders for Justice: Allan Tibbels." *US News and World Report* (August 20–27, 2001) 44–45.

Simon, David. "Interview with Bill Moyers." *Bill Moyers Journal*. April 17, 2009. Video interview. Online: http://www.pbs.org/moyers/journal/04172009/watch.html.

———. *Tapping the Wire with Charlie Brooker*. Directed by Steven Hore. Aired July 2007. United Kingdom: Zeppotron Limited and Fox International Channels. Online: http://www.youtube.com/watch?v=SVnNmw9dbNE.

Stehele, Vince. "Church in Depressed Baltimore Neighborhood Becomes a Dominant Force in Social Services." *The Chronicle of Philanthropy* 1 (1988) 9.

Tapia, Andrés. "Churches Wary of Inner-City Islamic Inroads." *Christianity Today* (January 10, 1994) 36–38.

11

Depravity and Hope in the City
Karl Barth in Conversation with *The Wire*

KEITH L. JOHNSON

MANY COMMENTATORS HAVE NOTED that *The Wire* is "bleak," and sometimes relentlessly so.[1] Despite the occasional redemptive moment, the show tends to leave its viewers with feelings of despair rather than hope. This despair arises from an overwhelming sense that the characters and the city—and, by extension, the viewer—are trapped in destructive cycles from which no escape can be found. Every attempt to improve or correct social ills is crushed by the bureaucracy; every vote cast for change only further entrenches a corrupt political class; every dollar spent not only upholds, but also undermines, the livelihood of someone struggling to survive; and every tax dollar invested, store patronized, or school funded contributes to a turf war between figures on both sides of the law who finally are concerned only with their own self-interest. Society is fundamentally broken, and our best efforts cannot fix it.

This bleak impression seems to be precisely what *The Wire* creator David Simon intended. In a 2006 interview, he noted: "We're worth less every day, despite the fact that some of us are achieving more and more. It's the triumph of capitalism. Whether you're a corner boy in West Baltimore, or a cop who knows his beat, or an Eastern European brought here for sex,

---

1. For example, see the remarks in Bowden, "Angriest Man in Television," 50–57.

your life is worth less. It's the triumph of capitalism over human value."[2] Note how Simon places human achievement in an inverse relationship to human value: no matter how hard we work or what we achieve, everyone becomes less important and less valuable at the end of the day. This leaves viewers with a sense that they are both perpetrators and victims: they have dirty hands due to their implicit or explicit participation a broken system, but they also can do nothing to clean them. Hence the despair. Something beyond our control is arrayed against us, twisting our efforts so that they become the means of our demise. So why fight at all? Is not *The Wire* simply "an elaborate, moving brief for despair and (ultimately) indifference," as one critic put it?[3] If we truly are caught up in the broken machinery of the system, then why should we attempt to resist its workings?

One reason to resist, of course, is that ceasing to do so would be fatal for society itself. Progressive political commentator Matthew Yglesias makes this point: "[David Simon's] vision of the bleak urban dystopia and its roots is counterproductive to advancing the values we hold dear . . . Simon believes that we are doomed; political progress requires us to believe that we are not."[4] In other words, to buy into *The Wire*'s portrayal of society's hopelessness is to surrender it as a lost cause, to concede that we will live always and only under the shadow of death. But for Yglesias, this cannot be: to live progressively in this context is to believe that the situation can be altered and, in some sense, redeemed. Most Christian would agree, since a surrender to the broken system would be a betrayal of our basic Christian identity, a pronouncement of the victory of the very enemies the church claims have been defeated in Jesus Christ. This point of agreement does not mean, however, that Christians would agree wholesale either with Yglesias' progressivism or his notion that Simon's bleak vision is misguided. In fact, from a Christian perspective, *The Wire* gets the human situation exactly right: we *are* trapped in a system from which there is no human means of escape, and there *are* forces arrayed against us that no human can defeat. Indeed, in my view, this accurate depiction of the reality of human life marks the great contribution *The Wire* makes to the life and work of the church. A church that watches this show and really *sees* it will be one that obtains a clearer grasp of the depth of human depravity, humanity's helplessness in the face of it, and the nature of the response that such depravity requires. It will be a church that, in light of what it sees, turns to scripture more closely,

---

2. Simon, "Behind the Wire," para. 4.
3. Salam, "Bleakness of *The Wire*," para. 3.
4. Yglesias, "David Simon and the Audacity of Despair," para. 2.

preaches the message of the gospel to the world more faithfully, and acts more courageously in its work for social justice.

This essay will explore this line of thinking by placing the *The Wire* into conversation with the theology of Karl Barth, and specifically with some of Barth's late insights about the church's relationship with society.[5] These insights show Barth at his most forward leaning, trying to describe what it might mean to be the church in the midst of the complexities of the modern world. The conversation between Barth and *The Wire* should lead to a mutual enrichment: Barth's material will help us see things in *The Wire* that we might have otherwise overlooked, and *The Wire* will help us make the implications of Barth's vision for the church more concrete. The goal will be to develop a vision for how the church might live faithfully and hopefully in a world marked by despair.

SIN AND THE POWERS

What *The Wire* depicts as a broken social system, the New Testament depicts as the consequence of human sin, which is at its root the human alienation from God. This alienation manifests itself in humans through their sinful acts and their state of being against God, other humans, and creation. This separation leaves humanity prey to the "powers" who are arrayed against it.[6] These powers are well armed, rule in darkness in the service of a dominion of evil, and work to corrupt creation until it succumbs to the final enemy, death itself.[7] As Barth notes as he reflects upon these powers, their presence is felt in every area of our life. They are "palpable in their impalpability in every morning and evening newspaper in every corner of the globe, the great impersonal absolutes in their astonishing willfulness and autonomy, in their dynamic, which with such alien superiority dominates not only the masses but also human personalities, and not just the small ones but also the great."[8] *The Wire* does not mention the powers directly, of course, but by depicting the stark reality of sin and its consequences, it portrays their work accurately. As in the Bible, so in *The Wire*: sin takes on a life of its own,

---

5. I draw primarily from lectures that were composed late in Barth's career, but only published posthumously. These unfinished fragments were gathered and published posthumously as *The Christian Life: Church Dogmatics Volume IV, Part 4: Lecture Fragments*, hereafter *Christian Life*.

6. Rom 8:38; 1 Cor 15:24; Eph 1:21.

7. Col 2:15; Eph 6:12–13; 1 Cor 15:26.

8. Barth, *Christian Life*, 219.

becomes an autonomous force that acts against human being, and holds humanity firmly in its grasp.

One of the ways sin works throughout Scripture and *The Wire* is by transforming order into disorder. In Scripture, for example, the very capacities God designed to secure human flourishing—human work and effort—are twisted into the traits that undermine this flourishing.[9] We see this, for example, in the creativity and work that are invested in the building of the tower of Babel in Genesis 11. Barth views this kind of transformation as sin's "denaturalizing" of humanity, the decommissioning of humans from their God-given task to be stewards of creation and one another and their commissioning into the act of destroying these very things. This shift occurs as capacities are transformed into "spirits with a life and activity of their own," forces that seem to work in distinction from human life to destroy humanity from without and within.[10]

Barth gives three concrete examples of this phenomenon, and all of them are illustrated in nearly every episode of *The Wire*. The first is *government*. Even though it was created to serve human beings, under the conditions of sin, government becomes a Leviathan working *against* humans. The problem, Barth argues, is that once the exercise of power becomes alienated from its context in God's sovereign plan for the world, its exercise is directed toward itself: "Power no longer protects the right, nor finds in it determination and limit. It subjects the right to itself and makes triumphant use of it. The state no longer serves man; man, both ruling and ruled, has to serve the state."[11] Under the conditions of sin, in other words, even the best governments are twisted until they exist for their own sake rather than for the sake of those for whom they were designed. We see this reality displayed again and again in *The Wire*. From politicians who use power to secure their own reelection, to a police bureaucracy that stifles the pursuit of justice, to a school administration that actually inhibits the learning of its students, the powers of the government are directed against the people more often than they are used to support them.

Lying behind all of these problems, in some way or another, is Barth's second example of the distortion of human capacities: *money*. Humans acquire and save wealth in order to find comfort and security,[12] but in reality, Barth says, "if his resources are to be faithful to him, to serve him and give

---

9. Gen 2:15.
10. Barth, *Christian Life*, 213–14.
11. Ibid., 220. I have left Barth's use of the masculine pronoun for "human beings" intact.
12. Luke 12:16–21.

him comfort, does he not have to be faithful to them and serve them?"[13] Once again, something that was originally intended to serve our good actually acquires power over us, so that our money possesses *us* in the sense that our lives are ordered around its pursuit, maintenance, and use. Again, *The Wire* displays this reality accurately. Union boss Frank Sobotka works with "the Greek" in order to acquire the money that he and his coworkers need to live, but this pursuit locks him into an underworld that leads to his demise. Politicians like Clay Davis exercise tremendous power and influence, but they also always are bound to both their contributors' wishes and their need to fund the next campaign. And drug dealers like Avon and Stringer sell drugs partly in order to make money that will help them escape poverty, but despite the wealth they acquire, they never are able to leave the very streets where they experience the forces of poverty most strongly.

Barth's third example, *ideology*, works more subtly, both in real life and in *The Wire*. An ideology provides a lens through which one can see and understand the world more clearly. This can be helpful inasmuch as it provides a framework from which a human can understand his or her presuppositions, approach problems, and propose solutions to these problems. The trouble, Barth explains, is that an ideology almost always leads the one who holds it toward a "numbness, hardening, and rigidity, and therefore an inertia in which he will cease to be a free spirit." Once a person is locked into a particular way of thinking, he "no longer has anything of his own to say" and "disappears behind the mask that he must wear as [the ideology's] representative."[14] This not only stifles creativity, but it also creates *partisans*: we fight for our side at the expense of the other side, and everyone who does not approach the world from our framework becomes an opponent who must be vanquished. We see this again and again in Baltimore. Politicians and police fight against one another even though they supposedly share the same aims, because they have different presuppositions about the goal of their organization. The dealers' "co-op" finally breaks down because Marlo approaches the drug trade with a particular vision that leaves no room for compromise. And the journalists find reporting the true story of Baltimore nearly impossible because they are bound both to the Baltimore political machine and the money-driven ideology of the paper's corporate owners. Again and again, something that was meant to help people approach the world more effectively actually hinders them by blinding them to reality, dividing them from one another, and forcing them to seek one another's defeat.

13. Barth, *Christian Life*, 222.
14. Ibid., 225.

BALTIMORE AND THE CITY OF CAIN

As he considers these particular forms of the "dehumanization" of humanity, Barth argues that they are merely modern manifestations of the single "twofold history" of humanity: the history of Adam, where the relationship with God was broken, and the history of Cain, the one whose violence brings Adam's sin to its fulfillment.[15] The one act leads to the other, and both acts provide a template from which all human history can be understood. Barth's move here is to read human history in light of the biblical story, so that the latter interprets the former.[16] This move provides insights when applied to the city of Baltimore as portrayed in *The Wire*. When seen within the trajectory of scripture, Baltimore can be viewed in light of a characteristic it shares with all human cities: it is a descendant of the very first human city, the one built by Cain after the murder of his brother Abel. We find the story in Genesis 4. After the Lord rejects Cain's offering but not Abel's, Cain becomes angry. Even though the Lord warns him that "sin is lurking at the door" (v. 6), Cain gives in to his anger, lures Abel into the field, and kills him. When the Lord asks about Abel, Cain lies: "I do not know; am I my brother's keeper?" (v. 9). The Lord then condemns Cain for the murder, puts a mark on him to protect him from vengeance, and casts him out to live as "a fugitive and a wanderer on the earth" (v. 12). This punishment corresponds to the nature of the crime. Before the murder, Cain had enjoyed the security of God's protection and a close relationship with his fellow humans and the earth. Now, this security has been shattered, Abel's blood soaks the ground, the bonds between God, humans, and creation have been broken. Cain is condemned to a life of insecurity, sentenced to roam the earth as a fugitive, fearful of those around him. After his exile, however, Cain does not wander long. Instead, he travels east to the land of Nod and builds a city, which he names "Enoch" after his son (v. 17). This name, which means "initiation" or "dedication," symbolizes Cain's rejection of God's sentence against him. Instead of wandering as a fugitive, he will start anew, rebuild a sense of order, and establish security and stability apart from God.

From a biblical perspective, all cities in some way reflect Cain's hopes for Enoch.[17] They are created with good intentions to be outposts of the future, stable centers that provide security against outsiders, social and economic order, and a space for the development and promotion of culture. But as human enterprises, every city betrays these aims in some way or another.

15. Ibid., 212.
16. This approach corresponds to what George Lindbeck would call an "intratextual" reading of scripture. See Lindbeck, *Nature of Doctrine*, 113–14.
17. For a book-length treatment of this theme, see Ellul, *Meaning of the City*.

Consider, for example, the security that cities are meant to provide. For all of our talk about either fearing or accepting "the other," it is often those closest to us, the ones whom we know the best, whom we have the hardest time embracing. This is especially true in cities, where the most basic form of violence is fratricide. Russell Jacoby examines this phenomenon in chilling detail in his book *Bloodlust: On the Roots of Violence from Cain and Abel to the Present*. He notes, for example, that in the years 2003–2005, nearly three-quarters of murder victims in New York City knew their attackers; that most rapes and assaults during the same period were committed by a spouse, ex-spouse, coworker, or acquaintance; and that gang members most often target other gang members rather than innocent bystanders.[18] These more recent examples follow an ancient trend repeated again and again throughout human history. "We prefer to stigmatize the strangers and the outsiders," he notes. "But most violence emerges from *within* the community."[19] This is the case in *The Wire*, where most of the violence takes place among those who are in "the game," and some of the most notable murders are performed by killers who know their victims well. Stringer Bell's murder-by-hire of D'Angelo Barksdale and Snoop's killing by Michael stand out prominently in this regard.

The Wire is unique, however, in that it makes its viewers *participants* in "the game." This happens at a general level simply because of the show's realism: Baltimore is a real place, the characters are based upon actual people, and the show's writers have firsthand knowledge of the situations and realities being depicted. But the viewer's participation goes much deeper, and it occurs from two directions. On the one hand, as the episodes pass, it becomes more and more difficult to make any character an "other," because those whom viewers initially may have set against themselves become increasingly sympathetic. Think, for example, of the drug dealers on the corners. We quickly learn that these "hoppers" are cogs in the machinery of a large and complex criminal organization, and many if not most of them have been drawn into their roles by the forces of poverty, hopelessness, and ironically, community. Over time, we begin to identify with them, and we might even be able to imagine ourselves standing on those same corners in the same situation. Characters like Stringer Bell and Omar remain abhorrent in many ways, but as their virtues are displayed alongside their vices, we begin to identify with and perhaps even admire them. Stringer's creativity in the face of tremendous complexity and opposition displays all the leadership qualities typically associated with success; and while Omar is a

18. See Jacoby, *Bloodlust*, xii.
19. Ibid., 32.

murderer and a thief, he also is unflinchingly loyal and, in an odd way, *likable* as a person. On the other hand, and at the same time, the characters many viewers might initially have been inclined to identify with become less and less sympathetic as the episodes pass. We discover that the police, politicians, journalists, and school administrators, despite being generally decent, are just as twisted in their own contexts as the criminals are in theirs. McNulty and Kima, for example, are "good police," fair, and fearless in their pursuit of the truth; yet they struggle with authority, sobriety, and familial obligations. Mayor Carcetti genuinely desires to use political power for the good of the people, but as he eventually gives in to workings of the system and its temptations, he becomes increasingly *unlikable* on a personal level. And the qualities that make Michael so sympathetic—his leadership, courage, and fierce loyalty to friends and family—become the very traits that make him a terrifying killer. All of these characters, both good and bad, are placed within a city that itself displays these same contradictory qualities at once: Baltimore is a place of both promise and despair, wealth and poverty, power and powerlessness, beauty and ugliness, generosity and corruption.

By placing viewers in the company of these characters in the midst of this city, *The Wire* causes its viewers to recognize the common humanity they share with these characters, so that they see that the bonds holding the characters' lives together and the forces driving their actions are the same ones that hold *our* families, cities, and nation together and drive our activities day by day. By the end of the series, there is no "other" anymore: Baltimore is *our* city, because we participate in the society that upholds it; the characters are our neighbors, or more accurately, they are *us*, because in so many ways, we are just like them. To watch *The Wire* is to bear witness to a fratricide, to see our kin struck down both by one another and the powers of the city machine. And because we are participants in this machine, we share in the guilt that covers it.

This insight leads us to the gift that *The Wire* offers to the church. Even though it never acknowledges the existence of the powers arrayed against humanity, *The Wire* depicts their effects powerfully. As we watch a broken government squandering its authority while its people suffer; see characters enslaved to money and the pursuit of it; and find that ideologies of every stripe are bankrupt in the face of the challenges of the streets, we are witnessing humans dehumanized to the point of becoming "worth less" before our eyes. This vision is shocking because *sin* is shocking, but also because modern technology and culture allows many of us to live sanitized lives that remain at a distance from sin's effects, most notably death. To watch *The Wire* is to encounter these effects in heartbreaking detail. And not only do we see the true nature of human depravity and the hopelessness of human remedies to address it, but we also come away with the sense that we are both a perpetrator and a victim of this same depravity. No one escapes this story clean: "All have sinned and fallen short of the glory of God."[20]

What *The Wire* does *not* give, as its critics note and the church should quickly recognize, is hope in the face of this reality. And how could it? If the problem depicted is the reality of sin, and if the despair is due to our enslavement to the "powers" that constrain our efforts, then there *is* no human solution. This marks the point where the church must step in, for Paul notes, God's divine order is that his wisdom will be revealed both to the powers and to humanity "through the church."[21] But how can the church fulfill this task? What concrete steps can the church take to offer hope in the midst of cities like Baltimore?

DIVINE ELECTION AND HUMAN CORRESPONDENCE

In his response to similar questions, Barth argues that hope is found only in the church's praying for the kingdom of God. For, as the critics of *The Wire* note in their own way, hope is precisely what the world under the dominion of the powers lacks. Despair and indifference arise when we no longer believe justice can be done, righteousness found, and order brought out of disorder; they come when we believe nothing we do matters, and that resistance against powers is futile. Barth argues that this kind of despair and indifference is precisely what the gospel of Jesus Christ overcomes, and that the church's great commission includes within itself the confrontation of these very things. "To bid man hope," he says, "and thus to mediate to him the promise that he needs, is [the Christian] task. Concern for this is their conflict."[22] This promise takes concrete shape as the church proclaims the kingdom of God as the alternative to the present state of the city. This preaching is not distinct from the preaching about Jesus Christ, in Barth's view, but central to it: to claim that "the kingdom of God is at hand" is to claim a victory over the powers, and this is identical to the church's claims about the salvation God achieves in and through Jesus Christ.[23]

Working behind Barth's argument here is his doctrine of election, which he develops in *Church Dogmatics* 2/2 around the claim that Jesus Christ is both the subject and object of divine election and thus the beginning and end of all created works. Barth sees this idea as the working out of

20. Rom 3:23.
21. Eph 3:10–11
22. Barth, *Christian Life*, 270.
23. Ibid., 249.

Paul's claim that God "chose us in Christ before the foundation of the world to be holy and blameless before him in love."[24] He argues that every created thing is determined in its inner depths by God's decision to enter into covenant with sinful humanity in and through Christ. This covenant is precisely what the Bible and church are talking about when they talk about God's grace, Barth says, and "[t]here is no such thing as a created nature which has its purpose, being or continuance apart from grace, or which may be known in this purpose, being or continuance except through grace."[25] This means the created order is intrinsically defined by the covenant, because it exists precisely in order to be the space where God's covenantal plan is executed.[26] Likewise, human being is intrinsically defined by the covenant, since Jesus Christ himself is the ontological ground of human existence, and true human being is found only in him. "It is not that [God] first wills and works the being of the world and [the human], and then ordains [the human] for salvation," Barth says. "But God creates, preserves and overrules [the human] for this *prior* end and with this *prior* purpose, that there may be a being distinct from himself ordained for salvation, for perfect being, for participation in his own being."[27] Barth's doctrine of justification shapes Barth's thought here: our relationship with God is a relationship by grace alone through Christ alone as we participate *in* Christ, and through him, in God. What we are intrinsically as humans is determined at every moment by our relationship to Christ, who as the fully human and fully divine mediator also remains utterly distinct from us in his unique relation to the Father. From the basis of this view of the nature of God's covenantal relationship with the world, Barth argues that the church can bring hope to the world inasmuch as its own human existence corresponds to both its and creation's being "in Christ."

To this end, Barth outlines four concrete ways the church can begin to live in correspondence to its being "in Christ" within the context of a fallen world. The first way is by *hearing* the Word of God. Specifically, the church must hear "the proclamation of the righteousness of God and in and with it the proclamation of the order of right, freedom and peace which is given to man."[28] As Barth sees it, the fact that all creation exists for God's covenant of grace means that any claim about God, creation, and human being—and

24. Eph 1:4.

25. Barth, *CD* 2/2:92.

26. Barth sees the covenant of grace as the created order's "material presupposition." See Barth, *CD* 3/1:232. For Barth's discussion of the relationship between creation and covenant, see *CD* 3/1:42–329.

27. Barth, *CD* 4/1:9.

28. Barth, *Christian Life*, 212.

thus any claim about the being of the church and the relationship of the church to the world—must be based upon the revelation of God found in the scriptural narrative of God's covenant with Israel and its fulfillment in and through the kingdom of God ushered in by Jesus the Messiah. If the church is to know Christ and his kingdom, it first has to listen to the revelation of Christ and his kingdom found in scripture. This listening orders both the church's internal life of worship as well as its external interaction with the world, particularly in its act of praying for the world. "Praying for the coming of the kingdom of God and his righteousness . . . Christians can look only where they see God looking and try to live with no other purpose than that with which God acts in Jesus Christ."[29] In other words, if the church is to live faithfully *as* the church in the midst of the world, the church first must listen to the revelation of God in Jesus Christ and then, on the basis of this hearing, live in correspondence to it by being like Christ and declaring the truth of what has been revealed about him to the world.

This insight relates to the second way the church corresponds to God's reality: through its *vision*. Barth insists that the church will be able to confront human unrighteousness only when it can envision the "possibility and necessity of human righteousness."[30] The disorder wrought by the powers cannot be seen as a "final reality that cannot be altered" but as a "phantom that is destined to disappear."[31] The development of this eschatological vision marks the point where the church brings its view of the external world into correspondence with the true inner reality of created being and human history, which is the reality of the covenant. To see humanity in light of God's plan for it, Barth argues, is to confess that the possibility of human righteousness already exists and is being fulfilled even now by God within human history. It is to declare that Christ's own righteousness—and the reality that through grace humans can be *in Christ*—creates and guarantees the possibility and establishment of human righteousness though Christ even within disordered systems of the powers. To base one's view of reality upon Christ, therefore, is to envision the world through the lens of Christ's atonement of sin on the cross; it is to look at the broken systems of Baltimore and see them, not in terms of their unrighteousness, but in the light of the reality of Christ's justifying work; it is to claim that the forces of death visible on the streets of Baltimore were conquered in the resurrection; and it is to look at the both the perpetrators and the victims and to declare that

---

29. Ibid., 266.
30. Ibid., 212.
31. Ibid.

one day, tears, death, and mourning "will be no more."[32] In short, a church with a God-centered vision of the world sees the world in light of Christ rather than the other way around, because it is a church that recognizes that because the history of the world is determined *by* Christ, the reign of powers that appears to be intractable actually is limited in nature and scope.[33]

This vision helps to explain the nature of the church's third act by which it corresponds to God's reality in Christ: *prayer for the kingdom*. Barth argues that Jesus Christ's command that his followers pray "Thy kingdom come" is an instruction for the church to exercise freedom over against sin and powers.[34] Prayer for the kingdom is a revolt against the disorder that dominates the world, a rebellion against despair, and a refusal to slip into inaction and indifference. This is not a human rebellion, because humanity as such cannot defeat the forces of sin and death; rather, it is a declaration that salvation—the restoration of order out of disorder—comes "from God, from above, from heaven."[35] This prayer proclaims the reality that God has acted and continues to act against the powers in and through Jesus Christ, and that despite the hopelessness that appears around them, humans are not "worth less" but worth more because their work is determined in Christ. It is a signal of the church's hope that the kingdom, which is at once manifested incompletely and yet truly in the life of the church, is "God himself in the victorious act of overcoming the disorder which still rules humanity" and thus "God himself in the act of normalizing human existence."[36]

This rebellious prayer for the kingdom leads to the fourth and culminating act of the church's correspondence with its reality in Christ: its *obedient deeds*. As an act aimed in a "vertical direction," Barth says, prayer for the kingdom leads to "the horizontal of a corresponding human, and therefore provisional attitude and mode of conduct in the sphere of freedom."[37] Prayer, in other words, leads to *action*. Christians cannot pray for the coming kingdom without "being projected into this corresponding action of their own which is provisional but nonetheless serious."[38] To pray for God's kingdom is to become "empowered, instructed, and summoned to fight against human unrighteousness."[39] If the church's confession about God's

---

32. Rev 21:4.
33. Barth, *Christian Life*, 252.
34. Matt 6:10.
35. Barth, *Christian Life*, 212.
36. Ibid.
37. Ibid.
38. Ibid., 213.
39. Ibid., 266.

righteousness in Christ is to ring true both within the church and to those outside of it, then this prayer must be accompanied by a "simultaneous and related revolt" against the unrighteousness that is in the world.[40] This means that the church's gospel preaching must be integrally related to its pursuit of justice: to preach and pray for the kingdom is to live in revolt against the powers. And this revolt must be an *active* one, going beyond mere non-participation in sin or a withdrawal from broken systems, because the church's claims arise from what God *has done* and is *still doing* in Christ and through the Holy Spirit. The church's resistance against unrighteousness corresponds to this divine action, and it marks the church's participation in it. As it prays for the kingdom to come, the church seeks to reflect the reality of this prayer in concrete ways by working to help the world begin to reflect the redemption coming to it. This work, Barth argues, marks the church's "entering into battle for [the kingdom's] actualization," a battle won solely by God, but one that does not exclude the active participation of his people.[41] Barth sees precedents for this battle throughout scripture, from Jacob's wrestling with God,[42] to Christ's struggle in Gethsemane,[43] to Paul's references to the "armor of God,"[44] athletic contests,[45] and fighting a "good fight."[46] The church of Christ has been commissioned to live in this same pattern: they are "citizens of heaven"[47] precisely in and through their active struggle against the "ungodliness" and "unrighteousness" that arise because of sin.[48] This struggle, Barth says, takes concrete form in ordinary acts of Christian faithfulness, so that the church's rebellion against the powers is "actualized in little steps" as Christians go about their daily lives, turning their hope for the kingdom into an ongoing and relentless fight against sin and its effects.[49] "As they may live by the great hope," Barth says, Christians "stand by others even in the little things, in hope venturing and taking with them little steps to relative improvements wherever they attempt them, even at the risk of often going astray and being disappointed with them."[50]

40. Ibid., 206.
41. Ibid., 207.
42. Gen 32:24.
43. Mark 14:32.
44. Eph 6:11.
45. 1 Cor 9:24; 2 Tim 2:5.
46. 1 Tim 6:12; 2 Tim 4:7.
47. Phil 3:20.
48. Rom 1:18.
49. Barth, *Christian Life*, 213.
50. Ibid., 271.

THE CHURCH FOR HUMANITY

Barth's vision for a church that pursues justice through daily actions gives the church a coherent approach to the task of addressing social problems, because it allows the church's pursuit of justice always to remain linked to its internal acts of worship and prayer as well as its reality of its being "in Christ" as a result of his saving work. We can draw two further implications as we consider how such a vision might be worked out in concrete ways. First, and on the one hand, it opens the door to the possibility that the church might engage in a real and vibrant partnership with other groups who also are working against unrighteousness and injustice within society, because their work can align with the church's own work even if it stems from different motivations. So, for example, in order to address the kind of social problems found in *The Wire*, the church could join forces with a political movement, social organization, or even the government. This might take the form of a partnership with the government to start and staff tutoring or job-training programs; working with social organizations to meet the needs of the elderly, young families, or children; partnering with police to establish crime-prevention programs and activities for young people living in gang-dominated neighborhoods; or investing in businesses in order to create job opportunities and foster a localized economy. Whatever the activity, the church can join with these other groups and practice together the "little steps and relative improvements" needed to work against unrighteousness and injustice. This fosters a distinct type of Christian politic, one that promotes and encourages involvement in the structures and programs of a society under the confession that this world is *Christ's* world, and that he actively works his will within it through his Spirit, the same Spirit who dwells inside believers.[51]

Second, however, and on the other hand, the church's work against unrighteousness always remains distinct from that of other groups because this work never exhausts the church's commission. The church is not called to struggle only against sin's effects, but against sin itself. This means that the church's pursuit of righteousness always includes within itself aims that go beyond those of the other entities fighting for the same thing, because the church's pursuit begins from the confession that the fight for justice is included within God's plan for the salvation of sinners in and through Christ. This distinct starting point leads to a unique perspective. For example, the church knows what all other groups do not: hardships, anxiety, persecution, hunger, nakedness, danger, and even violence can never separate anyone

---

51. John 14:16–26.

from the love of Christ, nor can they compare to the "glory about to be revealed."[52] Such evils, in fact, can be and are transformed by God so that they work for good, such as by increasing endurance, refining character, and turning one more fully to the hope found only in God.[53] This means that the church approaches the issue of justice always from within the larger context of God's providence, and this gives the church a level of patience and endurance that other groups lack.[54] The church can remain hopeful even in the face of the brutality of the bureaucracy and the seemingly intractable reign of the powers because it always acts under the presupposition that the powers' days are numbered: God will prevail over them, because they have been defeated by God in and through Christ. This knowledge helps the church resist the temptation to fall into the kind of indifference that too often grips those working for justice, because the church can proceed from the certainty that its actions matter even if they produce no tangible consequences. Neither the strength of the opposition nor the effectiveness (or lack thereof) of the church's efforts can ever be the church's primary focus. Rather, the church's chief concern is obedience: Christians fight for justice and against unrighteousness simply because that is what it means to follow Christ, and the goal is not success but a life lived in correspondence to him. This perspective provides Christians with the motivation to "swim against the stream regardless of the cost or consequences," because it gives them reason to continue their work against sin and its effects even when it does not make any sense to do so.[55] Such an approach makes all the difference in a city like Baltimore as depicted in *The Wire*, because it means that the church does not give up even when its work is stymied at every turn and failure, at least as some would define it, is a near certainty.

This insight leads to another particularity of the church's work in the world: among all the other organizations participating in the struggle for justice, only the church fights by working for *every* human being. Since the church first seeks God and on this basis struggles against the powers and their effects, its fight for justice can never be directed against any single entity, group, or person.[56] Political movements, social organizations, or governments tend to focus on an "other" that must be defeated, so that the pursuit of justice inevitably takes the form of a "friend-foe" dynamic. This is what we see in *The Wire*: the government, police, and citizens who struggle

---

52. Rom 8:18, 35.
53. Rom 5:3–5; 8:28.
54. Rev 13:10, 14:12.
55. Barth, *Christian Life*, 267.
56. Ibid., 210.

against injustice do so by fighting the people and groups they rightly or wrongly perceive to be the cause of these problems. But the actual problem is not these people but the *powers*, the forces that twist natural gifts and good efforts in misguided and problematic directions. The government, police, and good citizens have no solution to the problems on the Baltimore streets because none of them can grapple with their true foe, the actual enemy that remains beyond everyone's grasp while holding the city and its people in its sway and thwarting every move made against it. The church, in contrast, addresses its efforts against humanity's true enemies—sin and the powers— because it knows that history is defined by Jesus Christ's victory over these enemies through his life, death, and resurrection. The Christian God is the God who is for humanity in Christ, and this God awakens and enlivens his church so that it also exists for all humans by resisting, not other people, but the powers of sin and death that hold them in their grasp. To fight in this way is fight for *every* person, even "those with whom they may clash."[57] This is because every human—from the Christian in the church to the law-abiding citizen to the criminal—stands guilty of sin, the "disorder which both inwardly and outwardly controls and penetrates and poisons and disrupts all human relations and interconnections."[58] To fight against those who share this problem as if they were the enemy would merely confirm and increase the disorder fostered by the powers, to feed into the very cycle of sin that manifests itself at every turn. This is what we see happen again and again in *The Wire*. But to fight primarily against sin and the powers is to take the "cause of all people—wise and foolish, good and bad." It means not being "led astray either by the guilt of others toward them or by the idea that they themselves have no guilt whatever toward others."[59] Rather, it is to become a "peacemaker" (Matt 5:9), to turn the other cheek (Matt 5:39), to love one's enemies and persecutors (Matt 5:44), and to reverse Cain's indifference by becoming the "keeper" of one's brother, even when one's brother is the perpetrator of injustice. This, in turn, is to begin to live into the future of the kingdom and redeem the city made in Cain's image. No longer do we rely on the city to hold up human security or invest in its systems as ends in themselves. Rather, in and through its prayer, "Thy kingdom come," the church looks toward the heavenly city, the one that comes from the east where Cain once traveled (Zech 14:4), the one that comes with the promise of hope that all things will be made right. This new city marks the horizon of the church's hope, and by keeping their eyes fixed upon it, Christians in

---

57. Ibid.
58. Ibid., 211.
59. Ibid., 212.

the church continue to fight for every human even when it does not make any sense to do so, and even when everyone else has given up in despair.

CONCLUSION: IMAGINING THE KINGDOM

As Barth considers the despair caused by the powers and the church's response to it, he argues that the church must begin by starting with the reality of God's eternal decision to reconcile the world in Jesus Christ. The God Christians worship and serve is the God who created this world for Christ,[60] and we know Christ because he has come to us in the flesh in the fulfillment of God's covenant for humanity and creation.[61] This divine plan in and through Christ intrinsically defines all created being, including the being of every human. There is no part of creation that exists independent of this plan, and everything in creation can be seen in its light. From this posture, the church can envision the world around it in light of Christ rather than the other way around, giving it "ears to hear" and "eyes to see" Christ's ongoing work in creation, through his Spirit, "to reconcile to himself all things, whether on earth or in heaven, by making peace through the blood of his cross."[62] The "in heaven" part of God's reconciling work includes Christ's defeat of sin on the cross, where he "rescued us from the power of darkness and transferred us into the kingdom of his beloved Son, in whom we have redemption, the forgiveness of sins."[63] The "on earth" part is being worked out in time, according to God's plan, in part through God's work through his elect, his church, who were "created in Christ Jesus for good works, which God prepared beforehand to be [their] way of life."[64] The church, commissioned to live in obedience to God, prays for the coming of Christ and his kingdom. As they pray, they seek to correspond to their being "in Christ" by working out their salvation in concrete ways through daily obedience to Christ, knowing that God is at work in them enabling them to will and work according to his divine plan.[65] This work takes the form of living for others, which involves abandoning their own interests and putting others first in an imitation of the mind of Christ.[66] They exalt Christ through their work by seeking to make the world around them begin to reflect Christ's own will

60. Col 1:16.
61. John 1:14; Gal 4:4–5.
62. Col 1:20.
63. Col 1:13–14.
64. Eph 2:10.
65. Phil 2:13.
66. Phil 2:3–8.

for it. This is an act of worship, because it is an act of readiness: it marks the church's preparation for their coming king, so that when they go out to meet him at his coming,[67] they will do so as people who are "ready" for his arrival.[68] In the meantime, they pray for his coming and act in accordance with their prayer by seeking righteousness, a search that takes concrete form in lives given over to loving the people around them though proclaiming the gospel to them and seeking a justice for them that reflects God's own justice.[69]

This is a profound vision, but also a difficult one. Christians face opposition along the way from the "cosmic powers of this present darkness" that work against them.[70] The effects of those powers are on full display in *The Wire*. Viewed in isolation from God's coming kingdom, this display leads to despair, a hopelessness that all our efforts fail and we have no option but indifference in face of so great a foe. But when viewed in light of God's plan in Christ, the picture of humanity found in *The Wire* becomes a call to the church to enter into the city and struggle on behalf of humanity. This is *The Wire*'s clarifying contribution to the church mission, and it helps the church see how it might begin to link up with what God is doing in cities like Baltimore. These kinds of cities need people who will be willing to "speak the truth to [their] neighbors"[71] no matter what the cost, and they need citizens who, in the face of the powers, focus upon "building up, as there is need, so that [their] words may give grace to those who hear."[72] This work brings hope, not because it is merely another human work, but because it is a work performed through the church by God himself, the one "who by the power at work within us is able to accomplish abundantly far more than all we can ask or imagine."[73]

BIBLIOGRAPHY

Barth, Karl. *The Christian Life: Church Dogmatics 4/4: Lecture Fragments*. Translated by G. W. Bromiley. Grand Rapids: Eerdmans, 1981.
———. *Church Dogmatics 2/2: The Doctrine of God*. Translated by G. W. Bromiley et al. Edinburgh: T. & T. Clark, 1957.

67. Matt 21:8–9; 1 Thess 4:17.
68. Luke 12:32–39.
69. Rev 22:20.
70. Eph 6:12.
71. Eph 4:25.
72. Eph 4:29.
73. Eph 3:20.

―――. *Church Dogmatics* 3/1: *The Doctrine of Creation.* Translated by J. W. Edwards et al. Edinburgh: T. & T. Clark, 1958.

―――. *Church Dogmatics* 4/1: *The Doctrine of Reconciliation.* Translated by G. W. Bromiley. Edinburgh: T. & T. Clark, 1956.

Bowden, Mark. "The Angriest Man in Television." *The Atlantic* 301 (January/February 2008) 50–57.

Ellul, Jacques. *The Meaning of the City.* Translated by Dennis Pardee. Grand Rapids: Eerdmans, 1970.

Jacoby, Russell. *Bloodlust: On the Roots of Violence from Cain and Abel to the Present.* New York: Free Press, 2011.

Lindbeck, George. *The Nature of Doctrine: Religion and Theology in a Postliberal Age.* Louisville: Westminster John Knox, 1984.

Salam, Reihan. "The Bleakness of *The Wire.*" *The American Scene: An Ongoing Review of Politics and Culture* (January 2008). Online: http://theamericanscene.com/2008/01/01/the-bleakness-of-the-wire.

Simon, David. "Behind the Wire." Interview by Meghan O'Rourke. *Slate* (December 1, 2006). Online: http://www.slate.com/articles/news_and_politics/interrogation/2006/12/behind_the_wire.html.

Yglesias, Matthew. "David Simon and the Audacity of Despair." *The Atlantic* (January 2008). Online: http://www.theatlantic.com/politics/archive/2008/01/david-simon-and-the-audacity-of-despair/47692/.

12

On Naming the Work of God
Ecclesiological Witness and Theological
Transformation in *The Wire*

MYLES WERNTZ

INTRODUCTION

For Christians, the problem of how to "bear witness" to religious conviction has only become more complex; as cultural commonalities become more fragmented, Christians can no longer assume that there are preexisting bridges upon which to build from church to world.¹ As the narrative of *The Wire* unfolds, two things become particularly noticeable for people of faith looking to engage the world displayed by David Simon. First, religious figures continually surface within the matrix of *The Wire*, contributing to and complicating the problems of urban Baltimore life. But, secondly, religious figures are rarely successful in either bearing witness to the faith or in alleviating social ills. In this essay, I will be exploring what it means to bear

---

1. I do not take this to be an entirely unhelpful development. As John Howard Yoder pointed out nearly fifty years ago, secularization may be one providential way of reminding Christians upon what basis the faith exists, and that the Christian life is, in many ways, rooted in no other ontology than the work of God in Christ. Cf. Yoder, *Revolutionary Christianity*, 135–45.

witness within the world of *The Wire*, by explicating the various approaches seen in the show in conversation with contemporary ecclesiological theory. Regardless of how one thinks of the church, Simon offers no release from the world of *The Wire* for any church body; all church bodies are inevitably caught up in the machinations of the city. In accepting this presupposition, however, I am not relegating religious bodies to ethical irrelevance. Indeed, what I hope to show is that within *The Wire*, there is a way for Christian churches neither to abandon the common life of Baltimore nor simply to repeat the mistakes of the city's other failed institutions.

This essay will proceed in two main parts. First, I will explore one of the most dominant motifs in late twentieth-century ecclesiology, that of the church as "polis," a model which sees the church as a distinctive social form which bears witness to its distinctive social existence made possible by Christ through putting forth some aspect of its internal life as the mode of witness.

However, I will argue that when tested in the world of *The Wire*, this model renders Christian witness invisible at best, or at worst, collusive with other destructive forces in Baltimore. Secondly, I will lay out my proposal for how better to understand Christian witness not as testimony to the church's own distinctive social existence, but as testimony to the God who redeems the world. In contrast to polis ecclesiology, I propose that witness is done not by putting forth some internal aspect of the church's life (i.e., its socially distinctive practices), but by bearing witness to a God who frees creation to be fully creaturely. This will be done by directing our attention not to any of the high-profile religious figures of *The Wire* in Seasons 1–4, but by the dramatically understated presence of the church in Season 5.

NAMING THE PROBLEM

In the last two decades of work in ecclesiology, it has become common to describe the church as a "counter-polis," to view the church as a body of practices that, through its practices of liturgy and worship, presents an alternative to the corrupting practices of liberal democracy.[2] This thesis

---

2. The literature around this thesis has many instantiations. The modern genesis of this position is usually traced to Milbank, *Theology and Social Theory*, in which Milbank argues for the social existence of the church as a "counter-polis" to the pseudo-polis established by secular life. Drawing on Augustine's "two cities," Milbank contends that secular attempts to construct social life are, at their core, counter-theologies to Christian theology, and thus, secular social life is a parody of Christian existence in the church. Other notable works defending this thesis in a variety of keys include Hauerwas and Willimon, *Resident Aliens*, and Clapp, *Peculiar People*. Significant differences

assumes, in other words, that Christian witness in the world is achieved by displaying an internal good or practice of the church. Fostering the internal life of churches is not in and of itself a bad thing; as Dietrich Bonhoeffer argued, Christians receive the word of God in and through the words of one another.[3] Similarly, as Alisdair MacIntyre pointed out nearly thirty years ago, a moral life rooted in the knowledge of the individual duty or the individual experience is logically dubious, if only because one cannot make sense of terms such as "duty" or "experience" apart from a community of some form.[4]

The "church-as-counter-polis" argument as set out by John Milbank in his seminal work *Theology and Social Theory* can be summarized as follows: because secular ways of describing social existence—politically, economically, and sociologically—derive from theological concepts, churches exist as "other cities," true cities in contrast to the parodies of the secular. As Milbank argues, these counter-polities—if they are to be thick alternatives to secular polity—must bear witness to thick, visible communities. A similar (albeit decisively differently-grounded account) is that developed by Stanley Hauerwas, in which the church's description as a counter-polis rests less explicitly upon the ontological and institutional participation of the church in the triune life of God (as with Milbank), and more upon how the church's practices, practices which demonstrate the church as a social alternative to secular liberal politics.[5]

I do not wish to challenge the claim that the body of Christ is a visible one, one which bears witness to the good news of Christ in the world; if churches are following in the wake of the God who took on flesh, then churches cannot be Docetic in their own self-understanding. Again, to follow Bonhoeffer's lead, Christians should embrace the materiality of churches as intrinsic to being church, a worldly character which is not to be

---

appear between these works and Milbank's proposal, and it is not my intent to distill them all down to the same argument; the weight of Milbank's proposal, for example, rests upon the church's ontological participation in the triune life, whereas Hauerwas and Willimon, for example, emphasize the practices necessary for the church to be a social alternative to the world. My intent here is simply to point to the proliferation of this thesis concerning the church as a certain kind of alternate society, a thesis present both in the academy and in more popular writings.

3. Bonhoeffer, *Life Together*, 32.

4. Cf. MacIntyre, *After Virtue*, 204–25.

5. E.g., Hauerwas *Peaceable Kingdom*, 96–115, in which Hauerwas describes the nature of certain practices of peaceableness and friendship which present churches as visible alternatives to a world characterized by violence and agonism. Hauerwas has developed this thesis in a variety of ways throughout his career, most notably in *A Community of Character*.

derided.⁶ What I want to contest in "counter-polis" ecclesiology, however, is twofold. First, this ecclesiology describes participation in the internal life of the church as the telos of the Christian life. This description produces a secondary effect, namely, viewing internal goods of the church as the *means* by which witness is borne. If what is being witnessed to is the concrete life of the church, then, the argument goes, one must use internal goods to bear witness to this, lest what we are bearing witness *to* not match up with the *manner* of witness.

As John Flett has recently argued, in conversation with Reinhard Hütter's articulation of this ecclesiology, emphasizing the internal life of churches in witness has an unintended consequence. In prioritizing the internal life of the church as the telos of Christian existence, the practices and institutions of the church are left with the burden of having to bear witness to the outside world.⁷ If, as Flett argues, Christians name incorporation into the church as the telos of Christian witness, witness to the world consists of a kind of "propaganda" of the church's internal culture; if the Christian's witness *is* the way of life of the church, then Christian witness consists of propogating that culture in the wider world, for without that culture, the Christian message is an abstracted proposition rather than an embodied way of life.

Not all of those committed to the ecclesiology described above are implicated by the "propaganda" criticism which Flett highlights. Hauerwas in particular has long been suspicious of strategies of witness which seek to inject internal Christian goods into public discourse (seeing this as a kind of power play), and thus has expressed reservation about many of the kind of arguments made by Milbank in support of his ecclesiological proposals.⁸ What *The Wire* dares Christians to ask, however, is—whether conceived in terms of the church replicating its internal life into the public square in the form of policies and claims of authority (Milbank) or in terms of Christian practices which invite rather than coerce (Hauerwas)—if displaying internal goods of the church is the proper mode of witness for Christians. To put this question differently, does bearing witness to Christ involve replicating internal Christian teachings or practices in public, whether powerfully or weakly?

My assumption, following John Flett's argument, will be that this strategy of drawing on some internal aspect of church life in order to offer public witness confuses what church practices are for. As Flett writes, church

---

6. Bonhoeffer, *Discipleship*, 225–52.
7. Flett, "Communion as Propaganda," 457–76.
8. For Hauerwas on Milbank, see *Performing the Faith*, 169–84.

practices are not to be highlighted as that which makes Christ visible, but rather, church practices direct the people of the church outward into the world, so that they might attest to the God who has reconciled the world to himself, and identify this in the world in ways consistent with the biblical witness and the ongoing life of the body of Christ in the world.[9] In other words, the solution to how to bear witness in public is neither to replicate Christian acts and doctrines in public nor (as Jonathan Malesic has recently argued) to hide Christian acts away from the public in order to cultivate a truly formed church.[10] Though appearing to be polar opposite, I take these two proposals to be mirror images of each other, in that both assume that a church's identity exists *in toto* independent from its missional existence.

If the God of Scripture is a God of resurrection, then the practices of the Christian life are to be seen as waystations and "vision-forming" practices en route to mission within the world; as Craig Hovey has argued, the disciples of Scripture are depicted—even after the resurrection—not as being "in possession" of Christ, but as Christ's witnesses to the continued surprising work of the Spirit.[11] As Kevin Hector has recently argued, Christians are compelled into the world to offer witness about the continued work of God in Christ in the world, but without a guarantee that their witness will be uncontested by other explanations.[12] In sum, Christians bear witness to the work of God in the world, not because what is happening in the world is identical to the practices of the church, but because the nature of the worldly work is an echo of the work of God in Christ in the church.[13] The gifts of the church, such as worship, Eucharist, and discipline, can thus be simply what they are—gifts for formation and participation—and not expected to bear the extra weight of being mobilized outside the context of the liturgy.

For some, the analogous nature of what Christians bear witness to (as the work of God) and what may be explainable by other means is decisively

---

9. Flett, *Witness of God*, 251: "The nature of human reconciliation with God and with one another must itself correspond to the nature of God's self-revelation, that is, the community exists in her service of witness to the world.... She is thus revelatory in her movement into the world, for the fact of reconciliation includes within it the certain call to the whole of humanity."

10. Cf. Malesic, *Secret Faith in the Pubic Square*, 191–216.

11. Hovey, *Bearing True Witness*, 35–36.

12. Kevin Hector's recent *Theology Without Metaphysics* uses philosophy of language to argue persuasively that, while there may be other explanations for any number of kinds of God-talk, Christian descriptions of the world are assumed to be through the power of the Spirit and tested against the person of Christ for their truthfulness, creating an ever-unfolding chain of recognition which is ever new as Christians enter into new territory.

13. Hector, *Theology Without Metaphysics*, 73–102.

troubling, but this need not be so. The analogous nature of Christian witness to other accounts could be seen as an argument for the irrelevance of extrasensory claims. But if Christians know God in and through the creaturely world, then Christians need not fear competitive interpretations, as for Christians, this is nothing new.[14] To be certain, Christian liturgy does in fact demarcate something unlike other things; what I am suggesting, though, is that Christian witness in *public* consists more suitably of reading the acts of the world in light of Christ, testing for echoes of the world which conform to the person of Christ and the work of the Spirit, and naming them as such.

If Christians understand witness to be primarily about the work of God, then pointing to acts which Christians do as a matter of their worship to God seems to be confusing what God does with what Christians do as a *consequence* of what God has done. To put this differently, perhaps Christians offering witness consists of being able to name where the triune God is making *other* things visible than what is presently seen in and through the worship of the liturgical body, and being able to make space for the triune God to continue to bear witness to God's own self through the continual recreation of the world in conformity with the person of Jesus Christ.[15]

In what follows, I will be examining the various strategies of religious visibility which *The Wire* presents its viewers, contending that in the *The Wire*, when religious bodies seek to make the good news of Christ visible by highlighting some aspect of their internal life (either in doctrine, practice, or institution), the religious bodies ultimately end up replicating one of the pathologies of Baltimore. My goal in doing this is not to say that the various proposals articulated by "polis" ecclesiology cannot be sustainable, but rather, to show how within the world of *The Wire*, these proposals suffer from a variety of difficulties. To do this, I will now turn to four examples within the world of *The Wire* to explore how Christian witness occurs. In the first two, Christian witness is conceived as replicating some aspect of the church's own internal life in public. The third example breaks free of this pattern, and attempts to make Christian witness visible independent of church resources, but suffers difficulties of its own. In the fourth example,

---

14. One need only look to the Gospels to see that competitive interpretations of Jesus' person and of what counts as the activity of God in the world are nothing new to Christian theology.

15. John Flett has best characterized this as a "missio Dei" which speaks of the person of God bearing witness to God's self, calling Christians to follow God into creation. What is emphasized in this account is that the church must continually test what it finds in light of Scripture, expecting to find God's Spirit at work within the world as the church goes forth in witness. In sum, the work of God in the world should be freely and gladly received by the church. See DeCou, "Relocating Barth's Theology of Culture," 154–71.

however, witness occurs in conjunction with church resources (in agreement with the first two examples), but Christian witness occurs here not by replicating an aspect of the church's internal life, but rather by creating space for Christians to name what God is already doing in advance of the church's own liturgical presence.

TWO PROPOSALS FOR BEARING WITNESS: IDENTITY AND LITURGY

The first strategy used for Christian witness in *The Wire* is that of practical political actions. Because Christians engage in a pluralist society, the argument goes that Christian witness is best accomplished through acts of service before one's neighbors. Within the school of thought normally associated with what I have described as the "counter-polis" school, there are relatively few who opt for this proposal. But if the resources of the church's internal life are not only its doctrines but its moral commitments which are incumbent upon its members, then these are among the resources which can be externally offered as the mode of witness.

In *The Wire*, this appears in a group that could readily be drawn from nearly any context: the minister's council.[16] Based upon a real-life coalition of ministers within Baltimore, the ministers appear most prominently in Season 3, though the power and influence they represent reverberates in important ways in Season 4 as well.[17] In Season 3, as viewers are introduced to the inner workings of City Hall, we find that the coalition of ministers is an influential consideration for not only city councilman Tommy Carcetti, but also for the mayor, Clarence Royce, and his staff. As the ill-fated drug containment strategy implemented by Bunny Colvin (given the name "Hamsterdam" by the drug dealers) begins to disintegrate, both the police and the mayor's office give ample time and consideration to the question of how and whether to approach the ministerial alliance about this fiasco.

---

16. I freely grant that this particular mode is more common to certain theological veins such as Social Gospel on the one hand, and the so-called "Moral Majority" on the other, in that both of them conceive of the witness generated by Christian communities as consisting in the ways in which Christians engage in issues of public policy.

17. The "ministers" in *The Wire* are based upon a longstanding group of clergy known as the Interdenominational Ministerial Alliance, an advocacy group which proposes a certain policy, and which has been understood as one of the power-brokers within Baltimore life. The relevance of the ministers to political life has been called into question, most prominently in the 2011 mayoral race, in which the challenger Stephanie Pugh openly contested the endorsement of Mayor Stephanie Rawlings-Blake, thus questioning the power of the ministers' endorsement. Cf. Scharper, "Pugh Shakes Up Rawlings-Blake Endorsement."

All parties involved—Mayor Royce (trying to keep his job), Councilman Carcetti (trying to usurp the mayor), and the police (trying to keep their jobs)—know that however the blame unfolds, the ministerial alliance must be supportive lest there be a backlash among the voting populace.[18] In Season 4, we find that the ministers hold power not only with regards to procedural politics, but the city's racial politics as well. In the wake of the Hamsterdam debacle, Carcetti has launched his own bid for mayor, and is fully aware that he as a white Italian candidate has very little chance of securing the endorsement of the African-American ministers' group away from incumbent Clarence Royce, also African-American. Knowing that the ministers remain a significant power-broker to his electoral victory, Carcetti goes to the ministerial council, seeking their support while having qualms about their relevance to the political process.[19]

Within the world of *The Wire*, the minsters do not function as emissaries of religious bodies, but brokers of cultural and ideological currency vital to the functioning of the local politics of Baltimore. To put it differently, the way in which the ministers function is not as ministers, but as brokers of public concerns, speaking in the language of public concerns. As such, as is noted by Police Commissioner Ervin Burrell, the ministers are ultimately "voters," who represent in their actions and words, a voting bloc—not a peculiarly religious voice as such.[20] This view of the ministers is furthered during the mayoral election, as Carcetti is seen going to church and speaking with the minister after the service about the election, but is seen participating in religious life in no other fashion. After the election, the ministers are seen in only this capacity, used as political pawns by one force or another within the political life of Baltimore.[21]

---

18. In "Reformation," S3/E10 and "Middle Ground," S3/E11, we discover that though the ministerial council is opposed to the Hamsterdam operation, in which the police cordon off a vacant portion of the city as quasi-legitimate grounds for the drug trade to operate, not all ministers in Baltimore are opposed to this action; indeed, we find in "Reformation," S3/E10 that ministerial support letters are coming in thanking the police for the effects of their actions, namely, moving the drug trade to an isolated, circumscribed portion of the city instead of having it sprawl throughout Baltimore.

19. "Refugees," S4/E4. It is telling from this point forward that Carcetti, in his fundraising ventures, however, is not depicted calling the ministers for financial support, nor do the ministers appear in any of Carcetti's fundraising galas.

20. "Unto Others," S4/E7.

21. Cf. "Misgivings," S4E10 and "A New Day," S4E11, in which Herc's mistaken arrest of one of the ministers leads to his dismissal. Again, the administration's concern is that offending the ministers by not firing Herc will lead to political problems down the road for the administration.

Central to understanding the mode of witness seen in the ministers is how the ministers are consistently identified as "the ministers." But what the ministers—identified as the representatives of religious bodies—speak is the moral language of the common and public. In being named by their ecclesial identity, the ministers speak on behalf of the church's internal morals, though in publically understood ways, as seen in the Social Gospel.[22] But by speaking the internal identity of the church into the public in the shape of public concerns (such as who will be the police commissioner and how drug enforcement will be carried out) the advocacy of the ministers becomes shorn of anything which would identify the ministers' public witness as particularly religious, as indicated by the ministers being named ultimately as "voters."

As I have suggested already, by seeking to replicate something of the church's internal life externally, i.e., religious identity, the ministers are caught in a bind. If they speak in particularly religious language, they will be dismissed as a marginal voice which speaks of convictions that not all within public life can share. On the other hand, however, if they speak in a public idiom borne out of religious conviction (assuming that their internal identity as "minister" is sufficient for understanding their advocacy as not simply "moral" but specifically Christian), they join in the public process of political deliberation. Their approach is the latter, with the result that even their identities as "ministers" is transmuted into "voters," for what they bring forth is not particularly Christian, but universally democratic.[23] In other words, by letting an internal good (moral norms) bear the weight of witness independent of a liturgical context which renders them specifically Christian, the activism of the ministers becomes unintelligible except as that of "voters."

If putting forth internal moral norms becomes swept up into Baltimore politics, it is time to visit a second strategy for bearing witness: Christian practices of worship as evangelistic. As William Cavanaugh has put it recently, the Eucharistic celebration in conjunction with the corresponding acts of discipleship is what makes the church visible.[24] What Cavanaugh

---

22. The representative voice here is undoubtedly, for better or worse, Walter Rauschenbusch. On this point, see Rauschenbusch, *Righteousness of the Kingdom*, 79–116.

23. If one assumes that what is meant by "Christian witness" *includes* the concept of "good citizenship," then this proposal works fine, except for the glaring problem that no one whom the ministers address see "Christian" or "minister" as indicating anything *other than* "good citizen."

24. Cavanaugh, *Torture and Eucharist*, 234ff. Cavanaugh is arguing that, when the church receives the Eucharist as a penitent body, it is enabled by grace to "make the Amen true," i.e., to affirm that God's kingdom is among us in the person of Christ.

means by this is that the Eucharist creates "space" which "transgresses both the lines which separate public from private," thus "creating spaces for a different kind of political practice."[25] The practices of the liturgy, thus, are those practices and institutions which "constitute the Church as a distinctive public body." Through engaging in these liturgical practices, Christians, by the indwelling of Christ, are enabled to produce an analogous yet alternative configuration of common human activities (eating, drinking, establishing authority, etc.). Instead of diving into city politics in order to offer witness (as with the previous model), Cavanaugh argues that "the most fruitful way to dialogue with those outside of the Church . . . is through concrete practices that do not need translation into some putatively 'neutral' language to be understood."[26] Cavanaugh differs from the first approach in emphasizing that what Christians bear witness to—while having analogies—is not reducible to a common language. Thus, for Christians to have a visible witness, it is best done by thick Christian practices without attempting to translate these into a different language.

Throughout the seasons of *The Wire*, this is perhaps one of the more powerful visions of how Christian witness functions. Throughout the series, non-churchgoers regularly recognize the manner in which the liturgical practices and symbols of the church "speak" volumes. Take, for example, the episode "Slapstick," in which the Barksdale organization makes the scandalous decision to go after the drug-dealer robber Omar on Sunday morning, while Omar is escorting his grandmother to church.[27] While a seemingly reasonable decision (to attack one's enemy in a moment of surprise), both Omar and the Barksdale officials recognize that this is transgressing on a well-established law: one does not attack one's enemy in the presence of the church, or on a Sunday (the Lord's Day).

On the other hand, the specifically liturgical voice of the church is simply another locale for the struggles of Baltimore to be played out. In other words, while the liturgical settings are recognized as offering something "sacred" and distinct from other settings, this does not mean that the practices

---

Much of my own work is deeply indebted to Cavanaugh's work.

25. Cavanaugh, *Theopolitical Imagination*, 90. Other Protestant examples of this approach, though varied in their emphases, include Yoder, *Body Politics*, and Smith, *Desiring the Kingdom*. These works differ from Cavanaugh by emphasizing the performative nature of Christian practices as both constitutive of the church body and of Christian witness (in contrast to Cavanaugh, who speaks of the constitutive nature of the Eucharist, which in turn funds performance); these works agree, however, with Cavanaugh's approach in that what is constitutive of the church also forms the basis of how Christians bear witness in the world.

26. Cavanaugh, *Theopolitical Imagination*, 94.

27. "Slapstick," S3/E9.

or liturgies of the church will in and of themselves "speak" a clear alternative message to the violence of Baltimore without additional aid. If anything, asking the liturgy to offer a self-evident voice "without need of translation" invites the drama of *The Wire* to simply view the liturgical setting as one more place to conscript in the ongoing power struggles of Baltimore.

The most prominent example of this failure is in the background of the entire second season. Season 2, which focuses on how the dockworker unions play into the ongoing life of Baltimore, is a continual conflict between the police and what they (rightly) suspect to be a corrupted dockworker union. But what might otherwise appear as a routine investigation by the police of the docks has an ecclesial beginning. In the opening episode, Commander Stan Valchek goes to a local church with an offer to install a stained glass window in honor of the police department. Much to his dismay, the prime space has already been taken by Frank Sobotka, the union leader of the stevedores.

Lest we think that Sobtoka's gesture in providing the stained glass window is out of piety or devotion to the church, we find him going into the church later in the opening episode specifically *not* to confess his sins, but to seek the priest's political connections. With an envelope of money, Sobotka approaches the priest saying, "I need some face time with the Senator," who comes to the early mass in Polish. The priest responds, "You've made offerings way above what it would take to get that window up there," then attempts to change the topic by inquiring when Sobotka last came to confession. At this, Sobotka smiles and says, "I'll see you, Father."[28] The rest of the conflict between the police and the stevedores in Season 2 will escalate in the wake of this initial exchange conducted not (as with the ministers) outside the church, but within the context of what Cavanaugh takes to be the strongest self-evident witness of the church: the liturgy. Both Valchek and Sobotka rightly understand what the church offers in terms of its own practices (liturgy, confession, devotion via the architecture), but neither one are shown as being materially affected by these things. Rather, it is the *absence* of any additional explanatory function alongside these visible aspects of church life which allows Valchek and Sobotka to use the church for their own purposes.

---

28. "Ebb Tide," S2/E1. This dismissal of the church practices is reiterated later in the episode when Valchek returns later in the week to again try to get the police window installed, offering $2,500 for the spot, to which the priest responds, "At Sunday mass you can't be found, but early on Tuesday, you arrive with an army?" At this point, after offering an alternate spot to Valchek, which Valchek refuses, the priest leaves it to Valchek and Sobotka to "work it out."

In sum, in the world of *The Wire*, "counter-polis" ecclesiology functions well in terms of the maintaining the church as a public entity; what is called into question, however, is whether this kind of ecclesiology, as it has been articulated in contemporary discussions, can bear witness in public without either being misunderstood, marginalized, or dismissed. The examples from *The Wire* do not as such invalidate this approach, but it should call into question whether putting forth an aspect of the church as the *substance* of witness can work in public, given that these internal aspects are only intelligible once one is *in* the church.

ALTERNATIVE #1: WITNESS WITHOUT THE CONGREGATION

If the problem raised in our examination of "counter-polis" ecclesiology is using an internal aspect of church life as the means of witness, is the solution to do away with the congregation as intrinsic to Christian witness? Should we rather conceive of witness as something *disconnected* from congregational life? If witness is done not by replicating the internal life of the church but by seeking to embed oneself in the world on the terms of the world, should one not consider congregational life as unrelated to the act of witness? This too is presented as a possibility in the character simply known as the Deacon. Played by Melvin Williams, a former drug kingpin turned man of faith in real life, the Deacon appears most prominently in the third and fourth seasons.[29]

The Deacon (whose name is never given to the viewers) is a man of many resources. We first encounter the Deacon as he attempts to help the recently released Dennis "Cutty" Wiles obtain a GED. At this point, Dennis is wavering between re-entering a life in the drug game and doing something else. Notably, this first encounter between the two men takes place in a church sanctuary, though not during a service. In fact, what is notable about the Deacon is—like the ministers—the Deacon is known by reference to the church, but unlike the ministers, does not seek to speak on behalf of the church or to offer any resources of the church to any of the characters he encounters.[30] Throughout the series, the Deacon—instead of offering inter-

---

29. For the complicated story of Melvin Williams, aka "Little Melvin," see Smith, "Redemption Song and Dance."

30. In their first encounter in "Straight and True," S3/E5, the Deacon asks if Dennis is interested in going to church, while Dennis declines. The Deacon will not repeat this offer in their interactions. Similarly, in the Deacon's interactions with Bunny Colvin, there is no offer of church attendance, nor advocacy on behalf of the church body. In fact, only on one occasion ("Slapstick," S3/E9) do we hear the Deacon mention being

nal goods of the church to the figures he encounters—offers "reconciliation" in a secular key, connecting isolated figures to structures or resources which help those figures become more of themselves. In other words, the "witness" of the Deacon consists not in connecting them to the life of the church, but (as a Christian) in helping the people more deeply enter the circulations of Baltimore, more fully equipped than they were before.

The first example of this which displays this approach is the Deacon's engagements with Bunny Colvin, during the infamous Hamsterdam episode. The Deacon is taken by Colvin to see the contained drug trade, which horrifies the Deacon due to the deplorable conditions which have emerged. While not approving of the tacit legalization of the sale of drugs, the Deacon connects Bunny with various nonprofit agencies who provide the area with clean water, sanitation, and needle exchange.[31] Once Hamsterdam is exposed and Colvin forced to resign in disgrace, the Deacon appears again, connecting Colvin with researchers from the University of Maryland who are needing someone with Colvin's law enforcement background to help understand how to educate kids from the corners.[32]

In creating these connections for Colvin, the Deacon is helping Colvin become not a creature of the *church*, but more fully *himself*. Colvin's initial impulse for corralling the drug trade into a specific section of Baltimore is not only for the sake of helping the residents of Baltimore, but also for helping rescue the youth of Baltimore.[33] As such, with each connection that the Deacon makes, it is one that enables Bunny to flourish more fully as one who seeks to help the youth, but within the circulations present in the city. In other words, the Deacon enables Colvin not to escape the circulations or complexities of Baltimore by offering a "socially embodied alternative" to Baltimore, but rather by helping Bunny to function within the machinations of city life with the resources necessary to flourish *within* (not in spite of) that system.

A similar pattern emerges in the Deacon's dealings with Dennis. Soon after their initial meeting, Dennis comes to the Deacon, having decided not to reenter the life of drug dealing, but without the resources to do something different. It is at this point that the Deacon encourages him to work with the "hoppers" on the street that he knows so well, only for more constructive

---

on his way to church.

31. "Moral Midgetry," S3/E8.

32. "Home Rooms," S4/E3.

33. Ultimately, Colvin will adopt the son of an imprisoned member of the Barksdale organization. In Season 5, we see that Naymond, Colvin's adopted son, has moved from being a "corner boy," i.e., a runner for the drug trade, to an exemplary student, having left the life of the street behind.

ends. Thus, while working day labor, Dennis begins a gym for kids to train them in boxing. Dennis' new endeavor is not without its difficulties (including hospitalization). Thus, at key points, the Deacon appears to aid Dennis, first by putting him in touch with Roman, a community leader who is establishing a youth program, and then with Odell Watkins, a State Delegate who can help Dennis obtain the correct permits for his work.[34] Similar to the pattern we saw in the Deacon's interactions with Colvin, the Deacon's connections enable Dennis to find his vocation. As he goes down the road of helping rescue youth from the street and into his gym, Dennis—once again due to the help of the Deacon—obtains a job acting a "custodian," "mopping up" truant kids, so that Dennis is involved with rescuing children not only in the gym but through the school system as well.[35]

Dennis' story, however, proves to be a challenge to a narrative that would attribute the effectiveness of Dennis' change to the work of the Deacon. As frequently as the Deacon is engaged in making connections between Dennis and resources which can help Dennis flourish in the city, it becomes apparent that the Deacon's resources are coming up short; while Odell Watkins can help Dennis with the permits to establish the gym, neither he nor any of the Deacon's other legitimate contacts can help with funding. In the end, it is Avon Barksdale who provides the capital to get the gym off the ground, as Avon was a boxer in his youth.[36] But most powerfully, though the Deacon has aided Dennis in his quest to live within *The Wire* in a more fulsome way, Dennis laments that though he has reformed, there is nothing to hope for other than to live within the constant temptation of *The Wire*.

In other words, while Bunny sees the Deacon's witness as "deacon" as one which enables self-transformation, Dennis sees the Deacon's approach as not offering any reason not to turn to the provisions of the darker side of the streets, if the connections available through the streets are more effective than the "legitimate" connections of the Deacon. This, I contend, is the drawback to the Deacon's approach. By not expecting internal goods of the church to bear the weight of witness, the Deacon is able to enter more fully into the world of *The Wire* in creative ways, making connections rather than simply positing the church's stance (as with the ministers). But by displaying "witness" as "enabling personal flourishment"—in isolation from a new social existence within which to make sense of this transformation, we are left with Dennis' lament of having flourished in the ruins of *The Wire*, but having nowhere to go.

34. "Slapstick," S3/E9.
35. "Refugees," S4/E4.
36. "Reformation," S3/E10.

ALTERNATIVE #2: WITNESS AS RECOGNITION AND NAMING

The final possibility of witness in *The Wire*, and the one which I wish to put forth, is a witness of *recognition*. If the narrative of *The Wire* offers reason for pushing back on modes of witness which emphasize the internal goods of the church as sufficient to the task of witness, the final season of *The Wire* presents us with a different, if much more subtle, way of thinking about how to describe witness: naming acts of the world in terms of gospel, without first expecting that these acts either conform to liturgical parameters or describe themselves in Christian terms.

What I am putting forward here finds some agreement with both versions of witness treated thus far. In agreement with the "polis" ecclesiology, the form of witness I will advocate agrees that Christian witness is inextricably linked to the life of a community; as John Howard Yoder repeatedly argued, Christian witness cannot be reduced to simply what an individual does, as this misses the force of Scripture's narrative which describes the emergence of a community of God. But what I want to argue with is the presupposition that the practices of the community can or should bear the weight of witness. To be sure, Christian practices form the thinking, worship, prayer, and moral character of Christians. But since Christian practices require the context of communal life for the practices and habits of Christians to "make sense," the practices *in and of themselves* seem ill-fitted to be able to "speak" in a world where this communal life is not immediately present.

In other words, to put forward an aspect of Christian life *as* the witness struggles on two levels. First, it expects that the practice "speaks" sufficiently, whereas if *The Wire* is any indication, Christian practices independent of interpretative aid or the voice of Christians to name these practices or acts are either co-opted by other parties or ignored altogether. Secondly, putting forth an aspect of Christian life as the object of focus before the "watching world" (to borrow John Howard Yoder's phrase) confuses the God who creates the community with the community itself. As Hans Frei potently argued, there are no "Christ figures," in that to speak of a "Christ figure" is to make Christ a type which could be repeated; disciples are those who follow Christ, but not those who could be interchangeable with Christ.[37]

Rather, if it is in fact God in Christ who creates the community, the witness of the community is to the work of God in Christ, and not primarily to the practices of the church which arise as a consequence of Christ's work.

---

37. Frei, *Identity of Jesus Christ*, 63–73.

This approach, unfortunately, leaves Christians grasping for how then to witness, if not via their practices. It is here that I wish to suggest that Christians bear witness to Christ's work by learning to recognize the prevenient work of God in Christ in the world. This is not a kind of reading of all of creation as already "anonymously" Christian, but rather a way to aid Christians in recognizing that—if the life of the church in the world exists by the grace of God—then "bearing witness" to how the church exists means being able to identify "parables" of God's redemption in the world, and name them publically as such.[38]

It is at this juncture that my proposal likewise finds agreement and disagreement with the proposal seen in the character of the Deacon. While the ways in which the triune God renews the world are manifold and occur in spaces in which the institutional church is not present, this is *not* to say that this renewal will bear no resemblance to the work which God in Christ has accomplished in the visible body of the church, or that the work of Christian witness should occur completely independent of a Christian community. To speak of the God of Scripture is to speak of the narrative of Scripture as that which governs our vision of who this God is and the kinds of things this faithful God does. The work which Christians identify as the work of God will bear resemblance to that which is done within the church, though not being identical; because Christ is not only the founder of Christian redemption, but also the ongoing sustainer of that redemption, then the work of Christ will both resemble that work which is already done in the name of Christ (i.e., the worship of the church), and yet, will stretch Christians in ways which continually force us to reckon with the scriptural attestation that the call of the people of God is not to be focus on being self-formed, but to be formed in our following Christ into the world.[39]

In contrast to the more dramatic proposals already described, this proposal goes almost unnoticed in Season 5. Throughout the series, Reginald "Bubbles" Cousins struggles with a drug addiction which affects not only himself, but his relationships with his fellow addicts and his family. Though given counsel through his sponsor Walon (played by musician Steve Earle), Bubbles continues to float in and out of sobriety, unable to beat his habit. How exactly Bubbles rises up out of addiction moves toward the kind of "witness of recognition" that I have sketched above.

---

38. Cf. Barth, *CD* 4/3:111–14.

39. Again, Bonhoeffer's Christology pushes us in this direction, particularly in his reforming of Christology in terms of the promeity of Christ—that Christ is the one fundamentally who is "for me," compelling Christians to be the ones who are "for others." Cf. Jensen, "Real Presence," 143–60.

Throughout the series, Bubbles performs certain informant duties for the police, which secure him enough money to go back out into the streets and procure more drugs. Though the officers acknowledge this habit, they continue to say little to Bubbles about his habit, including Bubbles' cousin, Detective Shakima Greggs. In ways similar to the Deacon, the police provide Bubbles with resources which only lead to Bubbles surviving within *The Wire*, but not ultimately being able to withstand it. It is not until Season 5 that we find Bubbles rising up out of addiction, a drama played out against the backdrop of two Christian institutions—the Dorothy Day Catholic Worker house, and a nameless church which houses a Narcotics Anonymous program.

Following the death of one of Bubbles' associates, the teenager Sherrod, Bubbles seeks out help for his addiction. During this time, these two Christian settings are the scene of multiple transformations in Bubbles' own life, and subsequently, in the lives of others. Bubbles initially begins to volunteer alongside the other workers of the Catholic Worker house in the city out of a desire to do something constructive with his grief. Through this volunteering, Bubbles is gently encouraged by an unnamed volunteer not simply to work in the back scrubbing pots, but to engage with the people who come in. Bubbles is reluctant to do this, as he feels a great deal of guilt and grief over what has happened with Sherrod and others due to his actions. But over time, Bubbles moves into the front room, interacting with the neighborhood residents who come in.

As Bubbles works in the Catholic Worker house and attends his NA meetings—slowly coming to terms with his own addiction and past—Bubbles' gradual transformation emerges in these Christian spaces, though not in confessionally Christian ways. As he works in the Dorothy Day House, Bubbles slowly gains the strength in the NA meetings to tell his story, to confess his sins, and to come to terms with his own life; eventually, Bubbles is seen leaving the life of the streets and reconciling with his family. Importantly, the transformation that Bubbles undergoes—both in the shadow of the Catholic Worker house, and in the sanctuary of the church that houses the NA meeting—is not a result of an internal good of the church being externalized. Rather, the Christian communities in both places create space for the transformative work of God to occur, inviting a witness of recognition whereby the Christian communities are able to identify those things that God is doing.

This form of witness, as we see in the case of Bubbles, leads to Bubbles being transformed in such a way that it leads to further recognition as well: as Bubbles becomes transformed, his life leads to others recognizing the true nature of Baltimore's poverty and the depth of despair created by addiction.

In a continuing chain of effects, Bubbles' transformation opens up into further transformations.[40] Bubbles' confessions in NA help others gathering at the meetings to come to terms with their own addictions. Additionally, as Bubbles comes to terms with his life, he is able to open up to an eager newspaper reporter who comes to the Catholic Worker house looking for an easy human interest story, but instead has the complexities of Baltimore's poverty laid out before him.

While the spaces of the Catholic Worker house and the unnamed church provide space for God to work out in Bubbles a transformation, what is yet lacking is the *naming* of Bubbles' transformation as the work of God; Bubbles' movement from addiction to reconciliation is *accompanied* by Christians, but never *described* in Christian terms by any character. It is here that the door is opened for the Christian viewer of this program to go beyond *The Wire*, not by negating what Season 5 puts forth, but by supplementing it. *The Wire* correctly states that the way of witness is to create space to be, in Hovey's words, the God of the resurrection who must be anticipated, but not predetermined.[41] But *The Wire* does not go far enough, in my estimation, in that Simon is, in the story of Bubbles, not interested in making an explicitly religious statement about Christian theology as much as he is acknowledging the possibility of transformation. This is where Christians make their confession that—yes—Bubbles' transformation bears the contours of a christological transformation: that the resources for recovery are not outside our grasp, but readily available through the power of the Spirit of God.

As I suggested earlier, the fact that Bubbles' transformation or the reporter's enlightenment occur outside an identification of this being a work of God is not entirely problematic. Throughout the Scriptures, the people of God routinely identify as the work of God things that their neighbors resolutely misunderstand or misidentify, acts in history that *at that time* had no cognate in the experience or history of the people of God. Whether in the case of Cyrus as God's agent, or the plagues of Egypt as God's judgment, or Pentecost as the creation of a new people by the Spirit, the transformations of God in history always require the people of God to recognize God's work in new ways, and they are always open to misidentification. And yet, Christians bear witness that—though one could, for example, explain Pentecost as drunkenness—these things are the work of God in ways that

40. Cf. S4/E7, where Bubbles begins to open up the world of poverty to the reporter, and S4/E9 where Bubbles tells the story of Sherrod in the shadow of the cross in the church sanctuary. In both cases, Bubbles' transformation leads to other instances of "recognition" of what the world is.

41. Hovey, *Bearing True Witness*, 36.

cohere to God's work previously, though in ways that Christians could not have expected beforehand.

Thus I would submit that the reason the witness of the Catholic Worker house and the unnamed church of the NA meeting succeed where other more identifiably Christian witnesses fail within *The Wire* is precisely because it is not a witness to the church's life, but to the God who alone saves. In the cases of the Deacon, ministers, and the church liturgy, mobilizing an internal aspect of the church as the vehicle for witness fails precisely because that is not the purpose of these practices; to ask them to "bear witness" is to freight them with weight they were not meant to bear, and to confuse the material means of our transformation with the God who transforms. By contrast, the witness of the religious bodies of the final season of *The Wire* succeeds precisely by making room for Bubbles' transformation to occur within their spaces, but according to the contours of Bubbles' story. To put it differently, the former modes ask for there to be a transformation according to the specific contours of what *presently* is, whereas the latter acknowledge that God transforms in a way that is consistent with the person of Jesus, though perhaps not altogether consistent with what has already occurred.[42]

To be sure, while one can posit that Bubbles' transformation, from a Christian perspective, is only possible by the work of God, this is not to say that Bubbles himself identifies it as Christian transformation. This is precisely the point, however, where Christian proclamation, having identified the change in Bubbles as consistent with the gospel, steps in to bear witness to the nature of Bubbles' change: one enabled by God in Christ, who creates new life and creates in a differentiated unity.

BIBLIOGRAPHY

Barth, Karl. *Church Dogmatics 4/3: The Doctrine of Reconciliation*. Translated by G. W. Bromiley. Edinburgh: T. & T. Clark, 2010.
Bonhoeffer, Dietrich. *Discipleship*. Minneapolis: Fortress, 2003.
———. *Life Together; Prayerbook of the Bible*. Minneapolis: Fortress, 2005.
Cavanaugh, William T. *Theopolitical Imagination: Discovering the Liturgy as a Political Act in an Age of Global Consumerism*. Edinburgh: T. & T. Clark, 2002.
———. *Torture and Eucharist: Theology, Politics and the Body of Christ*. Malden, MA: Blackwell, 1995.
Certeau, Michel de. "How Is Christianity Thinkable Today?" In *The Postmodern God*, edited by Graham Ward, 142–55. Oxford: Blackwell, 1997.
Clapp, Rodney. *A Peculiar People: The Church as Culture in a Post-Christian Society*. Downers Grove, IL: IVP Academic, 1996.

---

42. Cf. Certeau, "How Is Christianity Thinkable Today?"

DeCou, Jessica. "Relocating Barth's Theology of Culture: Beyond the 'True Words' Approach of *Church Dogmatics* IV/3." *International Journal of Systematic Theology* (forthcoming). Online: http://onlinelibrary.wiley.com/journal/10.1111/%28ISSN %291468-2400/earlyview.

Flett, John G. "Communion as Propaganda: Reinhard Hütter and the Missionary Witness of the 'Church *as* Public.'" *Scottish Journal of Theology* 62 (2009) 457–76.

———. *The Witness of God: The Trinity, Missio Dei, Karl Barth, and the Nature of Christian Community.* Grand Rapids: Eerdmans, 2010.

Frei, Hans. *The Identity of Jesus Christ: The Hermeneutical Bases of Dogmatic Theology.* Philadelphia: Fortress, 1975.

Hauerwas, Stanley. *A Community of Character.* Notre Dame: University of Notre Dame Press, 1991.

———. *The Peaceable Kingdom.* Notre Dame: University of Notre Dame, 1984.

———. *Performing the Faith: Bonhoeffer and the Practice of Nonviolence.* Grand Rapids: Brazos, 2004.

Hauerwas, Stanley, and William H. Willimon. *Resident Aliens: A Provocative Assessment of Culture and Ministry for People Who Know Something Is Wrong.* Nashville: Abingdon, 1989.

Hector, Kevin. *Theology Without Metaphysics: God, Language, and the Spirit of Metaphysics.* Cambridge: Cambridge University Press, 2011.

Hovey, Craig. *Bearing True Witness: Truthfulness in Christian Practice.* Grand Rapids: Eerdmans, 2011.

Jensen, Matt. "Real Presence: Contemporaneity in Bonhoeffer's Christology." *Scottish Journal of Theology* 58 (2005) 143–60.

MacIntyre, Alasdair. *After Virtue.* 2nd ed. Notre Dame: University of Notre Dame Press, 1984.

Malesic, Jonathan. *Secret Faith in the Pubic Square: An Argument for the Concealment of Christian Identity.* Grand Rapids: Brazos, 2009.

Milbank, John. *Theology and Social Theory.* Malden, MA: Blackwell, 1990.

Rauschenbusch, Walter. *The Righteousness of the Kingdom.* New York: Mellen, 1999.

Scharper, Julie. "Pugh Shakes Up Rawlings-Blake Endorsement." *Baltimore Sun.* Online: http://weblogs.baltimoresun.com/news/local/politics/2011/07/pugh_makes_ surprise_visit_to_r.html.

Smith, James K. A. *Desiring the Kingdom: Worship, Worldview, and Cultural Formation.* Grand Rapids: Baker Academic, 2009.

Smith, Van. "Redemption Song and Dance: Little Melvin Williams Is Not the Deacon He Played on *The Wire*." *City Paper* (March 19, 2008). Online: http://www2. citypaper.com/eat/story.asp?id=15478.

Yoder, John Howard. *Body Politics: Five Practices Before the Watching World.* Nashville: Discipleship Resources, 1992.

———. *Revolutionary Christianity: The 1966 South American Lectures.* Edited and introduced by Paul Martens, Matthew Porter, and Myles Werntz. Eugene, OR: Cascade, 2011.

13

"It don't matter that some fool say he different..."
The Pretense of Frank Sobotka's Self-Sacrifice

JOSEPH WIEBE

Colvin: "Sometimes the gods are uncooperative."

Burrell: "If the gods are fucking you, you find a way to fuck them back. It's Baltimore, gentlemen; the gods will not save you."[1]

INTRODUCTION

Burrell sums up theology in *The Wire*: faith is the reprisal of things hoped for, the competition of things not seen. The show's epigraph, "This is America, man," tells us that "power is at the heart of every story."[2] Burrell's ribald comment captures the religious tenor of power—its decidedly bellicose rather than redemptive orientation. We are on our own; the divine does not give guidance but metes out arbitrary power. David Simon's gods, however, are what he calls postmodern, postindustrial institutions. The impetus of

---

1. "Dead Soldiers," S3/E3.
2. Wood, "This Is America, Man," 20.

the show is the frauds of Enron and Worldcom, and also the "institutional scandal of sexual abuse by priests and the self-preservation of the American branch of the Catholic Church."[3] The church, just like every other institution from policing to the drug trade and from unions to schools, has "something hollow and ugly" at its "institutional core."[4] American culture is not comprised of the aspects of society that rise above these problems; the failures of institutions constitute its essence. Institutions fail, and they have a proclivity to disown their failure. Paradoxically, the church claims that salvation comes in the form of failure on the cross; however, Simon observes that its behavior as an institution betrays a propensity to protect itself from all forms of failure. Simon's question to the church is a theological critique: how does the church continue to understand and articulate itself when things fall apart?[5]

A response must first attend to Simon's assessment of institutions. According to Simon, lies are at the core of institutions. *The Wire* famously depicts political pretenses: juked stats, the fantasy that free-market processes reward innovative individuals, and the illusion that institutions are steadfastly devoted to hard workers. These deceptions shape social life and public policies. Though lies are intentional, the people in power are more inept and ignorant than evil; more often than not they have conflicted and mixed motives. But *The Wire* never gives the impression that institutions should or can be eradicated. Rather than concentrating on the configuration of institutions per se, Simon is interested in people and the kinds of effects institutions have on them. There is a range of external influences and internal commitments that affect one's life, few of which act in harmony. *The Wire* shows the arbitrary quality of power through narratives with fully developed characters, denuding the pretensions of public discourse. That is, the purpose of *The Wire* is to dispel the myths—the pretenses—that are the funding currency of institutions.

---

3. Simon, "Introduction," 5.

4. Ibid.

5. My understanding of theology as church self-articulation follows Karl Barth's understanding of theology: human understanding of divine reality as it was present in the incarnate Word and experienced in history by witnesses to the Word who then founded the church to continue the proclamation of the work of God in the world. Theological claims cannot be proven by anything outside the life of the church; theology "can presuppose no help or buttress from the outside." That theology refers to the church itself is not meant as an alternate buttress but simply means that theology does not hover in "mid-air." It "depends actually upon God's living Word, on God's chosen eyewitnesses, and on the existence of God's people in the world.... The power of its existence is the power focused through those statements we have made about God's Word, God's witnesses, and God's people." Barth, *Evangelical Theology*, 49–50.

The Wire is a response to the betrayal of institutions that is constructively (not pedantically) didactic. Simon recognizes that stories are not neutral; they are used.[6] Simon uses his narratives for intellectual formation and political orientation. He portrays the lives of "the obscured, ignored, segregated" to show their relevance in America; the response he wants from "the ordinary" is "dissent." He wants the viewer "to think again": to become aware of the disjointed condition of culture and be open to possibilities beyond the current state of affairs.[7] At their best, Simon's stories bear a veracity that forms an alternative to deception as the basis for a social compact. Simon's commitment to authenticity and truthfulness in The Wire, which is an upshot of his affection for the city of Baltimore in which he resides, is not merely to expose the lies inherent in American society but also to imply genuine hope for American lives.[8]

Of course, narratives can also be a form of lying. Victories, happy endings, and life-affirming moments are dishonest representations of life in America. Satisfaction in these "Hollywood endings" cultivates a sense that things work out; The Wire's bleak perspective frustrates our desire for satisfying conclusions. And yet, according to Simon, there is hope in the dark corners of Baltimore. Simon homes in on the downtrodden in the city, putting his faith in the people whom the system has failed. Following Simon, then, The Wire's narrative stands in contrast to the church, whose

---

6. Hollywood not only reflects its own decadent world as normal, but also shapes narratives to fit with the economic system that enables its own success at the expense of the underclass. Simon disdains other police procedurals insofar as they "come down to us from on high." They "are all conceived in Los Angeles and New York by industry professionals, then shaped by corporate entities to calm and soothe as many viewers as possible, priming them with the idea that their future is better and brighter than it actually is, that the time is never more right to buy and consume." Simon, "Introduction," 2.

7. "We're after this: Making television into that kind of travel, intellectually. Bringing those pieces of America that are obscured or ignored or otherwise segregated from the ordinary and effectively arguing their relevance and existence to ordinary Americans. Saying, in effect, This is part of the country you have made. This too is who we are and what we have built. Think again, motherfuckers." Simon, "Interview with David Simon," para. 49.

8. "But in all of these Baltimore stories—Homicide, The Corner, and The Wire— there exists, I believe, an abiding faith in the capacity of individuals, a careful acknowledgment of our possibilities, our humor and wit, our ability to somehow endure. They are, in small but credible ways, a humanist celebration at points, in which hope, though unspoken, is clearly implied. . . . If the stories are hard ones, they are at least told in caring terms, with nuance and affection for all the characters, so that whatever else a viewer might come to believe about cops and dealers, addicts and lawyers, longshoremen and politicians, teachers and reporters, and every other soul that wanders through The Wire universe, he knows them to be part and parcel of the same tribe, sharing the same streets, engaged in the same, timeless struggle." Simon, "Introduction," 31.

propensity for "self-preservation" discloses a false hope that whatever makes the church efficacious is basically distinct from its worst parts. Rather than publically admit that its structure does not stave off immorality, the church, Simon accuses, defaults to a position of self-defense as a response to its sins and internal disorders.

Frank Sobotka is a product of the church; he reveals its worst aspects. Frank enacts the self-preservation that Simon says animates the church. As viewers, however, we are liable to be oblivious to this characteristic of Frank because he is subject to adverse external forces that we rightly denounce, and his reasons for defending himself against these powers are warranted. He appears to be virtuous; his narcissism is inconspicuous, veiled in loyalty. Frank's self-sacrifice hides—rather than transforms—his self-interest. It also misleads him; Frank is self-deceived. His principal motivation is not selflessness, but to prove himself to his union, coworkers, and older brother. In short, Frank's posture of altruism is a guise for power. This pretense brings harm and disorder to his family. Frank is heedless of the corollaries of his mode of being; he refuses every opportunity to change.

Though he is one of Baltimore's downtrodden, Frank embodies the degenerative quality of America's institutions. His pretense hides that which is ugly and hollow at his core. Frank is therefore not a source of hope but reveals a temptation for institutions, especially the church—namely, to give the appearance of virtue to augment power. The crux of the matter is construing rivalry as the quintessence of reality. Competition determines Frank's self-understanding; his faith and loyalty are techniques to empower his struggle within the field of power politics and ennoble his plight. Though he exhibits selfless generosity—he gives money to poor and lame workers, he shows no partiality for his son over other union members when assigning work hours—these actions are part of his struggle for power. Everything he does is for preservation, for "keeping what we had."[9] In his time of crisis, Frank is inattentive to the needs of others that do not concern union affairs.

With respect to the church, the specific theological problem of this temptation is to understand and evaluate its self-sacrifice in terms of strength. Virtues such as faith and charity are not ways to compete with the powers but rather name excellences of human character that facilitate a penitential turning toward victims. The church's assumption that it needs to protect its order—its structural constancy and integrity—to produce people of character takes for granted the apparent rivalry of the world. This assumption is a nervous attitude of self-defense, which is a frame of mind that understands the church as a countercultural community whose practices

---

9. "Bad Dreams," S2/E11.

are not aligned with any of the nefarious machinations of the nation and therefore needs to maintain a stance of self-protection. But this orientation leads to self-preservation and pretense; it produces an anxiety in the church to distance itself from its internal foibles to secure its self-defense against the external forces of the world. Such a trajectory is problematic insofar as strengths—what it considers to be its best practices and most virtuous characteristics—train people to become like Frank: closed off from those who perceive predicaments differently and harmful to those closest to them. The needs and concerns of those victimized by the members who represent church order are relativized by the commitment to the ongoing survival of the church as a credibly sacred institution.

Simply put, self-sacrifice is the right response to corruption—or any breakdown in human behavior and relationships—but the ongoing temptation for the church will be merely to appear selfless as a mode of self-preservation. For the church to be substantively distinguished by its compassion it first must eschew a competitive outlook on life, renouncing the idea that it is a central figure in political struggles between domination and resistance. I will focus on one difference between a substantive charity and the appearance of self-denial, namely, that the former cultivates ambivalence toward institutional procedures. Such equivocality does not abandon the church as an institution; rather, it enables openness to the needs of others in ways that profoundly exceed institutional obligations. Suffering is the form of this kind of openness, allowing the self to be consumed by the destitution and travails of neighbors. Theology is done from the place of the church's victims, which amounts to accepting the demands of the abused even if fulfilling those requests mars the institution that makes its theology intelligible.

There are two challenges *The Wire* puts to the church that this essay will address. The first examines whether self-sacrifice is a pretense for self-preservation or a substantive quality of character. The bulk of the analysis is a reading of Frank, who is rightly committed to the union as a central part of society that mediates personal and social interests, to be sure, but whose self-sacrifice is a pretense. He dramatizes techniques of disassociation, which is what Simon says the church uses as ways of dealing with institutional crises and scandals. Frank's narrative provides a framework for a theological response to Simon's critique against institutional self-preservation. Frank's gift to St. Casimir Church—a stained glass window of Herculean men unloading a ship by hand—manifests Simon's critique: the church is preoccupied with window dressing. Specifically, the imagery of Frank's window reveals a particular pretense of the church: it uses the guise of weakness as a form of power. In an especially telling confrontation, Frank refuses to move his window from the nave to the rectory, which might have appeased Valchek enough to dodge the impending investigation that catalyzes his downfall. At this point, Father Lew has already agreed to call a meeting with Senator Mikulski for Frank, which "didn't need a German window" or his excessive "offerings" to underwrite it.[10] Frank's inflexibility and combative habits reveal his fundamental qualities. The test of Frank's window is to determine whether the weakness of Christ on the cross is a façade for the desire to imagine participation in God's love as the visibly successful counter-dominance of opposition.[11] D'Angelo Barksdale provides a contrast to Frank as a character whose self-denial is not tactical.

The second test is the church's ability to account for Simon himself, whose love for Baltimore and all its inhabitants relativizes his loyalty to institutions. In other words, *The Wire* demonstrates receptivity to the particular interests and wants of his neighbors. This style of open-minded responsiveness is what Christians are called to incarnate; though he does not participate in the life of the church, he exhibits—through *The Wire*—the virtues of faith, hope, and love. Thus, the church must reckon with an instance of love that is non-Christian yet nevertheless displays its own understanding of God's love.

This essay seeks to uncover the ways in which we close ourselves off to the excesses of our social life. Frank's character is too ideological to be open to that which is beyond his hostile understanding of existence—which is encapsulated in Burrell's précis of Baltimore life in the epigraph above. At issue is the love that binds worshipers to one another and others in the world; does it foster open-ended conversation or only institutional patronage? Simon's drama puts his imagination and love for Baltimore at odds with both his characterization of Frank and the church. While Frank's love and commitments alienate him, David Simon's love for his city enables him to imagine the lives of those radically different from him. Ultimately, it is Simon's affection for the place where he lives that is informative for how the church can continue to understand and articulate itself when things fall apart.

"SMOKE FROM THE STACKS. BUT INSIDE . . ."

Frank Sobotka is a lynchpin for almost all the institutions presented in *The Wire*: the drug trade (both local and global), law enforcement, legal system,

---

10. "Ebb Tide," S2/E1.

11. Depictions of Jesus that present his weakness as a paradigm for strength and withstanding forces of power are easily found in popular culture, from Mel Gibson's *The Passion of the Christ* to www.jesusdidnttap.com.

government agency, city politics, the church, family, and the unions. His fate is not only the outcome of the conflict between these variously interested groups, but also a product of chance and irresponsibility. His ambitions are lofty and his intentions are legitimate; he has enough hubris to take on a police major in the Southeastern district, the head of a drug cartel, a state senator, and a union president in order to secure the livelihood of stevedores in Baltimore. Frank is a bulwark against the waves of unencumbered capitalism and its administrative appendages. That the impetus of the dissidence animating him is not only reasonable but also justifiable makes him a sympathetic character.

It is easy to be incensed at the injustice of his murder, to rail against the authorities that exploit his death, and to be depressed at the fallout from his failures. By the end of the season, we have forgotten all his injurious actions and monomaniacal desires that alienate his friends, coworkers, and family. Worse, these are overshadowed and excused in his undue execution. The power of external influences over the course of Frank's life and the termination of his objectives distracts us from his refusal to change. He is caught between competing institutions and is destroyed by his resolve. Unaffected loyalty is the point at which the relevant institutions converge, and we are left to answer the last question he asks: "I flushed my fucking family, for what?"[12]

The drama that draws out Frank's character takes place in Baltimore, but it is set within a changing world. By and large, the transformation is qualitatively described as progress—from inefficiency to productivity, from local to global. The world that is changing, however, is the configuration of the flow of capital. The port unions are the institutions that mediate the flux of global capitalism in America and yet they do not flourish in this position; they are both literally and metaphorically on the brink. The contents that move through the ports—from drugs to disposable diapers—are less important than how they move.[13] The "new world" is the one in which local interests do not obstruct or factor into a functioning global economy. The inauguration of the new world is a moment of crisis for Frank. He is given an apocalyptic vision of ports without humans, offering life for only salesmen and CEOs. There is a more insidious threat to the stevedores than supplanting "thick arms and strong backs" with robotics.[14] At stake in the perdurance of unions is not just the continuation of an economic livelihood, but also the determinants that direct that way of life: personal relations, filial

---

12. "Bad Dreams," S2/E11.
13. Alvarez, *The Wire*, 130.
14. Ibid.

piety, and social bonds. Put differently, "the new world" is the end of a relational mode of being.

Worlds are places, but also refer to orientations or motive forces for characters. Characters are developed through the complexity and confusion within the conflict between these worlds. Business and community are polar horizons for directing one's subjectivity. The "new world" trumpeted by the Greek[15] and FBI supervisor Amanda Reese[16] consists of unencumbered business and material prosperity of individuals at the expense of social institutions. Commodities are the new raison d'être;[17] capital is not the means to support one's household but has become itself the telos of life. Frank, along with other union members of his generation, is aligned with the "old world," which consists of social institutions at the expense of individual prosperity. Though he is frequently seen possessing and spending money, Frank's constant refrain is some iteration of "it ain't about me." Money is not life but the means of life. Frank is determined to secure a viable future for his family through the support of an operative union, even if it means personal suffering. From the perspective of the new world, Frank's commitment to the union is benighted; he is too enmeshed in institutions, too dutiful to the imperatives of social relations. From the perspective of the old world, the Greek's business practices are ruthless; the Greek is emotionally detached to the point of being undisturbed by fourteen murdered women.[18]

The history of Baltimore is—again, both literally and metaphorically—the background for the struggle over the fate of the ports. The events of Season 2 unfold within the two worlds' liminal field, but Baltimore itself provides it with a temporal landscape—elucidating the time between "old" and "new." The landscape, however, is contested; characters make divergent claims about this juncture—whether "the future is now" or if "we're back in the day"—and the show's intentional blur between fictional and actual Baltimore makes it difficult for viewers to make judgments for themselves. Season 2 begins with wide shots of rusted piers and decaying factories on the canal; both McNulty and Diggins have family members who were laid off by Bethlehem Steel in the 1970s. Baltimore has already undergone an economic shift, the results of which sit rotting on the underutilized waterfront. *The Wire*'s second season depicts the subsequent shift, which Baltimore currently experiences. Its time period is between two endings—first

15. "Duck and Cover," S2/E8.
16. "Storm Warnings," S2/E10.
17. The Greek tells Frank to buy "something you can touch: New car, new coat. It's why we get up in the morning" (S2/E8). The material examples are not random: Nick buys a new car; Ziggy buys a new coat.
18. He claims that no one gets into business "for love" (S2/E8).

the steel, then the docks. Whether or not these endings were/are inevitable is what is contested on-screen.

The hermeneutic for the difference between these worlds is economic. Each world is characterized according to its understanding of history as the relationship between past, present, and future. Either the past is mined for that which might withstand present adversities and provide favorable economic conditions for the future, or it is shrugged off in favor of a future whose economy is not subordinate to inexorable demands from the community. McNulty's and Diggins' historical specification marks the end of the Golden Age of post-World War II economic development, the circulation of which was aided by strong unions. Frank's list of union-busting adversaries spans from Bobby Kennedy to Ronald Reagan, signaling not only the history of anti-union labor politics but also a shift in capitalist development. Instead of maintaining security for the labor market through manufacturing and infrastructure, the economics of union busters culminate in the free-market ideology of financial capitalism. Or, as Frank summarizes the problem with American political economy: "We used to make shit in this country, build shit. Now we just put our hand in the next guy's pocket."[19] Frank's old capitalism is household economics; the state of the union is indicative of life at home. The new capitalism of the Greek is, as Nick says, "global like";[20] they have no household, no wives, no children. If the horizon for the Greek is the functioning of the new global economy, then Frank's horizon is the management of his household. Thus, the political fight Frank wages for his union is reflected in the order and condition of his *oikos*.

Frank's household is disordered. There are external and internal reasons for this condition. The external reasons are what make us sympathetic to his plight, what make the fall of his family seem so tragic. Corrupt politicians, vindictive police, crusading federal agents, opportunistic salespersons, and ineffectual religious leaders all obstruct the growth and development of Frank's world. These cultural forces help form an economy that devalues the labor of manufacturers and longshoremen. The heart of the issue is not the displacement of humans by robots but its condition of possibility: the diminishment of work and the trivialization of the desire to live by doing manual labor. This is the difference between Frank and Bruce DiBiago: while Frank is struggling to preserve "a future for the Sobotkas" on the waterfront, Bruce sends his son to Princeton so that he can do "whatever he wants."[21] Frank is astute enough to see through Bruce's vision of the

---

19. "Bad Dreams," S2/E11.
20. "Bad Dreams," S2/E11.
21. "Backwash," S2/E7.

American dream: even kids with economic versatility typically rehash their parents' lives just like everyone else. Sons of stevedores who drink Tang do not grow up to be astronauts; sons of lobbyists who go to Princeton "will grow up and squeeze a buck the way [their father's] did." The psychological dynamic Frank outlines here is that our desires and form of life precede us. Not everything can be understood as a matter of choice.

Frank's own performance of this psychological dynamic—his internal life—forms Ziggy's life. Ziggy tries and fails to be his father, but the portrayal of his failure is an imitation of Frank's desire for power and recognition. Ziggy's descent is catastrophic, but Frank is blind to his own participation in it. Though he is right that no one "could ever control" Ziggy, Frank is oblivious to his own best insight about Bruce's son.[22] Ziggy is and feels responsible for his murderous actions, but there are disorders in the family that prepare the way for his problems. Mr. Dizz tells Ziggy that Frank's father was often too drunk to find his way home.[23] Neither can Frank find his way home, it seems. We never see Frank's house; Beadie says the union hall is his house.[24] Ziggy has a younger brother who went to community college; in an environment that obsesses with succession, this kind of absence is symptomatic of either a breakdown in home or union—which amounts to the same thing.[25] Frank is abusive with Ziggy after he steals cameras, though Frank hardly says a reproachful word to Horse after he lifts four crates of vodka. There is also strain in Frank's relationship with his wife, who is addicted to the barbiturate Nembutal. Frank tells Ziggy that all his time spent away from home trying to get the canal dredged, schmoozing with politicians, and buying drinks for his union buddies was "work . . . for you, for your mother." The work he thinks will provide a future for his family turns out to be deleterious. Ziggy's self-destruction is a visible depiction of Frank's inward deterioration.

Lou provides Frank with an opportunity to learn from his failures and apply it at home. Frank is interrogated by the FBI and told to "come clean" in order to help himself and his union. Though he does not tell the FBI anything, these metaphors stay in Frank's mind. Immediately afterward, Frank tells his lawyers he needs to see his son in order to "get clean." At the end of

22. "Bad Dreams," S2/E11.
23. "Duck and Cover," S2/E8.
24. "Bad Dreams," S2/E11.
25. Simon makes the division clear-cut, though he is ambivalent about its advantage. "If you sensed the sea change and caught the wave—if you were smart enough to tear up your union card and walk away from your father's local to start over at a community college somewhere—then you are there in that world, perhaps, and not here in this one, and maybe it is all for the better." Simon, "Introduction," 8–9.

his conversation with Ziggy, though, he is far from feeling expiated. Frank feels "dirty" but instead of penitence he offers an excuse: "Everything I did, the cans I let through, the money we got from that went to keeping what we had."[26] It is not enough for Lou, whose son Nick has also been corrupted by Frank's actions. Lou reveals to Frank that Nick has always looked up to him as the model of strength and resolve: "Uncle Frank, with the big shoulders. If it was broke, 'give it to my uncle. He can fix it.'" Here the manifestations of Frank's desires are reflected back to him with all their pernicious consequences. Instead of saving the union and "keeping what we had," he enabled Nick's involvement in drug distribution. His strength and determination have betrayed him and damaged the life of his nephew.

Still needing to "get clean," Frank goes to the Local 47 hiring hall of the I.B.S. His substitutionary work for Little Big Roy is an attempt to show that, despite his arrest and indictment, he is committed to the union. His performance is a feat of strength, resembling both the image of the stained glass window in the church as well as Nick's perception of him. Frank continues to be the person he has been, the man that accords with Nick's admiration: a big, strong leader who tries to fix everything himself. Nat smiles and nods in appreciation, but the dockworker working with Frank refuses to help him unload a can. Frank assumes the leadership position, which alienates him from the worker. Nat rhetorically asks Frank about the origins of Moonshot's nickname, which lays bare Frank's endeavor: trying to accomplish a difficult task with the expectation that it will yield significant results. His work is a striving for atonement, but it is unsuccessful. "The grain pier is dead" and Frank is still "dirty."

Frank remains the unmoved, angry fighter until the bitter end. Both Nick and Ziggy completely break down in gut-wrenching scenes of regret, pity, and despair. The pathos in their characters is their grief, which is powerfully shown. Ziggy's final words are a sobbing denial of his father's kindred claim on him as a Sobotka, saying, "Fucked is what I am." He is last seen exiting the relatively safe interview room, only to be swallowed by elephantine prisoners who look down with scorn on his already mangled face. Nick falls apart on account of Ziggy's heinous deed and arrest, offering a kind of drunken eulogy for his cousin. He is last seen staring out through a chain-link fence at the rusting piers, crying while he trudges up an empty street accompanied only by a witness-protection federal agent. Frank does not externalize his defeat; he is too proud to give vulnerability such display. His eyes hardly moisten as he listens to his son's confession; he discreetly wipes his eyes while Ziggy rises so as not to be noticed. He

---

26. "Bad Dreams," S2/E11.

is again moderately tearful in his private conversation with Beadie, but he hides his face in shame. Frank's weakness is never presented as uninhibited or unintentional; we are denied his death as the camera zooms out on a crane shot above him and fades to white before he reaches his assassins. Even his corpse rises from the watery depths, the weights unable to hold down his lifeless body.

Frank has his opportunities to avoid this ending. He has conversations that occasion moments of decision, which give insight into his character but produce no change in his behavior. These encounters disclose his interior conflicts. Each one generates a moment of self-reflection, displaying Frank's inner life through four objects he beholds in four non-consecutive scenes: a grimy mirror, a defunct factory, a stolen can, the lost grain pier. These empirical things provide the means by which we see how Frank has placed himself at the center of his understanding of the world—that his account of his history and reality are not just descriptions—and how this perception prevents receptivity and transformation.

The first occasion is Frank retching alone in the bar bathroom.[27] A visibly distraught Frank stares at himself in a filthy mirror, appearing to evaluate himself in light of the fourteen murdered girls found on his docks. Frank has a guilty conscience. Though he is given the chance to testify—to confess—in front of a grand jury, he will not jeopardize his union. He assumes that the investigation is just a way to break up the union; he interprets every incident and relationship in terms of the union's future. Frank argues that his respect for women is reason enough to clear any suspicions about possible motive. His declaration is sincere, but incomplete. When pressed, mildly, Frank explodes; he is more sensitive about attempts to bust unions than about women's rights. He calls "Bobby Kennedy, Tricky Dick Nixon, Ronnie 'The Unionbuster' Reagan" and others "sons-of-bitches."[28] His guilt and respect for women have limits, namely the conditions for a prospering union. Though he seeks some type of reconciliation to satisfy his conscience, it cannot endanger the preservation of his union.

Frank gives the appearance of virtue but lacks substance. Frank is ostensibly oriented toward the end of common prosperity; the union provides a life of work for people regardless of class, race, or status. Thus, he claims to terminate his risky business partnership with the Greek because of the police investigation. At this, Spiros simply looks at one of Bethlehem's empty manufacturing plants, saying, "They used to make steel there, no? Smoke from the stacks. But inside. . ." Frank stares out at the plant—his second

---

27. "Hard Cases," S2/E4.
28. "Undertow," S2/E5.

moment of reflection—and considers his current situation in view of an empty factory on the horizon. Facing the end of his way of life, however, he is not open to anything beyond what he already knows and does. He caves in to more money despite alleging, "I don't need the trouble or the money."[29] The justification for capitulation is productivity; concessions are necessary for achieving an objective that will generate new economic potential. Nick says, "Today we got ships. . . . But the writin's on the fuckin' wall." Frank's response—"Fuck the wall"—expresses not only his hubris to confront fate but his own lack of intellectual depth; he thinks he has "no choice" but to continue to do business with the Greek. Spiros uses the vacant shipyard as a metaphor of postindustrial America and the future Frank has if he only relies on the docks for a sustaining economy. But the image could also apply to Frank: a hollow man blowing smoke.

Frank alienates himself from his son and brother. His dedication to the union's structure closes off Frank from his family. Instead of reacting to the story of Ziggy's misadventure in the scuffle with Maui—or Horse's disparagement of his son—Frank is distressed about his phone bill. He is incredulous, but also somewhat stirred, that his phone will stay connected without payment. Horse suggests, "Maybe you've been touched by an angel."[30] Following, Lou accuses Frank of bribery and is not interested in benefiting from his misdeeds. Frank again makes it a union issue, regarding his brother's principles as self-righteousness by calling him a "martyr" because his union went "belly up." Unlike Lou, Frank wants to be someone who opposes persecution, who determines the survival of his future. His focus on the union's viability within its political and economic climate construes the world in terms of persecution and resistance. Frank interprets the world according to his union's isolation; he identifies himself and his place in the world at the center of his union's battle for survival.

The next day, Frank is outside his office looking at a stolen can going to chassis, Serge climbing into his rig, and an undercover Kima on the radio. He has an insight into the invisible affairs around him; an intuition tells him something is wrong, that he should "change up." Horse calls him "paranoid"—the flip side to feeling "touched by an angel." Of course, the viewer knows he is right to be suspicious, but Frank's paranoia is part of his preexisting interpretation of the world. Anyone conducting illegal business would do well to be paranoid as a matter of course. Frank's paranoia, however, is not just the habit of looking over his shoulder; it signals his desire to control the outcomes of life. His struggle against the fate of his

29. "Undertow," S2/E5.
30. "Duck and Cover," S2/E8.

way of life indicates a claim to know the world's course. Frank's consciousness alienates him from both his family and yet-unimagined possibilities; the moment he gets the insight of being a part of something greater than himself he responds with attempts at mastery rather than humility. Instead of recognizing the risk he puts his family in, he goes on the attack.

The fourth and final potential moment of self-reflection is just prior to Frank's explicit attack on the gods. All his endeavors have come to naught and Beadie pleads with him to confess to the police. Appealing to his need for righteousness, she tells him, "You're better than them you got in bed with."[31] Frank informs the police detail that he is willing to testify "just to have it off my chest." It appears as though he has finally found atonement; he tells Nick, however, that he is not doing it out of contrition but for revenge. Confession is a strategy, a way to admit failure only in order to save his family and his union. Frank realizes he was mistaken to think that his partnership with the Greek "was wrong for the right reasons"; he admits that working with them to save the grain pier and dredge the canal was a complete disaster. But instead of reflecting on his own culpability and his responsibility to his already disordered household, he wants to avenge his losses: "I'm going to do to those cocksuckers what they did to me." Frank's willingness to meet with the Greek to help his family after everything that has happened shows that he has not learned anything. The rigid, belligerent loyalty they ask for is that which disordered his family; for his willingness to give it to the Greek he is killed. Frank's valor discloses his longing for control; he assumes he can master the fate of his family through true grit. He is wrong, and, given the other relationships in his life, he should have known better.

"IT DON'T MATTER THAT SOME FOOL SAY HE DIFFERENT . . ."

Frank's burliness and bravery are attractive: we are happy when he outsmarts the police and yet agonize over his mischance at confession; we want him to win over the politicians and dredge the canal and yet are furious at the corruption of elected leaders; we applaud his risky affiliation with the Greeks and yet protest his final assent to meet with them. Frank's steadfastness seems like Christian fidelity: a commitment to tradition tempered with some openness to ad hoc allegiances that must be renounced the moment they induce followers to sell out. Frank's corrupted character, rather than his failure, presents the analogy as a critique; his story is tragic not because

---

31. "Bad Dreams," S2/E11.

he remains steadfast against an implacable rival, but because it could have been otherwise. When put in a position of dire straits, Frank entrenches his convictions and uses weakness as a front for power to survive without change. His selflessness reinforces his habits and beliefs.

D'Angelo Barksdale, in Season 2, responds differently than Frank in his own moment of crisis. He is estranged from his family for the second time. At the end of Season 1 Dee is offered the possibility of a new life through confession. Compared to his family's life of violence, he remembers being "freer in jail than I was at home."[32] In order to enact this freedom, though, he thinks he needs to "start over.... Anywhere." He relents, yielding to Brianna's argument that the game suffocating Dee binds their family together; it is the source of their lives. He turns to drugs for transcendence; though he is denied bodily escape, he turns inward to "get my head up outta this shithole."[33] He stops using when Avon asks him to, but he quits altogether when he figures his uncle for orchestrating the hotshots that kill one of his friends. Wanting neither to be a part of the family nor the business, Dee "finds his own way."[34] The Barksdale's commitment to love and family is a façade for business operation. Though Avon's love for Dee appears genuine, Dee experiences it only as part of Avon's machinations. Avon's love is corrupted by business strategies.

Instead of turning to police for help this time, he turns to literature: *The Great Gatsby*. Through Fitzgerald, Dee undergoes a conversion experience of sorts. His account of how American lives are "all prologue" generates in himself a new consciousness, which attests to the possibility of "second acts" in life. Dee's whole self is redirected, changing his understanding of the world. Dee accepts that he cannot escape his past—he is stuck in prison and in his family—but his desires and way of life are not inevitable. He does not say he is "somebody new" nor does he give himself "a whole new story." It is not solely an internal change or mere pretense: "It don't matter that some fool say he different 'cause the only thing that make you different is what you really do, what you really go through."[35] Dee is unlike other characters insofar as he is "willing to get real with the story."

Dee is open to a life beyond those offered by his family and the police. His change in consciousness is reflected in his familial relationships. Dee's response to his mother's vexation at refusing Avon's help for early release recalls a childhood incident when Brianna forced him to fight two boys,

32. "Sentencing," S1/E13.
33. "Hot Shots," S2/E3.
34. "Undertow," S2/E5.
35. "All Prologue," S2/E6.

"whether I lose or not." The only life Brianna can imagine and prepare for her son is one of unrelieved competition—from which no one will save him, and there is no escape. For Dee to "live like I need to live" is to be inside the institution without letting it determine either his relationships or his understanding of the world solely in terms of rivalry. If the game will not let go, at least he will be free from it in jail. Unfortunately, the game also reaches into the prison. Dee learns from Fitzgerald that the desire to start over is self-deception; he incorporates his past and bears responsibility for his actions substantially differently than Avon and Brianna. Stringer, bearing the most likeness to Gatsby himself, cannot recognize Dee's life outside the concept of competition; his differently ordered desires are interpreted as "buckin' us."[36] Dee's openness to be faithful to those outside his family—namely his friend killed by Avon's hotshots—threatens its continued existence. Everyone in the game—even his own family—sees Dee as weak, but only Stringer takes that judgment to its utmost conclusion. According to the world of rivalry and retribution, Dee's life needs to be "snatched."

"IT'S A LOVE LETTER TO BALTIMORE"

The love of God disenchants people from the deceptions of civil society; Simon shows that love for his city, his place on earth, can do the same. Simon wants viewers to become better attuned to the structures of an American city and how they form our life together. *The Wire* is about "the City: It is how we in the West live at the millennium, an urbanized species compacted together, sharing a common love, awe, and fear of what we have rendered."[37] Simon's imagination, at its best, is not dialectical but poetic; *The Wire* educates our imaginations in the same way Fitzgerald educates D'Angelo. Important are the unmitigated receptivity and open conversations with others that lead to a penitential account of everyday life—more so than making life comport with unequivocal ideas about the nature and course of history.

Simon unquestionably desires authenticity in his storytelling, but he does not try to reproduce a "carbon copy"[38] of the city or claim the voices of

---

36. "Undertow," S2/E5.
37. Simon, "Introduction," 3.
38. Bowden, "Angriest Man in Television," 50–57. Mark Bowden argues that Simon's cynicism tends toward caricature rather than verisimilitude. Bowden contends that Simon uses fictional storytelling in order to present a finished image of the city that accords with his political passions and personal prejudices. Journalism, on the other hand, simply presents the facts and reflects "the real world." Simon's imagination, with its characteristic bleakness, is what makes *The Wire* untrue.

its denizens as his own.[39] As Michael Wood puts it, "[*The Wire*] isn't good because it's authentic, it looks authentic because it's good."[40] The quality and depth of Simon's research cannot be gainsaid, nor its style and finesse, but what makes *The Wire* so good is his love for Baltimore. It is what drives his fieldwork and motivates his aesthetic. In his words, his characters emerge from his "love [of] people"[41]; his Baltimore is rooted in his "affection for the place."[42] In short, this tragedy is a "love letter to Baltimore."[43]

The truth at the heart of *The Wire* is Simon's affectionate imagination. The deception of other police procedurals is their infantile depictions of good versus evil, which is ultimately more a result of a failure of imagination than inauthenticity; they do not enable the viewer to imagine the intricate lives of others. *The Wire* is helpful not because it is a portrayal of society without remainder, but rather because it is a presentation of characters and their relationships. The division between "ordinary" and "ignored" Americans is the absence of the latter in the minds of the former; people deemed disposable are not real in the popular imagination. Simon offers an account of living in America that is open to that which is beyond its renditions in popular culture and political campaigns. His imagination is formed through both observation and conversation and then filled out to make comments and criticisms of the limitations of institutional structures that shape people. Simon's love for his community connects him to anyone in it; his willingness to share a "dark corner of the American experiment"[44] enables him to tell stories about "another world" that can change our institutional relations.[45]

Where does this leave institutions? Simon's love for his city holds together the divided in America without belittling the tension intrinsic to the differences between them. Institutions are supposed to facilitate this tension rather than alleviate it. Churches, schools, unions, and other institutions

39. Simon was already confronted by this protest while producing *The Corner*. Charles S. Dutton, the director, was suspicious of a white writer distorting black stories. "I know that David Simon can visit and sit with as many black folks in this city as he wants to," Dutton says. "They can pay the families to get the stories. They can listen and walk around with dope fiends. They can write about murders, and they still won't know a damn thing about black people." See Scott, "Who Gets to Tell a Black Story?"

40. Wood, "This Is America, Man," 20.

41. Simon, "Interview with David Simon," para. 51.

42. Havrilesky, "David Simon on Cutting *The Wire*," para. 79.

43. Quoted in Moyers, *Bill Moyers Journal*, 85.

44. "Dead Soldiers," S3/E3.

45. "[I]f you stay in one place, say, if you put up your bag and go down to the local pub or shebeen and you play the fool a bit and make some friends and open yourself up to a new place and new time and new people, soon you have a sense of another world entirely." Simon, "An Interview with David Simon," para. 50.

are the mediating third between the individual and society. The church only offers false hope if it presents itself and the cross as relieving struggle. Furthermore, Baltimore is not a cipher for injustice in America; Simon is angry at the arbitrariness of power. Simon himself is committed to no less than two cultural institutions—unions and HBO.[46] His pessimism serves as a reminder that institutions are not perfect communities and cannot be fled to as refuges or answers to politically and economically systemic problems. This is the trope of the wire: the nexus of lives connected in the pattern of an urban environment, the "thin line between heaven and here."[47] There is no community without colliding wills and interests, no bonds that join society without constraint.

And what of theology? One lesson of *The Wire* is that the church should incorporate a form of institutional mediation that is not structured by opposition to domination. Instead, the church should mediate one's desires and actions through the interests and wills of others by way of open conversation that leads to a change in consciousness. The difficulty is that conversation and imagination cannot be institutionalized; they attest to, in Fitzgerald's words, "the inexhaustible variety of life."[48] The love of God facilitates such openness; good theology helps Christians discover the ideologies and desires that turn humans in on themselves rather than outward toward one another. The question, however, is not how to relate Simon's love of Baltimore to a Christian love of God; they are not categorically distinct. Instead, how the church can own its failures—even those that result from outside forces—by opening up in dialogue with neighbors is under consideration. The mode of theology should not be self-preservation in the face of crisis, but rather understanding the distinctly Christian life as formed by the motives, requirements, and commitments of others. Thus, important for the church is not only that it include outsiders in worship and confront its

---

46. David Simon frequently praises HBO for allowing the format that makes his storytelling possible. Of course, HBO is not only part of the privatized culture industry, it is self-consciously elitist: its tagline is "It's not TV. It's HBO." The viewers are congratulated for having sophisticated taste. Nevertheless, because its profit is based on subscription rather than advertising, writers do not have to organize the show around commercial breaks. Its format resists "simple paradigms of good and evil, of heroes, villains, and simplified characterization" that frames the tales of cable TV. Only HBO, Simon contends, offers the opportunity to oppose the tendency to make the show favorable for pedaling products: "the half-assed, don't rattle-their-cages uselessness of self-affirming, self-assuring narratives that comfort the American comfortable, and ignore the American afflicted; the better to sell Ford trucks and fast food, beer and athletic shoes, iPods and feminine hygiene products." Simon, "Introduction," 1–2. In other words, HBO is uniquely able to sustain Simon's imagination.

47. "Old Cases," S1/E4.

48. Fitzgerald, *Great Gatsby*, 40.

victims penitentially, but also to accept that there are forms of love outside the church that are truthful and therefore generative of virtue.

BIBLIOGRPAHY

Barth, Karl. *Evangelical Theology: An Introduction*. Grand Rapids: Eerdmans, 1963.
Bowden, Mark. "The Angriest Man in Television." *The Atlantic* 301 (January/February 2008) 50–57. Online: http://www.theatlantic.com/magazine/archive/2008/01/the-angriest-man-in-television/6581/2/?single_page=true.
Fitzgerald, F. Scott. *The Great Gatsby*. New York: Scribner, 1995.
Havrilesky, Heather. "David Simon on Cutting '*The Wire*.'" *Salon* (10 March 2008). Online: http://www.salon.com/2008/03/10/simon_2/.
Moyers, Bill. *Bill Moyers Journal: The Conversation Continues*. New York: New Press, 2011.
Scott, Janny. "Who Gets to Tell a Black Story?" *New York Times* (11 June 2000). Online: http://movies.nytimes.com/library/national/race/061100scott-corner.html.
Simon, David. "Interview with David Simon." By Nick Hornby. *The Believer* (August 2007). Online: http://www.believermag.com/issues/200708/?read=interview_simon.
———. "Introduction." In *The Wire: Truth Be Told*, by Rafael Alvarez, 1–31. Rev. ed. Edinburgh: Canongate, 2009.
Wood, Michael. "This Is America, Man." *London Review of Books* 32/10 (27 May 2010) 20.

14

Earthly Peace in the Halls of City Schools

PETER BOUMGARDEN
and KRISTEN DEEDE JOHNSON

INTRODUCTION

If the Greek tragedy is populated with a set of indifferent gods, woven through David Simon's *The Wire* is a similar ethos, albeit cast with a different adversary. In an interview with *The New Yorker*, Simon puts it thus: "What we were trying to do was take the notion of Greek tragedy, of fated and doomed people, and instead of these Olympian gods, indifferent, venal, selfish, hurling lightning bolts and hitting people in the ass for no reason . . . , it's the postmodern institutions . . . those are the indifferent gods."[1] In the same interview, Simon reflects, "It is perhaps the only storytelling on television that overtly suggests that our political and economic and social constructs are no longer viable."[2] In describing the framing of the show as such, Simon

---

1. Talbot, "Stealing Life," 153.
2. Ibid.

tells his colleagues, "As cynically as the rest of this stuff is ending, it will validate the one place we put any of our sincerity, which is individual action."[3]

So what makes institutions indifferent—indeed, indifferent to justice—especially given Simon's high view of the individual? *The Wire* movingly depicts individuals nested within a complex interplay of social systems, an ecosystem that collectively moves both to shape and reflect the desires of people set within. In this way, Simon shows through *The Wire* how individual desires, however pure in intent, are molded into action within a larger malevolent context. Simon's vision of institutions and the ecosystems they comprise can be clarified when cast in the language of St. Augustine of Hippo. Specifically, Simon depicts a world where individual action is shaped by a contextual molding of desires. Saint Augustine called this formation a shaping of the order of one's loves. More systematically, Augustine suggested that every earthly city or culture can be described in terms of the predominant objects of love that order and shape that city and its inhabitants. In Augustine's analysis, power, domination, and glory are the most common objects of love in the cities of this earth, whether the city of Rome in his own time or the city of Baltimore in Simon's. This lust for domination shapes institutions (such as the political, economic, and social constructs about which Simon is seemingly hopeless) and the individuals within. For Simon, a world that shapes the loves of its inhabitants towards maintenance of power is a world that does not change, and instead systematically reinvests itself in the same form. Nothing crystallizes this conviction more than the way that several neighborhood boys—Michael and Duquan, most specifically—mirror the destructive trajectories of older neighborhood presences—Omar and Bubbles, respectively. For Simon, the characters change, but the story remains the same.

Simon is clear that his story of Baltimore is intended to portray the "decline of the American empire"[4] and its consequences for the decaying institutions within the modern American city. Similarly, *City of God*, Augustine's most thoroughly recorded assessments of the political and social realities of the earthly city, was written in the context of and with focus on the decline of the Roman Empire. As John Rist notes, this involved "a decline in the prosperity of the cities which formed the building-blocks of the Empire itself. Mounting taxation, absentee landlords, decaying public roads and a widespread insecurity increasingly came to characterize large parts of the Christian Empire."[5] The stable institutions that had once

3. Ibid., 156.
4. Ibid., 153.
5. Rist, *Augustine*, 203.

marked Roman society increasingly began to resemble unstable facades.[6] This might very well be a description of Simon's Baltimore, in which the institutions of criminal justice, politics, education, and media are neither stable nor thriving.

When viewed together, Simon and Augustine have a good deal of overlap in their visions of the city and their understanding of the ramifications of prioritizing love of power and pursuit of glory over love of the good and pursuit of justice. Neither depicts an earthly city in which justice is flourishing. In *The Wire*, Simon is intentionally cynical, wanting to suggest that our contemporary institutions are not viable, our leadership is lacking, and, "no, we are not going to be all right."[7] Augustine would view this as a perennial problem, a necessary concomitant of humanity's disordered loves that prevents us from giving others their proper due. Through Augustine's extensive writings we can identify his severe diagnosis of the human and cultural condition, which leaves us with no hope of realizing true justice in earthly societies, a conclusion Simon seems to mirror based on the narrative developments in *The Wire*. And yet in Augustine we find more room for hope, especially if we change the language of the conversation from justice to peace. Despite his honest and sometimes searing assessment of the earthly city, Augustine nevertheless believes that we all have a desire for earthly peace and that this peace can be realized, even if it is a shadow of full, vibrant, heavenly peace.

In this essay, we explore where Augustine and Simon stand together, where their tales diverge, and how Simon's bleak vision might be supplemented with some Augustinian hopefulness. In both we see storytelling around a declining empire and its resulting impact on individuals. For Simon, a kind of despair emerges from how the systems of the city leave the city static in spite of its supposed "reinvention." Augustine's relationship to the need for, and value of, change is a bit more ambiguous—a fact observed by those who struggle to understand why he fails to argue for the need to overturn slavery.[8] Nevertheless, Augustine's tale mirrors Simon's in articulating how the earthly city fails to realize justice. Furthermore, in his own way, Augustine offers a way of thinking about the realization of peace east of Eden. Here we might find space for a temporal peace that can be cast in both the Roman Empire and the hallways of the Baltimore public schools.

---

6. Ibid., 204.
7. Talbot, "Stealing Life," 153.
8. For more on Augustine's understanding of slavery, see Rist, *Augustine*, 236–39.

EDUCATION AND THE HALTING OF JUSTICE

One setting in *The Wire* where thwarted justice is especially salient is within Baltimore's educational systems, most visibly depicted in Season 4. Consistent with the narrative arc of the show, Simon is quick to show that the problems facing education cannot be understood solely within the classroom context. Rather, Simon portrays a world where educational justice depends just as much on how educational institutions have to compete for a limited set of resources with the viable needs of other institutions. Furthermore, Simon shows how even the ability of a given teacher to influence and shape students depends upon the lived drama of the student herself—one shaped by family, friendships, the logic of the streets, and the value system(s) of the classroom.

Within this space, two stories related to education are especially illuminating—first in how justice is portrayed as a product of the dynamics internal to the school itself, and second in how justice depends on the way the school is seen as one of many possible areas of support in a world with resource limitations. As we explore these aspects of education portrayed in *The Wire*, we will learn more about Simon's understanding of power and justice in the earthly city and we will be able to explore this understanding in light of Augustine's vision of the earthly city.

Educational Justice in the School

The narrative close-up on education takes place on the stage of Edward Tilghman Middle School. Fictional Tilghman Middle is a part of the larger Baltimore public school system that is facing a significant budget deficit, a not-so-subtle echo of the $45 million deficit the real Baltimore public school system faced in 2004.

Within Tilghman, we see the school primarily through the classroom of its newest math teacher Roland Pryzbylewski. Earlier in the show, Pryzbyleweski was employed as an officer of the Baltimore Police Department before quitting in response to growing suspicion that his accidental shooting of a plainclothes black officer was racially motivated. From the beginning of Pryzbylewski's tenure, it becomes clear that he is facing a deck stacked heavily against his desire for social reform. Education is a low priority for students in his class, and as a result, the classroom experience is less about content and more about the status battles between students. Indeed, the classroom itself acts as an extension of the streets in how it reflects the streets' divisions of kids into those of "The Corner" and those of "The

Stoop"—the former being directly involved in crime, the latter being just observers. And why would we not expect the classroom to reflect these dynamics? Place is identity-shaping, and the corners where drugs are pushed are never just the location for a job, but instead act as a formative space of vocation and identity, one that in itself reflects a certain ordering of loves.

So how does Tilghman push educational outcomes while simultaneously managing such disruptive social dynamics? One approach is through innovation within current organizational structures. In Season 4 we see one such attempt initiated by a set of academics who pull in Major Howard "Bunny" Colvin, an "innovator" on the approach to managing crime from an earlier season. Specifically, in Season 3, Colvin created and maintained a drug-free zone in Baltimore—a self-titled "Hamsterdam." Colvin's under-the-rug attempt at monitoring but not prosecuting crime led to a significant drop in violent crime. Unfortunately, the eventual demise of Hamsterdam was written on the wall by the end of the season when the "politically incorrect" project leaked out to Colvin's superiors, the city government, and the larger media. As a result, Colvin was forced into retirement in exchange for a lower-grade pension.

While the project was controversial, one constituent who saw it for its benefits was the larger academic community where Colvin emerged with a reputation of a renegade social reformer. As a result, Colvin is approached at the start of Season 4 by a friend with links to the University of Maryland with an offer to act as a consultant to an experimental project at Tilghman Middle. Upon accepting the role, Colvin's recommendation is to "track" the corner kids by moving them out of the traditional classroom and into an experimental educational setting. The corner kids will then be overseen by Colvin and taught by one of the involved Maryland doctoral students. Amongst other things, this solution involved an unwillingness to offer "punishments"—like suspensions and corresponding escape from school—that would likely be viewed as rewards by someone whose loves already reflect the ordering of the streets.

As the initiative begins, we can see that Colvin has a certain kind of eye for projects that produce results. Specifically, like the success of Hamsterdam before, the experimental tracking begins to show progress. Prezbo's class begins to experience a greater degree of normalcy without the corner kids in it, and the alternative classroom setting begins a certain cultural shaping of the kids within it. As an audience, we see the most significant growth in one of the students, Namond, who forms a special connection with Colvin. In Namond, Colvin sees a kind of academic and personal potential that would be squandered without special attention—an individual who has just started to be crushed by the system. Once again, Simon's high view of the individual comes through. Colvin continues to mentor and shape Namond, and by the end of Season 4, he and his wife decide to adopt the boy as a way to get him off the street.

But the similarities to Hamsterdam do not end with their respective success. The storyline of tracking also follows that of the drug-free zone with the postmodern institution striking again with a destructive blow motivated by self-preservation. Specifically, the tracking program is shut down as a result of being assessed educationally and politically unviable despite its successes. In both situations, Simon shows positive pragmatic outcomes taking a backseat to the goals of maintaining the current state of the system and preserving the power of those who lead.

This thwarted progress is also evident in what happens within Prezbo's classroom itself across his first year. With growing fear that the school might get overtaken due to poor performance on standardized tests, and the possible consequences of this restructuring, Prezbo is pushed to change the content of his math class to English so that students demonstrate significant academic progress on a dimension where they have lacked in the past. The process is a clear reference to the No Child Left Behind Act, and specifically the Annual Yearly Progress (AYP) dimension, where schools are forced to plan for restructuring—and thus a large set of layoffs—to the extent they do not demonstrate sufficient testing improvement for three years in a row. In this narrative, Simon seems interested in demonstrating that policy, no matter its promise, can be problematic in how individuals and institutions respond, sometimes unpredictably, to its incentives.

Through Prezbo, for example, we witness a situation in which, after a difficult start with the students, a teacher had finally found ways to create an atmosphere in the classroom that fostered respect, trust, and learning. Students were coming to him with problems and spending time in his classroom and treating it as a safe and welcoming place. When Prezbo is forced to leave the subject of math to focus on teaching English for the upcoming test, he loses credibility and his classroom again becomes counterproductive and his significant gains seem lost. In both the tracking scenario and the pressure on schools to maintain AYP, Simon tells us a story of bureaucracy pushing individuals towards self-preservation over attentiveness to human need.

There is a particular moment, one of the most powerful of Season 4, that highlights the stronghold of administrative bureaucracy and the power of institutional self-preservation. When the principal of Tilghman announces the decision to focus on English in every classroom, she is questioned about whether teachers are being asked to "teach to the test." Sensing hostility in the question, another administrator reframes the goal as "curricular alignment," to an audience of rolling eyes. When asked for justification, the school's principal retorts, "There is nothing wrong with emphasizing the skills necessary to the MSA [Maryland State Assessment]." Prezbo, however, having been through similar situations with the Baltimore Police Department cuts to the heart of the situation. Softly to one of his fellow teachers, he dissects the motives behind this move. "Juking the stats," he identifies it. "Making robberies into larceny, making rapes disappear. You juke the stats and majors become colonels." Whether in the police department or educational institutions, there will be deception and corruption promulgated for the sake of institutional preservation and individual advancement.

This deception and corruption would not have surprised Augustine, who understood disorder to be a primary result of the fall. While he would have used different language, the portrait Simon paints of Baltimore's educational system would not have surprised him. In Augustine's understanding, disorder manifests itself within individuals, social structures, and institutions, all of which are marked by what he calls the *libido dominandi*, or the lust for domination. This "dominating lust" is, as Charles Mathewes aptly puts it, "the lust to dominate that is also the lust *that* dominates."[9] The earthly city places the pursuit of power over the pursuit of justice, or, in the language of *The Wire*, cares more about the path to becoming colonel than the duty of reporting rapes. Motivated by distorted love of self and greed for praise and glory, the earthly city seeks not the well-being of those in its midst but the possession of power. This, in Augustine's estimation, is what led to the downfall of the Roman Empire. Indeed, this was the downfall of the devil himself, whose "perversion made him a lover of power and a deserter and assailant of justice, which means that men imitate him all the more thoroughly the more they neglect or even detest justice and studiously devote themselves to power, rejoicing at the possession of it or inflamed with the desire for it."[10]

As Augustine understands it, perfect justice marked God's original and intended divine order, an order in which a hierarchy of goods each had its proper place in relation to God. Humanity turned away from the greatest goods at the top of this hierarchy (goods such as eternal peace and everlasting enjoyment of God and others in God) and chose self-love over love of God. This disordering of loves and goods was concomitant with a disruption in justice, for it is only when all goods are properly ordered that the just peace of God, a "perfectly ordered and harmonious fellowship in the

---

9. Mathewes, *Republic of Grace*, 117.
10. Augustine, *The Trinity* XIII, 17.

enjoyment of God, and of each other in God," can be realized.[11] To relate this back to the earthly city, without the reordering of desire that God offered in Jesus Christ, a soul "cannot with any kind of justice command the body, nor can a man's reason control the vicious elements in the soul. And if there is no justice in such a man, there can be no doubt that there is no justice in a gathering which consists of such men."[12] As Simon might put it, there is unlikely to be justice in the postmodern institutions created by these men.

Augustine's sense of order and justice means, as John Rist points out, that Augustine does not follow the classical philosophers who believed that justice was "the basic building block of human society and the key to an understanding of the state."[13] Rather than justice being the defining characteristic of earthly cities, Augustine offers love of power as the driving force. This sensibility leads to his famous suggestion that kingdoms can be understood as organized robber barons.[14] This seems like a sensibility with which Simon could concur. Indeed, the opening song of *The Wire* reminds viewers each time they begin another episode that "you gotta keep the Devil, keep him on down in the hole."[15] For Augustine, the devil's temptation results in a disordered desire for power, praise, and glory. He further believes that we can only avoid the devil's perverted desires by following God, who in Christ "deliver[ed] man from the devil's authority by beating him at the justice game, not the power game. . . . Not that power is to be shunned as something bad, but that right order might be preserved which puts justice first."[16]

For Simon, the source of the earthly city's prioritization of the power game over the justice game is less clear, although he displays the ramifications of this prioritization in the schools in a way that is both beautiful and heart wrenching. In this storyline, students who are just beginning to thrive under one committed and thoughtful teacher (Prezbo) are deprived again of the opportunity for justice when the disordered needs of the larger system, and those running that system, force changes in the classroom. Likewise, students are beginning to have their loves reordered through the alternative classroom offered to them as corner kids through the experimental program created by the visionary leadership of Colvin, before the larger system shuts the program down. Augustine describes the "just mind" as one that "knowingly and deliberately in life and in conduct gives each man what

11. Augustine, *City of God* XIX, 17.
12. Ibid., XIX, 21.
13. Rist, *Augustine*, 219.
14. Augustine, *City of God* IV, 4.
15. Waits, "Way Down in the Hole."
16. Augustine, *The Trinity* XIII, 17.

is his own."[17] Prezbo and Colvin are striving to carve out environments in which each student can receive his/her own, but their efforts are thwarted again and again. While Augustine sees in Christ and the Heavenly City hope for disordered loves to be reordered, and a just society realized (albeit eschatologically), Simon does not offer a hopeful vision—at least in this television show. Despite a few characters who manage to withstand the institutional pressures, the majority of characters in *The Wire*, many of whom the viewer has grown to love, suffer the consequences of broken systems and disordered loves.

This brokenness is intended to be particularly poignant in Simon's portrayal of one student named Duquan, or Dukie to his friends. In Season 4, Dukie is first shown getting harassed on the streets by a set of classmates because of his shy, awkward disposition and his odor. Without any sort of family support (his family members take and sell whatever he is given to support their drug addictions, and are regularly evicted from their living spaces, which have no running water), Dukie looks to his close group of friends and begins to lean into the support provided by the school, and specifically his teacher Prezbo. Prezbo goes out of his way to help provide for Dukie's basic needs, by doing things such as providing a place for him to keep his clothes, and arranging for him to be able to shower in the school gym. In part because of this support, and the potential of institutions to help individuals thrive, Dukie begins to thrive academically and finds a kind of success that would have been difficult on the streets given his lack of natural toughness. But just as Dukie begins to thrive, he is ultimately targeted by the school's administrators as a legitimate candidate to grade-up—a sign of juking the stats coming full circle to have real personal impact. Prezbo unsuccessfully tries to convince the administrators that Dukie is not ready for the change, an intuition that turns out to be correct as Dukie does not even have the courage to enter the high school building the following fall. With this failure (and yet another eviction of the relatives with whom he lives) comes an identity vacuum for Dukie. Though his close friends move back into the space left by this vacuum, the nature of their influence has changed significantly as his good friend Michael has migrated over the course of the season to the logic of the corner. In a heartbreaking scene towards the end of Season 4, Prezbo realizes that despite all his efforts, Dukie has ended up on the corner as well. In an even more heart aching scene in the show's finale, Dukie is shown strewn out on the streets as a drug addict. As one television commentator put it, we know what lies before Dukie just as we saw

---

17. Ibid., VIII, 9.

throughout all five seasons of the show what lay before Bubbles: misery.[18] And the seemingly hopeless storyline goes on.

Educational Justice within Public Policy

The second of the interwoven stories on education regards the ability of a system to thrive in a world of limited resources, which is inextricably linked to the story of those who hold the power to allocate those limited resources. The success of any initiative, including but not limited to educational systems, depends upon starting with sufficient capital—whether social or monetary. However, if there is a general capital deficiency, governments or other systems with the power to dole out capital resources have to choose between multiple goods, and sometimes even between competing ways to address the same problem. For example, how do you best serve Baltimore when deciding whether to spend money on fighting crime in the police department or supporting educational goals in the public school system?

The problem for Simon goes beyond the actual limited resources to the way in which people make decisions given such constraints. Specifically, decisions in Simon's version of Baltimore are not made pragmatically or rooted in a kind of utilitarianism—working to serve the needs of the greatest number of people—but rather are the outworking of those striving to maintain or build their own positions of power.

One place where this dynamic plays out most directly is in the character of newly elected Baltimore Mayor Tommy Carcetti. In Season 4, Carcetti is carefully considering what set of agendas to support based on both what looks best as the representative of the people of the city (justice concerns) and what it might mean for his anticipated candidacy for the governor of Maryland (power concerns). Finding the schools in significant financial trouble, the motivation for rallying around a schools agenda becomes even clearer given the perceived disarray of the Baltimore PD. It is from this standpoint that Carcetti approaches the current governor to plead his case for a bailout of the school system. Carcetti realizes that part of the system's

---

18. Here is former *Chicago Tribune* blogger Maureen Ryan's description of this harrowing ending to the story line of Dukie: "In Dukie's last scene, the camera remained distant. The viewer didn't see the needle piercing Dukie's skin—the wordless scene ended just before that moment. It's almost as if the filmmakers couldn't bring themselves to show the full extent of Dukie's downfall. We only see him preparing the syringe and bringing it up to his arm, but through *The Wire*'s unsparing depiction of Bubbles' life, we have a pretty good idea of what Dukie's existence will be from now on: misery. Dukie may not be real, Bubbles may not be real, but thanks to the show's masterful writing and acting, I won't soon forget them" (Ryan, "The Wire," pars. 10–11).

problem is related to limited resources, and he responds by working to increase the total pool.

Once again, Simon shows how any sort of systematic change is challenged by the misused power dynamics involved. While the governor initially offers to provide the support that Carcetti requests, he agrees to do so only on the condition that the mayor admits to the public to having pled for the governor's support, knowing that voters across the state will not appreciate having to bail out the city once again. The governor plays the power game rather than the justice game, and in response Carcetti does the same, turning down the funding because he knows it will undermine his ability to win the election. To his staff, and likely to himself, Carcetti justifies this decision using the logic that he can do more good for the public schools in Baltimore once he is elected governor of the whole state. Yet it is clear in Simon's portrayal of Carcetti that self-deception is a significant factor in this justification, and that this type of self-deception is unlikely to disappear upon moving up to the next rung of the ladder.

Applying an Augustinian lens to this aspect of Simon's storyline, given the disordered desire that marks both the earthly city's institutions and the individuals that compose those institutions, we should expect nothing more than for the governor and the mayor to succumb to the lull of power over the call to justice. The disruption in the proper ordering of goods that was concomitant with the fall of humanity disrupted the order and harmony within each person as well, so that each individual's inner desires and loves are disordered along with each individual's relationship with God, others, and the larger created world.[19] As Rowan Williams writes, "The *pax* of the individual soul and the *pax* of the universe are parts of a single continuum."[20] To put it in the negative, the disorder of the individual soul and the disorder of the earthly city are on a continuum, with love of self and lust for power dominating both. In Augustine's understanding, Jesus Christ offers the possibility that these loves might be reordered. As the mediator between God and humanity, Jesus took the disorder found in humanity and ordered it back to God, thereby opening the way for humanity to have its loves reordered.[21] In this reordering, it becomes possible for a person to love justly, giving both God and others their due, prioritizing the justice game over the power game.

---

19. See Augustine, *City of God* XIX, 13. See also Johnson, *Theology, Political Theory, and Pluralism*, 155–56.

20. Williams, "Politics and the Soul," 63.

21. See Johnson, *Theology, Political Theory, and Pluralism*, 158.

Augustine did not believe that the political order itself could be just; given how he understood justice and right order, true justice was only possible in the eschatological Heavenly City. He did, however, believe that Christians who had had their sinful desires reordered could make singular contributions to the political order by resisting the temptations of the *libido dominandi* and placing justice over power. Augustine urges judges and rulers to be just, merciful, humble, and gentle in light of the grace and mercy they have received, and he believes that ideally Christians love God and others more than themselves and their own glory.[22] That being said, Augustine recognizes that not many Christian rulers have actually ruled with such justice and love. This is because, as Robert Dodaro points out, true virtue resides in God so that even Christians can only know the virtue of justice imperfectly.[23] Penitence and confession are therefore an integral part of the picture of a just ruler. Augustine revises Cicero's portrait of the ideal statesman by offering the example of the Apostle Paul. In Dodaro's words, "Although the apostle exhibits strong moral character in the traditional sense, he is also aware of his own moral weakness, which he publicly confesses. Moreover, in Augustine's view, this awareness of personal weakness shapes Paul's compassion for other human beings, susceptible as they are to moral failure."[24] This penitential awareness of one's sinfulness enables the ruler to rely on divine grace for the reordering of his/her loves and to have compassion for others in their weakness, both of which are needed for the ruler to rule justly.

What is needed for Simon's fictionalized rulers to rule justly? This is not made clear in his portrayals. We certainly see evidence of weakness and sinfulness in these characters, but we are not given a vision of how they—the mayor, the governor, the leadership in the police department—could overcome the *libido dominandi* found in both themselves and the larger systems of which they are a part. From an Augustinian perspective, the approach taken by the leaders in Simon's *The Wire* will never allow them to move beyond love of power to love of justice. Once again Dodaro eloquently captures Augustine's reasoning: "Reason cannot arrive at truly just decisions, so long as its grasp is limited to contingent reality alone (*ratio scientiae*). To make just decisions, reason must reflect upon contingent reality against the horizon of transcendence, the abode of divine wisdom. This form of

---

22. See Augustine, *City of God* XIX, 5, 6, and Augustine's letters to Marcellinus, Apringius, and Macedonius in *Political Writings*, 61–99.
23. Dodaro, *Christ and the Just Society*, 111.
24. Ibid., 213.

reason as it relates to wisdom (*ratio sapientiae*) requires faith enlightened by grace."[25]

Outside of this divine grace, it is difficult to see how the desire for domination can end. As Charles Mathewes describes it, "Once we go down the road of domination, it is endless. It does not end in happiness, because it does not end. No amount of power will ever make us happy, because no amount of power will get us what we in our sin seek—namely, to control everything, to have complete mastery, to be God."[26] Mathewes is careful to note, however, that Augustine offers this diagnostic picture of the *libido dominandi* as a prelude to a different and better way. He does not want to leave us in despair but to point towards the love of God that can reorient all of our disordered loves. In Simon's portrayal of life in *The Wire*, we are left with the endless road of domination and not given a picture of how that road might end, either for an individual like Carcetti or for a city like Baltimore.

CRAFTING SPACE FOR SIMON'S NEW JERUSALEM

Watching *The Wire* can feel like an exercise in learned helplessness in how the streets are self-perpetuating and the city is, on the whole, redemptive for far too few people. In a telling contrast to other projects penned by Simon, *Treme* most notably, *The Wire* is a bleak tale. In contrast, Simon writes of his goal for *Treme* as "a way of making a visual argument that cities matter," all the more fitting given the setting of New Orleans for that show, a city in which "the musicians are already in the streets."[27] *The Wire* has no such ambition. As Simon himself suggests, "Because so much of television is about providing catharsis and redemption and the triumph of character, a drama in which postmodern institutions trump individuality and morality and justice seems different in some ways, I think."[28]

So if the show is more stasis than progress, what is the vision of justice that animates Simon? Though the answer does not clearly stand out in *The Wire*, two anecdotes from Simon's real life might be helpful in exploring the answer to that question.

On August 1, 2012, DeAndre McCullough, one of the inspirations for both the book *The Corner* and the show *The Wire*, was found dead in Woodlawn, Maryland. He passed away from heroin intoxication at the age of 35. In an obituary for D're left on Simon's blog, we hear the grief of a man who

25. Ibid., 119.
26. Mathewes, *Republic of Grace*, 118.
27. Talbot, "Stealing Life," 163.
28. Hornby, "David Simon," para. 8.

has clearly lost a friend. But beneath his grief is a hope for what should have been. He writes, "I once had the privilege to know a boy named DeAndre McCullough, who at the age of fifteen had led a life of considerable deprivation, but who nonetheless was the fine and fascinating measure of a human soul."[29] For Simon, there is something about the dignity of humanity that has to be acknowledged, what he refers to here as the human soul—a distinctly religious term that Simon retains despite acknowledging elsewhere that he is in effect more traditional than religious, per se. Indeed, it is that our institutions are indifferent to this very fact that grates at Simon. There is within all of us a soul worth honoring, a kind of dignity that is not seen in the abstract, but reflected in, amongst other things, societal participation and acknowledgment.

Simon's fictional Baltimore is caught in a cycle of self-perpetuated stagnancy that borders on despair, while Simon's fictional New Orleans offers a vision of a city that has hope for significance and celebration. Perhaps the hope that Simon finds in New Orleans is seen in the fact that its musicians are already in the streets in a form of participatory celebration and participatory justice. In the real world, Simon also seems to have more space for hope and change than *The Wire* itself reveales. In a blog response to President Obama's reelection in the fall of 2012, Simon fleshes out this vision further:

> Hard times are still to come for all of us. Rear guard actions will be fought at every political crossroad. But make no mistake: Change is a motherfucker when you run from it. . . . A man of color is president for the second time, and this happened despite a struggling economic climate and a national spirit of general discontent. He has been returned to office over the specific objections of the mass of white men. He has instead been re-elected by women, by people of color, by homosexuals, by people of varying religions or no religion whatsoever. Behold the New Jerusalem. Not that there's anything wrong with being a white man, of course. There's nothing wrong with being anything. That's the point.[30]

The hopeful language of "the New Jerusalem" here is striking. Simon anticipates a world that can no longer destroy the D'res or Dukies of this world—these men of dignity, joint participants in the march towards justice. And yet we can't entirely see within Simon what animates this hopefulness or how he believes we can move towards justice. Simon's vision is thus contradictory. In his personal life we see him yearning for, and identifying,

29. Simon, "DeAndre McCullough," para. 24.
30. Simon, "Barack Obama," para. 8.

signs of redemption that appear lacking in Baltimore. But in *The Wire*, he intentionally offers a bleak picture of Baltimore with only the vaguest signs of "inglorious redemption." Perhaps the words of the experimental poet/novelist Fanny Howe are relevant here: "We know our parts well, all of them individually. It is the whole we can't see or how our parts form an integrated contradiction."[31] Might Augustine offer a way to hold together Simon's "realistic" assessment of the dynamics of the fallen city of Baltimore with his espoused hope for change?

In his description of Augustine's sense of the earthly city, John Rist could easily have been describing Simon's perspective on Baltimore: "There is little sense of the public weal, though promoting public works and public shows is a necessary part of the route to power and influence. The world is a series of atomic factions, often struggling in the law-courts and even on the battlefield for predominance (though united in general support of the *status quo*, and certainly dedicated at least to maintaining their own status)."[32] And yet despite this assessment, Augustine continued to maintain that politics is a good and that earthly peace was worth pursuing. While arguing that no earthly city can be just because true justice requires giving God God's due, which is not possible outside of the Heavenly City, Augustine offers an alternative goal: earthly peace. This can be understood as a civic virtue, a proximate or shadow version of the heavenly virtue of peace, but nevertheless a good. Despite the many disordered loves to be found in the earthly city, Augustine maintains that all earthly cities also have a love of peace. A desire for peace is part of human nature and is evident even in those who declare war (for a victorious peace is still their aim). This earthly peace can be understood as a compromise between human wills about matters pertaining to earthly life.[33] Temporal peace, then, is a civic good and can be a love around which an earthly city is united. As Eugene TeSelle writes, Augustine "thought of political life as a *good*—indeed, perhaps the greatest of temporal values, since it seeks to establish conditions of earthly peace."[34] The pursuit of this earthly peace will not eradicate the *libido dominandi* evident in the institutions and individuals of the earthly city, but it can restrain it in significant ways. In so doing, it can carve out a space for some degree of human flourishing.[35]

31. Howe, *Indivisible*, 53.
32. Rist, *Augustine*, 211.
33. Augustine, *City of God* XIX, 17.
34. TeSelle, *Augustine the Theologian*, 275.
35. See Augustine, *City of God* XIX 17, 26. See also Johnson, *Theology, Political Theory, and Pluralism*, 166–69.

This pursuit of earthly peace would not usher in the New Jerusalem as Augustine understands it, but it might get Simon closer to his more restrained New Jerusalem vision. It does not over-promise what can be accomplished in the earthly city, in ways that would discount Simon's bleak portrayal of Baltimore and its disordered institutions and individuals. But neither does it leave us without any hope of change, which is where *The Wire* leaves its viewers even though this does not ultimately reflect Simon's hopes for this world. Individuals who yearn for such peace, especially while acknowledging its and their corresponding limitations, can act in a way that initiates social innovation and a corresponding movement towards justice in the earthly city. This is the ethos of the character Simon created in Major Colvin, and in the end this is perhaps the only way that institutions can move away from postmodern indifference, if only in part, and into a limited but lived version of earthly peace. We can follow Augustine and Simon in not naïvely thinking that we can create societies marked by robust justice, while also following Augustine and even Simon in hoping that it is possible to achieve an earthly peace that allows even the most disadvantaged students in the most disordered schools to have a chance.

BIBLIOGRAPHY

St. Augustine. *Concerning the City of God Against the Pagans*. Translated by Henry Bettenson. Harmondsworth: Penguin, 1972.

———. *Political Writings*. Edited by E. M. Atkins and R. J. Dodaro. Translated by Margaret Atkins. Cambridge: Cambridge University Press, 2001.

———. *The Trinity*. Translated by Edmund Hill. Edited by John E. Rotelle. Brooklyn: New City, 1991.

Dodaro, Robert. *Christ and the Just Society in the Thought of Augustine*. Cambridge: Cambridge University Press, 2004.

Hornby, Nick. "Interview with David Simon." *The Believer* (August 2007). Online: http://www.believermag.com/issues/200708/?read=interview_simon.

Howe, Fanny. *Indivisible*. Cambridge: MIT Press, 2000.

Johnson, Kristen Deede. *Theology, Political Theory, and Pluralism: Beyond Tolerance and Difference*. Cambridge: Cambridge University Press, 2007.

Mathewes, Charles. *The Republic of Grace: Augustinian Thoughts for Dark Times*. Grand Rapids: Eerdmans, 2010.

Rist, John M. *Augustine: Ancient Thought Baptized*. Cambridge: Cambridge University Press, 1994.

Ryan Maureen. "'The Wire' Comes Full Circle in Its Gripping Finale." Online: http://featuresblogs.chicagotribune.com/entertainment_tv/2008/03/the-wire-comes.html.

Simon, David. "Barack Obama and the Death of Normal." Online: http://davidsimon.com/inevitabilities-and-barack-obama/.

———. "DeAndre McCullough (1977–2012)." Online: http://davidsimon.com/deandre-mccullough-1977-2012/.

Talbot, Margaret. "Stealing Life: The Crusader Behind 'The Wire.'" *New Yorker* (October 22, 2007) 150–63.

TeSelle, Eugene. *Augustine the Theologian*. London: Burns & Oates, 1970.

Waits, Tom. "Way Down in the Hole." *Franks Wild Years*. Island Records, B000001FSR. 1987, compact disc.

Williams, Rowan. "Politics and the Soul: A Reading of the *City of God*." *Milltown Studies* 19/20 (1987) 55–72.

PART IV
Life after *The Wire*

15

The Communication of the Nameless

DANIEL COLUCCIELLO BARBER

GIVING ATTENTION TO COMMUNICATION

"ALL RELIGIONS, IN ESSENCE, direct and distribute time, attention, and devotion."[1] Philip Goodchild, with this remark, provides a compelling approach to the question of religion, one that is useful in a number of ways. We can begin by noting that this remark, because it insists on the tight connection between religion and attention, is able to discern very precisely how religion is operative in our present conjuncture, which Jonathan Beller has insightfully conceived in terms of an "attention economy."[2] We are still pious—how could we not be?—and this piety, today, is everywhere surfacing, as our capacity for attention is foregrounded more and more. It is harder and harder to ignore, amidst our contemporary society of communication, the way in which attention is essential to our existence. This fact, when taken in tandem with Goodchild's thesis, makes it similarly difficult to ignore the way in which religion, thus defined, remains an essential social category.

1. Goodchild, *Theology of Money*, 6.
2. Beller, *Cinematic Mode of Production*, 4.

In what follows, I pursue this connection between religion and attention in order to demonstrate how religion necessitates an *object* of attention, as well as how the enactment of such attention requires a ritual setting. Having thus delineated the problematic that emerges from this connection, I proceed to look at how our contemporary society of communication may be understood in terms of a ritual setting. Communication, I argue, raises a host of difficulties that we can see being negotiated—within *The Wire*—through the lives of Stringer Bell, Avon Barksdale, and Omar Little. Especially important, I contend, is the dramatic contrast between Stringer's conversion toward communication and Omar's commitment to invisibility. The resonance between Stringer's arc and a narrative of conversion allows us to investigate the genealogical link between contemporary communication and the history of Christian dominance. I propose that antagonism toward one demands antagonism toward the other, and it is in virtue of this demand that I address the alliance between Omar (the antagonist of communication) and Brother Mouzone (the antagonist of Christian religion). I conclude by conceiving the common condition of these antagonisms in terms of the namelessness of the divine, which I claim is enacted by Marlo Stanfield.

Returning, now, to the connection Goodchild makes between religion and attention, let us observe that if religion has to do with attention, then the naming of religion requires an account of the manner in which we give attention. This has to do with a *particular* naming of religion—that is, even if Goodchild has rightly located religion as such, religion in the generic sense, it still remains to define what religion is in a particular conjuncture or encounter. The intrigue is that our present conjuncture is one in which religion has to do with attention in particular. The task, then, is to think about the particularity of our attention *as communication*. Furthermore, to say that religion revolves around attention is to emphasize, even if only implicitly, that religion revolves around ritual. This is because attention does not happen without a practice, without a constellation of names, a set of habits, and a definite place that make a particular kind of attention possible. Not only must there be an object of attention, there must also be a ritual setting of this object. The ritual setting, in fact, is what enables the object of attention to emerge. Goodchild, in this respect, has incorporated Durkheim's now-classic intervention into the study of religion, an intervention that refused the notion that religion had to do simply with God or the gods. Buddhism, he noted, is not ultimately about divinities, they are not what finally matter in that ritual setting.[3] The upshot of this is that religion is not

---

3. Durkheim, *Elementary Forms of Religious Life*, 45.

the same as theology in the strict sense. One might imagine a religion for which theology is irrelevant, and so religion, in a generic sense, exceeds the scope of theology. This also allows us to highlight that "theology," when it is identified with religion, has to do not with religion generically but rather with a specific iteration of religion. If we are talking about religion in terms of theology, then the religion we are talking about is a specific one. To understand this theology, then, we must analyze its ritual setting as well as, more broadly, the way in which this ritual setting emerges over against other ones in order to give attention to God rather than to some other object.

It is with these points in mind that we can start to turn—now with some initial precision—to the conceptual nexus of communication and theology in *The Wire*. This television series is about a multitude of things, so much so that it is intrinsically risky to offer an account of its overall aim. That said, I would make the following wager: what *The Wire* is about, ultimately, is religion, understood in terms of attention and its ritual setting. In fact, I want to increase this wager by claiming not just that *The Wire* is about religion, but that, even more, it is at the vanguard of thought about religion. To see why this is the case, we should take a detour in order to observe a certain tension that is both irreducible and central to religion.

If religion is about attention, then we need to ask not just what the particular object of attention is, but also about the kind of object that is capable of playing this attention-gathering role. For instance, it is quite unlikely that a plastic bag would become a religious object, and this is because it appears as something that is relatively unimportant. It is not something worth much attention. Not only does it lack value relative to other objects, its value also seems incapable of being articulated as central to the value of these other objects. In other words, the limit of the plastic bag as religious object stems not just from its value as such, considered in isolation from other objects; it also stems from its tendency towards isolation, its apparent inability to become an object that galvanizes and gives value to other objects. The "religious limit" of a plastic bag is thus derived from its simultaneous lack of isolated value and lack of relational value.[4]

The limits of the plastic bag are instructive for our attempt to discern the kind of object that *can* become religious. The religious object will be one

---

4. It should made clear, of course, that we might imagine the overcoming of these limits and thus the possible emergence of the plastic bag as religious object. Perhaps it could play some valuable and galvanizing role in a perversely anti-ecological movement yet to come, or perhaps it could take on some attention-gathering power through the sacralization of artworks such as the Werner Herzog-narrated film, *Plastic Bag* (directed by Ramin Bahrani, 2009). Nonetheless, the present absurdity of such scenarios seems only to highlight the significant difficulties of the plastic bag's religious potential.

that succeeds where the plastic bag fails—that is, it will be an object that is valuable in its isolation and that is able to give value to all of the objects from which it is isolated. The religious object thus needs to be at once both distinctively superior and universally relevant. This is why Goodchild will also speak of religion's object in terms of "the value of values," for this object is more valuable precisely by being singularly capable of giving value to all others.[5] The religious object functions in a tricky manner, as it is both an object distinct from all others (for only in this way can it be *comparatively* greater than them) and an object that is in relation to all others (for only in this way can it give them value). It is here that we begin to see a fascinating problem whereby the religious object is constantly and necessarily in danger of undermining itself: it must be as universal as possible, but it must also insist on its singular superiority. This singular superiority must be maximally flexible yet rigidly demarcated, and it is for this reason that the religious object is in tension with itself. Religion, then, is not only about attention and ritual setting, it is about the intrinsically tensional interplay between the universality and specificity they involve. And, in order to conclude our detour, let us note that this is what *The Wire* is also about.

The possible counterintuitiveness of this last assertion can be dissolved by calling to mind some of the series' basic concerns, such as drugs, money, power, and information. What all of these objects have in common is a simultaneity of universalizing value and ritual setting: drugs are immensely valuable, but their value depends on a ritual setting that includes stash houses, practices of exchange, and habits that prevent contact with the state's aggression; money—and here it is probably enough just to say the name of Marx—has to do with contemporary value as such, but this purportedly absolute value depends on the establishment of a ritual setting for some version of quantification; power likewise is universal in scope yet depends on the ritual setting of institutions and corners; finally, information, which is perhaps the universal proper to our contemporary communication society, does not exist without the ritual setting of the titular wire, or the more advanced rite of securing and disposing of cell phones. Looked at from this vantage, we can see *The Wire* as religious through and through, and we can furthermore hear it screaming, amidst the regnant ideology of communication, that ritual settings matter. This, in fact, seems to be implied by series creator David Simon's frequent claim that the show is fundamentally about "institutions."[6] It is as if *The Wire* is, at essence, an aesthetically-inflected ethnography of ritual settings, which, when attended to, reveal the loose

5. Goodchild, *Theology of Money*, 5–7.
6. See, for instance, Simon, "*The Wire*: David Simon Q & A."

seams of our attention to communication.[7] The series forces us to look at what we tend not to see. In this sense, *The Wire* is a prophecy.

RITUAL SETTING AS "SET-UP"

To say that we live in a society of communication is to say that our social existence is one in which it has become increasingly impossible not to communicate. There are a number of ways of analyzing this development, but for our purposes the most useful analytical trajectory is one that sets this development against what Foucault called the disciplinary society. As long as a logic of discipline obtains, resistance tends to proceed in the name of liberation. The disciplinary predicament can be imagined in terms of boundaries. If these boundaries hem in desire, if freedom from the disciplinary order is prohibited, then the aim of revolution would seem to be that of a world without limit. Fluidity is posed against the sedimentation of boundaries. This, then, is the background against which communication emerges. Communication has become the means by which liberation proceeds, or by which the fluidity of desire renders porous and exceeds the limits of disciplinary boundaries. In short, the development of communication is the effect of successful resistance to the society of discipline. But is this liberatory? And if it is, then is this liberation genuinely revolutionary?

This was precisely the question at issue in an important interview with Gilles Deleuze, conducted in 1990 by Antonio Negri.[8] The essence of this interview may be located in a question that Negri asks about the difficulties and possibilities of the society of communication. He phrases this duality of communication as follows: "On the one hand this third scenario [the control of 'communication'] relates to the most perfect form of domination, extending even to speech and imagination, but on the other hand any man, any minority, any singularity, is more than ever before potentially able to speak out and thereby recover a greater degree of freedom."[9] Negri, it should be noted, is somewhat opposed to what we might call the pessimistic interpretation of communication. While he sees how communication could mean the emergence of a domination even greater in scope than that of discipline—for communication can control "speech and imagination"—he also sees a revolutionary possibility in communication. In fact, he goes on to suggest that communication supplies the "technology," or what I would

---

7. My sense of the connection between aesthetics and ethnography comes from my encounter with the work of Erin Yerby. See, for instance, her essay "Artificing Nature."

8. Deleuze, "Control and Becoming," 169–76.

9. Ibid., 174.

call the ritual setting, that makes communist revolution realizable, such that it is no longer a mere ideal of thought. He thus remarks that, with "the Marxist Utopia of the *Grundrisse*, communism takes precisely the form of a transversal organization of free individuals built on a technology that makes it possible."[10] This would indicate, Negri again suggests, that communication, far from posing a more radical form of domination, actually increases the viability of a communist society: "Is communism still a viable option? Maybe in a communication society it's less Utopian than it used to be?"

Negri's position is to valorize communication—not necessarily as it now stands, of course, but in terms of what it might become. In other words, even though the society of communication does not presently provide revolution, it does provide the ritual setting enabling revolution. Deleuze, in his response, is quite skeptical of such valorization. This is evident, first of all, in his insistence on identifying communication with control. He notes that, "We're definitely moving toward 'control' societies that are no longer exactly disciplinary."[11] Drawing on Foucault, he continues by defining control societies as those "that no longer operate by confining people but through continuous control and instant communication."[12] The liberation of communication opposes disciplinary society's confinement, but it does so in order to make domination more effective. As long as domination articulated itself in terms of boundaries, the freedom to communicate, to speak out in ways not allowed, posed a threat. So domination, rather than double-down on this prohibition of free speech, simply found a way to affirm expression, to give it a ritual setting that we now experience as the society of communication. This means that communication, though it may be outside discipline, is not outside control. Deleuze goes so far as to muse that, "Compared with the approaching forms of ceaseless control in open sites, we may come to see the harshest confinement as part of a wonderful happy past. The quest for 'universals of communication' ought to make us shudder."[13]

Deleuze's skepticism, expressed at a moment that is now over two decades in the past, has been more recently elaborated by Alexander Galloway and Eugene Thacker's brilliant book, *The Exploit*.[14] There they claim that "new media technologies" should not be welcomed as agents of liberation, as "ushering in a new era of advanced freedom." On the contrary, they "expect to see an exponential increase in the potential for exploitation and

10. Ibid.
11. Ibid.
12. Ibid.
13. Ibid., 175.
14. Galloway and Thacker, *Exploit*.

control through techniques such as monitoring, surveillance, biometrics, and gene therapy."[15] To communicate may very well be to speak out, to express oneself freely, but it is also—and immediately—to submit oneself to control. To speak out from below is to be kept track of from above. They even echo, in their own manner, Deleuze's attempt to put control in historical perspective, or to compare it to an era of discipline, by remarking that "the twentieth century will be remembered as the last time there existed nonmedia."[16] It will be recalled, in other words, as the last era during which there were modalities of social existence that were not immediately impelled to communicate. Social existence was not fully subsumed under communicative existence, whereas, "In the future there will be a coincidence between happening and storage."[17] The point here, as with Deleuze, is not to invoke affects of nostalgia, but rather to foreground the fact that communication is not ahistorical, that it is not eternal, that it is on the contrary something that has been constructed.

This characteristic no doubt applies to every ritual setting; there is no ritual setting that has not, in one way or another, been set up. So when does something that has been set up actually become a "set-up"? It is when, having been set up, the ritual setting makes us forget that it was set up, that once upon a time it was not. The "set-up," in other words, resides in the claim that the ritual setting in which we find ourselves is not just a contingent ritual setting but instead is necessarily progressive with regard to what came before, or is even an incarnation of the way things eternally are. (It is in this sense that communicative society can be seen as a repetition of Christian society.) Yet in order for things to be the way they are they had to become this way, and this is never a smooth transition. Things are the way they are because things violently unmade and produced ignorance of the way they were.[18]

DRAMAS OF NEGOTIATION

Give attention to the eternal truths of universal communication, not to the contingency and violence involved in the construction of its ritual setting, not to the lives being lived amidst this set-up—this is the command against which the *The Wire* consistently prophecies. Indeed, the series gives us, over

15. Ibid., 124.
16. Ibid., 132.
17. Ibid.
18. On this point I am indebted to the work of, and to my discussions with, Nathaniel Cunningham.

and over again, stories of such lives, dramas that variously tell of antagonisms toward, assimilations to, and negotiations with our ritual setting.

Recall, for instance, the arc of Stringer Bell, which is nothing if not a tale of conversion. Stringer's conversion is to the ritual setting that gives attention to communication. We can see this conversion in terms of his pursuit of educational advancement during his 'free time'—which, we should note, Deleuze saw as a central mark of the society of control[19]—or of his desire to be linked to the power of the state (in the form of Senator Clay Davis) and the power of business (in the form of real estate investment). But we can also see it in less obvious ways, such as his attempt to conduct drug trade meetings according to *Robert's Rules of Order*, or his posthumously-revealed possession of *The Wealth of Nations*. His attention has shifted.

One way of making sense of Stringer's story is to pose it against that of Avon Barksdale. Their contrast is clear: on one side, we have the cool-headed businessman who prefers profitably irenic relations, on the other, we have the hot-headed gangster who wants to decide conflict through force, or at least the threat thereof. Yet we can just as well see this contrast as indicative of a deeper commonality. Simon seems to be quoting another minority pairing, that of Coppola's Michael and Sonny Corleone. If Michael and Sonny are at odds, it is because they begin from the same position—that is, from a ritual setting at the margins, one that prevents them from ever fully entering the hegemonic ritual setting. The same holds for Stringer and Avon, and this is indicated by the scene, just prior to the former's death, where they reminisce about their shared past. The paths they choose are mutually exclusive, but each is governed by its own kind of marginality with regard to the dominant ritual setting. Stringer tries, and fails, to convert to communication. Avon never dreams of conversion, but this does not mean he is somehow free of any relation to communication—on the contrary, it is quite possible to see his attempt to reign within his own "alternative" ritual setting as analogically related to the sort of operations at work in the mainstream ritual setting. Indeed, if Stringer believes he can move from the drug trade to the world of business and state, then is this not because he already perceives a kind of analogy between them? The point ultimately made by the Stringer-Avon duality is not only that it is difficult, perhaps impossible, to convert from the ritual setting of the gangster to that of the "legitimate" communicative subject, it is also that it is difficult to consistently distinguish them from one another.[20]

19. See Deleuze, "Postscript on Control Societies," 182.

20. To attend to this indistinction is to take part in a long-standing American tradition.

"I ain't involved in none of that gangster bullshit anymore." So proclaims Stringer as he stands before Omar Little and Brother Mouzone, each of them with a gun pointed at him. He believes himself to have converted. Or, in any case, he believes at that moment that this is the right thing to say—that somehow he will be redeemed from his predicament by identifying himself with a new ritual setting. Is there not power in the real estate development where he stands, the existence of which is communicated in a sign—visible through the window behind him—that reads, "*Coming Soon, Residential/Retail Opportunities*"? After Stringer is shot, it is this sign, this icon of communication, to which the camera turns. In the wake of Stringer's death, the promise of opportunities on their way, coming soon, perhaps (as the theologians say of eschatology) *already here but not yet* . . . this is the object of our attention. It may be with these opportunities in mind that, after confessing his conversion, he tells his soon-to-be assassins about the money he could provide them in his new life. If you want money, he says, "I could be a better friend to y'all alive." This is to no effect, of course, as Omar responds by saying, "You still don't get it, do you? This ain't about your money."

Omar's attention is directed elsewhere than to money. He implies that Stringer's attention to money has failed not only to stave off death, but also to preserve friendship: "Your boy [Avon] gave you up. That's right. And we ain't had to torture his ass neither."[21] This is implicitly in contrast to Omar's own boy, who, when Brother Mouzone wanted information about Omar's location, gave it up only after extremely intense torture. We are thus given a clear contrast between Stringer and Omar, a contrast articulated in terms of differing objects of value or attention, but also in terms of differing relations to visibility. Stringer seeks to make himself increasingly visible, to enter into communication, whereas Omar maintains a notably low profile, keeping his location hidden and thus making invisibility into his ally. There is something about Omar's lyrical piracy, his affirmative juxtaposition of honor and robbery, or of stereotypical masculine power and queerness, that makes him incredibly compelling. Far from seeking conversion to a recognizable identity, he constructs an existence that affirms its independence from expectations. Omar turns unrecognizability into a milieu of freedom. Given all of this, it is easy to treat Omar heroically or hagiographically. This, it should be made clear, is not my aim. That said, his contrast with Stringer is important and needs to be insisted upon, for it presents a significant degree of asymmetry. In the pair of Omar and Stringer, unlike in that of Avon and Stringer, the difference is greater than the commonality. Avon did not

21. "Middle Ground," S3/E11.

share Stringer's desire for conversion, but this does not mean he practiced antagonism to communication. Omar did practice such antagonism, and this is because of his invisibility.

To get at why invisibility is significant let us return to Deleuze. He argued, in his interview with Negri, for a distinction between creation and communication: "Creating has always been something different from communicating."[22] In other words, to attach revolution to communication is to evade the demand for creation, which is central to any revolution worth its name. We need to speak out, to speak freely, but we will not succeed in this through communication, for communication is ultimately committed to the control of speech. We need speech, but the speech we need is "minority speech"—that is, speech that does not proceed from the majority, which is defined as the "model you have to conform to."[23] In the terms I have been using, the majority would be the ritual setting and object of attention associated with communication. To create, of course, is a complicated endeavor, for minority speech is presently non-existent and lacks a model. Furthermore, if speech must be created, and if speech is presently communicative, then the act of creation will need to be accompanied by a withdrawal from communication. It is for this reason that Deleuze observes, "The key thing may be to create vacuoles of noncommunication, circuit breakers, so we can elude control."[24] Once again, Galloway and Thacker elaborate this invocation by speaking of a contemporary need for practices of "cloaking," practices that would "make oneself unaccounted for." This is to bring about "nonexistence," but it is a nonexistence that is "full."[25] The fullness belongs to a practice that cannot be recognized by modes of control. The point, then, is not simply to cease existing or speaking, but to create modes of existence and speech that are asymmetrical to the dominant modes of communication.

My proposal is thus that Omar's invisibility should be seen as the sort of experiment about which Deleuze, along with Galloway and Thacker, are speaking. Omar's life is one that endeavors to find a ritual setting that involves "vacuoles of noncommunication" and that makes possible a "full nonexistence." Yet it is important here to avoid the sort of moralism that can creep into such analyses, and that would say, in this instance, that "Stringer is bad" and "Omar is good." This is not about morality, it is about the difficulties of creation amidst the limits that have been imposed on our existence. It is about experimentation with objects of attention and ritual settings. It is

22. Deleuze, "Control and Becoming," 175.
23. Ibid., 173.
24. Ibid., 175.
25. Galloway and Thacker, *Exploit*, 135–36.

about religion—and what this means, or what is ultimately at stake in this term, is the subject to which we now turn.

RELIGION AGAINST RELIGION

Stringer's religion is not Omar's religion. Yet Brother Mouzone's religion is different from both of theirs. We are able to understand the meaning of this religious distinction of Stringer and Omar, but only once we begin to conceive religion in terms of the ritual setting of attention. It requires much less to understand the religious distinction of Brother Mouzone; it is immediately visible, we recognize it right away. Brother Mouzone belongs to the Nation of Islam, a religion that takes difference seriously and that explicitly formulates itself as a response to Christianity's racist practice. This racist practice has a long history of constructing "visible" differentiation, to which the Nation of Islam has constructed a "counter-visibility." What is the significance of this visible religious difference? And what might the religion of Brother Mouzone have to do with his ability to enter into alliance with Omar?

I noted, in the first section of this essay, that theology should be seen as a subset of religion, for the religious object of attention is only sometimes, and not necessarily, God. This allowed us to conceive the society of communication in religious terms, and to do so in a manner consistent with any conception of theology. Communicative society is thus not a fall away from nor an overcoming of theology, it is simply one way of being religious (and theology is simply another way). Yet we now need to qualify this somewhat, for thus far I have talked about religion in univocal terms—and while that may be the case analytically, it is not the case historically. A genealogy of the concept of religion cannot be adequately provided in this space, but it is important to note that "religion" has never been consistent—which is to say that it has never been applied equally and pluralistically.[26] On the contrary, it was Christianity that invented the concept of religion, and it did so in order to articulate what made it not just different from, but also superior to, its others. The truth of religion meant Christianity, while all other religions (beginning with Judaism and Paganism, though there would be more), along with the "heresies," were identified as variants of false or imperfect religion. The invention of Secularism altered this arrangement, though it most definitely did not disturb the power hierarchy by which Europe, and eventually the neo-Europes, ruled over the rest of the world. Specifically, this invention was the distinction between secular and religious. Secularism

---

26. For an account of all this, see my *On Diaspora*.

was opposed, in principle, to religion, but the effect of this opposition was to distinguish once again the Christians—who now claimed to have overcome or privatized their religiosity—from their others, who were defined as religious (with the variety of these religions being less important than the common religiosity).[27]

What this very brief genealogy of the concept of religion demonstrates, then, is that all religion is not the same—or, more precisely, that the concept of religion has not served to treat all religion in the same way. I have made use of Goodchild's univocal account of religion, and this was because of its ability to discern the connection between religion and attention, and thus between religion and communicative society. But I have also claimed that our contemporary communicative society is one of control—and certainly not all religion is oriented towards this end. Furthermore, I have alluded to the fact that the omnipresence of communication, with its concomitant capacity to constantly extend the scope of control, draws on something akin to a conversionistic, missionary mentality. All of us must communicate, we are told—it's for our own good. It is with these points in mind that I propose a new sense in which communication is religious: not only because of its ritual setting of attention, but also because of its tendency to repeat, through its conversionistic, dominative tendencies, the (Christian) religion that created the concept of religion. In other words, the definition of religion in terms of attention cannot be allowed to obscure, and in fact must give way to, a distinction within religion: the distinction between religion-as-domination and religion-as-resistance.

If religion-as-domination is presently exemplified by communication, and in the historical past by Christianity, then what might exemplify religion-as-resistance? It is possible that Omar's resistance could play this role, but it is not immediately explicit how this would be the case. For a more explicit exemplification, within *The Wire*, of religion-as-resistance, we can turn to Brother Mouzone. He is religious, and visibly so, but his is not the contemporary communicative visibility sought by Stringer, much less the historically antecedent, Christian version of the majority's form of visibility. To say it once again: his is a counter-visibility, he is visibly minor. The consistent discipline demonstrated on an individual level by Brother Mouzone is inseparable from the larger religious logic of the Nation of Islam, for which the stakes of our social existence are clear: society is defined by racist domination, and because this domination is aided and abetted—if not produced—by Christian religion, antagonism toward racism must be

---

27. For an account of the link between Christianity and Secularism, see the work of Gil Anidjar, most notably *Semites: Race, Religion, Literature*.

articulated by religion, and specifically by a religion opposed toward Christianity in principle.

"A man got to have a code."[28] This statement is uttered by Omar, but it might just as well have been attributed to Brother Mouzone. A code is necessary, we surmise, because it enables the self to think and to act in ways that are not reactive. A code allows the self to imagine its aims independently of the range of possibilities—the "opportunities"—to which the dominant ritual setting calls attention. In other words, a code allows the self to rigorously focus its attention on matters that communication, or Christianity, wants to make disappear. If Omar's code helped keep his attention focused on an invisible existence from which communication wanted to convert him, then Brother Mouzone's code—i.e., that of the Nation of Islam—helped him attend to the facts of existence that Christian racism wanted him to forget. If Omar's code exemplifies what Deleuze referred to as "vacuoles of noncommunication," then Brother Mouzone's code exemplifies another imperative mentioned by Deleuze, the need to "hijack speech."[29] Omar's anti-visibility and Brother Mouzone's counter-visibility thus find a strange, code-driven convergence. Their convergence is indicated, after their execution of Stringer and in their final scene together, when Brother Mouzone, asking Omar to dispose of his gun, says, "I trust you to do it proper."[30] This trust cannot be communicated.

"MY NAME IS MY NAME"

We are not yet done with religion, or at least not with theology, which I here define as the naming of God. Brother Mouzone's counter-religion pits him against Christianity, but, theologically speaking, there is a common inheritance between the Nation of Islam and Christianity, for both religions intensively attend to the naming of God. So, what is God's name? When Moses asks this question to God, he is told that, "I AM WHO I AM."[31] This encounter has produced a wide variety of interpretations and disagreement, but one implication seems inarguable: the name of God does not resemble the names to which we are normally accustomed, so much so that it would be more accurate to speak of God in terms of namelessness. Again, there are many directions in which this implication might be taken, but I want to focus on the effect produced by the fact that the religious object of atten-

28. "Unto Others," S4/E7.
29. Deleuze, "Control and Becoming," 175.
30. "Mission Accomplished," S3/E12.
31. Exod 3:14.

tion introduces—like a radically vertiginous coefficient—the contagion of namelessness into the world.

If the value of values cannot be named, and if all names must articulate themselves in relation to this nameless value of values, then the "name" of God has the effect of ungrounding the act of naming. The propriety of each and every name has been called into question. This means, to put it bluntly, that names cannot be controlled. The sin of idolatry refers directly to the identification of the nameless God with a name, but it may be indirectly applied at a social level. If all individuals are, as theological traditions claim, fundamentally related to God, then the namelessness of God must have implications for the naming of individuals. In other words, if an individual is intrinsically related to a nameless God, then the name of that individual does not belong to others, it belongs only to God—and if God's name cannot be identified, then neither can the name of the individual before God. The naming of individuals, especially the imposition of a name on one individual by another, would thus contravene the prohibition of idolatry.

It is from this vantage that we should recall the name of the most famous member of Brother Mouzone's religion: Malcolm X. It was not his proper name, but, more importantly, it was not the name Christianity imposed on him. "X" marks his resistance to the social idolatry of Christianity—and brilliantly so, for it makes visible and communicates the disappearance of his real name at the same time that it asserts the invisibility, or the non-communicability, of such a name. I have argued that Omar's anti-visibility and Brother Mouzone's counter-visibility, when taken together, present a two-pronged opposition to communication and its repetition of Christian racism. We can now see how Malcolm X expresses their convergence.

Theologically speaking, then, an individual's name cannot be imposed, as this right belongs only to a God whose name also cannot be imposed. Yet what Christianity has enacted in the past, and what communication enacts today, is the desire to name everything, to control reality by controlling the act of naming. I have already suggested that *The Wire* is a prophecy, for it gives attention to the ways in which we give attention. It attends, as well, to experimental attempts to create modes of existence independent of these dominant modes of attention. Such experimentation is ultimately about extracting one's name from control and giving it to oneself. Some, of course, will argue that to give oneself a name is to repeat the sin committed by the other's imposition. Yet this is not the case, for these two acts of naming—like religion—are not univocal. When a name is imposed on the self from without, the aim is to control the thus-named self; when the self names itself—presuming that it does so in response to a situation in which its name is being erased or defamed—the aim is to free itself from control, to defend itself. These acts of naming are not reversible. The imposition of a name on the other is not just a denial of that other, it is also a denial of God, whereas the consequent defense by the other of its own name is a resistance not only of its own denial, but also of the denial of God (and it does not matter whether the imposed-upon other is conscious of resisting this latter denial).[32]

Let us conclude by recalling one last character from *The Wire*. Marlo Stanfield is in jail, and one of his crew mentions rumors, circulating on the outside, that portray Marlo as weak and fearful. "My name is on the street?!" When another member of his crew tries to console him—"It was bullshit, man, you ain't need that on your mind"—he takes this as nothing less than an attempt to control his attention. He responds without compromise: "What the fuck you know about what I need on my mind, motherfucker?" The denial of imposition, whether it comes from his friend or from the rumors on the street, does not end there. "My name is my name!"[33] Here we have a profane realization of Moses' encounter with the name of namelessness: "I am who I am." It is unlikely that Marlo saw his proclamation as theological, but that should not keep us from seeing its prophetic import: pay attention to the communication of the nameless.

BIBLIOGRAPHY

Anidjar, Gil. *Semites: Race, Religion, Literature*. Stanford: Stanford University Press, 2007.

Barber, Daniel Colucciello. *On Diaspora: Christianity, Religion, and Secularity*. Eugene, OR: Cascade, 2011.

Beller, Jonathan. *The Cinematic Mode of Production: Attention Economy and the Society of the Spectacle*. Lebanon, NH: University Press of New England, 2006.

---

32. To resist the imposition of names is to resist conversion. Malcolm X knew this. For him, this refusal takes place in the name of Islam, but what makes Islam paramount, on his reading, is its capacity to resist Christianity's conversion. As he puts it: "Only one religion—Islam—had the power to stand and fight the white man's Christianity for a *thousand years!* Only Islam could keep white Christianity at bay" (*Autobiography of Malcolm X*, 376). What Islam provides, then, is not a better conversion, but a placeholder for resistance to conversion, or for something like de-conversion. We can further see that this is the case by observing that his praise of Islam is contextualized by his praise of other developments, such as "non-white peoples returning in a rush to their original religions, which had been labeled 'pagan' by the conquering white man" (376). The value of Islam, then, emerges within the context of the liberation of a multitude of ritual settings from the logic of conversion. Continuing, he observes: "The Africans are returning to Islam and other indigenous religions. The Asians are returning to being Hindus, Buddhists and Muslims" (376). Islam is what enables one to name oneself.

33. "Late Editions," S5/E9.

Deleuze, Gilles. "Control and Becoming." Interview by Antonio Negri. In *Negotiations*, translated by Martin Joughin, 169–76. New York: Columbia University Press, 1995.

———. "Postscript on Control Societies." In *Negotiations*, translated by Martin Joughin, 177–82. New York: Columbia University Press, 1995.

Durkheim, Émile. *Elementary Forms of Religious Life*. Translated by Karen Elise Fields. New York: Simon & Schuster, 1995.

Galloway, Alexander R., and Eugene Thacker. *The Exploit: A Theory of Networks*. Minneapolis: University of Minnesota Press, 2007.

Goodchild, Philip. *Theology of Money*. Durham: Duke University Press, 2009.

Simon, David. "*The Wire*: David Simon Q & A." Interview by Alan Sepinwall. *What's Alan Watching?* (March 9, 2008). Online: http://sepinwall.blogspot.com/2008/03/wire-david-simon-q.html.

X, Malcolm. *Autobiography of Malcolm X*. New York: Ballantine, 1999.

Yerby, Erin. "Artificing Nature: From Fires and Forests to Mermaids and Sheep-Trees." *Thinking Nature* (forthcoming).

16

The Wire, Or, What to Do in Non-Evental Times[1]

SLAVOJ ŽIŽEK

"Who is David Guetta?" I asked my twelve-year-old son when he triumphantly announced he was going to a Guetta concert. He looked at me as if I were a complete idiot, replying, "Who is Mozart? Google Mozart, you get 5 million hits, google Guetta, you get 20 million!" I did google Guetta and discovered that he is indeed something like a contemporary art curator: not simply a DJ, but an "active" DJ who not only solicits but also mixes and even composes the music he presents, like those curators who no longer only collect works for an exhibition but often directly commission them, explaining to the artists what they want.

And the same goes for David Simon, "curator" of the multitude of directors and screenwriters (including Agnieszka Holland) who collaborated on *The Wire*. The reasons were not simply commercial. The collaboration also represented the nascent form of a new collective process of creation. It is as if the Hegelian *Weltgeist* had recently moved from the cinema to the TV series, although it is still in search of its form. The inner *Gestalt* of *The Wire* is in fact not that of a series— Simon himself has referred to *The Wire* as a single sixty-six-hour movie. Furthermore, *The Wire* is not only the result of

---

1. Originally appeared as chapter 8 of *The Year of Living Dangerously* (London: Verso Publishers, 2012), pp. 91–112. Reprinted with permission.

a collective creative process, but something more: real lawyers, drug addicts, cops, and so on, played themselves; even the names of some characters are condensations of the names of real individuals ("Stringer Bell" is a composite of two real Baltimore drug lords, Stringer Reed and Roland Bell). *The Wire* thus provides a kind of collective self-representation of a city, like the Greek tragedy in which a polis collectively staged its experience.

If *The Wire* is an example of TV realism then, it is less an objective realism (a realistic presentation of a social milieu) than a subjective realism, a film staged by a precisely defined actual social unity. This is signaled by a key scene whose function is precisely to mark its distance from any crude realism, the famous "all-fuck" investigation.[2] In an empty ground-floor apartment where a murder had been committed six months previously, detectives McNulty and Bunk, witnessed by a silent housekeeper, try to reconstruct how it happened. But the only word they say during the scene is "fuck" (or variants thereof). They say it thirty-eight times in a row, in so many different ways that it comes to mean just about anything, from annoyed boredom to elated triumph, from pain or shock at the horror of the gruesome murder to pleasant surprise, and it reaches its climax in the self-reflexive reduplication of "Fuckin'fuck!"[3] Imagine the same scene in which each "fuck" is replaced by a more "normal" phrase ("Just another photo!" "Ouch, it hurts!" "Now I get it!" etc.). The scene works on multiple levels: (1) as a taboo-breaking use of a prohibited word; (2) as a point of seduction (after several hours of "serious stuff," it is designed to function as the moment at which a typical viewer will fall in love with *The Wire*); (3) as a pure phallic joke marking the programs distance from "proper" social-realist drama.

So, once again, what kind of realism are we dealing with here? Let us begin with the title. "Wire" has multiple connotations (walking along a wire, or, of course, the wearing of a wire or bugging device), but the main reference of the title, according to Simon, is "to an almost imaginary but inviolate boundary between the two Americas,"[4] between those participating in the American Dream and those left behind. The topic of *The Wire* is thus the class struggle tout court, the Real of our times, including its cultural consequences. As Fredric Jameson observes: "Here, in absolute geographical propinquity, two whole cultures exist without contact and without interaction, even without any knowledge of each other: like Harlem and the rest of Manhattan, like the West Bank and the Israeli cities that, once part of it,

---

2. "Old Cases," S1/E4.
3. See the detailed analysis in Burdeau, "Fuck."
4. Quoted in Potter and Marshall, *The Wire*, 228.

are now still a few miles away."⁵ The two cultures are separated in the basic manner of their relating to the Real: one stands for the horror of addiction and consumption, while in the other, reality is carefully screened.⁶ On the horizon, one can even make out the contours of the rich as a new biological race, secured against disease and enhanced through genetic intervention and cloning, while the same technologies are used to control the poor.⁷

Simon is very clear about the concrete historical background of this radical split:

> We pretend to war against narcotics, but in truth, we are simply brutalizing and dehumanizing an urban underclass that we no longer need as a labor supply. . . . *The Wire* was not a story about America, it's about the America that got left behind. . . . The drug war is war on the underclass now. That's all it is. It has no other meaning.⁸

This bleak general picture provides the background for Simon's fatalistic worldview:

> *The Wire* is a Greek tragedy in which the postmodern institutions are the Olympian forces. It's the police department, or the drug economy, or the political structures, or the school administration, or the macroeconomic forces that are throwing the lightning bolts and hitting people in the ass for no decent reason.⁹

---

5. Jameson, "Realism and Utopia," 369–70.

6. For example, the claim that waterboarding is not torture is obvious nonsense—why, if not by causing pain and fear of imminent death, does waterboarding make hardened "terrorists" talk?

7. The premise of Andrew Niccol's movie *In Time* is that by 2161 genetic alteration has allowed humanity to stop aging at twenty-five, but on reaching that age people are required to earn more time or die within a year. "Living time," which can be transferred among individuals, has replaced money and its availability is displayed on an implant on a persons lower arm: when the clock reaches zero, the person dies instantly. Society is divided by social class into specialized towns called "Time Zones": the rich can live for centuries in luxurious districts, while the poor live in ghettos where youth predominates, and must work each day to earn a few more hours of life, which they must also use to pay for everyday necessities. This dystopian vision of a society in which the expression "time is money" is taken literally, and in which rich and poor are becoming two different races, is emerging as a realistic option with the latest biogenetic developments.

8. Moyers, "Straight Dope," para. 39.

9. Simon, "Interview with David Simon," para. 5.

Over the last few years, we do indeed seem to have witnessed the rise of a new form of prosopopoeia where the thing which speaks is the market itself, increasingly referred to as if it were a living entity that reacts, warns, makes its opinions clear, etcetera, up to and including demanding sacrifices in the manner of an ancient pagan god. To take just a couple of examples from recent media reports: "When the government announced its measures to combat the deficit, the market reacted cautiously." "The recent fall of the Dow Jones . . . signals a clear warning that the market is not so easily satisfied—more sacrifices will be necessary." It may seem that there is an ambiguity as to the precise identity of these "Olympian forces": is it the capitalist market system as such (which is causing the working class to disappear) or the state institutions? Some critics have even proposed reading *The Wire* as a liberal critique of bureaucratic alienation and inefficiency. It is true that a basic (and often described) function of the state bureaucracy is to reproduce itself, not to solve society's problems—even to create problems in order to justify its existence. Recall the famous scene from Terry Gilliam's *Brazil* in which the hero, who is having problems with his electricity supply, is secretly visited by an illegal electrician (Robert de Niro in a cameo appearance) whose criminality consists of simply repairing the malfunction. The greatest threat to bureaucracy, the most daring conspiracy against its order, comes from those who actually try to solve the problems the bureaucracy is supposed to deal with (like McNulty's group of detectives, who set out actually to break up the drug gang). But does not the same hold for capitalism as such? Its ultimate impetus is likewise not to satisfy existing demands, but to create ever-new demands so as to facilitate its continuous expanded reproduction.

It was Marx who formulated early on this idea of the arbitrary and anonymous power of the market as a modern version of Fate. The title of one essay on *The Wire*—"Greek Gods in Baltimore"—is thus quite appropriate: is not *The Wire* the realist counterpart of recent Hollywood blockbusters in which an ancient god or half-god (Perseus in *Percy Jackson*, Thor in *Thor*) finds himself trapped in the body of a confused U.S. adolescent? How is this divine presence felt in *The Wire*? In telling the story of how Fate affects individuals and triumphs over them, *The Wire* proceeds systematically, each successive season taking a further step in the exploration: Season 1 presents the conflict, drug dealers versus police; Season 2 steps back to its ultimate cause: the disintegration of the working class; Season 3 deals with police and political strategies to resolve the problem and their failure; Season 4 shows why education (of black working-class youth) is also insufficient; and, finally, Season 5 focuses on the role of the media: why is the general public not adequately informed of the true scope of the problem? As Jameson has pointed out, the basic procedure of *The Wire* is not to limit itself only to the harsh reality, but to present utopian dreams as part of the world's texture, as constitutive of reality itself. Here are some of the main examples:

1. In Season 2, Frank Sobotka uses drug-trade money to build up his own contacts, in view of his ultimate project, which is the rebuilding and revitalization of the port of Baltimore: "He understands history and knows that the labor movement and the whole society organized around it cannot continue to exist unless the port comes back. This is then his Utopian project, Utopian even in the stereotypical sense in which it is impractical and improbable—history never moving."[10]

2. Also in Season 2, D'Angelo grows more and more ambivalent about the drug trade. When the innocent witness William Gant turns up dead, D'Angelo is shaken, assuming his uncle Avon ordered the killing as revenge for Gant's testimony. D'Angelo is brought in for questioning by McNulty and Bunk who trick him into writing a letter of apology to Gant's family. (In a wonderful Lars von Trier-style manipulation, they show him a photo of two young boys, taken from the desk of a fellow policeman, but presented as photo of Gant's now orphaned sons.) The mob lawyer Levy arrives and stops D'Angelo before he can write anything incriminating, and he is released. Later, having been arrested again, D'Angelo decides to turn states witness against his uncle's organization; however, a visit from his mother convinces him of his duty to his family, and he backs out of the deal. Because of his refusal to cooperate, he is sentenced to twenty years in prison. Is not the mother who convinces D'Angelo not to testify also mobilizing the family utopia?

3. In Season 3, Major Colvin conducts a novel experiment: without informing his superiors, he effectively legalizes drugs in West Baltimore, creating a mini Amsterdam, dubbed "Hamsterdam," where the corner dealers are allowed to set up shop. By localizing the drug dealing, which he knows he cannot stop anyway, Colvin eliminates the daily turf battles that drive up the murder rates and dramatically improves daily life for most of his district. Calm returns to terrorized neighborhoods, and his patrolmen, freed from their cars and the endless pursuit of drug-dealing corner boys, return to real police work, walking the beat, getting to know the people they serve. (The real model here is Zurich, not Amsterdam, where back in the 1980s a park behind the main railway station was proclaimed a free zone; there was a similar experiment in Baltimore itself a decade or so ago.)

---

10. Jameson, "Realism and Utopia," 371.

4. Also in Season 3, friendship itself is rendered as utopian. Avon and Stringer betray each other, but just before Stringer's murder, the two enjoy one last drink together at Avon's harbor-side condominium, reminiscing about the past and acting as if their old friendship were intact, despite their mutual betrayal. This not simply fakery or hypocrisy, but the expression of a sincere wish for how things might have been—as John Le Carré put it in *A Perfect Spy*: "Betrayal can only happen if you love."

5. In Season 4, focused on education, the utopian element is to be found in Pryzbylewski's classroom experiments with computers and his repudiation of the evaluation system imposed by state and federal bodies.

Is not Stringer Bell himself a utopian figure: a pure criminal technocrat, striving to sublate crime into pure business? The underlying ambiguity here is that if these utopias are part of reality, and what makes the world go round, are we then beyond good and evil? In his DVD commentary, Simon points in this direction: "*The Wire* is really not interested in Good and Evil; it's interested in economics, sociology and politics." Jameson is also too hasty in his dismissal of the "outmoded ethical binary of good and evil":

> I have elsewhere argued against this binary system: Nietzsche was perhaps only the most dramatic prophet to have demonstrated that it is little more than an afterimage of that otherness it also seeks to produce—the good is ourselves and the people like us, the evil is other people in their radical difference from us (of whatever type). But society today is one from which, for all kinds of reasons (and probably good ones), difference is vanishing and, along with it, evil itself.[11]

However, this formula seems all too facile. If we discount the premodern (pre-Christian, even) identification of Good with people like us (what about loving one's enemy/neighbor?), is not the properly ethical focus of *The Wire* precisely the problem of the ethical act: what can a (relatively) honest individual do in today's conditions? To put it in Alain Badiou's terms, these conditions (at least a decade ago, when *The Wire* was in the making) were definitely non-evental: there was no potential for a radical emancipatory movement on the horizon. *The Wire* presents a whole panoply of the "types of (relative) honesty," of what to do in such conditions, from McNulty and Colvin up to Lt. Cedric Daniels who, with all his readiness to compromise, sets himself a certain limit (he refuses to meddle with statistics). The key point is that they all have to violate the Law in one way or another. For

11. Ibid., 367.

Žižek | The Wire, or, What to Do in Non-Evental Times 291

example, recall how in the final season McNulty aptly manipulates the fact that

> villainy in mass culture has been reduced to two lone survivors of the category of evil: these two representations of the truly antisocial are, on the one hand, serial killers and, on the other, terrorists (mostly of the religious persuasion, as ethnicity has become identified with religion, and secular political protagonists like the communists and the anarchists no longer seem to be available).[12]

McNulty decides to secure funding for the Marlo Stanfield (the crime boss who takes over after the fall of Avon) investigation by creating the illusion of a serial killer on the loose, in order to draw media attention to the police department. He interferes with crime scenes and falsifies case notes as part of his scheme. However, the basic lesson here is that individual acts are inadequate. A further step is needed, going beyond the individual hero, towards a collective act that, in our present conditions, can only appear as a conspiracy:

> The lonely private detective or committed police officer offers a familiar plot that goes back to romantic heroes and rebels (beginning, I suppose, with Milton's Satan). Here, in this increasingly socialized and collective historical space, it slowly becomes clear that genuine revolt and resistance must take the form of a conspiratorial group, of a true collective.... Here Jimmy's own rebelliousness (no respect for authority, alcoholism, sexual infidelities, along with his ineradicable idealism) meets an unlikely set of comrades and co-conspirators—a lesbian police officer, a pair of smart but undependable cops, a lieutenant with a secret in his past but with the hunch that only this unlikely venture can give him advancement, a slow-witted nepotistic appointment who turns out to have a remarkable gift for numbers, various judicial assistants, and finally a quiet and unassuming fixer.[13]

Is not this group a kind of proto-communist cell of conspirators, or a group of eccentrics from a Charles Dickens novel or a Frank Capra film, with the dilapidated basement office they are allocated as their secret conspiratorial lair? G. K. Chesterton's famous formula of law itself as "the greatest and most daring of all conspiracies" here finds an unexpected confirmation. Included in this group of eccentrics, as an informal member from

---

12. Ibid., 368.
13. Ibid., 363.

the other side of the divide, is the character of Omar Little: Omar's motto can be expressed as the reversal of Brecht's from the *Beggar's Opera*: what is the founding of a bank (as a legal action) compared to robbing a bank?[14] Omar can be placed in the same lineage as the titular hero of *Dexter*, a series which debuted in 2006. Dexter is a bloodstain-pattern analyst for the Miami police who moonlights as a serial killer. Orphaned at the age of three, he is adopted by Miami police officer Harry Morgan. After discovering the young Dexter's murderous proclivities and to keep Dexter from killing innocent people, Harry begins teaching him "The Code": Dexter's victims must be killers themselves who have killed someone without justifiable cause and will likely do so again. Like Dexter, Omar is also a perfect cop in the guise of its opposite—his code is simple and pragmatic: only kill those who have the authority to order the deaths of others.

But the key figure in *The Wire*'s group of eccentrics is Lester Freamon. Jameson is justified in praising his genius

> not only to solve... problems in ingenious ways, but also to displace some of the purely mystery and detective interest onto a fascination with construction and physical or engineering problem solving—that is to say, something much closer to handicraft than to abstract deduction. In fact, when first discovered and invited to join the special investigative unit, Freamon is a virtually unemployed officer who spends his spare time making miniature copies of antique furniture (which he sells): it is a parable of the waste of human and intelligence productivity and its displacement—fortunate in this case—onto more trivial activities.[15]

Lester Freamon is the best representative of "useless knowledge"—he is the conspirators' intellectual, rather than an expert, and as such is effective in proposing solutions to actual problems.

So what can this group do? Are they also caught up in a tragic vicious circle in which their very resistance contributes to the system's reproduction? We should bear in mind that there is a key difference between

---

14. Similarly, the Brechtian lesson in relation to the privatization of the intellectual commons is thus: what is intellectual property theft (piracy) compared to the legal protection of intellectual property? This is why the struggle against the Anti-Counterfeiting Trade Agreement (ACTA) is one of the great emancipatory struggles today. ACTA aims to establish an international legal framework for combating counterfeit goods, generic medicines, and copyright infringement on the internet, and its work should be regulated by a new governing body outside existing forums (another "apolitical" technocratic institution).

15. Jameson, "Realism and Utopia," 363–4.

Greek tragedy and the universe of *The Wire*. As Simon himself explains: "Because so much of television is about providing catharsis and redemption and the triumph of character, a drama in which postmodern institutions trump individuality and morality and justice seems different in some ways." In the climactic catharsis of a Greek tragedy the hero encounters his truth and attains sublime greatness in his fall; in *The Wire*, the Big Other of Fate rules in a different way—the system (not life) just goes on, with no cathartic climax.[16]

The consequences of this shift from ancient tragedy to the contemporary form are easy to discern: the absence of narrative closure and of catharsis, the failure of the melodramatic Dickensian benefactor to appear, and so on.[17] The TV series as a form also finds its justification in this shift: we never arrive at a final conclusion, not only because we never discover the ultimate culprit (because there is always a new plot behind the current one), but also because the legal system is really striving for its own self-reproduction. This insight is rendered by the final scene of *The Wire*, in which we see McNulty observing the Baltimore port from a bridge, accompanied by a series of flashbacks and glimpses of daily life throughout the city. What we get here is not an ultimate conclusion, but a kind of proto-Hegelian absolute standpoint of reflexive distance, a withdrawal from direct engagement: the idea being that our various struggles, hopes, and defeats are all part of a larger "circle of life" whose true aim is its own self-reproduction, or this very circulation itself. A similar point was made by Marx when he noted that although from the finite subjective standpoint the goal of production is the product—objects that will satisfy people's (imagined or real) needs; use-values in other words—from the absolute standpoint of the system as a totality, the satisfaction of individuals' needs is just a necessary means to keep the machinery of capitalist (re)production going.

The narrative openness of the form is thus grounded in its content. As Jameson puts it, *The Wire* is a whodunit in which the culprit is the social totality, the whole system, not an individual criminal (or group of criminals). But how are we to represent (or, rather, render) in art the totality of contemporary capitalism? In other words, is not totality always the ultimate culprit? What is so specific about contemporary tragedy? The point is that

---

16. Jon Stewart once remarked that he wished every new U.S. president, upon being elected, was taken to meet five unknown people who would explain how things really work in the United States.

17. Is *The Wire* then a "Dickensian" work? Bill Moyers has said that "one day, while screening some episodes of HBO's *The Wire*, it hit me: Dickens was back and his name is David Simon." However, what is missing is precisely the Dickensian melodrama of the last-minute intervention of a kind benefactor.

the Real of the capitalist system is abstract, the abstract-virtual movement of Capital—here we should mobilize the Lacanian difference between reality and the Real: reality masks the Real. The "desert of the Real" is the abstract movement of capital, and it was in this sense that Marx spoke of "real abstraction." Or, as *The Wire*'s coproducer, Ed Burns, puts it: "we only allude to the real, the real is too powerful."

Marx described the mad, self-enhancing circuit of capital, whose solipsistic path of self-fecundation reaches its apogee in today's metareflexive speculations on futures.[18] It is far too simplistic to claim that the specter of this self-engendering monster pursuing its path without regard for any human or environmental concern is nothing more than an ideological abstraction, and that behind it there are real people and natural objects on whose productive capacities and resources capital's circulation is based and on which it feeds like a gigantic parasite. The problem is not only that this abstraction is part of our financial speculators' misperception of social reality, but that it is also real in the precise sense of determining the structure of material social processes. The fate of whole strata of the population and sometimes of whole countries can be decided by this solipsistic speculative dance of Capital, which pursues its goal of profitability in blessed indifference as to how its movements might affect social reality.

Marx's point was not primarily to reduce this second dimension to the first, or to demonstrate how the theological dance of commodities arises out of the antagonisms of "real life." Rather, his point was that *one cannot properly grasp the first (the social reality of material production and social interaction) without the second*. It is the self-propelling movement of Capital that runs the show, that provides the key to real-life developments and catastrophes. Therein resides the fundamental systemic violence of capitalism, much more uncanny than any direct pre-capitalist socio-ideological violence. This violence is no longer attributable to individuals and their "evil" intentions, but is purely "objective," systemic, anonymous. Here we encounter the Lacanian difference between reality and the Real: the former is the social reality of actual people involved in interaction and in the productive process, while the Real is the inexorable, "abstract," spectral logic of Capital that determines what goes on in social reality. This gap becomes palpable when one visits a country in which life is obviously in a shambles,

---

18. The stages in the predominant mode of money seem to obey the Lacanian triad of RSI: gold functions as the Real of money (what it is "really worth"); with paper money we enter the Symbolic register (paper is the symbol of its worth, worthless in itself); and, finally, the emerging mode is a purely "Imaginary" one—money will increasingly exist as a purely virtual point of reference, of accounting, without any actual form, real or symbolic (the "cashless society").

marked by ecological decay and human misery, and yet economic reports nonetheless inform us that the country is "financially healthy"—the reality does not matter, what is important is the situation of Capital.

Once again, the question is: what would be the aesthetic correlate of such a Real, what might something like a "realism of abstraction" be?[19] We need a new form of poetry, similar to what Chesterton imagined as a "Copernican poetry":

> It would be an interesting speculation to imagine whether the world will ever develop a Copernican poetry and a Copernican habit of fancy; whether we shall ever speak of "early earth-turn" instead of "early sunrise," and speak indifferently of looking up at the daisies, or looking down on the stars. But if we ever do, there are really a large number of big and fantastic facts awaiting us, worthy to make a new mythology.[20]

At the beginning of Monteverdi's *Orfeo*, the Goddess of Music introduces herself with the words "Io sono la musica"—is this not something that soon afterwards, when "psychological" subjects invaded the stage, became unthinkable, or rather, unrepresentable? One had to wait until the 1930s for such strange creatures to reappear on the stage. In Brecht's "learning plays," an actor enters the stage and addresses the public: "I am a capitalist. I'll now approach a worker and try to deceive him with my talk of the equity of capitalism." The charm of this procedure resides in the psychologically "impossible" combination, in one and the same actor, of two distinct roles, as if a person from the play's diegetic reality can also, from time to time, step outside himself and make "objective" comments about his actions and attitudes. This is how one should read Lacan's "*c'est moi, la vérité, qui parle*" from his essay on "*La Chose freudienne*": as the shocking emergence of a word where one would not have expected it—it is the Thing itself that starts to speak.

In a famous passage from *Capital*, Marx resorts to prosopopoeia to bring out the hidden logic of the exchange and circulation of commodities: "If commodities could speak, they would say this: our use-value may interest men, but it does not belong to us as objects. What does belong to us as objects, however, is our value. Our own intercourse as commodities proves it. We relate to each other merely as exchange-values."[21] Can we imagine something like an operatic prosopopoeia: an opera in which commodities

---

19. I take this expression from Toscano and Kinkle, "Baltimore as World and Representation," para. 16.
20. Chesterton, *Defendant*, 50.
21. Marx, *Capital*, 176–77.

themselves sing, rather than the people who exchange them? Maybe this is the only way one could stage Capital.

Here we encounter the formal limitation of *The Wire*: it has not solved the formal task of how to render, in a TV narrative, a universe in which abstraction reigns. *The Wire*'s limit is the limit of psychological realism: what is missing in its depiction of objective reality, including its subjective utopian dreams, is the dimension of the "objective dream," of the virtual/Real sphere of Capital. To evoke this dimension, one has to break with psychological realism (perhaps one way is to embrace ridiculous clichés, as do Brecht and Chaplin in their representations of Hitler in *Arturo Ui* and *The Great Dictator*).[22]

The very psychological-realist "concrete" totality that would encompass social reality, including the lived experience of individuals that are part of it, is in a more radical sense abstract: it abstracts from the gap that separates the Real from its subjective experience. And it is crucial to see the link between this formal limitation of *The Wire* (its remaining within the confines of psychological realism) and, at the level of content, Simon's political limits. His horizon remains that of a "faith in individuals to rebel against rigged systems and exert for dignity." This faith bears witness to Simon's fidelity to the basic premise of the American ideology that postulates the perfectibility of man—in contrast to, say, Brecht, whose motto is "change the system, not individuals": "Mr. Muddle thought highly of man and did not believe that newspapers could be made better, whereas Mr. Keuner did not think very highly of man but did think that newspapers could be made better. 'Everything can be made better,' said Mr. Keuner, 'except man.'"[23]

This tension between institutions and the resistance of individuals limits the political space of *The Wire* to a modest social-democratic individualist reformism: individuals can try to reform the system, but the latter ultimately always wins. What this notion cannot properly grasp is the way these individuals themselves lose their innocence in their struggle—not so much in the sense that they become corrupted, but rather that even if they remain honest and good their acts simply become irrelevant or misfire ridiculously, providing a new impetus to the very force they oppose. We get an intimation of this in *The Wire*'s very first scene, in which McNulty and a

---

22. This move beyond psychological realism is clearly signaled by the fact that the symbol of the OWS protesters became the well-known smiling mask (from *V for Vendetta*), which should not be read simply as means of hiding their identity from the police, since it harbors a much more refined insight: the only way to tell the truth is to wear a mask, or, as Lacan put it, the truth has the structure of fiction.

23. Brecht, *Stories of Mr. Keuner*, 64–65.

black kid commenting on the death of Snot Boogie come across like a Greek chorus:

> McNulty: So your boy's name was what?
>
> Kid: Snot Boogie.
>
> McNulty: God. Snot Boogie. . . . This kid, whose mama went to the trouble to christen him Omar Isaiah Betts. . . . You know, he forgets his jacket, his nose starts running and some asshole, instead of giving him a Kleenex, he calls him "Snot." So he's Snot forever. Doesn't seem fair.
>
> Kid: I'm sayin', every Friday night in an alley behind the Cut Rate, we rollin' bones, you know? I mean all them boys, we roll till late.
>
> McNulty: Alley crap game, right?
>
> Kid: Like every time, Snot, he'd fade a few shooters, play it out till the pot's deep. Snatch and run.
>
> McNulty: What, every time?
>
> Kid: Couldn't help hisself.
>
> McNulty: Let me understand. Every Friday night, you and your boys are shootin' craps, right? And every Friday night, your pal Snot Boogie . . . he'd wait till there's cash on the ground and he'd grab it and run away? You let him do that?
>
> Kid: We'd catch him and beat his ass but ain't nobody ever go past that.
>
> McNulty: I've gotta ask you: if every time Snot Boogie would grab the money and run away . . . why'd you even let him in?
>
> Kid: What?
>
> McNulty: Well, if every time, Snot Boogie stole the money, why'd you let him play?
>
> Kid: Got to. It's America, man.[24]

Here is a tragic vision of a meaningless (life and) death, redeemed only by hopeless resistance—the underlying ethical motto is something like "resist, even if you know that in the end you will lose." Snot (real name Omar) is, of course, a metaphor for the later central character, Omar Little: each

---

24. "The Target," S1/E1.

time he is beaten, he gets up again and again until he is killed. Not only will you lose, but your death will be a nameless death, like that of Omar Little towards the end of the last season. We see his body in the city's morgue, and all that identifies him now is a nametag, one which was initially misplaced on another body. His murder will remain unaccounted for, he dies without ceremony, with no Antigone demanding his burial. However, this very anonymity of death nonetheless shifts the situation from tragedy to comedy, a comedy harsher than tragedy itself: Snot's death is no tragedy for the same reason that the Holocaust was no tragedy. Tragedy is by definition a tragedy of character, the failure of the hero being grounded in a flaw in his character, but it is obscene to claim that the Holocaust was the result of a Jewish character flaw. The comic dimension is also signaled by the utter arbitrariness of the name: why am I that name? Omar becomes "Snot" for totally external arbitrary reasons. There is no deep reason for his name, in the same way that, in Hitchcock's *North by Northwest*, Roger O. Thornhill is in a totally arbitrary way (mis)identified as "George Kaplan."

But Snot, Omar, McNulty, Lester, and the others, they continue to resist. Later in the first season, McNulty asks Lester why he ruined his career by pursuing a culprit against the orders of the deputy commissioner, and Lester replies that he did it for the same reason McNulty is now pursuing the Barksdale gang against the wish of his superiors, who merely want some quick street arrests—there is no reason, just the presence of a kind of unconditional ethical drive that links the members of the conspiratorial group. No wonder the series' final scene repeats the beginning: like Snot or Omar, McNulty (along with the others) persists in his Beckettian repeated failure, but this time, finally, the loser is not only beaten, he really loses—loses his job, experiences professional death. McNulty's last line is "Let's go home"—home, that is, outside the public space.

The Wire is often read through the lens of a Foucauldian topos of the relationship between power and resistance, or the law and its transgression: the process of submissive regulation generates what it "represses" and regulates. Recall Foucault's thesis, developed in his *History of Sexuality*, regarding how the medical-pedagogical discourse disciplining sexuality produces the very excess it tries to tame ("sex"), a process begun already in late antiquity when the Christians' detailed descriptions of every possible sexual temptation retroactively generated what they were supposed to suppress. The proliferation of pleasures is thus the obverse of the power that regulates them: power itself generates resistance to itself, the excess it can never control, and the reactions of a sexualized body to its subjection to disciplinary norms are unpredictable. But Foucault here remains ambiguous, shifting the accent (sometimes almost imperceptibly) from *Discipline and Punish* and the first volume of the *History of Sexuality* to the second and third volumes: while in both cases power and resistance are intertwined, Foucault's initial emphasis is on how resistance is appropriated by power in advance, so that power mechanisms dominate the entire field and we become the subjects of power precisely when we resist it. Later, however, the accent shifts to how power generates the excess it cannot control—far from manipulating resistance, power thus becomes unable to control its own effects.

The only way out of this dilemma is to abandon the entire paradigm of "resistance to a *dispositif*": the idea that, while a *dispositif* determines the network of the Self's activity, it simultaneously opens up the space for the subject's "resistance," for its (partial and marginal) undermining and displacement of the *dispositif* itself. The task of emancipatory politics lies elsewhere: not in elaborating a proliferation of strategies of "resisting" the dominant *dispositif* from marginal subjective positions, but in thinking about the modalities of a possible radical rupture in the dominant *dispositif* itself. In all the talk about the "sites of resistance" we tend to forget that, difficult as this is to imagine today, from time to time, the very *dispositifs* we resist are themselves subject to change.

This is why, in a profoundly Hegelian way, Catherine Malabou calls on us to abandon the critical stance towards reality as the ultimate horizon of our thinking, under whatever name it may appear, from the Young Hegelian "critical critique" to twentieth-century Critical Theory.[25] What such a critical stance has failed to accomplish is the fulfillment of its own gesture: the radicalization of the subjective negative-critical attitude towards reality in a full critical self-negation. Even if it means exposing oneself to the accusation of "regressing" to the Old Hegelian position, we should adopt the authentically Hegelian *absolute* position that, as Malabou points out, involves a kind of speculative "surrender" of the Self to the Absolute, a kind of *absolution*, or release from engagement, albeit in a Hegelian-dialectical way—that is, not an immersion of the subject into the higher unity of an all-encompassing Absolute, but the inscription of the "critical" gap that separates the subject from the (social) substance it resists into this substance itself, as its own antagonism or self-distance.

The reflexive withdrawal rendered in the very last scene of *The Wire* stands for precisely such a "surrender to the Absolute." Here this gesture refers specifically to the relationship between the law and its violations. From the "absolute standpoint," it becomes clear that the (legal) system not only tolerates illegality, but indeed requires it, since it is a condition of the system's own ability to function. From my military service (in 1975, in the

---

25. See Butler and Malabou, *Sois mon corps*.

infamous Yugoslav People's Army), I remember how, during a class on law and patriotic values, the instructing officer solemnly declared that international regulations prohibit shooting at a paratrooper while he is still in the air; in the next class, on how to use a rifle, the same officer explained how to aim at a paratrooper in the air (taking into account the velocity of his fall and thus aiming a little bit lower, etc.). Somewhat naïvely, I asked the officer whether there was not a contradiction between what he was now saying and what he had said an hour earlier; he gave me a look full of scorn as if to say, "How can anyone be so utterly stupid as to ask such a question?" More generally, it is well known that most "Socialist" states were able to function only by relying on the black market (which provided, among other things, 30 percent of the food available)—had one of the regular official campaigns against this network succeeded, the whole system would have collapsed.

In the world of *The Wire*, the crucial question with regard to this relationship between the legal order and its transgression does not concern the status of drug dealing, etcetera, since it is clear that the legal system itself generates much of the crime it fights. The central question is more insidious and unsettling: what is the status of the (utopian) acts of resistance portrayed? Are they also merely a moment in the totality of the system? Are the individual acts of resistance on the part of Snot and Omar, Freamon and McNulty, also just the obverse of the system that ultimately sustains them? If so, then the answer is obvious, if counterintuitive: the only way to stop the system from working is to stop resisting it.

Here a (perhaps surprising) detour through the novels of Ayn Rand may help us to clarify the point. The true conflict in the universe of Rand's two novels is not that between the prime movers and the crowd of second-handers who depend on the prime movers' productive genius—with the tension between the prime mover and his feminine sexual partner being a mere sub-plot of this principal conflict. Rather, the true conflict is between the prime movers themselves, in the (sexualized) tension between the prime mover, the being of pure drive, and his hysterical partner, the potential prime mover who remains caught up in a deadly self-destructive dialectic (between Roark and Dominique in *The Fountainhead*, between John Galt and Dagny in *Atlas Shrugged*). When, in *Atlas Shrugged*, one of the prime-mover figures tells Dagny that the prime movers' true enemy is not the crowd of second-handers but Dagny herself, this is to be taken literally. And Dagny is aware of it: when prime movers start to disappear from public life, she suspects a dark conspiracy, a "destroyer" who is forcing them to withdraw and will thus gradually bring all of social life to a standstill. What she does not yet see is that the figure of the "destroyer" she identifies as the ultimate enemy is the figure of her true Redeemer. The solution comes when the hysterical subject finally escapes her enslavement and recognizes the "destroyer" as her savior. But why? Second-handers possess no ontological consistency of their own, which is why the key to finding the solution is not to break them, but to break the chain that forces the creative prime movers to work for them. When this chain is broken, the second-handers' power will dissolve by itself. The chain that links a prime mover to the perverted existing order is none other than her attachment to her productive genius: a prime mover is ready to pay any price, up to and including the utter humiliation of feeding the very force that works against her, just to be able to continue to create.

What the hystericized prime mover must embrace is thus a fundamental existential indifference: she must no longer be willing to remain hostage to the second-handers' blackmail, she must be ready to give up the very kernel of her being, that which means everything to her, and accept the "end of the world," the (temporary) suspension of the very flow of energy that keeps the world running. In order to gain everything, she must be ready to go to the zero-point of losing everything.[26]

Mutatis mutandis, exactly the same goes for *The Wire*: in order to make the step from reformism to radical change, we must pass through the zero-point of abstaining from acts of resistance which only keep the system alive. In a strange kind of release, we have to cease to worry about other people's worries, and withdraw into the role of a passive observer of the system's circular self-destructive movement. For example, in relation to the ongoing financial crisis that threatens the euro and other currencies, we should stop worrying about how to prevent financial collapse in order to keep the whole system going. The model for such a stance is Lenin during World War I: ignoring all "patriotic" worries about the motherland in danger, he coolly steps back to observe the deadly imperialist dance while laying the foundations for the future revolutionary process—his worries were not the worries of most of his countrymen.

As was clear to Rand, if we want to see real change, then our own worries and cares are our main enemy. We need to stop fighting small battles against the inertia of the system, attempting to make things better here and there, and instead prepare the terrain for the big battle to come. The

---

26. We can imagine a strike conducted, not by the Randian mythic "achievers" but by what one can call the "inherent transgressors": those who, in "resisting" the system and transgressing its rules effectively make it viable. Imagine the black marketeers in today's Cuba suspending their activity: arguably the economic system would collapse in weeks. Something similar occurs in Western countries as the "work to rule" strike: when state employees in a sensitive branch, like the customs or health services, simply follow the rules to the letter, thereby bringing the system virtually to a halt.

standpoint of the Absolute is simple enough to achieve; one merely has to withdraw to the (usually aestheticized) position of totality, as in the popular song the "Circle of Life" from *The Lion King*:

> It's the Circle of Life
> And it moves us all
> Through despair and hope
> Through faith and love
> Till we find our place
> On the path unwinding
> In the Circle
> The Circle of Life.[27]

The song is sung by, of course, the lions: life is a great circle, we eat the zebras, the zebras eat grass; but then, after we die and return to the earth, we also feed the grass, and the circle is closed—this is the best message imaginable for those at the top. The crucial thing is the political spin we give to such "wisdom": is it a matter of simple withdrawal or of withdrawal as the condition for a radical act?[28] In other words, yes, life always forms a circle, but it is still possible (sometimes) not just to climb or descend its hierarchy, but to change the circle itself. Here we should indeed follow Christ, as the paradox of the Absolute itself renouncing the standpoint of the Absolute and adopting the radically "critical" stance of a finite agent engaged in a terrestrial struggle. This stance is deeply Hegelian, Hegel's main thesis being precisely that of an Absolute strong enough to "finitize" itself, to act as a finite subject.

In other words, reflexive withdrawal into the standpoint of the Absolute does not entail a retreat into inactivity, but the opening up of a space for radical change. The point is not to resist Fate (and thus only aid its accomplishment—like the parents of Oedipus and the servant from Baghdad who fled to Samara), but to change Fate itself, its basic coordinates. Jean-Luc Godard once proposed the motto "*Ne change rien pour que tout soit différent*" (change nothing so that everything will be different), a reversal of "some things must change so that everything remains the same." In some political constellations, such as the late capitalist dynamic that requires constant self-revolutionizing to maintain the system, those who refuse to

---

27. Rice and John, "Circle of Life."

28. Can we imagine a slight change to the film *Life Is Beautiful*, with the father singing a similar song to the son? "The Nazis are killing us here in Auschwitz, but you should see, my son, how all this is part of a larger Circle of Life: the Nazis themselves will die and turn into fertilizer for the grass, which will be eaten by the cows; the cows will be slaughtered and we will eat their meat in our pies."

change anything are effectively the agents of true change: effecting a change in the very principle of change.

Therein resides the ambiguity of *The Wire*'s finale: does it suggest a resigned and tragic form of wisdom or the opening up of a space for a more radical act? This ambiguity clouds the bright vision of *The Wire* as "a Marxist's dream of a series" (as one sympathetic leftist critic dubbed it). Simon himself is clear here. When asked if he was a socialist, he declared himself a social democrat who believes that capitalism is the only game in town: "you're not looking at a Marxist here ... I accept that [capitalism] is the only viable way to generate wealth on a large scale."[29] But does not his own tragic worldview contradict this reformist social-democratic vision? While putting his faith in rebellious individuals, he is nevertheless "doubtful that the institutions of a capital-obsessed oligarchy will reform themselves short of outright economic depression (New Deal, the rise of collective bargaining) or systemic moral failure that actually threatens middle-class lives (Vietnam and the resulting, though brief commitment to rethinking our brutal foreign-policy footprints around the world)."

Are we not today approaching an "outright economic depression"? Will such a prospect give rise to a properly collective counterinstitution?[30] Whatever the outcome, one thing is clear: only when we fully embrace Simon's tragic pessimism, accepting that there is no future (within the system), can an opening emerge for a radical change to come.

BIBLIOGRAPHY

Aarons, Kieran, and Grégoire Chamayou. "Contradictions." In *The Wire: Reconstitution Collective*, edited by Emmanuel Burdeau and Nicolas Vieillescazes, 63–89. Paris: Capricci, 2011.
Aloisi, Silvia. "Israeli Film Relives Lebanon War from Inside Tank." *Reuters*, September 8, 2009. Online: http://www.reuters.com/article/2009/09/08/us-venice-israel-idUSTRE5873TK20090908.
Brecht, Bertolt. *Stories of Mr. Keuner*. San Francisco: City Lights, 2001.
Burdeau, Emmanuel. "Fuck." In *The Wire: Reconstitution Collective*, edited by Emmanuel Burdeau and Nicolas Vieillescazes, 9–33. Paris: Capricci, 2011.
Butler, Judith, and Catherine Malabou. *Sois mon corps. Une lecture contemporaine de la domination et de la servitude chez Hegel*. Paris: Bayard, 2010.
Chesterton, G. K. *The Defendant*. New York: Dodd, Mead, 1902.
Jameson, Fredric. "Realism and Utopia in *The Wire*." *Criticism* 52 (2010) 359–72.
Marx, Karl. *Capital*. Vol. 1. Translated by Ben Fowkes. Harmondsworth: Penguin, 1976.

---

29. Toscano and Kinkle, "Baltimore as World and Representation," para. 12.
30. I rely here on Aarons and Chamayou, "Contradictions," 86–87.

Potter, Tiffany, and C. W. Marshall, editors. *The Wire: Urban Decay and American Television*. New York: Continuum, 2009.

Rice, Tim, and Elton John. "The Circle of Life." *The Lion King Soundtrack*, Walt Disney Records, 1994. Compact disc.

Simon, David. "Interview with David Simon," by Nick Hornby. Online: http://www.believermag.com/issues/200708/?read=interview_simon.

———. "The Straight Dope." Interview by Bill Moyers. Online: www.guernicamag.com/interviews/2530/simon_4_1_11.

Toscano, Alberto, and Jeff Kinkle. "Baltimore as World and Representation: Cognitive Mapping and Capitalism in *The Wire*." Online: http://dossierjournal.com/read/theory/baltimore-as-world-and-representation-cognitive-mapping-and-capitalism-in-the-wire.

Contributors

Nekeisha Alexis-Baker, Anabaptist Mennonite Biblical Seminary

Brian Bantum, Assistant Professor of Theology, Seattle Pacific University

Daniel Colucciello Barber, Fellow, ICI Berlin Institute for Cultural Inquiry

Peter Boumgarden, Assistant Professor of Management, Hope College

Anmol Chaddha, Doctoral Fellow in the Multidisciplinary Program in Inequality and Social Policy, Harvard University

James H. Coston, Senior Pastor, Calvary Baptist Church, Waco, Texas

Jacob L. Goodson, Assistant Professor of Philosophy at Southwestern College

Fredric Jameson, William A. Lane, Jr., Professor of Comparative Literature, Professor of Romance Studies, Duke University

Keith L. Johnson, Associate Professor of Theology, Wheaton College

Kristen Deede Johnson, Associate Professor of Theology and Christian Formation, Western Theological Seminary

Whitney Johnson, Academic Program Associate, Bainbridge Graduate Institute

David Matzko McCarthy, Fr. James M. Forker Professor, Mount St. Mary's University

Jonathan Tran, Associate Professor of Religion, Baylor University

Myles Werntz, Postdoctoral Research Associate in Theology and Ethics, Baylor University

Joseph Wiebe, Adjunct Instructor, McMaster University

William Julius Wilson, Lewis P. and Linda L. Geyser University Professor, Harvard University

Joseph Winters, Assistant Professor, Religious Studies, UNC Charlotte

Slavoj Žižek, senior researcher at the Institute of Sociology, University of Ljubljana, Slovenia

Index

Adorno, Theodor, 130
aesthetics, 273
African-American community, 6, 8, 34–35, 42, 44, 52, 176, 183
black masculinity, 128–29, 139, 143
Aimee (character), 78
Alcoholics Anonymous, 92, 184
America, United States of, 34, 69, 102, 122
American Dream, x, 10, 239, 286
Christianity, 13, 15, 231
economy, 21, 238
experiment, 111–12, 190, 246, 250
South, 27
urban, 3, 4, 31, 36, 65, 109, 175, 231–32, 245
Annapolis, Maryland, 105
Apostle Paul, 5, 85, 199–200, 203, 260
Aquinas, Thomas, 157
Aristides, 16
Atlanta, 46. 56
Augustine, ix, x, 148, 149, 172, 211, 250–52, 255
City of God (*De Civitate Dei*), 110–111, 115, 121, 125, 256–65
De Doctrina Christiana, 71, 73
authenticity, 77, 81, 85, 130, 188, 232, 245–46

Baltimore, 3, 5–9, 14, 17–30, 33, 39, 47, 64, 92, 95–96, 105, 109, 111–12, 115, 121–22, 125–26, 143–47, 160, 167, 179–81, 195–201, 205, 208, 210–15, 220–26, 230–35, 245–48, 251, 261–63, 288–89, 293
Board of Education, 187
churches, 178, 182–85
City Hall, 19,
City Office of Sustainability, 17–18
Community Foundation, 19
economics, 41–45, 238
housing, 46,
Neighborhood Energy Challenge (BNEC), 19, 22, 30
Police Department, 6, 21, 116, 148–51, 153–54, 157, 167, 169–70, 252, 255, 258
Sun, 4, 32, 81, 182
United in Leadership Development (BUILD), 180–181
West Baltimore, 21, 24, 26, 40, 63, 78, 184, 191, 289
Barksdales (characters), 89, 98, 123
Avon (character), 7, 10, 34, 38, 62, 82–84, 98–100, 106, 113, 118–19, 133–34, 151–57, 159, 166, 169, 171–72, 177, 195, 223, 244–45, 270, 276–77, 289–91
D'Angelo (character), 37–38, 51, 53, 79, 83–85, 90, 93, 117, 119, 129, 133–37, 139, 141–42, 197, 235, 244–45, 289
organization, xi, 8–9, 28, 33–34, 38, 40, 82–84, 101, 111, 118–19, 129, 133–39, 141, 156, 195, 197, 219, 289
Barth, Karl, xi, 193–96, 199–206, 207–8, 215, 228–29, 231, 248

Index

belonging, 109–11, 114–23, 125–26
Bell, Russell "Stringer" (character), 9–10, 12, 38, 62, 82, 84, 100–101, 107, 113, 118–19, 134–37, 141, 152–57, 159–61, 166, 169–73, 195, 197, 245, 270, 276–81, 286, 290
Bennett, William, 150, 172
Bible, 8, 184, 193, 200, 228
  Scripture, 6, 59–60, 192, 194, 196, 201, 203, 214, 215, 224, 227
Black Power, 130–31
Blanchard, Pooh, 133–35
Blocker, Wendell "Orlando" (character), 79
Broadhus, Preston "Bodie" (character), 38, 41, 62, 117, 133–34, 137–39, 143, 157–58
Bonhoeffer, Dietrich, 212–13, 225, 228–29
Boogie, "Snot" (character), 297–300
Boys & Girls Club, 14, 185
Brandon (character), 90, 118, 133, 136–37, 157
Brecht, Bertolt, 292, 295–96, 303,
Brice, Namond (character), 51, 87, 186, 188, 222, 253–54
Brice, Roland "Wee-Bey" 34, 51, 79, 134, 139
"Bubbles" (character). See Cousins, Reginald "Bubbles" (character)
"Bug" (character), 165, 286
Burns, Edward, 4, 20, 32, 182, 265, 294
Burrell, Commissioner Ervin (character), 8, 81, 89, 149–50, 179–80, 217, 230, 235
Butler, Judith, 128, 135, 143, 229, 303

Cain, 113–14, 196–97, 206, 209
capital
  cultural, 49–50, 54, 96
  financial, 107, 223, 236–23, 258, 295–96
  social, 44, 258–59,
capitalism, ix, 5, 63, 118, 173, 177, 191–92, 236, 238, 288, 293–95, 303–4
Capra, Frank, 291

Carcetti, Tommy, (character), 5–8, 11, 81–82, 178–80, 198, 216–18, 258–59, 261
Carr, Malik "Poot" (character), 11, 38, 133–34, 136–38, 158
Carver, Ellis (character), 79–81, 86 116–17, 124
Catholic Worker House, 91, 226–28
Cavanaugh, William, 218–20, 228
Cavell, Stanley, 67, 70, 75, 172
Charles, Slim (character), 10
Chesterton, G. K., 291, 295, 303
Chicago, 16, 31, 33, 42, 45–46, 49–50, 54–56, 108, 144, 173, 188, 190, 258, 264
Christ, Jesus, 5, 12–13, 15, 59–60, 73–75, 135, 175, 186, 192, 199–208, 210–12, 214–15, 218–19, 224–25, 228, 235, 256–57, 259–60, 264, 302
Christianity, 4, 7, 11, 13–14, 15, 74, 77, 92, 178, 279–82
  ethics, xii, 11, 92, 149ff, 199–206, 214,
  leaders, 4, 180–182
  members, 9, 15, 75, 124, 199–200, 206–8, 212–29, 235, 244, 247, 260
  Orthodoxy, 73,
  scripture, 60,
  speech, 5, 59, 61, 66,
Christie, Agatha, 98, 108
Chrysostom, John, 92, 94
church, ix–x, 5–12, 61, 74, 77, 85, 179–90, 210–29
  African-American, 175–76, 178, 188, 217
  Catholic, 6, 13, 112, 231,
  ecclesiology, 211, 213, 215, 221, 224
  institutions, 4, 6–7, 10–11, 13–15, 26, 40, 175, 181, 187–88, 220, 230–35, 240, 247–48
  Bethel A. M. E. Church, 178, 182–87, 190
  Garden of Prayer Baptist Church, 182, 185, 187
  New Song Community Church, 182, 184, 187, 189

Index

St. Casimir, 234
  programs, 188–89
  relationship with society, 193, 204–8
citizenship, xii, 8, 18, 109, 111–12, 118–25, 171, 177, 203–5, 208, 218
Clapp, Rodney, 211, 228
class, 29, 34, 40, 42, 76, 97, 110, 140, 159, 184, 191, 241, 286
  hierarchy, 35
  middle-class, 27, 37, 40, 45–47, 181, 186
  positions, 35
  underclass, 174, 177, 232, 287
  working class, 39, 41, 183, 288
classroom, 87, 101, 108, 122–23, 186–87, 252–56
Clinton administration, 44–45
"code", 141, 281, 292
  masculinity, 133, 135,
  streets, 10, 37–38,
Cold War, 104
Coles, Romand, 129, 140, 144
Colvin, Lt. Howard "Bunny" (character), 5, 21–22, 87, 108, 122, 124–26, 176–77, 186, 216, 221–23, 230, 253–56, 264, 289–90
community, 44, 66, 80, 130, 168, 175, 189, 212, 222–24, 233, 239, 246–47, 253
  church, 7, 14, 92, 178, 185–88,
  civic, 10, 13, 14–15, 22–24, 34, 100, 179–82, 185–89, 237
  inner-city, 37
  organizations, 19–22
  volunteers, 22, 28
  white, 42
confession, 7, 92, 122–23, 126, 202, 204, 226–27, 241, 243–44, 260
Connolly, William, 150–151, 172
corruption, xi, 64, 82, 92, 104–5, 107, 198, 234, 243, 255
counter-insurgency, 151, 159–72
Cousins, Reginald "Bubbles" (character), 8–11, 34, 91–93, 111, 134, 142–43, 179–80, 225–28, 258
crime, xi, 23, 31–33, 35–37, 46, 52, 78, 82, 94–99, 101, 108, 118, 126, 131, 172, 196, 204, 253, 258, 290–291, 300
cross, 4, 10, 11, 201, 207, 227, 231, 235, 247

D'Agostino, Theresa (character), 83, 120–121, 179
Daniels, Cedric (character), 86–87, 113, 117, 119, 121, 150–151, 172, 290
Das, Veena, 67–68, 75
Davis, Senator Clay (character), 179, 195, 276
Deacon (character), 4–7, 176–79, 181, 184, 186, 221–23, 225–26, 228–29
degradation, 21, 80, 85
Deleuze, Gilles, 273–76, 278, 281, 284
democracy, ix, 129, 144, 211, 218, 296
Diamond, Cora, 147–48, 172
Dickens, Charles, 33, 54, 96, 291, 293
dignity, 22, 79, 84, 177, 262, 296
discrimination, 32, 40, 159–71
domination, 77–78, 80, 93, 110, 112, 116, 140, 234, 247, 250, 255, 261, 273–74, 280
Donald, James, 115, 126
Donette (character), 83–84
Dozerman, Kenneth (character), 89
drugs, 150, 154, 169, 185, 189, 236, 244, 277
  legalization, 108, 177, 289
  trafficking, 38, 87–90, 97, 105, 113, 134, 137, 147, 156, 166, 195, 222, 226, 253
  War on Drugs, xi, 34, 149–51, 157, 159–60, 170–73
Durkheim, Émile, 270, 284
dysfunction, x, 76, 78, 83, 85, 87, 93

economics, 54, 154–55, 178, 238, 290
  illegal economies, 19, 41, 51, 90, 134, 182, 287–89
  money, 103–7, 111, 114, 118, 123, 156, 178, 185, 194–95, 198, 220, 226, 237–42, 258, 277
Edward Tighlman Middle School, 177

education, ix, 13, 25, 32–33, 41, 48–52, 54–55, 108, 177, 186–89, 251–55, 258, 276, 288, 290
Elba, Idris, 9, 100
election
  political, 5, 114, 181, 217, 259, 262
  theological, 199
Ellul, Jacques, 114, 126, 196, 209
empire
  American, 250
  Roman, 214, 251, 255
  worldly, 14, 251
employment, 21, 36, 39–44, 55, 180
Enoch, 114, 196
environment, 18–22, 32, 50, 54, 89, 129, 140, 187, 239, 247, 257
equality, 25, 52, 103
eschatology, 277
ethics, 126–27, 140, 148–49, 155, 159–62, 165, 167, 170–73
evil, 15, 61, 67, 103–4, 141, 155, 161, 163, 165, 173, 185, 193, 205, 231, 246–47, 255, 290–91, 294
exploitation, 21, 62, 169, 274

family, 28, 35–36, 38, 42, 51, 56, 63–64, 78, 84, 87, 92, 94, 103, 107, 136, 142–43, 175, 189, 198, 225–26, 233, 236–39, 242–47, 289
food desert, 24–25, 30
Foucault, Michel, 112–14, 116, 126–27, 148, 173, 273–74, 298–99
Fitzgerald, F. Scott, 244–45, 247–48
Flett, John, 213–15, 229
Freamon, Lester, (character), 3, 80, 86, 89, 100, 119–22, 151, 172, 292, 300
Frei, Hans, 224, 228–29
friendship, 79–80, 85, 92, 212, 252, 277, 290
Freud, Sigmund, 98, 128, 136–37, 144

Galloway, Alexander, 274, 278, 284
"game," 83, 85, 91, 110, 112, 117–19, 125, 133–37, 139, 149, 151–56, 166, 174, 186, 197, 221, 244–45
gang culture, 10, 34, 37–38, 40, 52, 64–65, 69, 97–98, 101, 185, 204

Gant, William, 135–36, 289
globalization, 107, 112, 115
God, 14–16, 59, 66, 71–72, 74–75, 77, 110, 114, 118, 171, 183, 194, 196, 200–208, 211–15, 250, 255, 260–61
  acknowledgment of, 10, 185
  faithfulness of, 77, 85, 199
  "gods" 5, 112, 230, 243, 249, 270, 288
  kingdom of, ix, 14, 199, 201, 224,
  love of, 235,
  name of, 60–62, 279–83
  peace of, 256
  people of, 225, 227
  presence, xi, 7, 193
  revelation of, 59, 71–72, 201
  word of, 200, 212
  work of, 214–15, 224–28
Goodchild, Philip, 269–70, 272, 280, 284
government
  federal, 44, 150,
  local, ix, 44–47
grace, 5, 10–11, 30, 92, 200–201, 208, 218, 225, 255, 260–61, 264
Gray, Tony (character), 6
Great Gatsby, 244, 247–48
Greggs, Shakima "Kima" (character), 79–80, 85–87, 93, 118, 149, 198, 226, 242
Griffiths, Paul, 72,75
Guetta, David, 285
guilt, 10, 92, 122, 132, 138, 198, 206, 226, 241

Habermas, Jürgen, 103, 108
Habitat for Humanity, 13, 185
Hamsterdam, 5, 21–22, 30, 124, 176–77, 180, 216–17, 222, 253–54, 289,
Harlem, 69, 106, 286
Hauerwas, Stanley, 129, 144, 148, 172–73, 211–14, 229
Haynes, Augustus "Gus" (character), 81–82
Hector, Kevin, 214, 229
Hauk, Thomas "Herk" (character), 8, 79–81, 116–17, 217

Index 311

hierarchy, 10, 38, 80, 134, 141, 184, 255, 279, 302
Holmes, Arthur, 148, 173
Holocaust, 103, 298
Holy Spirit, 75, 183, 203, 215
Holzer, Harry, 36, 42, 54–55
hope, x, 30, 83, 99, 109, 112, 171, 189, 191, 247, 262–64, 293, 302
 HOPE IV Program, 46
 hopelessness, 73, 124, 151, 192, 197–98, 202, 208, 250, 258, 297
 melancholic, 124, 130, 140, 143, 154
 personal change, 73–75, 114–15, 118, 262
 political hope, 21, 23–24, 26, 174, 182, 186, 196, 232–33, 251
 virtues, 148, 171, 191, 199–200, 202–3, 205, 208, 235, 257
Hornby, Nick, 248, 261, 264, 304
housing projects, 3, 12, 19, 39, 40, 45–46, 147, 165, 167, 185, 189
Hovey, Craig, 214, 227, 229
Hütter, Reinhard, 213, 229
hypocrisy, 81, 290

ideals, idealism, 19, 78, 82, 99, 130, 160, 291
identity, x–xi, 18, 30, 86, 88, 115, 120, 123, 131–33, 143–44, 192, 214, 216, 218, 224, 229, 253, 257, 277, 288, 296
incarceration, 32–37, 54–56
incarnation, xi, 59–61, 71–74, 275
industrialization, 20, 30–33, 102, 107
 deindustrialization, 36, 39–45, 47, 107
 postindustrialism, 20, 109–10, 115, 118, 129, 139, 230, 242
infidelity, 82–86, 88
injustice, 20, 25, 29, 128, 148, 161, 165–67, 171, 204, 206, 236, 247
inner-city, x, 20–21, 26, 31, 36–41, 44–56, 61, 63, 69–70, 175, 178
Innes, Shardene (character), 83–86,
Interdenominational Ministerial Alliance (IMA), 7, 178, 180, 216
isolation, social, 40, 44, 49, 93, 233, 242

Jameson, Fredric, 126, 286, 303

Jay-Z, 132, 144
joblessness, 21, 35, 36, 39–40, 42, 44–45
Jongman, Albert, 158, 159, 171, 173
just war theory, 148, 159, 165, 167, 171
Kenard, (character), 142
Kennedy, Bobby, 238, 241
killing, 83, 87, 93, 98, 100, 121
 accidental, 142
 gang, 38, 133–34, 153, 243–45, 289
 ethics, 64, 121–22, 154, 156–58, 166, 168–69, 171, 292
 hired, 105, 197
 murder, 38, 50, 65, 72, 84, 97, 114, 131–39, 168, 196–98, 236–41, 286, 289, 298
 retribution, 64–65, 74
 serial killers, 93, 104, 119, 291–92
Klebanow, Thomas (character), 81–82

Landsman, Sergeant Jay (character), 88–89, 91, 93, 111, 118
language, 110–11, 113, 116, 121, 131, 149, 160, 170,
 human language, 60–62, 66–67, 69–71, 74, 250
 domination, 77, 79, 82
 institutional language, 80, 82
 ordinary language philosophy, xi, 61, 66
 public language, 217–19
 sexual language, 78–82, 85, 89, 90
 theological language, 60–61, 71, 73–74, 77
labor market, 19, 21, 31, 36, 40, 42, 46, 51, 54, 238
Lee, Micheal (character), 86–87
Levitt, Steven, 38, 56
Levy, Maurice, 136, 289
Little, Omar (character), 9–10, 38, 61–62, 69, 90–91, 93, 111, 113, 133, 136, 142, 153–57, 197, 219, 250, 270, 277–82, 292, 297–300
Lindbeck, George, 196, 209
Lincoln, Eric, 175–76, 178, 189,
liturgy, 6, 211, 214–16, 219–20, 228,

love, 60–61, 67, 71, 76–77, 200, 235, 244, 290, 302,
  Baltimore, 245–47
  disordered, x, 115, 250–51, 253, 256–57, 259–61
  enemy, 172, 206,
  God's love, 15, 72, 205, 235, 247–48
  self-love, 62, 255–56, 259
  transcendent, 11
loyalty, 38, 84, 123, 152–53, 155, 198, 233, 235–36, 243
Lupton, Robert, 9, 16
Lukács, Georg, 97

Machiavelli, Nicolo, 62, 104
MacIntyre, Alisdair, 212, 229
Malatov, Sergei (character), 242
Malcolm X, 282–84
Mamiya, Lawrence, 175–76, 178, 183, 187, 189–90
marginalization, 9, 69, 112, 218, 221, 276, 299
marriage, 82–83, 85–86, 92–94
Marshall, C. W., 143–44, 173, 286, 304
Marx, Karl, 140, 272, 288, 293–95, 303
materialism, xii, 14, 154, 212, 294
Mathewes, Charles, 255, 261, 264
McCabe, Herbert, 67, 75
McCullough, DeAndre, 261–62, 265
McDougall, Harold, 176, 181, 183–85, 190
McNulty, Elena (character), 82
McNulty, Jimmy (character), 62, 79, 82–93, 96, 111, 119–22, 126, 135, 139, 151, 157–58, 166, 172, 198, 237–38, 261
metaphysics, 59, 66–67, 74, 101, 214, 229
Milbank, John, 211–13, 229
media, ix, 46, 108, 251–53, 274, 288, 291
mediation, 136, 189, 247
  mediating space, 124
  Mediation in Christ, 199–200, 259
Ministers, The (characters), 8, 9, 178–80, 188, 216–18, 221, 223, 228
money. *See* economics, money
Monk (character), 157–58

Moreland, Bunk (character), 62, 79–80, 89, 135, 154, 286, 289
Mouzone, Brother (character), 90, 155–56, 270, 277, 279–82
Mr. Dizz (character), 239
murder. *See* killing, murder

naming, 18, 62, 97–99, 105, 114, 153, God, 60–62, 270, 279–83
  God's work, 211–29
  religion, 270
Narcotics Anonymous, 10–11, 26, 226
Nation of Islam, 279–81
networks
  crime, 105, 152
  family, 175,
  homosocial, 85
  power, 122,
  social, 22, 44, 77–78, 91, 175–76, 299–300
New Federalism, 44
New York City, 105, 197
newspaper, 81, 86, 91, 108, 193, 227, 296
Nietzsche, Frederick, 66, 103, 113, 115, 126, 290
nihilism, 110–11, 115–16, 125,
No Child Left Behind Act, 254

Oakley, Deirdre, 45, 55
O'Dog (character), 158
O'Donovan, Oliver, 149, 159–60, 167–71, 173
Ogbu, John, 49, 54
Ochs, Peter, 69, 75
Oldenburg, Ray, 25, 30
Orlando's Strip Club, 83, 118, 135

Pakusa, Thomas "Horseface" (character), 239, 242
Partlow, Chris (character), 64–65, 67–69, 157–58, 169
Pearlman, Rhonda (character), 82–83, 85–88
Pearson, Snoop (character), 64–65, 67–69, 85–86, 157–58, 165, 197
Pentecost, 227
Perry, Imani, 132–33, 144

personhood, xi, 118, 123,
The Pit, 133–34, 137, 139
Polish, 6, 106, 112, 181, 220
police, 63, 65, 95, 96–105, 109, 120, 186, 195, 216, 242, 288–89
    abuses, 8, 86, 156, 158, 179, 238
    department, 12, 21, 37–38, 79, 116–18, 141, 148–54, 157, 167–71, 220, 252, 255, 258, 260, 287, 290
    institution, 21, 32–33, 37–38, 79, 81, 88–93, 96, 99, 182, 194–98
    officers, 6–7, 34, 52, 87, 111, 118–20, 122, 124, 149–51, 153, 170, 204, 218, 220, 236
    procedural, x, 95, 97, 105, 232, 246
    "real police work," 21, 37–38, 82, 87, 93, 119, 121, 186, 289
Politics, 4, 16, 44, 46–47, 54, 56, 80–82, 93, 95, 104, 121, 140, 144, 172, 178, 183, 195, 209, 212, 217–19, 228–29, 233, 236, 238, 251, 259, 263, 290, 299
Porter, Jean, 160, 173
postmodernism, 5, 95, 105–6, 112, 118, 228, 230, 249, 254, 256, 261, 264, 287, 293
poverty, ix, 9, 16, 18, 22, 24, 29, 31–33, 36, 40, 42, 45–46, 53–55, 70, 172, 182, 195, 197–98, 226–27
power, x, xi, 3, 7, 18–19, 62–63, 85, 110, 114–27, 216, 230–231, 236, 239, 244, 247
    brokers, 6, 29, 174, 179, 217
    civic, 6, 7–8
    dynamics, 78, 84, 88, 90, 116, 259
    enactment, 110–12, 116–26, 297–301
    inequalities, 51, 79, 129, 160, 250–61
    institutions, 51, 88, 112, 124, 178, 179, 220, 276,
    political, 8–9, 12, 15, 179, 197–99, 232–33
    redemptive, 11, 15
    sexualized, 78, 85, 129, 132
Powers, 6, 91, 112–14, 123–24, 168, 189–95, 198–208, 233

Pryzbylewski, Roland "Prez" (character), xi, 86–88, 93, 110–11, 115–26, 186, 253–57
Princeton, 12, 16, 108, 149, 239
Prison, 15, 34–37, 51–52, 91, 106, 119, 134, 168–71, 240, 244–45, 289
Project Succeed Academy, 118
Public housing, 40, 45–46, 54,
Putnam, Hilary, 160, 173

race/racism, ix, 18–19, 27, 29–31, 34, 40, 54, 69, 76, 97, 106, 109–11, 127–28, 131, 143, 183, 189, 241, 248, 280–83, 287
Ramsey, Paul, 149, 159–67, 170–173
Rand, Ayn, 300–301
Rauschenbusch, Walter, 218
Rawlings-Blake, Stephanie, 181, 216, 229
Rawls, Major William (character), 79, 88–90, 113, 149–50
Read, Jason, 152–55, 173
Reagan, Ronald, 44–45, 238
realism, xi, 70, 77, 92, 95, 97–98, 107–8, 110, 112, 126, 141, 173, 197, 286–87, 289, 292, 295–96, 303
reconciliation, 30, 92, 184, 209, 214, 222, 227–28, 241
redemption, 4–5, 10–11, 13, 77, 124, 182, 199–200, 202–4, 207, 221, 225, 229, 231, 261, 263, 293
redistribution, 189
Reed, Stringer, 286
reform, xi, 7, 78, 85, 89, 93, 107, 119, 126, 156, 171–72, 175, 179, 182, 189, 217, 223, 225, 252–53, 296, 301, 303
Reid, Frank, 6, 178–79
religion, xii, 75, 77, 104, 112, 209, 262, 269–72, 279–83, 291
revelation, 4, 60, 201, 214
Royce, Clarence (character), 6, 47, 81, 180, 216–17
Royce, Josiah, 155
Russell, Beadie, 83, 86–87, 93

Sandtown, 184–85, 187

Santangelo, Officer Michael (character), 79
segregation, 40, 42, 48–49, 76, 183
sexuality
  autoeroticism, 88, 90–91
  celibacy, 90–92
  heterosociality, 78, 85–88, 91, 133
  homosexuality, 85, 89–90, 104, 130, 262
  homosociality, 78, 85–91
  prostitution, 83, 93
Sherrod (character), 10, 92, 142, 226–27
Simon, David, ix, 3–7, 9–12, 15–16, 20, 32, 62, 82, 96, 109–10, 112–13, 115–16, 126, 136, 172, 174–75, 182, 191–92, 210–11, 227, 230–35, 239, 245–65, 272, 276, 285–87, 293, 296, 303
sin, 77, 92, 193–207, 220, 226, 233, 260–61, 282
Sobotka, Frank (character), xi, 41, 106–7, 181, 195, 220, 230–48, 289
Sobotka, Lou (character), 240, 242
Sobotka, Nick (character), 77–78, 237–43
Sobotka, Ziggy (character), 91, 237–42
social commentary, 9, 65, 71, 77, 81, 84, 124
social policy, 36, 44–48, 52, 80, 135, 150–151, 216, 254, 258, 303
solidarity, 80, 89, 106
Spinoza, Baruch, 155–56
Stanfield, Marlo (character), 9, 28, 62–65, 70, 72, 74–75, 86–87, 99, 111, 123, 139, 142, 151–52, 157–60, 165–66, 169–72, 182, 195, 270, 283, 291
Stewart, Joseph "Proposition Joe" (character), 155, 182
suburbanization, 12–14, 21, 39–40, 53, 65, 105, 112, 165, 184
suffering, 5, 9–10, 26, 68, 92, 128–31, 134, 136–40, 142–43, 179–80, 183, 185, 198, 234, 237
suicide, 84
Templeton, Scott (character), 82

Terrorist, 68–69, 104, 122, 141, 152–53, 157–73, 289–91
Tertullian, 15–16
"The Greek" (character), 95, 99, 107, 195, 237–42
Theology, xii, 71, 73, 193, 230–234, 247–48, 271, 279, 281
  Christian, 215, 227
  Natural theology, 70,
  Resources, x,
Theology and the city, 13, 111
Theology of language, 59–61
Theology of the suburbs, 14,
Trenton, New Jersey, x, 3–4, 10–15

unions, 6, 38, 41, 44, 52, 80, 85, 91, 105–7, 195, 213, 220, 231–43, 247
University of Maryland, 222, 253
urban inequality, 31–53, 76, 140, 183
utopianism, 95–108, 110, 112, 118–19, 125, 274, 287, 289–92, 300, 303

Valcheck, Stanislaus "Stan" (character), 7, 87, 112, 116, 121, 181, 220, 235
violence, 15, 22, 46, 61, 79, 125–26, 185–88, 204, 275,
  drug violence, 25, 83, 189
  family, 195–97, 244,
  ordinary violence, 62–70
  personal acts, 37, 52, 90–93, 113–14, 132–33, 135, 196
  restraint, 153–54, 159,
  sexual, 79, 134,
  social/systemic, 9, 38, 50, 61, 85, 113, 116–19, 136–41, 152, 179, 294,
vulnerability, 24, 45, 91, 115, 118, 121, 128–43, 174, 180, 241

Wagstaff, Randy (character), 123
Wallace (character), 37–38, 53, 105, 117–18, 129–39, 142
Walon (character), 10–11, 225
Watkins, Odell (character), 6, 179–80, 223

weakness, 122, 129–30, 133–43, 181, 234–35, 241, 244, 260
Weeks, Johnny (character), 92, 134–35,
Weems, Duquan "Dukie" (character), 87–88, 93, 123–24, 257–58, 262
Western District, 21, 80, 178–79, 182
Williams, Melvin, 4, 176, 221
Williams, Rowan, 61, 71, 259
Wise, Dennis "Cutty" 4–7, 34, 78, 120, 122, 176, 221

witness
  bearing witness, 22, 198, 210, 212–15, 219, 221, 225, 227–28, 296
  legal, 133, 135, 139, 171, 241, 286, 289
  prophetic, 3, 11
Wittgenstein, Ludwig, xi, 66–68
Wright, Richard, 33

Yoder, John Howard, 210, 219, 224

Zenobia (character), 141

www.ingramcontent.com/pod-product-compliance
Lightning Source LLC
Chambersburg PA
CBHW021344300426
44114CB00012B/1074